RADCLIFFE AND CROSS
THE ENGLISH LEGAL SYSTEM

FIFTH EDITION

BY

LORD CROSS OF CHELSEA

One of the Lords of Appeal in Ordinary;
a Privy Councillor; and a Past Fellow
of Trinity College, Cambridge

AND

G. J. HAND

of King's Inns, Dublin, Barrister;
Lecturer in Legal History, University
College, Dublin.

LONDON
BUTTERWORTHS
1971

ENGLAND:	BUTTERWORTH & CO. (PUBLISHERS) LTD.
	LONDON: 88 Kingsway, WC2B 6AB
AUSTRALIA:	BUTTERWORTHS PTY. LTD.
	SYDNEY: 586 Pacific Highway,
	Chatswood, NSW 2067
	MELBOURNE: 343 Little Collins
	Street, 3000
	BRISBANE: 240 Queen Street, 4000
CANADA:	BUTTERWORTH & CO. (CANADA) LTD.
	TORONTO: 2265 Midland Avenue,
	Scarborough, M1P 4S1
NEW ZEALAND:	BUTTERWORTHS OF NEW ZEALAND
	LTD.
	WELLINGTON: 26-28 Waring Taylor
	Street, 1
SOUTH AFRICA:	BUTTERWORTH & CO. (SOUTH AFRICA)
	(PTY.) LTD.
	DURBAN: 152-154 Gale Street

ISBN   Casebound: 0 406 64701 1
Limp: 0 406 64702 X

PRINTED IN GREAT BRITAIN BY OFFSET LITHOGRAPHY BY
BILLING AND SONS LTD., GUILDFORD AND LONDON

PREFACE TO THE FIFTH EDITION

Mr. Hall was not able to take part in the preparation of this edition and Dr. Hand kindly agreed to revise the first half of the book in his place. In doing so he has paid particular attention to constitutional and administrative matters. The last seven years have seen a number of changes in the legal system the effect of which I have tried to incorporate in the later chapters without destroying the continuity of the narrative. The last chapter has been almost wholly rewritten since many of the changes foreshadowed in 1964 have been made and the "pressure points" are now different.

GEOFFREY CROSS

March, 1971

PREFACE TO THE FOURTH EDITION

SOME thirty years ago in my early days at the Bar I became a part time lecturer at the Law Society's School of Law of which Geoffrey Radcliffe was then the Principal. He suggested to me that we should write this book which first appeared in 1937. A glance at the table of contents will show that it contains much more historical matter than any lawyer needs to know for any ordinary professional purpose. But professional purposes are not everything and we thought that some students—and possibly even some general readers—who would never tackle Pollock and Maitland or Holdsworth might enjoy reading a more connected and detailed account of the development of our legal system than was contained in the existing students' text books. When new editions were needed in 1946 and 1954 Radcliffe revised the historical portions while I revised the later chapters; but he is no longer here to take part in the preparation of the fourth edition of a book which but for him would never have been written. Research into legal history has not stood still in the last ten years, but I have not kept pace with it and Mr. Derek Hall has been good enough to undertake the revision of the first fourteen chapters. I have tried to bring the later chapters up to date and I have added a final chapter setting out what appear to be the principal current criticisms of the legal system as opposed to the substantive law.

GEOFFREY CROSS

February, 1964

PREFACE TO THE FIRST EDITION

THIS book makes no claim to embody the results of any original research. Its purpose is to supply a want, which we have felt as teachers, of a book which should contain within a reasonable compass at once a short history of our legal institutions and an account of the existing organisation of our courts of law.

We have not thought it desirable in a book intended for students beginning the study of the law to encumber the text with a mass of references to the authorities. Our indebtedness to the labours of such writers as Maitland and Sir William Holdsworth, and to the great mass of material published by the Selden Society since its first volume appeared more than fifty years ago, will be apparent on every page to those who are already familiar with the subject.

Our chief difficulty has been that of selection. We trust we have included everything about the past history and present constitution of our courts which anyone beginning the study of our substantive law ought to know. We hope that what else is added will not be found unprofitable as showing those who will help to shape the professional opinion of lawyers in the future what causes have helped or hindered the development of our law in the past.

Dr. Radcliffe wishes to add that though the book has been planned, and revised, in common, Mr. Cross has contributed by far the larger share to its actual execution.

G. R. Y. R.
G. C.

April, 1937

vii

CONTENTS

CONTENTS

1

THE ANGLO-SAXON PERIOD

A GENERAL history of England must include some account of its early inhabitants and of their conquest and rule by Rome, but the historian of the English legal system has no need to push his enquiry so far back into the past, for though England was for more than three centuries a province of the Roman Empire, and, as such, governed by the Roman Law the Anglo-Saxon invasions of the fifth century A.D. destroyed all traces of the old legal order and replaced it with institutions which were, in their origin, purely Germanic. At various stages in its history English Law was deeply influenced by ideas derived from Roman jurisprudence, but this was due in part to the return to England of a measure of Roman Law embedded in the Canon Law of the Church, and in part to the study of Roman Law itself by English judges, and is not at all attributable to any surviving traces of its old dominion here.

Our starting place, then, is the invasion of England by the Anglo-Saxons, and our first period stretches from that date to the Norman Conquest. It is a long period—from the coming of the English to William the Conqueror there is as long an interval as between William the Conqueror and William III—but our knowledge of the law which our ancestors brought with them from Germany and of its development among them here in those early centuries is very scanty, and much of what we do know is of purely antiquarian interest. All that can be attempted in a book of this sort is to give a short sketch of the history of the Anglo-Saxon period and a description of those features in its legal system which must be borne in mind if the work of the Norman and Angevin kings in laying the foundations of our modern legal order is to be appreciated.

The Anglo-Saxons did not invade this country as a united people, but as a number of separate tribes. Gradually in the course of the seventh and eighth centuries, through conquest or the intermarriage of ruling families, larger units began to emerge—such as the kingdoms of Wessex in the south, of Mercia in the Midlands, and of Northumbria in the north. Meanwhile, in these centuries the English were converted to Christianity by missionaries from the Continent and received from them a first faint contact with the traditions of Roman civilisation, which had been to some degree preserved by the Christian Church. It was under this influence that English tribal chieftains came to reduce into writing their rude attempts at legislation and to employ written conveyances in their grants of lands to their retainers ; it was from the Church, too, that men learnt to dispose of their property by will. Then in the ninth century there came fresh invaders, the Danes, who ousted the Anglo-Saxons from the north-east coast of England and settled there themselves. Alfred, the King of Wessex (878–900), headed the Saxon resistance to their further advance, and at last, in the course of the tenth century, Alfred's son and grandson succeeded in merging the Danish districts—" the danelaw "—in the rest of England and in uniting the whole country into one kingdom. It is with the legal system as it existed in the united Anglo-Saxon state in the last century before the Norman Conquest that the rest of this chapter is concerned.

The England of the tenth century was divided into shires, though the northernmost parts of the country were not " shired " until after the Norman Conquest. But the oldest division of local government in the Anglo-Saxon system appears to have been a lesser one, the Hundred. No one can now state with confidence how it arose, but in historic times its basis was thought to have been a hundred hides—the hide was a unit of land, originally the amount considered necessary for the sustenance of a peasant household. Perhaps because of this economic origin, both the amount of land in a hundred and the number of hundreds in a shire varied very much. Each hundred was itself made up of a number of " townships " or " " vills." [1] Though many English villages have kept through the centuries the name of an Anglo-Saxon township, the manner of life of their inhabitants and their law and its administration have been completely transformed. An Anglo-Saxon township was a little community which was often separated from its neighbours by a belt of uncleared woodland, and lived an isolated existence with very little interference from any central authority. Agriculture was the livelihood of almost every man, and commerce, beyond an occasional sale of cattle, was almost unknown. In such conditions there are few subject-matters of litigation. Injury to person and property and the simplest contracts of sale or loan make up the bulk of it, and we shall not be surprised to find that the law and its administration are alike very primitive.

The law courts of the Anglo-Saxons corresponded to the territorial divisions of the country. The township indeed was, it seems, too small a unit to have a law court of its own, but once a month a court was held in each hundred and two or three times a year a court of the shire assembled. It is important to remember that these local courts were not staffed by professional judges administering a law of which they had made a special study, but were rather in the nature of public meetings which assembled to transact any public business that there was to be done, including incidentally the judging of cases. The transaction by autonomous communities

---

[1] " Township " was the Anglo-Saxon word. " Vill " is derived from the Latin " villata." It must be remembered that " town," as the widespread use of the suffix " ton " in place-names shows, did not denote (as it does to-day) a centre of population. A town in the modern sense was called a " borough " in the Middle Ages.

of all their business—legislative, administrative and judicial—through a single organ and the application to that organ of government of the name " court " run through the whole history of the Middle Ages and were, as we shall see later, of importance in national as well as local institutions.

The shire court, which will become the " county " court after the Norman Conquest, was the gathering in which royal power encountered more ancient popular institutions. It is first expressly mentioned in the reign of Edgar (957–975). As it operated under the later kings it consisted of the free men of the shire [1]—at least nominally ; later there will be the refinement of owing " suit " to the county court because of holding a particular piece of land.[2]   In effect, however, the court was conducted by royal officials.   At first the head was the alderman, later the earl.   But, with a tendency to group shires into the care of a single alderman or earl, a subordinate official, the shire-reeve, the sheriff, came to the fore.   The shire-reeve seems to have developed from the king's reeve, the local official who looked after various interests of the king in a given area.   The bishop, though not technically a royal official, should also be there in the Anglo-Saxon period ; and his presence is a reminder that Anglo-Saxon society did not know a distinction between Church and State in the form which was to become familiar under the Normans.

The sheriff had important functions in the hundred also.   In the later Anglo-Saxon period the hundred

---

[1] In Anglo-Saxon times a large part of the population was slave or only partially free.

[2] The words " suit " and " suitors " have undergone a distinct change of meaning.   Derived from the Latin " secta " they referred originally to the privilege of following and attending the court in order to take part in its proceedings as a doomsman or judge : a privilege which came to be regarded as an onerous obligation, so that " suit of court " became a recognised feudal burden.   Later the word " suitor " became transferred to a person who attends the court in the capacity of a litigant.

came to the fore as the unit of police and public order. It kept the peace. Its manner of doing so has led to its being called " lynch law legalised " [1] ; and though the anachronism of the phrase is unhappy it makes a valuable point. The hundred court met under the presidency of the hundred-reeve, a subordinate of the sheriff. Sometimes, however, the sheriff came to the hundred and in this practice there was a measure of closer control.

In the courts of Anglo-Saxon England king and people co-operated under the law. The medieval idea of law and law-making was markedly different from either that of classical times or that we know to-day. Law was primarily the custom of the community. At first it was insisted upon, though, as society grew more complex, perhaps with less conviction, that this law could not be added to, it could merely be declared and clarified and the details of its administration regulated. " The king derived new law from the revelation of an existing law, in which all new laws were already latent but not formulated." [2] King and people alike were under the law and the king needed the co-operation of his people. When the Northumbrian king, Edwin, was considering the adoption of Christianity in 627, so the historian Bede tells us, he first discussed the matter " with his principal advisers and friends," " his wise men," his *witan*.[3] Victorian historians often yielded to the temptation to see in a meeting of these wise men (a *witenagemot*) a kind of forerunner of the Parliament of modern times. Such views are now substantially discredited. The *witan* seems to have been made up of members of the royal family, earls, bishops, men who may be called " thegns of the royal circle" —landowners on whom the king relied most in what administration there was, and some clergy of the royal chapel and writing-house, who attended to the

[1] J. E. A. Jolliffe, *Constitutional History of Medieval England* (4th ed., 1961), p. 121.
[2] P. E. Schramm, *A History of the English Coronation* (1937), p. 179.
[3] Bede, *Historia ecclesiastica*, II.13.

written work of government.   The *witan* were consulted
by the king before he made important declarations of the
law ; they formally witnessed important grants of land ;
they helped in occasional great judicial affairs ; they
might be asked for advice during a political crisis.   But
they were not a body with fixed membership, rights, and
functions, nor were they representative of the nation in
any sense we should find adequate to-day.   They were
men of importance in the community whom the king consulted because he and they were under the same law and
because he could not play his own part without the co-
operation of the community at large.

In passing from institutions to the substance of the
law which they administered it is essential to bear in mind
that the law to-day plays a far more active and compelling part in social relations than it did then.   Nowadays the law is in many cases enforced irrespective of any
submission of the parties to its jurisdiction.   If a contract
is broken it rests with the injured party whether he will
pursue his remedy at law or not, but if a crime is committed the law is normally set in motion against the
criminal whether the injured party wishes it or not; and
we regard that state as very ill-regulated which does not
provide an adequate machinery of police for the purpose
of bringing criminals to justice.   In primitive times, however, the law court is like the arbitrator of to-day, who
can only hear a case if both parties submit themselves to
his jurisdiction, and the law has gradually grown to its
present majesty from a stage when resort to it was little
more than an optional alternative to self-redress.   In
those days an injury done was primarily the affair of the
party injured and of his kindred—for in proportion as the
bond of the community at large was weak the bond of
the family was strong.   It was for him and them to avenge
the wrong on the wrongdoer and his kin, and to prosecute
a " blood feud " against them until the wrong originally
done was wiped out by retaliation.

In quite early times, however, we find the community

as a whole attempting to put some limits to these private feuds by inducing the wrongdoer to offer, and the injured parties to accept, compensation for the wrong ; and a large part of the extant laws of the Anglo-Saxon kings is occupied in laying down a minute tariff of compensation (bot) for injuries, based on the extent of the wrong done and the rank of the sufferer. Thus we can read in the laws of King Alfred, " If the great toe be struck off let twenty shillings be paid to him as bot. If it be the second toe, fifteen shillings ; if the middlemost toe, nine shillings. If the fourth toe, six shillings. If the little toe be struck off let five shillings be paid him "; and in the laws of Ethelbert, " God's property and the Church's 12-fold. A bishop's property 11-fold. A priest's property 9-fold. A deacon's property 6-fold. A clerk's property 3-fold."

If compensation is refused the law has no means to enforce its payment. The feud must be prosecuted and the most that the law court can do is to assist the injured party by declaring the wrongdoer an " outlaw " who can be pursued and slain by anyone with impunity like a wild beast. It is to be noticed, however, that even in these times there were many offences which could not be completely atoned for by compensation paid to the sufferer but also entailed a fine (wite) payable to the king through the medium of his officer the sheriff. Further— and this is of great importance in the future—there were some offences which in the later Anglo-Saxon period no compensation could wipe out. They were " botless," were punishable with death or mutilation [1] and entailed a forfeiture of the offender's property to the king. From the point of view of the royal finances it was desirable that the number of " botless " offences should be maintained and if possible extended, and we find in several of the later Anglo-Saxon codes lists of such offences under the heading of royal rights. Thus, in the laws of Canute it is laid down that the rights which the

[1] Punishment by imprisonment seems to have been unknown.

king enjoys over all men in Wessex are " Breach of the King's peace, housebreaking, ambush, the receiving of outlaws and neglect of the summons to the army " [1] unless indeed the king has granted the right of taking the profits of such cases to a favoured subject.

The only one of these royal rights which needs any explanation is the first. To-day we consider that any illegal violence is a " breach of the peace," and from this standpoint " breach of the King's peace " might seem to cover most of the other offences and many more. But it is only gradually that the " King's peace " has come to have such an extended meaning. In Canute's day the " King's peace " did not extend to all places at all times, but only to all places at some times and to some places at all times. For instance, it covered the king's own household and his officers and the few great roads of England (" the King's Highway ") at all times, and it reigned everywhere on the great festivals of the Church.[2] But there were many places and occasions in which it could be claimed that an act of illegal violence was no breach of the king's peace—though maybe it was a breach of some lesser man's peace. Every freeman had a " peace " of his own the breach of which was an offence varying in gravity with the importance of its owner,[3] but it was only very gradually that the " King's peace " ate up all lesser " peaces " so that any act of violence anywhere was a breach of the king's peace though the king was not in any way directly affected by it.[4]

In these early lists of " royal rights," or " Pleas of the Crown " as they came to be called later, we can see the first beginnings of the English Criminal Law. Similarly, in some other provisions of the Anglo-Saxon codes we

[1] These are translations of Anglo-Saxon words, the precise meanings of which are not in all cases certain.

[2] For the " peace " of the itinerant justices see *Select Cases of Procedure without Writ under Henry III*, Selden Society, vol. 60, pp. xxxvii–xli.

[3] This conception of the peace of an individual survives in the proverb " An Englishman's home is his castle." [4] See p. 35, below.

can see the beginnings of an attempt by the community to ensure that men charged with offences shall be brought before the court. To a large extent it is still the business of the complainant to produce his adversary before the judges ; but the laws of Edward and Ethelred insist that every man—and especially any man who has already had charges brought against him—must find people who will be pledges or security for his due appearance in court if he should be accused. In this way, if an offence is committed there will be others besides the injured party interested in securing the appearance of the defendant.

So far we have assumed that there has been a breach of the law and have dealt with the question of redress. But in many cases, of course, there is a preliminary question of fact to be settled. Some thieves are caught red-handed : sometimes a man admits a breach of contract ; but often a charge is met by a denial and the court must in some way decide who is speaking the truth. To us to-day it seems obvious that both sides ought to be allowed to bring witnesses to give evidence in support of their stories, that the parties themselves and their witnesses should be cross-questioned by the other side so that their evidence may be tested, and that the court, whether it be judge or jury, should weigh one case against the other and make up its mind between them. All this, however, was far beyond our Anglo-Saxon ancestors. When faced with two conflicting stories the suitors of the shire or hundred court would decree which party was to have the onus—or maybe in some cases it was the benefit—of having to prove his case. They would further decree how he was to prove it and what would be the results of his failure to prove it, but his failure or success in the actual process of proof did not rest with them. They had told him what the test was to be. God would see to it that if he was innocent he would succeed in the test, and that if he was guilty he would fail. No doubt in trivial cases or where the defendant was a man of good character the proof required would be simple, while in serious criminal charges where appearances were against the accused or he was of bad repute, the test would be one in which he would be likely to fail. To this extent there was an element of rationality in the proceedings, but there was always something of the supernatural too, for the actual decision of the case was out of the control of the judges. One man might fail in the easiest test, another might pass through the severest ordeal. The nature of the tests or mode of proof employed was very varied. In what we should call civil cases proof by "oath helpers" (compurgators) was the commonest form, that is to say that the party who had to prove his case must find a certain number (generally twelve) persons to swear solemnly that the oath which he himself had sworn before the court was a true oath, a procedure which was known as "wager of law." If he could produce the requisite number of oath helpers and they took their oaths in the proper form with no slips, the proof was made. To our eyes this seems farcical enough, but in days when the consequences of taking a false oath were generally regarded as very grave indeed, it was probably not so easy to find oath helpers in a bad case as modern experience might suggest. In serious criminal charges "ordeals" were often employed. In the ordeal by fire, for instance, the accused must carry a red-hot iron a distance of nine feet. His hand was bound up and unbandaged three days afterwards. If the wound was healed he was innocent : if it was still an open sore he was guilty. In the ordeal by water he was bound and lowered into a pool. If he sank a certain distance he was innocent; if not, guilty.[1] Such ordeals were obviously direct appeals to the supernatural and were conducted with solemnity under the ægis of the Church.

It remains to mention a development of the legal system in the later Anglo-Saxon period which added

---

[1] The ordeal by water survived for centuries in a modified form in the test applied to persons suspected of sorcery. "Swimming a witch" was known as late as the seventeenth century.

greatly to its complexity : that is, the growth of private jurisdictions. Side by side with the courts of the hundred and shire we can see in existence a crop of private law courts held by the larger landowners, and to understand their presence it is necessary to say something of the conditions under which the land was owned and cultivated in these times. Originally, perhaps, in the period immediately succeeding the Anglo-Saxon invasions, the land in the various townships in England had been owned in common by groups of two or three families which had settled down in each, but long before the end of the Anglo-Saxon period communal ownership, if it ever existed, had given place to private holdings. If we bear in mind that land and cattle were the chief—practically the sole—forms of wealth, and that without a footing on the land, in however humble a capacity, it was difficult to subsist at all, it is not surprising to find that those who were fortunate or able enough to acquire large interests in the land were persons of far greater importance in the community than the large landowner of to-day, and that those less fortunate tended to drift into a position of dependence. In times when violence was rife and the state did little to protect the subject against it, the small landowner would be glad to seek the protection of the greater, and in return for it to acknowledge that he held his land as a tenant of his lord, while the landlord on his side would be willing enough to grant out portions of his estates, which his supply of serfs did not enable him to cultivate, to free tenants, who would become his vassals. From above, too, there were causes operating to concentrate large estates, and with them large powers over their tenants, in the hands of a few landlords. The Anglo-Saxon king was in name the ruler of an extensive kingdom, but he had no extensive machinery of government or large official class with which to exercise an effective control over it. It was natural for him to reward those who had stood by him in the past and whose support and services he wished to secure for the future with grants of lands. In these royal grants there are often included rights of jurisdiction over the humbler folk living on the land so granted; some landowners, it may be, usurped such rights. The extent of the jurisdiction varies and sometimes no more than a share in the profits of justice may be in question ; sometimes the lord may hold a court to decide cases concerning the land held by his tenants ; sometimes he has a criminal jurisdiction also over them and a private gallows to hang thieves caught on his estates. Sometimes in rare cases, as the extract from the laws of Canute given above shows us, the grantee has even jurisdiction to hear the pleas of the Crown itself arising on his lands.

The development which we have tried to discuss in the last paragraph is sometimes referred to compendiously as " the growth of feudalism." It is important to remember that in Anglo-Saxon England it never attained to uniformity either as a system of land-holding or as a system of private jurisdiction. On the eve of the Norman Conquest there were many " townships " where much of the land was still held in independent ownership and where no large landowner claimed to hold a court which ousted the jurisdiction of the local hundred court. Many " townships," on the other hand, had become communities of tenants who held their land of a lord and brought some at least of their litigation to his court. A unit of land held in this way by dependent tenure came to be called a " manor," [1] and it often happened that the same area of land which was a township in what we may call the national subdivision of England into shires, hundreds and townships, was a manor in its feudal subdivision into a hierarchy of dependent land-holdings, and also a parish for ecclesiastical purposes. [2]

[1] The word " manor " (manerium) does not appear to have been used in England before the Conquest—but the thing which it described already existed in many parts of the country.

[2] While the above account has treated private jurisdictions as primarily a matter of royal grant the possibility of a continuance of ancient rights of jurisdiction cannot be excluded in some cases.

II

THE NORMAN PERIOD
1066–1154

THE Norman Conquest of England was of a very different character from the Anglo-Saxon invasions. These had been migrations of whole peoples and in the course of them the earlier inhabitants of the land were largely exterminated or expelled ; but the result of Duke William's victory at Hastings was only to impose on the Anglo-Saxon population a relatively small foreign governing class. Further, the Conqueror claimed to be the lawful successor of Edward the Confessor. He assured the citizens of London that it was his will that " you be worthy of all the laws that you were worthy of in the time of King Edward," [1] and, though he made changes in the Anglo-Saxon legal system, he did not replace it as a whole with Norman institutions. Nor, indeed, had he done so, would the change have been very great, for the Norman law of the eleventh century so far as it is known to us [2] seems to have borne a considerable resemblance to contemporary Anglo-Saxon law and was certainly no less primitive. At first sight, therefore, it may look as though the Norman Conquest was not an event of great importance in our legal history. In fact, however, it was all-important, and before we discuss in detail the few immediate changes which resulted from it, it will be well to sketch in outline the nature of its ultimate effects.

[1] *English Historical Documents, 1042–1189,* p. 945.
[2] Pollock and Maitland : *History of English Law* (2nd. ed.), vol. I, pp. 79–110. (This work is hereafter cited as " P. and M.") The student is advised to use the re-issue (1968) with elaborate introduction and select bibliography by Professor S. F. C. Milsom.

Some two centuries before the Conquest, at about the time when the Danes were invading England, Scandinavian freebooters were also ravaging the coasts of Northern France, and in 911 Rollo, the leader of a host of these marauders, in return for his acknowledgment of the nominal suzerainty of the French King Charles the Simple, received from him the right to settle in and reign over the province which came to be known as Normandy, the land of the Northmen. The invaders soon amalgamated with the native French inhabitants, and by the middle of the eleventh century the Normans, combining, as has been said, the strength of the Viking with the vivacity of the Celt, had become a powerful people led by a feudal aristocracy endowed with a vigour and enterprise unequalled in Europe. In Duke William they had a leader who was one of the ablest statesmen of his time. It was not likely that such a man with such resources, having England at his feet, would be content with the feeble control over it which the Anglo-Saxon kings had exercised, particularly when we remember that in France he had had ample personal experience of the results of weak monarchies and powerful feudal vassals. At once after the Conquest he gathered round him as a nucleus of his royal court—the Curia Regis—a group of skilled administrators such as no Anglo-Saxon king had had at his command, and through them the royal authority was made effective in England in a manner hitherto unknown in Europe.

In the reign of the Conqueror and his sons the activity of the Curia Regis was mainly directed to matters by which the King's own interests were immediately affected—notably to the collection of a revenue—while ordinary litigation continued for the most part to come before the old local and private courts unhampered by any control from the central authority. Gradually, however, in the reigns of the early Angevin kings the Curia Regis came to offer itself as a law court in which the suits of private individuals could be judged, and, as its law and procedure were far superior to anything which its rivals had to offer, it extended its jurisdiction more and more at their expense. Eventually, about two centuries after the Conquest, the royal court had become the normal tribunal for the dispatch of most of the important litigation in the country, and its law, the Common Law of England, had taken the place of the variety of customary rules upon which justice had been administered in the local and private courts.

It is natural to ask what was the character and origin of this "Common Law" administered by the royal court. In form, of course, it was chiefly a French law. French was the language of the Norman and Angevin sovereigns and their courtiers, and French continued to be the language of the common law courts long after it had ceased to be the language of the upper classes in England.[1] In substance the common law may be said to have been a new law created by the royal courts in the twelfth and thirteenth centuries. Many of the materials with which the royal judges worked can, of course, be traced to the law of Anglo-Saxon England or pre-Conquest Normandy, but these materials they built into a new building with additions of their own, and so far as they were indebted in their achievement to anything beyond their own abilities it was to the law of Rome rather than to any other that the credit must go.

The eleventh century saw a renaissance of Roman Law in Europe based on the study of the original texts of Justinian in the law schools of Northern Italy, and side by side with it a development of the canon law of the Church, which now for the first time was reduced into a logical system not unworthy to be compared with the

[1] See P. and M., vol. I, pp. 80–87. The written records of the common law courts were kept in Latin, but the oral pleadings in them were in French. English supplanted French as the language of the ruling classes in the later fourteenth century, but French continued to be used in legal literature until the seventeenth century.

magnificent order of the Roman civil law.[1] To turn to
these two bodies of law from the primitive confusion of
the customary law of the shires and manors of England
was to pass from darkness to light, and the judges of the
Curia Regis, who were in this period most of them
Churchmen and many of them students of the Roman
civil law as well,[2] found in these systems much to help
them in their task of building up the common law.
After about 1300 Roman and canon law ceased almost
entirely to influence the development of the Common
Law, but in their day they helped to make it a system not
wholly unsuited to the needs of the English state, and
thus it came about that when in the fifteenth and sixteenth
centuries many continental states abandoned their own
mediæval law in favour of a wholesale reception of the
law of Rome, in England the mediæval common law
supplemented by equity and reformed by statute has
survived into modern times to share the legal empire of
the world with systems derived directly from the Roman
jurisprudence. This is a matter of importance in our history
and can be traced to the fact that the Norman Conquest
gave us at such an early date a strong central monarchy
which was able to supplant the old legal order with its
own royal law.

With so much by way of introduction we must pass to
the few immediate changes in the legal system which
were brought about by the Norman Conquest. Before
we consider the royal court or Curia Regis we must look
at the local, feudal (" seignorial ") and franchise courts
which covered the country, and first at the changes in the
organisation of the local courts. The early Norman kings
appear to have insisted that the courts of the shire and

---

[1] See P. and M., vol. I, pp. 111-135, and *Cambridge Mediæval
History*, vol. V, Chapter 21. Hitherto Western Europe had known of
the Roman Law chiefly through the truncated and barbarised version of
it issued by the Visigothic King Alaric II.

[2] See p. 382, below.

hundred should be held regularly as of old,[1] but after the Conquest both bishop and earl disappeared from their meetings. William was a supporter of the movement of reform in the Church which is associated with the name of his great contemporary Hildebrand, afterwards Pope Gregory VII. The movement emphasised the independence of the Church from secular control and in particular its right to exclusive jurisdiction over matters regarded as ecclesiastical. William ordained that ecclesiastical causes (and the profits from them) should be excluded from the hundred courts; and by a slower evolution the bishop and his affairs withdrew from the shire court.[2] As for the earls, he was determined that so far as might be there should be no hereditary viceroyalties in England, and though the title of earl continued to be conferred from time to time on some great baron as a mark of honour it became in most cases a mere title which of itself gave its holder no powers of government in the shire whose name he bore. The so-called " Palatinates " were exceptions to this rule.[3] On the Welsh and Scottish borders the constant danger of invasion made it necessary for large powers of government more or less unhampered by control from the centre to be concentrated in a single hand, and in the Palatine Earldoms of Chester and Lancaster and the Bishopric of Durham the Earl or Prince Bishop enjoyed a vice-regal authority for some time after the Conquest.

The importance of the sheriff was naturally increased by this removal of his two rivals from the shire court, and

[1] The sessions of these courts seem to have become more frequent in the twelfth century—the shire court meeting once a month and the hundred once a fortnight. P. and M., vol. I, pp. 538 and 557.

[2] *English Historical Documents, 1042–1189*, pp. 604–5 (probably April 1072) ; see C. Morris, " William I and the Church Courts " (1967), 82 *E.H.R.* 449–63. For the jurisdiction of the ecclesiastical courts, see Chapter 14, below.

[3] P. and M., vol. I, p. 533. See as to the position of the earls in Norman times, Stenton, *English Feudalism 1066–1166* (2nd. ed., 1961); pp. 227–235.

in Norman and Angevin times he wielded enormous power in his county as the sole representative in it of the royal authority.   He was appointed and removable by the king, and the Crown was successful after a struggle in preventing the office from becoming hereditary [1]; but even so his power aroused at once the distrust of the Crown and the jealousy of the great landowners.   By Magna Carta, clause 24 he was prohibited from holding Pleas of the Crown.   The royal courts, as we shall see, in time deprived him of most of the remainder of his jurisdiction, and the justices of the peace of his control over local administration.[2]   By the end of the Middle Ages his office had become one of honour rather than of power and profit.   Such duties as still remained to him, notably the conduct of Parliamentary elections, and the execution of judgments, including the " execution " of criminals, were in fact carried out by a Deputy Sheriff, who was normally an attorney, and permanently employed in that capacity by successive Sheriffs.   The only duty which he still performs personally is the ceremonial one of attending the judges of assize with trumpeters and javelin men.

The procedure of the shire and hundred courts remained largely unchanged.   The chief suitors of the court were now no doubt Normans and not Anglo-Saxons, but they gave the judgments of the court in the old way and according to the old customary law, assessing the " bot " or " wite " to be paid and fixing the appropriate mode of proof.   One innovation there was.   Trial by battle—a Norman institution—took its place beside the ordeals by fire and water as a mode of proof in some cases.   At first the new ordeal may not have been imposed

[1] The border shire of Westmorland alone retained an hereditary sheriff, and the office was vested in the Earls of Thanet as late as 1831. The City of London was also powerful enough to secure from the Crown the right to elect its own sheriffs and to hold the shrievalty of Middlesex in farm, and the two sheriffs of the City of London were always also appointed by the City as sheriffs of Middlesex.

[2] See pages 76, 78, below.

on Anglo-Saxon litigants,[1] but in time, with the disappearance of the distinction between the two races, trial by battle became a universal mode of trial in certain classes of case in all courts and survived as a possible mode of trial long after the ordeals of fire and water had been abolished.[2] Further, the Norman kings made important improvements in the methods of bringing criminals to justice. Their Norman followers, few in number and living among a recently conquered population, had to be protected. Hitherto, as we saw, the duty of bringing a suspected criminal before the court was laid chiefly on the injured party or his kin, but the murdered Norman might have no kin in England, and so William introduced a system of communal responsibility for crime. In the first place, if a man was found murdered and he could not be proved to be English, he was presumed to be Norman, and the hundred in which he was found was liable to pay a " murder " fine.[3] Secondly, by an extension of the law of the Saxon King Edward to which we referred, every man who had not substantial property or a man of rank to answer for his conduct, had to be enrolled in a group of ten men known as a " tithing." If one member of such a group committed an offence the other nine must secure his production in court or be fined for their failure to do so and make reparation in his place. Twice a year the sheriff held a special session of each hundred court in his shire [4] at which he reviewed the operation of this system—known as the " frankpledge " system—enquired whether every man who ought to be

[1] Ten Articles, no. 6 (*English Historical Documents, 1042–1189*, p. 399) ; but this is a document of doubtful authenticity.

[2] Trial by battle was a possible mode of trial in an appeal of murder until the year 1819. See p. 70, below.

[3] The process by which the hundred proved to the sheriff or royal officer that the deceased was English was known as the " presentment of Englishry."

[4] It is not strictly accurate to say that the sheriff always held this session, for many hundred courts were in the hands of private lords who maintained the right to exclude the sheriff and take the view of frankpledge themselves.

enrolled in a tithing was so enrolled and collected the fines due from the hundred townships and tithings for any breach of this system. This special session of the hundred court for the view of frankpledge, afterwards known as the " sheriff's tourn," came to play an important part in the administration of criminal justice in the Middle Ages.[1]

Next we must speak of the effect of the Conquest on feudalism and feudal courts. We saw that in later Anglo-Saxon times there was a growing tendency for land instead of being owned by its cultivators to be held by one man as tenant of another as lord. The Conquest completed at a blow a development which might otherwise have been spread over a century or more, for William claimed the whole land of England as forfeited to him and laid down the principle, which is still a part of our land law, that the Crown alone is the owner of land and that all others are but tenants holding their land directly or indirectly from the Crown. Much of England the Conqueror retained in his own hands. There were royal manors in nearly every shire, and the king was by far the greatest landlord in the realm.[2] The rest he granted out to his chief followers, lay and ecclesiastical—nearly all of them Frenchmen—in fiefs of varying sizes which they held of him in return for some defined service, generally the service of providing armed horsemen for the royal army in number proportionate to the value of the land granted. The king's tenants-in-chief in their turn granted out (subinfeudated) a large number of the manors granted to them to others to hold under them by some form of ser-

---

[1] For the nature and origin of the frankpledge system, see Holdsworth: *History of English Law* (hereafter cited as " Holdsworth "), vol. I, p. 13, and W. A. Morris, *The Frankpledge System*.

[2] A computation based on the Domesday Survey reckons the annual value of all the lands at William's disposal (exclusive of the income derived from the boroughs) at about £73,000, and the value of royal manors at about £12,500 a year, *i.e.* about a sixth. *Cambridge Mediæval History*, vol. V, p. 508.

vice, and the sub-tenants [1] again often subinfeudated a
portion of their holding, so that there might be many
rungs on the ladder stretching from the king to the serf
who held a small patch of land in a manor in return for
his labour in cultivating the demesne land of his lord.
Naturally this re-allotting of the soil of England was not
accomplished without great hardship to the Anglo-Saxon
population. The great English landlords were for the
most part expropriated,[2] and many of the lesser men who
had previously looked on themselves as owners of their
land were converted into tenants holding it of a foreign
master. Where there had been an English overlord the
Norman stepped into his shoes and exercised the rights
which his predecessor had exercised : where there had
been no lord before one appeared now, and in place of
the variety of conditions of men and landholding which
had obtained in the Anglo-Saxon era, we find the few
definite forms of tenure (free and unfree) which were
worked out by the genius of Norman lawyers in the two
centuries after the Conquest.

The details of the feudal tenures are to be sought in
books on real property, but the complete " feudalisation "
of our land law had important effects on the legal system
of this country, for it came to be a principle of English
feudalism that every man who had tenants under him
holding land of him by any sort of tenure had a right, and
indeed a duty, to hold a court for those tenants in which
certain disputes which might arise between them ought
to be settled. Of these courts, based on the existence
of the relation of landlord and tenant, and which are
commonly termed " seignorial " courts, there were
three grades, but the evidence on which our knowledge
of their jurisdiction and procedure is based comes from

---

[1] Many of the sub-tenants were, of course, Anglo-Saxons.

[2] A very few took William's side and retained their lands, but the vast
majority of the tenants-in-chief—about 170 in all—were Frenchmen.
Cambridge Mediæval History, vol. V, p. 508. *Cf.* also F. M. Stenton,
Anglo-Saxon England (Oxford History ; 2nd ed.), pp. 671–2.

the thirteenth and later centuries, and it is not to be assumed that the principles and distinctions then recognised had been clearly marked in the twelfth century.[1]

The widest and most valuable jurisdiction was that of certain tenants in chief of the Crown in the courts of their baronies or honours, of which many manors, sometimes situated in different counties, might be held. It seems that all these courts claimed as of right not only the normal feudal jurisdiction to try disputes regarding land held of the lord, but also the franchise of " view of frankpledge " and with it the right to hold all the personal pleas, such as debt, covenant and replevin, which were normally tried in the hundred and county courts, and which in the baronial courts were commenced by oral plaint without writ.

Next in order came the Courts Baron of single manors. The principle of trial *per iudicium parium* required that there should be at least two free tenants of a manor, other than the litigants, to try a case of free tenement, and many manors had no free tenants. The lord who had a sufficiency of free tenants, his " barons,"[2] could hold a Court Baron. Primarily their jurisdiction was confined to the trial of disputes as to the ownership of land held of the manor and the enforcement of the various customary rules which governed the rights of lords and tenants in the common fields and waste. Cases of crime—whether paltry transgressions or those serious offences which were Pleas of the Crown—were for the hundred and the county, or in later times the royal courts.

The third and lowest type of seignorial court arose from the distinction between the free and villein tenants

---

[1] By far the most illuminating account of these private tribunals is to be found in the introduction to *Select Pleas in the Manorial Courts*, by F. W. Maitland (Selden Society, vol. 2). The introduction to *Brevia Placitata* (Selden Society, vol. 66) by G. J. Turner should also be consulted. *Cf.* also D. W. Sutherland, Quo warranto *Proceedings, 1278–1294* (1963), chs. i and xi.

[2] " Baron " in Norman French primarily means " man " as in the phrase " baron et feme " for " man and wife."

of the manor. For the trial of actions about the tenements of villeins, who held their land by the custom of the manor, the lord would hold a Court Customary.

With the difference of jurisdiction went a difference in procedure. In the courts which dealt with free tenements, as in the local courts, the suitors gave the judgments and the lord's steward only presided; the modes of proof were compurgation, ordeal and trial by battle. In the Customary Court the suitors were only witnesses, and the steward was judge.

A manorial court which enjoyed the view of frankpledge was known as a " Court Leet."

We must look last at the franchise courts. Cases of crime—whether paltry transgressions or those serious offences which were Pleas of the Crown—were tried not in the feudal courts but in the hundred and the county, or in later times the royal courts. In fact, however, as we saw, many landowners in Anglo-Saxon times had claimed to exercise a criminal justice over their humbler neighbours, and the Norman lords who stepped into their shoes claimed the same privileges as their predecessors. According to the theory of the royal lawyers of the thirteenth century, such a claim could only be based on the existence of a special grant from the king [1]—whether some old " landboc " of an Anglo-Saxon monarch or a recent charter of a Norman or Angevin sovereign. It was not an incident of the relation of lord and tenant, but a special privilege or " franchise." We must not think, however, that such franchises were rare. In the England of the thirteenth century—and it is only then that our knowledge of these matters begins to be at all satisfactory —a very large number of the hundred courts were in the hands of private lords who took the profits of them to the

---

[1] This was the foundation of the royal claims in the Quo Warranto enquiries of Edward I. Nothing shows the continuity between Anglo-Saxon and Norman times better than the fact that many claims to franchises in the thirteenth century were based on Anglo-Saxon grants.

exclusion of the sheriff.[1]   Where the lord claimed the franchise of the view of frankpledge there appears to have gone with it the jurisdiction of the hundred court in paltry crime, and in debt, covenant and replevin, commenced by plaint.   It was only rarely that a franchise extended to jurisdiction over serious crime.[2]

England, then, in the first century after the Conquest was covered with a network of different kinds of courts— courts of shires and hundreds, courts of honours and manors and franchise courts.   Often they had a concurrent and competing jurisdiction and the law which they administered was for the most part the customary law of the district laid down by the suitors of the court and varying from place to place.   The Conquest, so far from lessening, had added to this confusion by increasing the number of manorial courts and introducing a certain number of customs which were only applicable to the Norman part of the community, and the difficulty which there was in ascertaining the law on any given subject in any given place is reflected in the legal treatises of the Norman period which attempt with indifferent success to give a coherent statement of the existing system.[3]   But the Norman Conquest had given the country a strong central government, and above the local and manorial courts with their conflicting laws there towered the majesty of the royal court whose law was everywhere and at all times the same. It remains for us to say something in detail of the composition and activity of this tribunal in the Norman period.

[1] Thus of the thirty-nine hundred courts in Wiltshire in 1255, sixteen and a half were in the hands of the king and subject to the sheriff, and twenty-two and a half in the hands of private lords. P. and M., vol. I, p. 558.

[2] See *Select Pleas in Manorial Courts*, p. xxv and *Brevia Placitata*, p. lxi. Sometimes, however, though the royal judge tries the case the profits go to the lord and the criminal is hanged on the lord's gallows.

[3] *E.g.* the so-called "Leges Henrici Primi," and "Laws of Edward the Confessor," two treatises composed in the early twelfth century; see T. F. T. Plucknett, *Early English Legal Literature* (1958), ch. ii; H. G. Richardson and G. O. Sayles, *Law and Legislation from Æthelberht to Magna Carta* (1966), ch. ii.

We have seen that the local courts of the Early Mediæval period were meetings which assembled for the transaction of the public business of the district which they represented and were as much occupied with what we should call administrative work as with the judging of cases.   This was as true of the " Curia Regis " as of the county and manorial courts.   The Curia Regis as a law court was only one aspect of a single body which carried on the whole central government.   Nowadays we are apt to conceive of all central governments as necessarily split up into a number of different organs with different functions and in particular with different organs for their legislative, their executive and their judicial work. This is the famous principle of the " Separation of Powers " upon which Montesquieu fixed as the secret of the relative freedom enjoyed by the subjects of George II as compared with those of Louis XV, and which had so great a vogue in the eighteenth century that it deeply influenced the constitutions of the American and French Republics.   It may be doubted whether it was really true to say that any rigid separation of powers existed in the English constitution of the early eighteenth century, and the farther back one goes the less true it becomes.   In Norman and Angevin times there was no such separation at all.   Whatever powers of central government the king had were exercised through one and the same body—his royal court.   As we shall see, the composition of this body was of a very fluctuating character and depended almost entirely on the king's will.

The king's council, his *curia*, was no longer composed of *witan* but of " barons "—it was the court of the tenants of a feudal lord.   True, much the same kind of people (including the bishops and other prelates) might attend : " the barons in the king's *curia* were the old *witan* feudalised." [1]   Just as a manorial court was the

---

[1] R. C. van Caenegem, *Royal Writs in England from the Conquest to Glanvill* (Selden Soc., vol. 77), p. 27.

proper tribunal for disputes between tenants of the manor among themselves or with their lord, so the Curia Regis, as the chief feudal court, was the proper tribunal for disputes between the tenants-in-chief or between a tenant-in-chief and the sovereign. In such cases the tenants-in-chief—the suitors of the court—were themselves the judges, though we may suspect that the influence of the king himself often counted for much when his interests were at stake.[1] Besides their functions as the highest feudal tribunal, the tenants-in-chief were generally parties to what we should call important acts of legislation. Just as the laws of the Anglo-Saxon monarchs had been promulgated with the co-operation of the witan, so the laws of William the Conqueror and Henry I, to some of which we have referred, were most of them expressed to have been decreed with the advice of the chief men of England, though it is very doubtful whether anything but the will of the sovereign really counted on such occasions.

But day-to-day government required something more than occasional gatherings of tenants-in-chief. The Curia Regis in the narrow sense was primarily composed of what might be called great ministers of state and—admittedly with greater anachronism—working civil servants. These latter were clerks, for only those in clerical orders could be relied upon to have the literacy necessary for the conduct of administration. Unquestionably, the Norman monarchy made great strides in the field of central administration. Its first great exploit in this connexion was the compilation of the survey of England known as Domesday Book, though it is right to add that the Doomsday survey could hardly have succeeded without the substructure of Anglo-Saxon local government.

---

[1] Still the tenants-in-chief were the judges and they supported the saintly Anselm, Archbishop of Canterbury, against William Rufus, though the king shouted in his rage, " By God's face if you will not condemn him as I wish I will condemn you."

For the purpose of revising the assessment of the
" geld " or " land tax," King William sent officials of
the Curia over the greater part of the kingdom to enquire
of the value of every parcel of land in it. For the
purpose of the enquiry the whole county visited was
represented before the royal commissioners, the larger
landowners appearing in person and the smaller landowners and the peasantry appearing by representatives
sent from each hundred and township. A list of questions concerning the nature and value of each unit of
land—each " manor "—was submitted by the commissioners to those who appeared from the locality in
question, and their questions had to be answered on oath.[1]
The land tax assessed on this new basis was not collected
by officials of the Curia, but by the sheriff, and accounted
for by him twice a year to the central treasury along with
the other revenue of the shire.

It may indeed have been that the union of dominions
separated by a sea-crossing helped to impress the need for
a strong administration ; certainly, the impossibility of
the king, the pivot on which all turned, being in two
places at once helped to bring about the emergence of a
new and highly important official, the Chief Justiciar, the
king's other self.[2]   Though this office was not fully established until after 1154, it was foreshadowed in the position of such men as Roger of Salisbury, Henry I's
Treasurer.   Under Roger, too, there emerged a distinct
financial office, the Exchequer (probably about 1110–
1120).   It was to the Exchequer that the sheriffs came
twice a year, as we have already mentioned, and it was the
Exchequer which kept the first of the great series of public
records which to-day form the riches of the Public Record

---

[1] For extensive materials in translation, see *English Historical Documents, 1042–1189*, pp. 854–78.

[2] See F. J. West, *The Justiciarship in England, 1066–1232* (1966).
It is significant that after the office faded out in England (where, after the
loss of Normandy, the king was usually to be found) its Irish imitation
remained (for the king was scarcely ever there).

Office.   The first surviving Pipe Roll in fact comes to us
from 1130, but it is certain that it had predecessors.
Upon the Pipe Roll the accounts of the sheriffs and others
were carefully recorded in a most elaborate way and the
Exchequer soon developed a professional pride and *esprit
de corps*.[1]

Revenue was the great concern of the Conqueror and
Henry I, and naturally the class of litigation in which
they were most interested was that which produced
revenue for them, namely, the " Pleas of the Crown."
We have a list of these from the reign of Henry I[2] which
is far longer and contains a far greater variety of matters
than the list in the laws of Canute to which we referred.
But there is not yet any broad general principle that all
acts of violence, or even all serious crimes, are royal pleas
and entail a forfeiture to the king.   The pleas of the
crown were still, generally speaking, tried before the
sheriff in the county court and the resultant fines and
forfeitures accounted for by him to the Exchequer, but
on occasions for a case of great importance the king would
send down a member of the Curia Regis to hear a case;
and such a trial before a royal commissioner was regarded
as a trial before the Curia Regis itself.   There were two
respects in which such a trial differed from one in any
other court.   In the first place, the parties were summoned to it by a command—a writ—from the king
himself under the royal seal kept by the Chancellor,
disobedience to which might entail very serious consequences.[3]   Secondly, the Curia Regis was not bound by

[1] A generation later the *Dialogue of the Exchequer* is at once the first text-
book on English administration and of some value for legal history as well:
edition with translation by C. Johnson (1950) and translation only in *English
Historical Documents, 1042–1189*, pp. 490–569.   Because the Exchequer
was a stable centre of government, though secondary to the itinerant
king himself, the justiciar developed a specially close relationship with it.

[2] Leges Henrici Primi, 10 (1) : *English Historical Documents, 1042–
1189*, p. 459.

[3] Contempt of a royal writ was one of the Pleas of the Crown in the
list referred to above.

the procedure of other tribunals, and though it might decide a case by compurgation or trial by battle it might use the procedure employed in the Domesday Survey and insist on arriving at the facts by means of an " inquest " of persons likely to be acquainted with them.   As we have said, the Curia Regis in this period did not, generally speaking, concern itself with private litigation.   That was for the local or manorial courts.   But obviously the superior procedure of the royal court was an inducement to the private litigant to get his case brought before it if possible, and there is evidence to show that the Norman kings occasionally granted the privilege of a trial before a royal judge with the royal procedure in an ordinary private case.   Such a proceeding was, however, exceptional, and no doubt the royal writ was only purchased at a high price.

The functioning of the royal court in this period was, we have seen, of an exceptional and irregular character, Except in the department of the exchequer it can hardly be said to have evolved any fixed rules or any normal procedure.   Ultimately everything depended on the will of the sovereign, for there was not yet any tradition of continuity which would enable the court to function independently of the will of its head.   William the Conqueror and Henry I were both men of extraordinary force of character who wielded a despotic authority in England, but their authority was largely personal and not due to the inherent strength of the machine of government.   Therefore, when Henry was succeeded by Stephen, who was a man of a feebler stamp and whose succession to the throne was disputed, civil war broke out, and in the resultant confusion the authority of the royal court largely vanished.   Its restoration and extension by Henry II will be the subject of the next chapter.

III

THE EARLY ANGEVINS
1154–1215

HENRY II, the son of Geoffrey Plantagenet, Count of Anjou and husband of Eleanor of Aquitaine, was by reason both of the extent of his dominions and his remarkable personal endowments one of the greatest, perhaps indeed the greatest, of the European princes of his age. King of England was for him only one of many titles. As Duke of Normandy and of Aquitaine and Count of Anjou he reigned subject to the shadowy suzerainty of the French king over the greater part of Western France and more than half his time was spent out of this country. His personality impressed itself deeply on his contemporaries. Friend and enemy alike agree that he was a man of energy and passions far beyond the normal run of men. One trait in his character is of particular interest for our purpose—his love for the details of law and administration. He relished legal argument and delighted to sit in judgment.

The thirty-five years of Henry's reign have a good claim to be considered the most important of our legal history. To appreciate their importance one must compare the England of Stephen with the England of Richard I. In Stephen's reign the " King's Peace " was still a limited conception. Many grave crimes if they were punished at all were punished in local or private courts. Similarly, the feudal land law was still administered in feudal courts. It was to his lord's court and not to the king's court that the tenant looked for protection. In Richard's reign, on the other hand, though the king himself was almost continuously absent from the realm, the royal court held the centre of the stage.

the twelve leading thegns and the reeve were to come forward and swear that they would accuse no innocent man and conceal no guilty one.[1] Of course, such a procedure may not have been universal in Anglo-Saxon England ; but a tradition of communal responsibility, if it did indeed exist, was no doubt strengthened by the " murder fine " [2] and the " frankpledge system." [3] Men were thus made vigilant to prevent crime and to inform against suspected criminals. Though to us the system may seem arbitrary, in the enclosed rural communities of medieval England the possibility of the truth coming to light in this way was far greater than in a more complex society. At all events, in 1166 the Assize of Clarendon gave the system of communal accusation much greater organisation and severity.[4]

Whatever the detailed history, by the end of the twelfth century the administration of the criminal law had greatly advanced. All serious offences involving a breach of the peace are now Pleas of the Crown, and most Pleas of the Crown are now heard in the royal court. The more serious crimes—homicide, for instance, and the graver cases of theft—wherever committed, place life and limb in the king's hands and are the subject of prosecution at the suit of the king and not merely at the suit of the injured party. Further, while the lesser criminal offences

---

[1] III Æthelred 3.1 (translation in *English Historical Documents, c. 500–1042*, p. 403). Dismissed by Maitland, Holdsworth and Plucknett (*Select Pleas in Manorial Courts*, pp. xxxvi–xxxvii ; *History of English Law*, i.12 n ; *Concise History of the Common Law*, 5th ed., pp. 108–9) the linking of Æthelred's law with the later " jury of presentment " has been favoured by Dr. N. D. Hurnard and Richardson and Sayles (" The Jury of Presentment and the Assize of Clarendon " (1941) 56 *E.H.R.* 374–410 ; *Governance of Medieval England*, pp. 182–4). For a broader view, see S. F. C. Milsom, *Historical Foundations of the Common Law* (1969), p. 357.

[2] See p. 19, above.

[3] See p. 19, above.

[4] *English Historical Documents, 1042–1189*, pp. 407–10 ; *cf.* Richardson and Sayles, *Governance of Medieval England*, pp. 438–49.

[5] *English Historical Documents, 1042–1189*, pp. 410–13.

are still tried in the local or franchise courts, a system of discretionary money fines payable to the Crown or the holder of the franchise takes the place of the old system of compensation. Further, as a result of the Assize of Clarendon in 1166 and of the Assize of Northampton in 1176 which supplemented it a duty was cast on twelve representatives [1] of each hundred in every county, and also on four representatives from each township in each hundred, of reporting or " presenting " to the authorities all persons whom they suspected of having committed crimes in their district. These presentments were made in the first instance to the sheriff in his " tourn " round the hundred courts, but he could only punish those accused of lesser offences. [2] Those accused of the graver crimes (which were coming to be known as " felonies ") were kept in detention until a justice of the Curia Regis should come round to the county and were then " presented " to him by the jury of the hundred in question. For fifty years or so after 1166 the presented suspects were sent by the royal judge to the ordeal by water. If they failed they were in peril of their lives [3]; if they came through it they went free unless they were men of very bad repute with their neighbours. Such men, even though the ordeal had declared them innocent, had to leave the country, but they kept their goods and land, whereas the property of those who failed at the ordeal was forfeited, the goods to the king and the land to the lord of whom it was held.

There are several points of importance to notice in the system established by the Assize of Clarendon. The juries of presentment are, of course, the ancestors of the

[1] The bailiff of each hundred chose four knights of the district, who themselves chose twelve freemen to form the jury of this hundred.

[2] For the preliminary presentment at the tourn and the punishment of misdemeanours there, see Holdsworth, vol. I, pp. 76–80.

[3] The idea that William the Conqueror abolished the death penalty in favour of mutilation can be disregarded: N. D. Hurnard, *The King's Pardon for Homicide* (1969), pp. 5–6.

Grand Jury which survived in England until 1932 ; but in those early times far more extensive duties were cast on them than was latterly the case, for in the absence of any police force it was their task to see that suspected persons were brought to justice. Secondly, it is to be noted that suspected felons presented under this system could only be tried by a royal judge, and that for this purpose justices of the Curia Regis began to be sent round the country on regular circuits to try these felonies. Thirdly, one can see that trial by ordeal was falling into discredit. Some fifty years later it disappeared altogether and it became necessary to find a new method of trying the suspects presented by the juries of the hundreds.

It must not be supposed that the method of public accusation of criminals instituted by these assizes at once supplanted the older method of accusation at the suit of the injured party or his kin. For a century and more after 1166 it was at least as common for a criminal to be brought to justice by way of a private action in the royal court—known as an " appeal of felony "—as for him to be indicted at the suit of the king under the assizes of Clarendon and Northampton, and in the case of murder an " appeal " continued in theory possible until 1819. The great difference between the two was that appeals were normally [1] decided by battle between the parties, whereas persons presented under the assize were tried originally by ordeal and later—as we shall see—by petty jury. The chief ground for the survival of the older private procedure was perhaps that in some cases it offered advantages to the injured party which he would not obtain if the criminal was merely prosecuted at the suit of the king.[2]

We must now pass from Henry's reform of the criminal law to the intervention of the royal court in

[1] But see p. 69, below.
[2] *E.g.* the stolen goods which would be forfeit to the king if the thief were convicted under the assize could be recovered by the owner in an appeal of larceny (see Holdsworth, vol. II, p. 361).

suits concerning land.   Land was by far the most important article of property in the Middle Ages and a large
proportion of all litigation was connected with it.   By
feudal principles the appropriate court for the determination of such questions was normally the court of the lord
of whom the land affected was held, and Henry did not
attempt directly to deny the principle or to make a frontal
attack on feudal jurisdiction ; but he was successful in
undermining that jurisdiction and facilitating its eventual
supersession by the royal courts through the application
of two rules to litigation about land.   The first was that
the king's writ was necessary for the commencement of
litigation about freehold land in any court, the second that
a person claiming land in the possession, or seisin as it
comes to be called, of another must not help himself, but
must recover the land by action in the appropriate court.
As to the first of these rules, it became an established
principle under Henry II that no suit touching the title
to land held by free tenure [1] should be started without a
" writ " from the king.   Such a writ, known generically
as a " writ of right," took on two different forms.   Where
the disputed interest in the land was not a fee held of the
king in chief but a fee held of a " mesne lord " the writ
was directed to him bidding him do full right between the
parties in the matter of the land in question under pain of
the case being removed from his court to the sheriff's
court if he failed to do justice.   This removal was
effected (if necessary) by the process known as " tolt "
under which the sheriff on a complaint to him in his
county court of a failure of the lord to do justice ordered
his bailiff to attend the lord's court and take away the
plaint into the county court.[2]   Once in the county
court the case could again be removed into the royal

[1] The royal courts refused to interfere in questions touching land held
by unfree tenure until the very end of the Middle Ages.

[2] " Tolt " is commonly referred to as a writ, but it was only a precept
of the sheriff.   See the precedent in the *Proceedings on a Writ of Right
Patent*, Blackstone's Commentaries, vol. III, Appendix 1, No. 2.

court by a writ of " pone " directed to the sheriff.
But where the dispute was between two tenants-in-chief
and the appropriate court, even on feudal principles, was,
accordingly, the Curia Regis, the writ, which was known
as a " præcipe," was addressed to the sheriff and directed
him to order the defendant either to yield up the disputed
land to the plaintiff or appear in the royal court to answer
why he had not done so.[1]   In these writs we have the first
of the writs known as original writs, *i.e.* writs starting
litigation, which soon took on a great number of different
forms and exercised a great influence on the development
of our law.[2]

In the seignorial and shire courts the recognised method
of trial of questions touching the right to land held by free
tenure was trial by battle.   In Henry II's reign, as we can
see from the provisions of the Assize of Clarendon, ordeals
of any sort were beginning to be felt to be unsatisfactory,
and in response to this feeling an ordinance by the Curia
Regis gave the defendant to a writ of right the option of
declining battle in the seignorial or shire court and insisting on the case being decided by the verdict of an inquest
in the royal court.   This ordinance [3] was known as the

[1] See Maitland, *Forms of Actions*, p. 376, for the two forms of a
writ of right.

[2] Writs are simply commands from the king and may just as well
concern administrative as judicial business, *e.g.* a writ of summons to
Parliament. Writs dealing with ordinary litigation fall into three classes :
(*a*) original writs which start the action in question ; (*b*) writs of " mesne
process " for carrying on the proceedings, *e.g.* a writ of *venire facias*
summoning a jury to try the case (see p. 185, below) ; and (*c*) writs of
" final process " for executing judgment, *e.g.* a writ of *fieri facias* (see
p. 189, below). The student should also remember the " prerogative "
writs, which stand on a somewhat different footing ; see p. 60, below.

[3] The ordinance in question seems to have been made in 1179. The
word " assize " means primarily a " session " of a court. Then it comes
to mean an ordinance made at such a session, *e.g.* the Assize of Clarendon.
Then it comes to mean some procedure laid down or made available by
the ordinance in question. It is in this sense that the words " Grand
Assize " and " Possessory Assize " are used. Finally, it comes to mean
the court which deals with cases involving that procedure, so that we
talk of " assize courts " or of judges " taking the assizes."

" grand assize," and the defendant who availed himself of
it was said to " put himself upon the grand assize." If
he did so a writ went from the Curia Regis to the sheriff
directing him to summon four knights of his shire whose
duty it was to choose twelve other knights of the district,
not related to either of the parties, to decide by their verdict
which of the two parties had the greater right to the land
in question.[1] Two points are to be noticed about the
grand assize. In the first place it was only open to
defendants : the plaintiff might still have to rest his claim
on the issue of battle. Secondly, it was only available in
the royal court : the king would not allow feudal or local
courts to use his own special procedure by inquest, so that
if the defendant put himself on the grand assize the case
had to be transferred to the royal court.

But it is of no avail to offer adequate remedies in courts
of law if men are free to help themselves. Even to-day it
often happens that a man who thinks that he has a better
right to some object of property than the possessor of it
will take the law into his own hands, and eight centuries
ago resort was far more often had to self-help than it is
to-day. Obviously self-help tends to breach of the king's
peace, and Henry did his best to discourage it so far as
land was concerned by devising summary remedies for
those who had been dispossessed of freehold land, by
which they could be put back in possession even though
the other party might possibly have a better right to the
land. If he had, he should bring a " writ of right " to
assert it. These summary remedies were known as the
" possessory assizes."[2]

The two chief among them were the assize of " novel
disseisin " and " mort d'ancestor." " Seisin " was the
technical term for possession of an estate of freehold in
land, and the plaintiff in an assize of novel disseisin

---

[1] For a specimen of this writ see Holdsworth, vol. I, p. 651.

[2] On the real actions, see the powerfully original views of Professor
Milsom, not yet fully assessed by other scholars, in his " Introduction "
to P. and M., pp. xxvii–xlix, and *Historical Foundations*, ch. 6.

complained that he had suffered a recent (novel) deprivation of seisin and asked the king's court to restore him to possession of the land. But men can be deprived of their property without an actual dispossession or " disseisin," and the assize of mort d'ancestor was devised to meet the case (apparently a common one) of a man dying seised of land and of his lord or some third party entering upon the land in reliance on some alleged right before the heir who had a *primâ facie* right to be clothed with his ancestor's seisin had time to enter himself.[1]

The procedure under the possessory assizes was as follows. Self-help was rigorously limited and the person disseised was only permitted a space of a few days to recover his seisin for himself if he could.[2] Thereafter, if he applied quickly to the royal court he might have a writ [3] directed to the sheriff bidding him empanel a body of twelve free men of the neighbourhood who should view the land in question and then appear before the royal judge when he next came to that county ready to answer whether the defendant had disseised the plaintiff of his freehold " unjustly and without a judgment "[4] within the time limited for bringing the assize, or, in the case of the mort d'ancestor, whether the plaintiff's ancestor had died seised of the land for an estate in fee within the time limited and whether the plaintiff was his next heir. These possessory assizes, it will be seen, differ in several respects from the grand assize. They deal with possession, not with ownership : the question put

---

[1] Mort d'ancestor was introduced in 1176. The traditional date for novel disseisin is 1166; but see R. C. Van Caenegem's *Royal Writs in England* (Selden Society, vol. 77), pp. 261-315, and Milsom, " Introduction " to P. and M., p. xxxix, and *Historical Foundations*, pp. 116-19. The other possessory assize was " darrein presentment," which dealt with possession of an advowson.

[2] The time allowed depended on the circumstances of the case, but four days was the normal period: P. and M., vol. II, pp. 49-50.

[3] For a specimen, see Maitland, *Forms of Action*, p. 377.

[4] As opposed to a recovery of seisin by the verdict of the grand assize or success in trial by battle.

to the inquest is not " Who has the better right ? " but
" Was the plaintiff disseised ? " or " Did the plaintiff's
ancestor die seised ? " Proceedings by writ of right
may start in the feudal court, and if so, can only be
transferred into the royal court at the defendant's option,
while the possessory assizes in all cases begin in the royal
court. Thirdly, the possessory assizes on their first
introduction were a very summary remedy. They had
to be brought quickly so that if the disseisee delayed he
might find himself too late and be thrown back on the
writ of right.[1]   On the other hand, the defendant in them
could be forced to appear in court and was not allowed
the manifold opportunities for delay allowed to the
defendant to a writ of right.   In time, however, as we
shall see, the procedure even of the possessory assizes
became so technical that suitors avoided them if they
could in favour of newer forms of action.

These assizes of Henry II, under which many
questions concerning freehold land could be litigated in
the royal court, may seem to us simple affairs enough, but
to the men of those days their introduction was a great
event.   The book known as " Glanvill " because of its
improbable ascription to Henry II's justiciar, Ranulf de
Glanvill, and written c. 1187–1189,[2] describes the grand
assize proudly as" a royal benefit granted to the people by
the goodness of the king acting on the advice of his
magnates : it takes account so effectively of both human
life and civil condition that all men may preserve the

[1] In Glanvill's day novel disseisin could only be brought for disseisin
" since the King's last passage to Normandy," and Henry II was seldom
in England for more than twelve months at a time.   Later the period
of limitation was fixed from time to time by royal ordinance, but
eventually when it had got up to 1242 it remained unaltered until the
16th century, so that the adjective " novel " (recent) came to be deprived
of all meaning.

[2] *Tractatus de Legibus et Consuetudinibus Angliae* (ed. G. D. G. Hall ;
Selden Society, 1965).   Various authors have been suggested for the
book ; in any event the author was a royal official who knew what he was
talking about.

rights which they have in any free tenement, while avoiding the doubtful outcome of battle," [1] while elsewhere Bracton [2] speaks of the possessory assizes as worked out at many a late sitting of the royal court. The success of these new remedies was extraordinary. The rolls of the royal court which began to be kept in the closing years of the reign and of which many examples from the reigns of Richard and John are preserved show us records of hundreds upon hundreds of these assizes brought often by quite humble persons in respect of quite small plots of land. To meet this demand it was, of course, necessary to send delegates from the Curia Regis round the country at fairly frequent intervals to " take the assizes " and such visitations accustomed men to the activity of the royal court and to its special procedure by the verdict of an inquest. Instead of the old method of trial by which the suitors of the court decreed the mode of proof and the issue was left to God, men came to approve of the submission of issues of fact to a body of persons likely to be acquainted with them and to the decision of incidental questions of law by the royal judge.[3] Here, of course, we have the germs of our trial by jury—but we must not overlook the great change which has come over the institution since those days. A modern jury is not supposed to be acquainted with the facts of the case which it is called upon to hear, but learns of them from witnesses or documentary evidence. The assize inquests of Henry II, on the other hand, were composed, like the Domesday inquests before them, of persons who were supposed to know the facts in advance.[4]

[1] Glanvill II, c. 7.

[2] At f. 164b of his *De Legibus et Consuetudinibus Angliae*, written towards the middle of the thirteenth century ; see p. 95, below.

[3] But clause 39 of Magna Carta shows that many of them retained a regard for the older modes of trial. See p. 50, below.

[4] Accordingly it was essential that they should be drawn from the neighbourhood (vicinetum). This is the origin of the strict rules of " venue " which made it necessary for actions to be tried in the county in which the cause of action arose before a local jury.

Indeed, the very writ which summoned them propounded the question which they were to decide, and they appeared before the court " prepared to answer " [1] whether A or B had the better right or whether A disseised B as the case might be.

The grand and possessory assizes and the Pleas of the Crown formed the great bulk of the business which came before the royal court in the later years of Henry II —but not all of it.   Glanvill tells us of a considerable variety of other jurisdiction.   In the first place there were a number of writs by the issue of which the Curia Regis could contest the activities of other tribunals —for instance, " writs of prohibition " to the ecclesiastical courts restraining them from hearing a case which the king's court considered to be outside their jurisdiction and writs such as the " pone " or the " tolt " by which cases could be removed from the communal and feudal court to the royal court on the ground of the refusal or delay [2] of the inferior court in hearing it. Then there are several other forms of action concerning freehold land besides the assizes, for example, writs of dower enabling the doweress to have her dower assigned to her and writs available to mortgagors and mortgagees to redeem or realise their securities.[3] Finally, there were a few actions of the type which afterwards came to be known as " personal."   But the distinction between the " real " and " personal " actions and the development of the personal actions can be more conveniently discussed in a later chapter.[4]

Evidently, the royal administration has been recog-

[1] " Parati recognoscere," " venit assisa recognitura."

[2] There was no "appeal" in our sense of the word from the lower to the higher court.   The case was removed to the royal court because of denial of justice below, not because of error (see P. and M., vol. II, p. 666).

[3] The mortgage in Glanvill's day was something essentially different from the classical English mortgage which we know.   The mortgagee was " in possession " from the first (see P. and M., vol. II, pp. 117 et seq.; Holdsworth, vol. II, pp. 128-131).

[4] See Chapter 6, below.

nising a great deal of new law in Henry II's reign by means of the invention of new writs. But we ought not to think that the appearance of a writ is the first appearance of a remedy or that, even after a writ has been provided, other procedural means to a remedy do not survive.[1] Only at a later time did the common law become imprisoned in an apparently rigid formulary system. "In the first place many of the ordinary writs were probably even less than Maitland thought the product of definite acts of creation."[2] To take the writ of novel disseisin, for example, one finds a pre-history of " executive " writs—mere orders, on the royal authority, to replace someone in possession—before " judicialisation " sets in with the inclusion of some such phrase as " if he has been unjustly disseised."[3] The Londoners believed that their local procedure, the assize of " fresh force," analogous to the royal remedy of novel disseisin, was older than it.[4] Secondly, one great area of legal administration remains almost wholly in darkness to us, for the county courts are not represented by masses of surviving public records, merely by a few pathetic fragments of parchment; if we knew more of their workings much might seem evolutionary rather than revolutionary. Thirdly, we know that extensive use was made, certainly until the early fourteenth century, of procedure without writ in the central royal courts and in proceedings before justices in eyre.[5] Usually " bills " written in French,

---

[1] What is said above is conspicuously indebted to Professor Milsom : " Introduction " to P. and M., pp. lxiv–lxvii.

[2] *Ibid.*, p. lxiv.

[3] van Caenegem, *Royal Writs in England*, pp. 261–316. But his " evolutionary " view of " judicialisation " has been powerfully attacked by Lady Stenton, who sees creative innovation consciously at work under Henry II : *English Justice between the Norman Conquest and the Great Charter, 1066–1215* (1965), ch. 2 (" The Angevin Leap Forward ").

[4] M. Bateson, *Borough Customs* (Selden Society, vol. 18), i.232 ; *Eyre of London, 14 Edw. II* (Selden Society, vol. 85), p. lxx.

[5] The best account is by G. O. Sayles, *Select Cases in the King's Bench*, vol. iv (Selden Society, vol. 74), pp. lxvii–lxxxvi ; see also : G. J. Hand, *English Law in Ireland, 1290–1324* (1967), pp. 67–79.

rather than in the Latin of the writs, were employed to initiate such an action, but even oral plaints are not unknown. However, in the thirteenth century at least, no man could be compelled to answer concerning his freehold without a writ and the main scope of the " bill " was in personal actions involving relatively small sums. There are pervasive hints that a sum at issue of forty shillings marks a dividing line.

Nevertheless, the appearance of the writs of Henry II's reign is a landmark not merely in procedure but also for the future of substantive law. Once created, writs were soon *de cursu*, issued freely as of right, though particular writs in particular situations might be *de gratia*, of grace, requiring a not very substantial fee.[1] Secondly, each writ, as created, became a mould for the law, for each was tailored in a particular way ; it was not just a bare order to appear which left the cause of its issue uncertain and which was in the same form in every case.[2] It contained a statement of its purpose and defined from the start the scope of the proceedings which it initiated, and these proceedings might differ very materially in different forms of action. Thus some actions were started by writs which merely directed the sheriff to summon the defendant,[3] while in others the writ directed him at once to obtain security from the defendant for his appearance.[4] Some forms of action gave many opportunities for delay [5] ; others were relatively speedy.[6] In some the mode of proof may be by compurgation or battle : in others by the verdict of an assize inquest or a jury. When once you had selected your writ you were committed to a prescribed form of procedure and could not wander from the path which you had chosen. This variety of forms of action quickly made the common law a very technical system, but so long as new

---

[1] *Brevia placitata*, pp. xlviii–li.

[2] Contrast the enormous variety of common law " writs " with the Chancery "subpœna," which was the same in every case (see p. 147, below).

[3] *E.g.* debt.   [4] *E.g.* trespass.

[5] *E.g.* the writ of right.   [6] *E.g.* novel disseisin.

forms were freely devised to meet new circumstances the law had no difficulty in meeting the needs of the times. As we shall see, a time came when the Chancery was no longer free to invent new forms of action in this way.

The great extension of its jurisdiction as a law court naturally affected the organisation of the Curia Regis and led to a distinction growing up between those of its members who were competent to deal with the judicial business and those whose talents and training were purely executive. It is clear that " Henry II rendered justice, even in his own person, in a court held before him, but it had no regular staff, no regular procedure, no regular records, and when he left the country it went overseas with him." [1] Now Henry was frequently overseas in his last years, and Richard I spent less than six months of his ten years reign in England. In such circumstances the Chief Justiciar and the Exchequer were the core of the routine administration of justice, though matters peculiarly affecting the king continued to go *coram rege* and so the court about the king himself became the forerunner of the later court of King's Bench. From the Exchequer there went forth the itinerant justices, who took the possessory assizes and tried criminals presented under the Assizes of Clarendon and Northampton. Sometimes, indeed, the justices itinerant were given an even more extended commission and were empowered not only to try " all pleas " both criminal and civil arising in the county in question, but to pass in review the enforcement of all the various royal rights which were ordinarily the responsibility of the sheriff and to supervise his conduct and that of other royal officials. This " General Eyre " had constantly before it the financial interests of the Exchequer, for justice was a great source of profit and such judicial proceedings were often the only means of enforcing public obligations. But it was to the Exchequer that the justices returned after their work in the

[1] G. O. Sayles, *The Court of King's Bench* (Selden Society Lecture, 1959), p. 8.

counties and it was in the Exchequer that we find the beginnings of a central court to dispense justice of the kind available to private parties from the justices itinerant.[1] It may well have been that the eagerness of litigants for speedy justice, without waiting for the next itinerant visitation, was, as much as the difficulties presented by the royal absences, the stimulus of this new court settled at Westminster, the Bench or Court of Common Pleas. But as yet there is no great distinction and cases are heard by one tribunal rather than another on grounds of pure convenience and likewise there is no clear distinction of personnel, for the justices were in effect interchangeable.[2] Finally, we may note that it seems to have been towards the end of this period that records of the judicial business which came before the court began to be kept. Exchequer business had been recorded for some half-century past, but now the Pipe Roll of the exchequer begins to have companions in the Plea Rolls of the courts—records in Latin [3] of the cases coming before the royal court which have been continued unbroken from then to the present day.

The system left behind him by Henry II functioned fairly smoothly during the reign of Richard I, who was interested above everything in foreign adventure and left the management of his English kingdom to men who had worked under his father. With John, however, there was a change. His unsuccessful foreign policy,[4]

[1] See also p. 93, below.

[2] Earlier accounts of the origins of the central courts should be read with Professor Milsom's re-assessment in *Historical Foundations*, ch. i. It may be that he overstresses when he writes (p. 24) of the Bench " the most regular institution of the middle ages therefore started, not as a part of the regular routine of government, but as a provision for exceptional cases ; " and this stress has not been followed above. It is interesting that in the following century the Irish Court of Common Pleas can be seen clearly emerging from the court of itinerant justices.

[3] Until 1731. Since then in English.

[4] It was, of course, in John's reign that Normandy was lost to Philip Augustus of France. Its loss hastened the consolidation of royal government in England by making the king largely resident.

his disastrous quarrel with the Papacy and the arbitrary measures, suggestive of mental derangement, by which he strove to extricate himself from his difficulties aroused against him a coalition of the Church, the baronage and the boroughs which extorted from him the Great Charter of Liberties.[1] This is not the place to speak in detail of this famous document : we can only mention those few of its many clauses which bear directly on the system of royal justice. Naturally the great extension of the royal jurisdiction had not been entirely acceptable to the feudal barons, and in clause 34 John is made to promise that " the writ called *Praecipe* shall not in future be issued to anyone in respect of any holding whereby a freeman may lose his court." The reference is to the difficulty the lord of a feudal court might have in reclaiming from the king's court a case which should have by rights gone to the lord's court; the effect of the clause, it is now accepted, was to permit the issue of an appropriate writ of prohibition on behalf of the lord and to lead to the use of a special form of *praecipe*, *praecipe in capite*, where the tenure was in fact of the Crown.[2] But it cannot fairly be said that the Charter shows any marked hostility to royal justice. Indeed, there are several clauses which definitely favour it. Thus clause 24 provides that the sheriffs shall not hear the Pleas of the Crown, and seems to show that in criminal cases more confidence was reposed in a court presided over by a royal commissioner than in one dominated by the great local officer. Then again, clause 17, which provides for the " common pleas " being held in one fixed place instead of following the royal person appears to have been intended to restore the Bench, which John for a time had merged with the court

---

[1] A more favourable view of John, which credits him with a lively and intelligent interest in the common law but may underestimate the disruptive effects of this interest, has been suggested by Lady Stenton in *King John and the Courts of Justice* (British Academy Raleigh Lecture, 1958).

[2] J. C. Holt, *Magna Carta* (1965), p. 225, and references.

coram rege itinerating with himself.   Clause 18, which
promises that justices shall be sent quarterly to take the
possessory assizes, " probably sought more justice than
was possible." [1]   Finally, we must mention clause 39,
which is the most famous in all the Charter and the one
the meaning of which has been the most hotly debated.
" No free man shall be taken or imprisoned or disseised
or outlawed or exiled or in any way ruined, nor will we
go or send against him, except by the lawful judgment
of his peers or by the law of the land."   While the
provocation behind the clause was John's unbridled proceedings by *voluntas*, his arbitrary will, *ira* and *malevo-
lentia*, his anger and spite, its sweeping phrases gave it
great future fertility.   But its issue included the legend
that " judgment of peers " referred to trial by jury.
That is clearly not so.   A jury does not, and never did,
pronounce a judgment, but gives an answer to a question
of fact propounded to it in a court presided over by a
royal judge who himself applies the law and delivers the
judgment.   In claiming the " judicium parium " the
barons were not thinking of this novel royal procedure,
but of the traditional method of trial by which the suitors
of the court—who were the equals of the parties in the
case—themselves as a body gave the judgment of the
court unfettered by any control from above.   At the
same time it could not reasonably be claimed that a
free man should in no case lose land or life without a
judgment of his peers—the charter itself, for instance,
definitely recognised the possessory assizes and under
the verdicts of assize juries hundreds of free men were
being put out of their seisin every year by the royal court
in favour of those whom they had dispossessed.   It is
reasonable to suppose that it was to meet this difficulty
that the words " vel per legem terrae "—words which
were, one imagines, intentionally wide and vague—were
added to the clause.   We shall see that, in fact, it was
only in a very limited class of cases that the claim to a

[1] Holt, *op. cit.*, p. 224.

judgment of one's peers was maintained against the level-ling influence of royal justice.[1]

Before we take leave of the early Angevin achievement, one other event deserves a mention, though its impact on the development of the English legal system was marginal and collateral. The law taking shape in England was for the first time exported over sea when the Anglo-Norman invaders brought it with them to Ireland. Thus there occurred the first of those extensions which have made the common law one of the great legal systems of the world, shared with its early home by the United States of America and by many other lands.

[1] *I.e.* in the trial of " peers " for felony ; see p. 224, below.

IV

THE DEVELOPMENT OF PARLIAMENT AND THE CENTRAL COURTS

ONE document has for centuries held its place as the most famous in the legal and constitutional development of England: the Great Charter, first granted by King John in 1215 and many times afterwards confirmed.[1] Some of the honour it has enjoyed has been due to the " myth of Magna Carta,"[2] the notion that it enshrined ideas of personal liberty and of democratic control which were in fact far in the future. Even amongst contemporaries the Great Charter meant different things to different people; and perhaps to most it meant a confirmation of the " Liberties "—we should rather say, " privileges "—of the baronial classes and the Church against the Crown. To the historian's eye it is first and foremost a feudal document, dealing with the technicalities of feudal society and feudal law. Yet to the lawyer—who can easily be lost in those technicalities— it should also stand, however imperfectly, for ideas that have played their part in the workings of the Common Law ever since. We may smile at the language of seventeenth-century parliamentarians and Victorian liberals; we may even think that they looked upon the " liberties " they saw in the Charter in terms of class interest quite as much as the barons who first sought them; but a residue of great importance remains.

---

[1] The best study is: J. C. Holt, *Magna Carta*. Students should note that the original issue of 1215 (the " historian's Magna Carta ") differed in important respects from the issue of 1225 in which it took permanent shape (the " lawyer's Magna Carta ").

[2] This was the title of a very influential article by Edward Jenks in (1905) 4 *Independent Review* 260–73.

What Maitland wrote can still claim validity : " And yet, with all its faults, this document becomes and rightly becomes a sacred text, the nearest approach to an irrepealable ' fundamental statute ' that England has ever had.   In age after age a confirmation of it will be demanded and granted as a remedy for those oppressions from which the realm is suffering, and this when some of its clauses, at least in their original meaning, have become hopelessly antiquated.   For in brief it means this, that the king is and shall be below the law." [1]

In this history of the legal system, which is of course our main concern, the Great Charter has had this general influential role and more.   It contains one clause, as we shall see, which had a direct and important impact on the development of the central courts.   But, before we turn to that, we should consider the institution which is so often coupled with Magna Carta in the English tradition, though their historical links are tenuous enough, the High Court of Parliament.

Few matters in English history are more controverted than the origins of parliament and a student who approaches the literature on the subject may well feel that the historians have been incapable of seeing the wood for the trees.[2]   In England, a brief generation after the Great Charter, we begin to meet the word " parliament "—which could mean simply a " parley " between groups of people or their representatives—in the sense of some sort of special and formal gathering about the king.[3] It is an occasion as yet, rather than a body or an institution.   At certain times the king reinforces his council with the attendance of other people for judicial business.

[1] P. and M., i.173.

[2] G. L. Haskins, *The Growth of English Representative Government* (1960), and P. Spofford, *Origins of the English Parliament* (1967) might together form the best introduction.   Richardson and Sayles, " Parliaments and Great Councils of Medieval England " (1961), 77 *L.Q.R.* 213–36 and 401–26, is a forceful statement of one of the rival positions.

[3] The earliest known official use comes from 1236 : Richardson and Sayles, (1967), 82 *E.H.R.* 747.

By the end of the century, though judicial business was still the mark of a true parliament, other business was also being transacted and a European movement in favour of " representation " was having its effect in England.   In particular, in addition to great tenants-in-chief, representatives of other sections of the community are often called in.   At a later date still, the representation will harden into two knights elected by the freeholders of the shire and two burgesses from each recognised " borough ".

Parliament was a time for doing justice and for hearing petitions from the king's subjects.   To-day only the faintest shadows of this beginning remain and, on the other hand, it has long been recognised that only an Act of Parliament can alter the law and that there is no law that such an Act cannot alter.   In, say, 1300, neither of these propositions was true.   It was convenient, rather than essential, to promulgate a law in parliament, an obligation of political and administrative commonsense rather than of constitutional law.   There was much law, too, which was regarded as unalterable.[1]   Similarly, the use of parliamentary gatherings to secure money grants to the Crown was much less important than it was later to become.   When Edward I died in 1307 the association of parliament and taxation was still far from clear-cut.

Because parliament began as a strengthened meeting of the king's council, the body of his ordinary advisers, the council remained at the heart of parliament for a long time.   (A last relic was the extension of certain special rights in debate to privy councillors.)   Only gradually did the Council become distinct from the Parliament and the change was very roughly parallel to the disappearance

---

[1] It is only since the seventeenth century that it has been generally admitted that Acts of Parliament can override the " natural " or " divine " law and must be enforced by the judges whatever their contents may be. Of course, by another line of development, some countries of the common law (notably the United States of America and the Republic of Ireland) have a system of " judicial review " of statutes by a Supreme Court.

of ordinary judicial business from Parliament in the course of the fourteenth century. To-day it is only at the ceremonial opening in the House of Lords when the Queen is on her throne surrounded by her great officers of state and, supported by the presence of non-Parliamentary counsellors, such as the judges, faces her Peerage and Commons that the picture of mediaeval Parliament is, for a moment, revived.[1]

While in the thirteenth century Parliament had gradually been taking its shape, the royal Curia had been itself tending to split up into a number of separate bodies. To put it another way, certain administrative offices were beginning to go " out of court," to become quasi-independent bureaux, no longer directly expressive of the king's immediate personal will. We have seen that in the twelfth century the only specialised branch of the government was the Exchequer, in which all the chief officers of state assembled for the audit of royal revenue. By the close of the century, however, the Chancellor seems to have established a separate office of his own and to have left behind him to deal with the secretarial work of the Exchequer a subordinate—the Chancellor of the Exchequer—who has grown as great a figure as the Chancellor himself. Of the functions of the independent " Chancery " which grew up in the thirteenth century the most important for our purpose was that of issuing under the great seal the original writ with which most actions in the royal court were started by an ordinary litigant.[2] It is, however, with the separate judicial organs that split off from the Curia that we are more particularly concerned for the moment, and of them we must speak in some detail.

[1] " Parliament " in strict law is still perhaps only to be found not in the separate meetings of the Houses but when the Sovereign or his Commissioners under the Great Seal meet both Lords and Commons in the Lord's Chamber. The Speaker of the House of Commons is indeed called " Speaker " just because on such occasions he alone can speak ror the Commons.

[2] See p. 45, above, for proceedings without writ.

We have seen that even as early as the end of Henry II's reign a separate class of "judges" was growing up within the circle of royal councillors and that some of these judges sat at Westminster while others followed the king. Clause 17 of Magna Carta, which provided that the "Common Pleas," *i.e.* ordinary civil suits between subjects, "shall not follow our court but be heard in some fixed place" emphasised the distinction between the judges sitting at Westminster [1] and the judges appointed to sit "before the king himself," and though the distinction was obscured during and after the minority of Henry III it reappeared as the result of legal reforms which took place in 1234. "From henceforward there should be two main central courts of common law, one peripatetic with the King, the other stationary at Westminster." [2] From 1234 onwards we have two separate series of rolls, the "Coram Rege" rolls and the "De Banco" rolls. The separation is further marked by the disappearance of the office of a single "Justiciar" and the appointment of two Chief Justices, one of the "King's Bench" in 1268 and one of the "Common Pleas" in 1272. From this moment one may fairly consider "the Bench," or "the Court of Common Pleas" to give it its more usual name, as an independent court. Its jurisdiction covered by far the largest part of the work coming before the royal law courts in the Middle Ages and can be classified under three heads [3]: First it was pre-eminently a court for civil litigation in which common pleas (pleas between common people) were heard, e.g. the real actions concerning land of which we spoke in the last chapter and personal actions such as debt, detinue, covenant and account of which we shall say something in the next chapter : it also exercised,

---

[1] The provision that there should be a "fixed place" did not necessarily imply Westminster, but the Common Pleas very seldom sat anywhere else.

[2] G. O. Sayles, *Select Cases in the King's Bench*, vol. *IV* (Selden Society, vol. 74), p. xxxi.

[3] See Holdsworth, vol. I, pp. 194–203.

concurrently with the King's Bench, a civil jurisdiction in cases of trespass, which became increasingly frequent towards the end of the thirteenth century. Secondly, it exercised a supervision over the local and manorial courts which in the thirteenth century at least still had a considerable mass of cases coming before them. By " tolt " and " pone " [1] plaints pending before a local or seignorial court could be transferred into the Common Pleas for hearing, and by various other writs the court had a limited power of correcting the errors of these inferior courts. Thirdly, the court—like most mediæval courts—claimed an exclusive jurisdiction over cases in which its own officials were concerned whether as plaintiffs or defendants.

Meanwhile, side by side with the growth of a separate Court of Common Pleas, we can trace the beginnings of a second separate royal law court—the Court of Exchequer.[2] In Glanvill's time the Exchequer was simply an administrative body and in no sense a court of law—but soon after his day it came to be seen that many questions habitually arose on the audit of the royal revenues which raised issues of law rather than of accountancy and could be more conveniently dealt with and recorded separately. Such questions might take several forms. Thus the liability to pay might be disputed altogether or a prior payment to some subordinate royal accountant might be pleaded ; or again, the debtor, while admitting his liability to the Exchequer, might plead that he could not meet it by reason of the failure of his debtors to pay him their debts. This last was a very frequent plea, and gradually the principle grew up that as it was a matter of interest to the Exchequer that its debtors should be financially able to meet their liabilities to it, the Crown debtor could obtain a writ from the Exchequer summoning his own debtor before it to

---

[1] See p. 38, above.

[2] See the Introduction to *Select Cases in the Exchequer of Pleas* (Selden Society, vol 48), edited by Hilary Jenkinson.

answer him " ùna cum domino Rege " or to pay him " in partem solutionis debitorum quae X debet domino Regi." As well as these disputes touching the royal revenue, the Exchequer, like the Common Pleas, claimed an exclusive jurisdiction over its own officials. Further, it was not uncommon for the king to grant private individuals, especially private merchants, the right to recover their own debts by proceedings in the Exchequer. By the end of the thirteenth century there was already a recognised distinction between the Exchequer of Account and Receipt,[1] and the Court of Exchequer or " Exchequer of Pleas," and there were even complaints that cases were being brought before the Court of Exchequer which were not in any true sense " revenue " cases and which should have been brought in the Common Pleas.[2] It is doubtful, however, whether there was at this early date any conscious desire on the part of the court to extend its jurisdiction by the use of fictions which afterwards became so common.[3] As yet its business was very slight compared with that of the Common Pleas, and its judges, the Barons of the Exchequer, were still government officers rather than lawyers, and were not regarded as the equals of the judges of the other royal courts.[4]

[1] The Exchequer of Account and Receipt is, of course, the direct ancestor of the modern Treasury.

[2] It may be surmised that the growth of a jurisdiction in the Exchequer was facilitated by the fact that the Angevin kings on their frequent journeys abroad left a duplicate of their Great Seal in the Exchequer, and even after that duplicate had become a merely departmental seal, in the custody of the Chancellor of the Exchequer, it is significant that it was still used to test the writs by which actions were begun in the Exchequer of Pleas, and which were not issued from the Chancery. See the article on Departmental Seals in *Archæologia*, 1936, and Introduction to *Select Cases in the Exchequer of Pleas* (Selden Society, vol. 48), both by Hilary Jenkinson.

[3] See p. 170, below.

[4] Only the Chief Baron of the Exchequer was normally a professional lawyer in the Middle Ages. It was not until 1579 that the " puisne " barons were invariably chosen from the serjeants-at-law as the other judges were.

Finally, above the Common Pleas and the Court of Exchequer there rose a third royal court—that held before the king himself and which still accompanied him on his progresses. As yet, however, this court was no pure court of law staffed exclusively by trained lawyers, but rather a judicial session of the inner Curia Regis. There were, it is true, justices assigned to sit in this court, but the king himself often presided, and a larger or smaller number of lay councillors was generally present. The appointment in 1268 of a special chief justice to preside over the " coram rege " judges shows, indeed, that the professional element was slowly gaining the upper hand in the court, but throughout the thirteenth century it is often difficult to distinguish sittings of the " Coram Rege " Court from sittings of the Royal Council, and the same sets of rolls may record all the business, judicial and administrative, which came before the royal council, including that before it in parliament. The jurisdiction of the " Coram Rege " Court—or the King's Bench—in the thirteenth century has been the subject of recent study.[1]   The jurisdiction has often been contrasted with that of the Common Pleas in a way which suggests that the King's Bench was concerned mainly with crime and the Common Pleas with civil cases. For the thirteenth and fourteenth centuries this is misleading. The King's Bench at this time left pleas of the crown to be indicted and judged locally before itinerant justices ; its dealings with crime were mainly confined to the hearing of appeals of felony,[2] a jurisdiction which it shared with the Common Pleas.   So far as civil cases were concerned, the bulk of common pleas was, as we have said,[3] left to the Common Pleas ; but the King's Bench also heard common pleas when the King had an interest or wished the case to be heard there, and the two courts shared the

---

[1] See G. O. Sayles, *Select Cases in the King's Bench, vol. IV* (Selden Society, vol. 74), pp. xxxii–xxxviii.

[2] See p. 37, above.　　　　　[3] See p. 56, above.

growing jurisdiction over civil trespass.[1] The general
picture is one of parallel jurisdiction, amicably exercised
by both courts. In one important respect, however, the
King's Bench stood apart and superior : it had an
inherent jurisdiction to correct and to supervise the proceedings of other courts both local and royal, including
those of the Common Pleas. This jurisdiction developed
in two ways. It led first, as we shall see, to an important
jurisdiction in appeal, or error as it was called.[2] It also
led to a system of control based on a number of special
writs—the so-called " prerogative writs "—by the issue of
which the King's Bench could control the activities of
inferior authorities throughout the realm. Thus, by the
writ of " habeas corpus " it could cause any person to be
brought before it even if detained by the order of some
other tribunal : by the writ of " prohibition " it could
forbid an inferior court to hear a case which it considered
to be outside its jurisdiction ; by " quo warranto " it
could challenge the legality of a claim to jurisdiction or to
any royal franchise ; by " mandamus " it could compel
the due exercise of its functions by some inferior body or
local official ; and by " certiorari " it could call up for
review the decisions of many inferior courts and annul
them if they had been made irregularly or without
jurisdiction. These prerogative writs had a great history
before them, and to-day they are the chief means by
which the law courts exercise such control as they can
exercise over the actions of the executive government.

The differentiation of the organs of government and
central justice—the beginnings of which in the thirteenth
century we have sketched already—continued throughout the following century, so that by the time of the accession of Henry IV (1399) Parliament, the Council and the
three royal law courts may be said to have become entirely

[1] See Chapters 6 and 10 on the development of the writ of trespass
which brought much ordinary civil work into the King's Bench.
[2] See Chapter 13, below.

independent bodies.   To trace this development in detail through the fourteenth century would be a task far beyond the scope of this book, but it is necessary to give some account of it in outline.[1]   We have seen that in Edward I's reign the king's council was the centre of government, reinforced regularly by summons to the great tenants-in-chief and by causing elected representatives of communities to be present in parliament; and that such reinforcement was a matter of expediency, as was legislation or taxation in parliament.   Further, intimately associated with the Council, there was the King's Bench, the highest of the law courts below the afforced Council in Parliament, and the king might himself preside in judicial sessions, which decided important cases and reviewed the decisions of the Bench or Common Pleas.

In the twelfth century, when " feudalism " was still a reality and the power of the central government proportionately feeble, the right of the king to appoint what men he chose to his Council had not been contested. The reforms of Henry II had, however, permanently strengthened the central power, and the question of who was to exercise it—the question of the composition of the Royal Council—became of ever-increasing importance. Henry III's reign was a prolonged battle between king and baronage on this point : Edward I—one of the greatest of our kings—had his way more easily than his father.   In fact, " all the evidence seems to agree that the normal council of the thirteenth century was essentially ministerial." [2]   The struggle continued with varying success throughout the fourteenth century, the barons— or " magnates "—striving to gain control of Parliament and the Council, and to keep the officials—the " curiales "

[1] The works of Professor B. Wilkinson, *Constitutional History of England, 1216–1399* (3 vols., 1948–58), and *Constitutional History of England in the Fifteenth Century* (1964) have particular merit as introductions, since they offer texts in translation and fair summaries of opposing views, as well as the author's own (not always widely shared) interpretations.

[2] B. Wilkinson, *Studies in the Constitutional History of the Thirteenth and Fourteenth Centuries* (2nd ed., 1952), pp. 158–9.

—in a proper position of subordination, while the king was always trying to free himself from baronial control. Edward II fell in this contest ; Edward III, after a certain success in it—the result of the prestige acquired by his French victories—gradually allowed the day to go against him ; Richard II, after a long minority, struck suddenly and by a series of assassinations and judicial murders seemed for a moment to have brought the " magnates " to the ground ; but his tyranny gave his enemies a fresh opportunity, and in 1399 he was replaced by the House of Lancaster, which owed its elevation to the throne to the baronial party, and save for a few years under Henry V depended more than was consistent with the good government of England on baronial support.[1]

Gradually in the course of this conflict the judges and officials were excluded from effective membership of Parliament. Even in Edward III's reign the magnates contended that they were there for consultation only, and in the fifteenth century the judges themselves admitted the correctness of this contention. Their right of voting in Parliament was already obsolete when in 1539 it was formally taken away. Even to-day, however, the royal judges and the King's Attorney and Solicitor-General still receive their writs of summons to Parliament and attend its ceremonial opening, and it has always been the right of the House of Lords to require the attendance of some of the judges to advise them when the House is exercising its judicial functions. Since the creation of the " Law Lords " in 1876 this right has been used sparingly, but the judges attended in 1896 in the great case of *Allen* v. *Flood*, and were regularly summoned when a peer was tried for felony.

The exclusion of the non-baronial element from Parliament was accompanied by the growth of the doctrine of " peerage." Just as no man, other than a representative knight of a shire or burgess, could sit and vote in Parlia-

[1] See Chapter 7, below.

ment unless he was a " baron," so the theory grew up that once a man had been summoned to Parliament as a baron he acquired a dignity which was transferred to his descendants.   Thus the discretion of the Crown to withhold a summons was taken away and the foundations of a hereditary chamber, a House of Lords, were laid. Recognising themselves as a separate caste in the community, the magnates in the fourteenth and fifteenth centuries began to claim exclusive privileges for themselves, and in particular contended that though for other men trial by jury might be good enough, they could claim, in serious criminal cases at least, a trial by their own order, that " judgment of their peers " which Magna Carta had asserted to be the right of every free man.[1]   In those centuries the magnates completely overshadowed the representative element in Parliament, and the gradual growth of a separate House of Commons took place in the shadow of the more sensational rise of the House of Lords.   Nevertheless, it should be borne in mind. Early in the reign of Edward III the knights of the shire and burgesses had begun to deliberate apart from Parliament as a whole, first in the refectory of Westminster Abbey, and later in the Chapter House.   By 1377 they had begun to elect one of their number as their speaker, their spokesman when they appeared in the Parliament chamber before the king and the lords.   Finally, by the end of the century they began to claim certain privileges for themselves as the magnates had done before them.

Just as the officials and judges were excluded from Parliament, so in the same period we can trace a similar development within the Council.   Many of the officials became mere administrators with no control over policy, while the judges were confined to purely judicial business. They might be summoned to the Council board to give advice, but they had ceased to be members of the Council in the full sense of the word.   The Council had fallen by the time of the accession of the House of Lancaster

[1] See Chapter 13, below, for the later history of " Trial of Peers."

almost entirely under the control of the magnates, and was a smaller body than it had been in Edward's day. Naturally, in view of this separation between judges and councillors, the court held before the king himself (coram rege) became in the fourteenth century a far more purely professional court than it had been in the thirteenth. The king ceased to preside in person, lay councillors ceased to attend, and the King's Bench becomes a Court of Common Law similar, though superior in dignity to, the Common Pleas and Exchequer.

This development had two important consequences which we must mention. So long as the King's Bench had been closely connected with the Council and with Parliament it had been the highest court in the land. Now that it was a separate professional tribunal it was clear that this was no longer the case ; but who was to receive appeals from its decisions—the Council proper or Parliament ? We shall see that in this contest Parliament was successful.[1] Secondly, the separation of the common law courts from the central government which was completed in the fourteenth century by the final break between the Council and the King's Bench, meant that henceforth the administration of the common law was handed over entirely to professional lawyers who would have little inclination and perhaps not much power to keep the law abreast of the times by the infusion of new principles. This partial atrophy of the common law may have been important in the rise of the Court of Chancery, of which we shall speak in a later chapter.

By 1400, then, Parliament, the Council and the three common law courts are completely separate bodies, each with its own set of records and its own forms of procedure. The courts are staffed by judges, animated by a strong professional feeling under whose guidance the common law is rapidly becoming a very technical and inelastic system. These judges are summoned on occasion to Parliament or the Council board to give advice

[1] See Chapter 13, below.

on legal matters, but in general they are not full members
of either body.   Parliament and the Council, meanwhile,
are largely dominated—and will be dominated throughout the first half of the fifteenth century—by the aristocracy ; later (as we shall see) they will be once more
dominated by the Crown.   But though normally litigation in the King's Court goes to one or other of the three
separate law courts whose growth we have traced, neither
Parliament nor Council—both of which consider themselves   superior   to   the   common   law   courts—have
entirely abandoned the judicial field to them.   Parliament
hears appeals from the King's Bench, and the Council,
as we shall see in more detail in Chapter 7, claims to
exercise on behalf of the Crown a residue of judicial
power which will enable it to supplement the ordinary
courts with its own extraordinary justice.

V

THE CRIMINAL LAW IN THE THIRTEENTH AND FOURTEENTH CENTURIES

IN the last chapter we described how in the course of the two centuries which lie between the granting of the Great Charter and the accession of the House of Lancaster (1215–1399) the Curia Regis—the central government of England—finally lost its unity and developed into a number of separate organs. One branch which grew out of the old trunk was formed by the three royal law courts, and in this chapter and the next we must turn back to the beginning of the thirteenth century and state, as briefly as may be, how the system of law administered by those courts—that is the common law of England—had itself developed in this period. In this task it will be convenient to deal with each of the main divisions of the law—the criminal and the civil law—in separate chapters, and first to treat of the former.

Already by the end of the twelfth century serious crime had become a matter for the royal rather than the local or private tribunals. Here and there one could, of course, find a great lord whose " franchises " extended to the trial of such cases in his own court,[1] and the fact that it was necessary in Magna Carta to protest against the hearing of the Pleas of the Crown by the sheriffs [2] shows that the exclusion of the county court from this sphere was not yet quite complete, but, broadly speaking, the generalisation is correct. The accused might, however, be brought before the royal tribunal on a charge of felony in either of two quite different ways. He might

---

[1] Even then the trial was often before a royal judge or at least in the presence of a royal official, though the lord, by virtue of his franchise, might take the profits of the proceedings.

[2] Clause 24.

be presented by a local jury under the procedure instituted
by the Assize of Clarendon,[1] or he might be the object of
a private accusation—an " appeal of felony "—brought
by the injured party or his representative.   The first of
these methods was tending to grow in importance during
this period at the expense of the second, but even in
1400 the appeal in cases of murder at least was still a
living thing. We must, therefore, say something of
each.

For some sixty years after the Assize of Clarendon
persons presented in the county court before the king's
itinerant justices by a jury of one or other of the hundreds
in the county were normally sent to the ordeal.   In consequence, however, of the decision of the Church (taken
at the Lateran Council in 1215) no longer to lend the
weight of its authority to these " judgments of God," the
ordeals—other than trial by battle [2]—soon fell into
disuse, and since there could obviously be no trial by
battle in the case of persons indicted in the name of the
Sovereign by public testimony under a royal ordinance,
some other method of ascertaining guilt or innocence had
to be devised.   This was a moment of extreme importance in the history of English criminal law, for it might
well have happened that the royal judges would have
taken upon themselves the decision of the question of
fact—of guilt or innocence—with the result that our
criminal procedure would have taken an " inquisitorial "
turn and have developed in a manner parallel to the law
of France.   In the result, however, after a good deal of
hesitation and uncertainty in the thirteenth century, the
rule was established that the question of the guilt or
innocence of the persons presented by the jurors of the
hundred should normally be submitted to a second jury
for decision.

Just as the jurors of the hundred are the ancestors of
the Grand Jury of modern times, so the second jury is,

[1] See p. 35, above.
[2] Trial by battle survived both in criminal appeals and in writs of right.

of course, the ancestor of our petty jury. In early days it was common, in spite of the obvious injustice to the accused, for some at least of the members of the jury of presentment to be empanelled on the petty jury, but in 1351 a statute was passed enabling the accused to challenge a juror on this ground, and from this time the two juries were completely distinct.[1]   In the infancy of trial by jury in criminal cases it was thought to be unfair to a man charged with felony to compel him to submit to this substitute for the judgment of God when he was ready to be tried by ordeal, and consequently if he refused his consent he could not be tried by jury but could only be kept in prison until he changed his mind. Gradually, as the reason for the rule disappeared, the imprisonment became more and more rigorous and developed into torture (the " peine forte et dure ") designed to extract a submission to trial by jury from the accused, but it was not until 1772 that a " standing mute of malice " or refusal to be tried by jury in a case of felony was made equivalent to a confession.[2]   If it be asked why any men were found ready (as a few were) to die under torture rather than be tried by a jury of their countrymen, the answer is that in such cases they did not die " convicted felons " and therefore suffered no escheat of lands or forfeiture of goods.   Similarly, it was considered improper in the thirteenth and fourteenth centuries when the true meaning of the " judicium parium " claimed in Magna Carta had not been entirely forgotten, for a man to be convicted by a jury composed of persons inferior to him in social status, and we find cases of a knight insisting with success on being tried by a jury of knights.   But this sentiment soon dis-

---

[1] See Holdsworth, vol. I, pp. 324–5.
[2] If a prisoner refused to plead, a jury was empanelled to enquire whether he stood mute " of malice or by the visitation of God." See p. 200, below. The " peine forte et dure " was not used in cases of treason or mere misdemeanours. In them a refusal to plead was always equivalent to a confession.

appeared, and it was only in the trial of peers themselves that any relic of the "judicium parium" survived.[1]

Trial by jury, then, became the ordinary mode of trial
of those indicted at the suit of the king by the presentation of the juries of the hundred. In private
criminal appeals, by contrast, the accused could in a
normal case offer to defend himself by battle. He did
not, however, always have this privilege, for if there was
a violent presumption of his guilt he might be convicted
and hanged at once. If, on the other hand, appearances
were on his side he might, if he chose, avoid the issue of
battle by complaining that the accusation was brought
against him out of malice and not from any genuine
belief in his guilt and offer to put himself on a jury. The
royal judges did their best to discourage appeals, both by
multiplying the technicalities that the appellor must
observe in a successful prosecution of his appeal and also
by lending a ready ear to appellees in their objections to
this form of procedure. Under this disfavour from the
royal court the appeal in cases other than murder almost
died out in the later Middle Ages,[2] but appeals of murder
were still so common in the fifteenth century that in
1486 we find a statute passed regulating the priority of
indictment and appeal in the same case. By the common
law no indictment could be brought for homicide for a
year and a day after the death, since that was the period
allowed by the Statute of Gloucester (1278) for bringing

---

[1] The "judgment of peers" was not, of course, originally a trial by
jury at all, but a trial in which the *judges* are the equals of the accused.
But in this insistence on having no social inferiors on the jury, one sees
the beginning of the process of misunderstanding which leads to the
identification of trial by jury with the "judicium parium."

[2] A different use of the appeal continued common throughout the
Middle Ages. This was the appeal by an approver. "An approver was
a medieval 'King's evidence.' A felon himself, if he successfully
maintained his appeals against a certain number of others who had committed felonies in his company and secured their conviction, he escaped
hanging and was allowed either perpetual imprisonment or to abjure the
realm": R. F. Hunnisett, *The Medieval Coroner* (1961), p. 69.

an appeal, but the Act of 1486 declared, more sensibly, that the indictment could be brought at once, but that an acquittal should be no bar to a subsequent appeal. In the following three centuries there are a few examples of appeals of murder brought by relatives of the deceased who were dissatisfied at the acquittal of the accused on indictment. The last example was the case of *Ashford* v. *Thornton* in 1818, in which the appellee chose to offer battle rather than face a second trial by jury. The appellor abandoned the proceedings rather than accept this offer, and in the next year the " appeal " was abolished.

The court of King's Bench had the administration of the criminal law as its especial province—but, as we have said, it was not usual for ordinary criminal trials to be held before that court itself. Normally " felonies "—as serious crimes were coming to be called—were tried by royal commissioners on circuit sitting either under special commissions [1] empowering them to try criminal matters only or under a general commission which included the trial of felons with much other business.[2] These commissions were issued not only to justices of the King's Bench and Common Pleas [3] but also to a number of " serjeants-at-law " and to prominent laymen. In the early Middle Ages laymen frequently acted as itinerant justices both under criminal and civil commissions, but later, though their names continued to be included in the commission, they came not to take any active part in its execution, but left the work to the justices and serjeants.

Obviously a great deal of preliminary work had to be

---

[1] The two principal criminal commissions were those of " oyer et terminer " and of " gaol delivery," see p. 193, below.

[2] See below, p. 93, for the " General Eyre."

[3] In this period, though the Chief Baron was usually a lawyer, the puisne Barons of the Exchequer were generally laymen. It was not until 1579 that they came to be always chosen from among the serjeants like their brethren in the King's Bench and Common Pleas. Consequently it was not until after that date that they normally rode the circuits, though the Chief Baron (if a lawyer) often did so at an earlier date.

done in the various counties before any batch of suspected felons was presented to the royal commissioner on his visit to the county court. Local enquiries had to be conducted, local juries to be empanelled, suspects had to be arrested, a list of them kept, and the various escheats and forfeitures incident to their conviction had to be supervised and checked. One might suppose that all this business would be entrusted to the sheriff, and in the twelfth century it had been, but the Crown was very distrustful of its sheriffs in matters which touched the royal revenues as closely as the Pleas of the Crown, and in the thirteenth and fourteenth centuries we find subordinate local officers set up to assist or watch the sheriff in his criminal work.

First there were the " coroners," or keepers of the Pleas of the Crown, in each county, whose office seems to have been specially created in the year 1194. It was their chief business to keep a roll of local crimes which was handed to the royal justice on his visitation so that he could check the accuracy of the presentments made to him by the hundred jurors. They also received abjurations of the realm made by felons who had taken sanctuary ; they heard confessions of felons and appeals of felony made by approvers.[1] Finally, they held enquiries or " inquests " in cases of deodand [2] and unexplained death. The last still survives as the chief remaining function of the coroner, though its object has

---

[1] See p. 69 n. 2, above.

[2] Deodands were an instance of the principle of the noxal surrender of property causing injury, which is to be found in other archaic systems of law. A deodand was any animate or inanimate thing which "moved to the death" of a human being. It was forfeited to the King or to the lord of the manor to be devoted by him to pious uses "for the appeasing," as Coke says, of God's wrath. When railway engines began to be claimed as deodand, deodands were abolished by statute 9–10 Vict. c. 62. The assertion that coroners held inquests into treasure trove and wreck, which was made by contemporary text-writers and repeated by later authorities, is not supported by the evidence of coroners' rolls ; see R. F. Hunnisett, *The Medieval Coroner*, pp. 6–7.

been changed from that of adding to the royal revenue to that of satisfying the public conscience, but for some reason (perhaps for the reason that their office was elective and not the subject of royal appointment) coroners have never played the great part in our criminal law which has been played by the holders of the next local office to be erected as a check on the sheriff—that of the " justice of the peace."

Throughout the thirteenth century local men of influence, laymen not lawyers, had been appointed as keepers of the peace (*custodes pacis*). Their duties, like those of coroners, were of an administrative and police nature. They could receive appeals and indictments, arrest the suspects and keep them in gaol pending the coming of the royal justices. In the course of the fourteenth century a series of statutes increased their powers. One important increase was the giving of power to try and punish offenders, which first appeared in the commission of the peace for 1329 : government policy towards this new jurisdiction varied, but from 1368 onwards the commissions always included power to determine criminal cases, including felonies. Shortly before 1368 the title " justice of the peace " finally replaced that of " keeper." [1] An increase of power of a different kind arose indirectly out of the Black Death of 1349. This plague, which carried off a large part of the labouring population of England, raised an economic problem of some difficulty. There was a great shortage of labour and in consequence a demand for wages on a scale which seemed excessive to an employing class which was used to an ample supply of villeins. To meet the difficulty so-called " justices of labourers " were appointed in every county to fix a rate of wages to be observed in the district, and the duty of executing the Statutes of Labourers was often entrusted

[1] Recent work on the keepers and justices is summarised in Holdsworth, vol. I (7th ed., 1956), pp. 24*–27*. The decline of the general eyre and of other special judicial commissions contributed to the rise of the justices.

to the men who were justices of the peace. This was the first important administrative function of the justices but by the end of the Middle Ages they were, as we shall see, to become the local government authority for the county in place of the sheriff and his courts. Regular meetings of the county justices became necessary, and in 1362 they were directed to meet together in session four times a year. This is the origin of the modern " quarter sessions " of the justices before which tribunal a great part of the serious crime committed in this country is tried to-day. From the earliest times the most serious or difficult cases of all have been re-served for trial by the royal commissioners on assize, but the jurisdiction of quarter sessions, though fluctuating from time to time, has always been wide, and there is no doubt that the conferring of judicial powers on the justices of the peace relieved the royal commissioners on circuit of a great mass of work. Indeed, it was probably the existence of quarter sessions which enabled the criminal commissions to be executed by a small number of professional commissioners without the assistance of laymen. A justice of the peace was not then, any more than he is to-day, of necessity a trained lawyer, and no effective provision was made for the presence of a qualified lawyer at quarter sessions.[1] A trial at quarter sessions was, however, conducted in the same manner as a trial at assizes, that is to say, the accused was presented by the Grand Jury and tried by a petty jury. In the exercise of their functions, both judicial and admini-strative, the justices of the peace themselves were under the general control of the court of King's Bench.

It is not within the province of a book like this to describe the various forms of offence which were recog-nised as " felonies " in the later Middle Ages, but it is necessary to say something of a rule of procedure which applied equally to all felonies short of treason, and which had a considerable effect on the whole development of

[1] See p. 195, below.

our criminal law ; that is, the so-called " benefit of clergy." [1] We have seen that, after the murder of Becket, Henry II accepted the view championed by the Archbishop that a cleric accused of serious crime could only be tried in the ecclesiastical courts, where, it was presumed, he would be convicted if guilty, degraded from his orders and thus exposed to the arm of temporal justice if he lapsed again. This system obviously depended for its proper working on the efficiency of the trial in the ecclesiastical courts, but even as early as the thirteenth century the trials of " criminous clerks " in them were becoming something of a farce, and before long an acquittal was practically a foregone conclusion.[2] Gradually, too, the privilege of " clergy " was extended to persons even indirectly connected with the church, and to overcome the difficulty of establishing whether or not a claimant was entitled to it the royal courts introduced as a test ability to read.[3] In the Middle Ages, no doubt, this qualification was some slight evidence of clerkship, but in time the reading test became a fiction, so that " clergy " could be claimed by practically any male.[4] In face of these developments the royal courts changed their procedure in these cases. Instead of admitting the plea of clergy as a bar to a trial in the lay court, they tried the prisoner and allowed him to plead his clergy after conviction. As a convicted felon his goods were forfeit even if his body was handed over alive to the ecclesiastical tribunal. But a state of affairs in which serious crimes could be committed practically with impunity by educated criminals was obviously unsatis-

[1] Holdsworth, vol. I, pp. 75*-77*, vol. III, pp. 293-302.

[2] The standard account is by L. C. Gabel, *Benefit of Clergy in England in the later Middle Ages* (1929). The normal procedure of trial in the ecclesiastical court was " compurgation."

[3] The test eventually imposed was the reading of verse 1 of the 51st Psalm, which thus became known as the " neck verse."

[4] Women, other than nuns, were not entitled to " benefit of clergy " in the Middle Ages, but the privilege was extended to them in the seventeenth century.

factory, and from the end of the Middle Ages a series of statutes limited the effect of the plea and confined it to a small number of felonies. Here we can only mention a few of these statutes. In 1487 a statute directed that all who pleaded their clergy and were not actually in Holy Orders should be branded on the hand to prevent their pleading it a second time; and another statute of 1576 enabled the courts to pass a sentence of imprisonment of one year on such persons. In 1547 benefit of clergy was taken away in cases of murder, burglary and house-breaking, and, as new offences were made felonies by statute, it was often expressly provided that the privilege should not extend to them. As a result of this development benefit of clergy became in the sixteenth to eighteenth centuries a method by which first offenders [1] could avoid the extreme consequences of a conviction for felony in the case of those crimes, chiefly larcenies, which were felonies by the common law, and from which the privilege had not been taken away. Misdemeanours, as opposed to felonies, were not the subject of benefit of clergy at all.

So far we have spoken only of the graver crimes, the felonies, which were punishable with death and entailed a forfeiture of lands and goods. In the thirteenth century lesser offences, which came to be called "misdemeanours" and were then generally known as " trespasses," were not ordinarily brought before the royal justices on assize but were dealt with by the sheriff in his " tourn " in the hundred court or (if the tourn jurisdiction was in private hands) by the lord's steward in the " Court Leet." In the tourn and the leet the procedure was by presentment of offenders by local representatives just as it was in the more exalted tribunals. The sheriff or the steward (as the case might be) addressed a list of questions known as the " articles of the tourn " to the

---

[1] Peers and clerks in Holy Orders were not branded, and escaped all punishment for the first offence. Indeed, clergymen could plead the privilege any number of times.

representatives of the various townships in the hundred just as the royal justices in eyre addressed articles of the eyre to the various bodies representing the county who stood before them in the county court. The articles of the tourn required the presentment of persons suspected of a great variety of offences and also the answers to a number of questions affecting the good government of the district in question. Those accused of serious crimes were reserved for the assizes, while the smaller offenders were fined by the court. But after the establishment of the justices of the peace it came to be felt that they would form a far more satisfactory tribunal to deal with the work done in the tourn than the sheriffs, or rather their deputies, who were frequently accused of oppression in their exercise of this jurisdiction. From the middle years of the fourteenth century the justices of the peace were dealing in quarter sessions with a great volume of indictable trespasses.[1] A statute of 1461 deprived the sheriff of much of his power of arresting or inflicting fines.

We shall see [2] that in the sixteenth century the arrest and preliminary examination in cases of serious crime and the trial and punishment of lesser offences was largely [3] vested in the justices. This jurisdiction, however, was not always exercised by all the justices of the county collectively in quarter sessions, but often, as statute provided, "out of sessions" in much smaller and more frequent gatherings which came eventually to be known as Petty Sessions, and of which we must speak in greater detail in a later chapter.

[1] See the Introduction to B. H. Putnam's *Proceedings before the Justices of the Peace* (Ames Foundation). By this time royal justices on circuit were also trying indictable trespasses under commissions of oyer and terminer.

[2] Chapter 12, below.

[3] Courts Leet preserved their independence longer than the tourn.

VI

THE CIVIL LAW IN THE THIRTEENTH AND FOURTEENTH CENTURIES

WE saw that by 1215 a great part of the litigation concerning freehold land was already coming before the royal rather than the feudal courts. The courts of common law continued in the thirteenth century to extend their jurisdiction over such cases further and further, so that by 1300 it is true to say that the courts "baron" as opposed to the courts "customary" of the manors had little work to do. The thirteenth century also saw the beginning of the drawing away of other civil litigation—disputes over the possession of chattels, the enforcement of debts and civil injuries generally, from the local to the royal tribunals. In Glanvill's day the royal court knew little of this class of work, which then came chiefly before the county or hundred courts (and sometimes the ecclesiastical courts also), but by 1300 it was already well acquainted with it, and by 1400 the sheriff's courts had lost all but the smallest litigation.

As we have seen, the encroachment of the royal courts on feudal jurisdiction principally affected suits concerning land. Their encroachment on local courts affected other civil business and we must now say something about it. This business could originate in the county court in two different ways, by oral plaint, or by a writ from the Chancery ordering the sheriff to do justice in a case. Such writs were known as "viscontial," because addressed to the "vicecomes" or sheriff, and are mostly writs of the family known as "justicies" because the opening clause requires the sheriff to "justice" the defendant.

Debt, detinue, covenant, account and trespass could all be commenced either by justicies or by plaint. Such actions could also be commenced by writ in the Common Pleas but these writs were much more expensive than the corresponding justicies triable in the county. The county court was, therefore, the natural choice of a plaintiff seeking speedy and cheap justice, and such cases normally found their way there. Indeed, the Statute of Gloucester (1278) laid down that writs in which less than forty shillings was in dispute must not be pleaded in the royal courts. But the appetite of the royal judges grew with eating, and the restrictions which they placed on the competence of the local courts to hear important business, coupled with the better remedies and methods of trial available in the royal court, brought about the decline of the former tribunals. Soon after the Statute of Gloucester was passed the judges construed its provision to mean that suits involving more than forty shillings could not be heard in the county court, and though forty shillings was then and for many years to come a substantial sum of money, it became in time a very low maximum which deprived the sheriff's court of all important business.

Before we pass from the county and hundred courts we may observe that their decay as courts of law was by no means an unmixed blessing. It would indeed have been impossible for the suitors of the local courts to have administered a uniform system of law of growing complexity, but the development of that law was secured at a high price when it led to the absurdity of the twelve judges of the Common Law Courts attempting to deal in London or on circuit with practically all the civil litigation of the county. In the field of criminal law, where the interests of his "peace" were at stake, the king saw to it that efficient local tribunals, the courts of the justices of the peace, relieved the judges of the superior courts of a part of their work. But a system of efficient local courts for disposing of small civil litigation was not an obvious necessity of good government, and it was not until the nineteenth century and in the teeth of considerable professional opposition, that the administration of civil justice was again partially decentralised by the creation of the modern county court system.

We must now describe those " better remedies and methods of trial " which the royal courts could offer to the suitor in them. An action in the royal court was normally started, we have seen, by an original writ obtained from the Chancellor, which might take one of a number of forms adapted to the varying circumstances of the case. Often it happened that no existing form of writ would meet the circumstances in question, and if it appeared to the clerks at the cursitor office [1] that the case was one for which a remedy ought to be available in the royal court, a new form of writ might be devised to meet it. It was by this invention of new writs initiating new forms of action that the royal court extended its jurisdiction, and in a period of rapid expansion of the common law, such as was the reign of Henry III, the number of original writs available to suitors increased enormously. Early in Henry III's reign the Register contained some fifty writs: by Edward I's time there were nearly five hundred.[2]

It is not surprising to find that this making of new law by the Chancellor and his clerks by way of the granting of new writs came to be viewed with some suspicion in the course of the thirteenth century as the distinction between legislative and administrative acts began vaguely to be realised, and the Provisions of Oxford (1258) laid it down that the Chancellor should seal no writs save the existing writs " of course " without the sanction of the king and Council. Nevertheless, it was generally obvious that a certain discretion must be left to the officials, and by a clause in the Statute of Westminster II (1285) it was enacted that in addition to the existing writs the clerks in the Chancery might agree in making a new writ " whensoever it shall happen that in one case a writ

[1] The clerks who issued these writs were known as " cursitors " and Cursitor Street, Chancery Lane marks the site of their office.
[2] Maitland: *Register of Original Writs* in *Collected Papers*, vol. II.

is found and in like case (in consimili casu) falling under like law and requiring like remedy is found none." The modified power of framing new writs allowed by this statute was perhaps little used and the spectacular development of " actions on the case " which began in the late fourteenth century was the result not of this statute but of judicial willingness to accept experimental writs devised by persuasive litigants and complaisant Chancery clerks.[1]

An accurate knowledge of the Register of Writs and of the form of action which each writ originated was the foundation of the professional knowledge of a mediæval lawyer. He must first know whether the facts of the case before him were such that they fell within the scope of an existing writ. If they did not, a question might arise whether it was a case which the Chancery would be likely to meet by framing a new writ. Supposing this was out of the question, the only advice which the lawyer could give his client was that he should present a humble petition to the King's Council or Parliament setting out the facts of his case in his own words and asking for some special relief outside the ambit of the common law. In fact, such petitions were very frequently presented, and became in time (as we shall see) the method by which the equitable jurisdiction of the Chancellor was invoked. Suppose, however, that the facts of the particular case brought it within the scope of the common law, a question of great difficulty might arise, for it might well happen that two or more writs were equally available, and a choice had to be made between them. Each writ, as we have said, initiated a different form of action, with its own process for compelling the defendant's appearance, its own methods of trial and its own appropriate form of judgment. Further, some forms of action could be brought in all three of the royal courts, while others were peculiar to one of them. When one reflects that in addition to this knowledge of the exact

---

[1] *Early registers of writs*, ed. Hall (Selden Soc., 87), p. cxxvii.

nature of each form of action the practitioner was bound
to employ a meticulous exactitude in his pleading of his
client's case, one will realise that the " learning " of a
a mediæval lawyer was no empty form and left him very
little time for anything but professional knowledge.

Naturally, as the number of writs in the register increased, attempts were made to classify the forms of
action which they initiated.   A very frequent classification—and one which has left a deep mark on our law—
was that into real actions and personal actions.   In the
first the plaintiff claimed—and if he was successful
would recover—a specific object of property (a " res ").
In a personal action, on the other hand, the plaintiff
sought to enforce a general claim to compensation in
damages from the defendant for some injury done to his
person or property.[1]   Broadly speaking, the only objects
of property which were recoverable in specie in the
developed common law system were estates of freehold
in land.   The actions by which title to such estates could
be asserted were the " real actions " *par excellence*, and the
estates themselves came in consequence to be called " real
property."   We have already described the earliest of
the real actions—the writs of right and the possessory
assizes.   We must now say something of their development in the thirteenth and fourteenth centuries.

Clause 34 of the Great Charter contained a protest by
the baronage against the drawing away of cases touching
the title to freehold land from the feudal to the royal
courts.   The king was not for the future to issue the
writ " præcipe " commanding a tenant of a mesne lord
to appear in the royal court to answer for his land holding.   The plaintiff must obtain his writ of right in proper
form directed to the feudal lord and start his action in the
feudal court, or else persuade the lord to waive his juris-

---

[1] A third, less important, category was that of mixed actions—" suits
partaking of the nature of the other two, wherein some real property is
demanded, and also personal damages for a wrong sustained " ; Blackstone's *Commentaries*, vol. III, p. 118.

diction, so as to permit the writ to issue in the form *quia dominus remisit curiam ruam*.   On the other hand, where mere possession (seisin) and not title to the freehold was in issue, the royal court had a free hand, for so far from attacking the use of the possessory assizes the Great Charter sought to make this procedure more easily available to litigants.[1]   This distinction between proprietary and possessory actions must be borne in mind, for in the thirteenth century the royal court extended the application of possessory actions so that they came to do the work of the writ of right.   It is impossible in a book such as this to trace this development in any detail, but its outline is not hard to grasp.

The two chief possessory assizes—novel disseisin and mort d'ancestor—if brought in time, enabled the man disseised to recover his seisin from the disseisor and the heir to recover the seisin of his ancestor, but they were generally speaking inappropriate in cases where the seisin improperly obtained had been transmitted before the disseisee took action.   For instance, if A disseises B and dies leaving C his heir, B cannot have the assize against C, still less against an alienee from C.   Yet if the events were recent and notorious it was obviously hard that B should be forced to rely on a writ of right and have to run the risk of trial by battle in order to recover the land.   Then there is another class of case that the assizes will not meet.   A man who is in possession —and rightly in possession—of land makes an alienation of it which he has no right to make and which prejudices his successor.   Thus a life tenant conveys the fee simple [2] or a husband alienates his wife's lands of which he alone has control during the marriage.   In each of these cases

---

[1] Clause 18 of 1215 originally provided that the possessory assizes should be held four times a year in each county ; but this was altered in later issues to an annual visitation.

[2] It must be remembered that in our early land law a conveyance—or feoffment—by a man who was seised of the land was in some cases capable of passing a greater estate than the feoffor had any right to convey ; it was said to have a tortious operation.

the alienee gets a seisin which is obviously improper as against the remainderman after the expiry of the life estate and the wife after her husband's death, but there has been no " disseisin " for which the assize will lie, and unless the court can invent some new remedy the remainderman or the wife, as the case may be, must have recourse to the writ of right.

The new real actions which the royal court invented in the thirteenth century to meet these—and many other —difficulties, were called the " writs of entry." In form these writs resembled the præcipe—that is to say, that by them the defendant was ordered to give up the land in dispute to the plaintiff, who claimed title to it, or answer for it in the royal court ; but then, unlike the præcipe, a writ of entry went on to state the recent flaw in the defendant's title which would justify the bringing of such an action in the royal court. The following examples may make this clear : " To the Sheriff of Berkshire, Greeting. Command (præcipe) X, that justly and without delay he render to A one messuage with its appurtenances in Abingdon which he claims to be his right and inheritance and *into which the said X had no entry save* through Y who demised it to him and who unjustly and without a judgment disseised B the father of the said A of it since the passage of our Lord the King to Gascony " or " *into which the said X had no entry* save through K once the husband of the said A who demised it to him and whom A, as she says, could not oppose during his life," and in each case the sheriff is directed if X refuses to surrender the land to summon him to Westminster before the royal justices to answer for it.

It is difficult to say whether these writs of entry ought to be classed as actions affecting the title or only the possession of land. In a sense they were merely possessory, for they were not conclusive of the title even between the parties, since it might happen (though not as easily as in the case of the original possessory assizes) that the plaintiff who was successful in a writ of entry and recovered the seisin of the land would be subsequently adjudged to have no title to it against his opponent when the latter brought a writ of right against him. Further, the writs of entry were originally subject to a rule about " degrees." There was a limit to the number of transactions in the land between its leaving the seisin of the demandant or his ancestor and its coming to the present tenant, if the writ of entry was to be available against the latter. This made for the protection of the feudal jurisdiction in writs of right. But after the limit was abandoned for certain writs of entry by the Statute of Marlborough (1267) it was rapidly abandoned in general, producing a new crop of writs of "entry in the *post* "—a simple allegation that the tenant had entered " after " some event, which constituted the flaw. When this was established the writ of entry had in substance become a means of trying title to land in nearly every case. Indeed, almost the only bound to its use was set by the fact that the flaw relied upon had to be subsequent in date to the period of limitation for bringing the action which was in force at the time. The mediæval method of providing for the limitation of actions was to fix upon a definite date since which the plaintiff's cause of action must have arisen and when that date had receded too far into the past a new one was fixed. The last occasion when this was done was by the Statute of Westminster 1275, when the coronation of Henry III (1216) was chosen for the writs of entry ; the same statute appointed the coronation of Richard I (1189) for writs of right.[1] As time passed the number of actions which could not be covered by writs of entry but only by writs of right grew

[1] For acquisition of rights by prescription the common law requires enjoyment of the right " during the time whereof the memory of man runneth not to the contrary " ; the courts adopted 1189 as the limit of " legal memory " and did not change this date for purposes of prescription when later statutes introduced a fixed period of years within which real actions must be brought. So 1189 is still today the technical limit of legal memory.

fewer and fewer, and by the close of the Middle Ages a writ of right was already a rarity.

From the " real " we must pass to the " personal " actions. Before the reign of Edward I the list of those common in the royal courts was indeed a short one : debt and detinue, covenant, and account. We have written " debt and detinue " advisedly to imply a unity of origin for these, the most important actions on the list. For Glanvill, for the clerks who made the rolls, and for the *Register of Writs* there is one heading of " debt," applicable equally to the recovery of a money debt or of a specific chattel.[1] But lawyers came to distinguish two actions : debt for the recovery of a liquidated, *i.e.*, a fixed, sum of money and detinue for that of a specific chattel lent or bailed by the plaintiff to the defendant. Viewed as contractual actions, therefore, they were available only where the consideration had been executed on one side by the loan or deposit—that is to say, the obligation created was what Roman lawyers would call " re "; and the form of the writs was a *praecipe quod reddat* ordering the defendant to return the money or the chattel to the plaintiff or to answer in the royal court for his failure to do so.

By the fourteenth century, a further refinement had led to debt becoming merely a claim for the return of equivalent, not identical, coins, while the rule grew up that in detinue a tender of the value of the chattel was sufficient and that specific restitution could not be claimed. Though the actions thus effectively lost the " real " aspects of their beginnings, they retained one mark of their great antiquity in the fact that in them the normal method of trial was by " wager of law "[2] and not by the

[1] See the important discussion of debt and detinue in Milsom, *Historical Foundations*, pp. 219–35.

[2] A defendant could not wage his law against the King. Consequently there was no wager of law in actions in the Exchequer on a quo minus (Co. Litt. sect. 514) and actions of debt continued to be brought in that court after they had been generally supplanted by actions of assumpsit in the King's Bench and Common Pleas.

verdict of a jury. This was not the only disadvantage attendant on them. Debt could not be brought for unliquidated damages or against the executors of the debtor, and it was doubtful whether detinue lay except in cases of bailment and against the original bailee.

The other two actions which we have mentioned can be disposed of quickly. Covenant lay for breach of an agreement made under seal.[1] Account speaks for itself. It was usually brought by landowners against their bailiffs. There was one other personal action which it would be natural to class with the four which we have named, the action of replevin. This was the appropriate remedy for testing the legality of a distraint, or distress, and still gives its name to the equivalent procedure in our courts to-day. Replevin has all the signs of great antiquity : its proceedings are described by Bracton as something quite well settled, the defendant could wage his law, and the plaintiff, if the distress were wrongfully eloigned pending judgment, could have the reprisal known by the archaic Saxon name of Withernam. But though replevin was commenced by a writ issued out of the Chancery, the writ was a viscontial one which gave the sheriff jurisdiction to determine the lawfulness of the distress in his own court and unlike other viscontial writs never had a counterpart returnable in the Common Bench or on circuit. The Statute of Marlborough 1267 introduced a new and simpler form of replevin by mere complaint to the sheriff without a royal writ, which in most cases superseded the proceedings by writ. In course of time it became the invariable practice for proceedings in replevin, begun by writ or plaint in the sheriff's court, to be removed into the royal court by a writ of pone or recordari,[2] which the defendant could not

[1] See p. 87 n. 1, below.

[2] A " record " is technically a document which proves itself in court without evidence. Such were the writs issued from the Chancery and the records of their proceedings kept by the royal courts. But the local courts were not " courts of record " and consequently proceedings in a county court, which had been commenced by plaint, and not by writ, could only be

oppose, and replevin became one of the commonest
causes of action litigated in the common law courts ;
but it was in fact an unusual survival of the original
jurisdiction of the sheriff's court.   The action was known
as replevin, because where a lord or lessor had entered on
the premises out of which his dues or rent issued and had
seized and impounded some chattels found there, the
owner of the chattels if he alleged that the distraint was
illegal was allowed to replevy, that is, to redeem, the seized
goods on the terms of bringing an action for illegal distress at once and meanwhile giving security to the sheriff
for the payment of the dues or rent if he lost his action.

It appears from this brief account of the older personal actions that they were very far from covering the
field of civil law even as it existed then.   In particular
there was no civil action for damages for injury to person
or property or for failure to perform an executory [1]
agreement, unless it was under seal.   If the injured
party could bring himself to assert that his adversary
had acted " feloniously " he might proceed against him
in some cases by way of a criminal appeal of felony, and
indeed the appeal of theft was the common remedy for
conversion of personal property.   But an appeal might
end in battle, and the injured party might want damages,
not a fight ; and, further, the royal judges steadily
discountenanced appeals for minor injuries.   If an
appellor alleged " wickedly and in felony you struck the

---

removed into the royal court by an order to the sheriff " recordari facias
loquelam " " cause a record to be made of the proceedings." For a
precedent see *Brevia Placitata*, p. lxvi.

[1] *I.e.* an agreement where neither party has performed his side of the
bargain as opposed to a contract where the consideration has been executed
on one side. " It might well have seemed, indeed, that Covenant was
destined to fulfil the promise of its name and to provide a general contractual remedy. That this expectation was disappointed was due to the
introduction of the technical rule that the writ would lie only upon a
writing under seal ": Fifoot, *History and Sources of the Common Law*,
p. 257. The " technical rule " was finally settled early in the fourteenth
century.

4—E.L.S.

dust from my cap " the justices, says Bracton, must quash the appeal even if the appellee should be ready to fight. There was great need, therefore, for a comprehensive action designed to give damages for injuries to person or property which, though wrongful, fell short of being felonious, and it was to meet this need that the action of trespass was developed during the reign of Henry III.

In the thirteenth century trespass meant wrong. It embraced not only the direct interference with the plaintiff's body, goods or land which we now call trespass but also many other wrongs of an indirect non-forcible kind. Trespass in this wide sense was normally dealt with in the local courts and especially in the county court. But certain types of trespass came to the royal courts, both King's Bench and Common Pleas. The writs in such cases were either general writs in which the act complained of was clearly wrongful, or special writs which set out special matter explaining why the act was a wrong to the plaintiff. The royal courts heard such cases either because the local courts were forbidden to deal with them (cases involving breach of the peace ; these were the subject of general writs and correspond roughly to our modern trespass for direct interference) or because there was some other royal interest (e.g. cases involving abuse of a franchise or non-performance of a public duty ; these were the subject of special writs and would often involve no direct interference with the plaintiff). Towards the end of the thirteenth century there seems to have been an attempt to restrict the flow of trespass cases into the royal courts and to insist more strongly on the requirement of royal interest ; the Statute of Gloucester (1278) says that " pleas of trespass shall be pleaded in the counties." As a result the words " vi et armis et contra pacem domini regis " (" by force and arms and against the peace of our Lord the King ") spread to all general writs : these words became the hallmark of trespass writs for direct interference and they ensured the continued favourable reception of such writs in the royal courts. A further result was that the development of special writs was held back for nearly a century. But by about 1370 the requirement of royal interest was abandoned and special writs of a new sort began to appear in the royal courts. Unlike the older special writs the new ones made no pretence of royal interest but relied solely on the wrongfulness of the conduct in question, which was specially recited in the writ. For example, where a man undertook to cure a horse but his treatment led to its death, this could not be general trespass because the delivery of the horse to the defendant to cure contradicts the necessary allegation of force and arms nor could it be special trespass so long as royal interest was insisted on : but an action of "'trespass on the case" or " case ", as the new special writs were called, would lie in such a situation.[1] We shall see in a later chapter how these writs came to cover the branches of the law now known as negligence and nuisance, and how, too, since the breach of an undertaking frequently involves the tort of negligence, a variety of " case" known as " assumpsit " became the foundation of the modern law of contract.[2]

Now that we have mentioned the principal " forms of action " available in the royal courts in the later Middle Ages it remains for us to say something of the mode in which these actions were tried. As we have seen, each form of action was started by a different writ and had its own peculiarities, but there was one characteristic possessed by nearly all of them, the submission of issues of fact to a jury. It is true that the common law knew

---

[1] This account is based on three articles by S. F. C. Milsom in (1954) 74 L.Q.R. (1958) ; see also his *Historical Foundations*, ch. II. The traditional view was that trespass in the thirteenth century was a definite tort with the essential ingredient of direct forcible injury which had grown out of the appeal of felony and from which there developed in the late fourteenth century actions on the case for indirect injuries, framed in reliance on the " in consimili casu " clause of the Statute of Westminster II: this view is now difficult to accept.

[2] See further Chapter 10, below.

of other methods of trial ; appeals of felony and writs of right might result in trial by battle, and the defendant in an action of debt or detinue could resort to " compurgation " ; but, broadly speaking, one may say that actions in the common law courts were tried by jury. We may recall that the first examples of this method of trial were afforded by the grand and possessory assizes of Henry II, but one must observe that there was a considerable difference between the jury, or " inquest," used in those assizes and the jury used, for instance, in the actions of trespass or case. The " assize " jury used in the possessory assizes was called together by the very writ which initiated the proceedings and appeared before the justices on assize ready to answer the questions which had been propounded to them in that writ, *e.g.* whether A had disseised B of his free tenement in Blackacre since the last passage of our Lord the King from England to Normandy. The writ of trespass by contrast contained no reference to the summoning of a jury. It was only after the parties to the action had appeared and pleaded before the court and arrived at some issue of fact which had to be decided between them that a jury was summoned, and summoned, of course, by a separate judicial writ different from the original writ which initiated the action.

Both forms of jury, the assize jury (assisa) and the ordinary common law jury (jurata) were, of course, very different in character from a modern English jury. A modern jury relies on the evidence given before it and is even discouraged from relying on any knowledge obtained " aliunde." A mediæval jury, by contrast, was expressly selected from among people who might be supposed to know or to be in a position to ascertain the facts—from neighbours of the parties to the action—and they were expected to answer the questions put to them without the assistance of witnesses. It is true that by the fifteenth century this system showed some signs of breaking down and witnesses began to be called to supplement the knowledge of the jurors, but as yet the rules of evidence were in their infancy. Any witness ran some risk of a charge of " maintenance," and evidence by the parties to the action themselves was then, and for centuries to come, rigorously excluded.

From the jury we must pass to the other chief characteristic of the common law system, the trial on circuit. The headquarters of the common law were, of course, at Westminster, but one must not suppose that all actions in the common law courts were tried there in all their stages. Henry II had, as we have seen, laid the foundations of a " circuit " system in England for the trial of serious crimes under the Assize of Clarendon and for the trial of possessory assizes under some ordinance which is lost to us, and Magna Carta had expressly approved the circuit system in the latter case. But in the case of other forms of proceedings no provision had been made for a trial elsewhere than at Westminster, and accordingly in grand assizes, writs of entry and all personal actions the sheriff was ordered to summon parties and jurors to Westminster on the appointed day. If one reflects on the difficulties of travel in those days it will at once be clear that this was an intolerable hardship which could not long survive the increase of business in the royal courts which came in the thirteenth century, and in 1285—in the Statute of Westminster II—we find the first step taken in the direction of making a general provision for the trial of all issues of fact in any common law action on circuit.

This statute included in the commissions of assize, which had hitherto been confined to the hearing of the possessory assizes, the hearing of actions of trespass and of civil pleas generally depending in the courts of King's Bench and Common Pleas. In such actions the sheriff was still ordered (as before) to have the jurors at Westminster by a certain day, but only " unless before " (*nisi prius*) that day the justices of assize came to his county. In practice, of course, it was arranged that the assizes should always be held in the county before the day in question. This system, initiated in 1285, was further developed in the fourteenth and fifteenth centuries. Thus it was extended to civil proceedings of every sort, including grand assizes and writs of entry. Further, it was laid down that the commissioners of assize sitting under this extended commission must be men of law. In the early days of the common law the commissions of assize were frequently issued to local magnates, and, as we shall see later, laymen continued to take an active part in the criminal commissions of " oyer " and " terminer " and gaol delivery down to the seventeenth century ; but the growing complexity of the civil law made the hearing of civil actions by laymen impossible at an early date. The commissions of assize, therefore, became confined to the justices of the King's Bench and Common Pleas, the serjeants-at-law who had not yet been promoted to the Bench and the Chief Baron of the Exchequer if a lawyer.

We must not suppose, of course, that the whole action was disposed of by the trial on assize, or at *nisi prius*, as it came to be called. The *nisi prius* system was pushed no further than was necessary to secure its object of avoiding the fetching of jurors, parties and witnesses to London. Thus the action was commenced at Westminster, the pleadings (in the days when the pleadings were oral) were conducted before the court at Westminster, and it was only if and when an issue of fact emerged which necessitated a trial by jury that the action was sent for trial at *nisi prius*. Further, the commissioner of assize, who presided at the trial, and who was not, of course, necessarily a judge of the court in which the action was depending, had no power to enter judgment. A note of the verdict of the jury was added to the record of the case, and this record was then remitted back to Westminster, where legal arguments of various sorts might take place before the court there before judgment was entered for one side or the other.[1]

[1] Chapter 11, below, for a fuller account of the proceedings at *nisi prius* and before the court *in banc*.

Before we leave the system of itinerant justices we must say something of a type of commission which died out in the course of the fourteenth century, but which at one time occupied a place of great importance in the government of England. This was the commission " ad omnia placita," or the " general eyre." To-day it seems natural to us to consider the circuit system as a useful, even a necessary, element in the dispensing of justice, but it was not a desire to administer justice to their subjects that was the chief motive of our mediæval kings in sending out their justices " on eyre " round the shires. An itinerant justice played an important part in the government of the country.[1] He was expected to enquire into and report on the conduct of county administration by the sheriff and the local courts, and was expected to bring a contribution to the royal exchequer both in the form of fines for maladministration and by the exaction of all royal fiscal rights. From time to time, normally, in the late thirteenth century, once every seven years, each county had to endure a protracted inquisition into its affairs by royal justices acting under a wide commission which enabled them not only to hear the ordinary judicial pleas but also to overhaul the whole county administration. For the purposes of this so-called " general eyre " a special session of the county court was summoned to meet the royal justices. The great men were present in person and every local community was present by representatives.[2] The justices then put to the county a long list of questions known as the " articles of the eyre " (capitula itineris) which covered the whole field of county administration and comprised, for example, enquiries into the neglect of their police duties on the part of the county, its hundreds, townships and

[1] He continued to play this part even in the sixteenth and early seventeenth centuries, see p. 110, below.

[2] It has been reckoned that from 1,500 to 2,000 persons were present before the royal justices at Canterbury at the Eyre of Kent in 1313–1314. Bolland : *The General Eyre*, pp. 35–7.

boroughs, into the misdoings of all the county officials
and into the various proprietary rights of the Crown,
such as escheats and wardships. The object of these
enquiries (which extended back to the date of the last
eyre held in the county) was to extract from the juries
which represented the various county communities
information on every subject which might possibly
afford a ground for imposing a fine on someone or
seizing some property into the royal exchequer. In this
game the justices had a most unfair advantage in that they
had before them on the bench the records of the Pleas
of the Crown kept by the sheriff and coroners, and could
check from them the accuracy of many of the answers
which the juries had to give from memory of the occur-
rences in question ; and for a false answer the jury was
liable to a fine. Naturally, the general eyre was intensely
unpopular with all sections of the community ; we are
told that in 1233 the men of Cornwall took to the moors
and woods rather than face the justices, and in the early
fourteenth-century protests were heard in Parliament.
The financial attraction of the General Eyre for the
Crown were outweighed by newer means of taxation and
the last completed eyre was in 1337.

It remains for us to say something of the general
character of the English legal system in the later Middle
Ages, and for this purpose it is necessary to distinguish
the thirteenth century from the fourteenth and the
fifteenth. Exact boundaries cannot, of course, be drawn
in matters of this sort, but one may fairly say that round
about 1300 a considerable change came over English
law caused by its increasing technicality and the growth
of a legal profession to administer it. The thirteenth
century, especially the reign of Henry III, was a period
of rapid development and expansion of the common law.
Unhampered by Parliament and unfettered by tradition
the royal justices, who were then usually ecclesiastics with
some knowledge of the Canon and Roman Laws, and often
men of some general culture as well, in co-operation with

the Chancellor and his clerks, freely admitted new forms
of action to meet fresh circumstances, and with some
borrowings from the law of Rome and much native
imagination moulded the English common law to the
needs of the time and of its own ever-increasing jurisdiction.

This period has left a perpetual memorial of itself in
the work of Henry of Bracton—one of Henry III's
judges—who wrote a treatise on the law of England
which in comprehensive scope was unrivalled until the
works of Sir Edward Coke. The extent of Bracton's
borrowings from the Roman Law has been the subject
of some dispute. Undoubtedly in the form of his work—
which was far superior to anything that English law
could point to for centuries to come—he relied very
largely on the great Italian commentators on the civil
law, especially on Azo of Bologna, but it may be that the
substance of his borrowings has been somewhat exaggerated. It is at least of interest to observe that in some
parts of his work he referred to and relied upon decisions
of some of his predecessors on the English bench. There
were as yet, of course, no published reports of such
decisions but a record of the pleadings, issues and
decisions was entered in Latin in the rolls of the court.
Bracton had in his possession several of these rolls recording cases tried before such judges as William Raleigh and
Martin Pateshull, and he evidently regarded some of the
law to be found in them as authoritative and incorporated
it in his treatise. Bracton may therefore be considered
the originator of the specifically English system of reliance
on reported decisions.

As the common law grew in bulk it became hard for a
man to be a master of it who had not devoted his life to
its study. About 1300 we can see the beginnings of an
organised legal profession in England. The Inns of
Court were founded and gradually the tradition is established that the judges of the royal courts must be drawn
from the ranks of the most eminent practitioners of the

law. At the same time—in the fourteenth century—as
we saw in Chapter 3, the common law courts were rapidly
losing their original connection with the king and his
council and drifting away from the fountain head of fresh,
extraordinary justice. The common law was tending to
become a closed system and he who sought an exceptional
remedy must seek it by petition to the Crown or Council.
We must not exaggerate this tendency, nor need we
altogether deplore it. What we have said of the development of the action of trespass in the fourteenth and
fifteenth centuries shows that the common law was by
no means wholly inelastic in the later Middle Ages, and
if it had been less technical and professionalised than it
was it might have succumbed in the sixteenth century to
a wholesale reception of the law of Rome—a reception
which might very well have adversely affected the growth
of our parliamentary constitution.

The fourteenth and fifteenth centuries saw the beginnings of written pleadings in the common law courts in
place of the old oral statement and answer by the opposing
counsel. They also saw the beginnings of the English
law reports. From about 1270 we have notes—at first
they can hardly be called reports—of the facts and the
arguments of counsel in a vast number of cases in the
common law courts.[1] It soon became customary to
collect these reports into annual volumes called Year
Books which run in a broken series down to the middle
of the sixteenth century. The Year Books had no
official sanction and seem to have been the notes taken
by students of the points of practice which might be of
use to themselves and their successors ; but in course of
time they improved very much in quality. Those of the
fifteenth century are generally distinctly superior to those
of the fourteenth. They were, of course, written in

[1] For these early notes and later history see W. H. Dunham, *Casus
Placitorum* (Selden Society, vol. 69), pp. xlii–lxx and 45–141. Many
Year Books of Edward II's reign have been edited and translated by the
Selden Society and some of Richard II by the Ames Foundation.

the French which until the middle of the fourteenth century was the language of the upper classes of England and remained the professional language of the lawyers after it had given way to English as the language of everyday life. Naturally this "law French" tended to become more and more polluted with "anglicisms," but in a debased form it continued to be habitually used in law reports and textbooks until the middle of the sixteenth century, and did not die out altogether until the end of the seventeenth.[1]   Meanwhile the records of the courts were written, as they always had been, in Latin, and continued to be so written until 1731.

[1] "Those who disparage the mediæval French of our law courts would do well to remember that it was a living language spoken by men of learning; and very different from the so-called French of the seventeenth century law reporters which was unspoken, little studied, and written grotesquely. It had undoubtedly then become a mere jargon." G. J. Turner, *Brevia Placitata*, p. xxxvii.

VII

THE COUNCIL AND THE COURT OF STAR CHAMBER

WE saw in Chapter 4 that in the course of the thirteenth and fourteenth centuries the common law courts and Parliament gradually developed as independent organs of government. By 1300 this development was not complete even for the common law courts and far from it in the case of Parliament. The King's Bench was still in a special relationship with the Council and the Council in Parliament; though the rolls of the King's Bench and the Parliament Rolls were separate series of records the same matter might appear on both. The judicial function of Parliament still was at its heart and the legislative function had not yet matured; both were guided by the Council, the core and essence of Parliament. But in the fourteenth century, perhaps especially in the vital but mysterious constitutional changes of the reign of Edward II (1307–1327), development proceeded apace; by its end it makes sense to regard the Council, the common law courts, and Parliament as three distinct organs. What were to be their precise spheres of action?

The standpoint of the Council, if one may formulate it in modern terms, was that though the private disputes of the king's subjects were normally to be tried in the king's common law courts by the course of common law, and their grievances were normally to be ventilated in Parliament and redressed by statutes duly passed there, yet the existence of these bodies had not taken away from the king his original inherent prerogative of governing his people. In cases of necessity there remained in him a reserve of power by which he could supplement the activities of Parliament and the law courts; and his

Council, being in constant session and in close contact with his person, was the natural organ of this prerogative. Parliament and the common law courts in the later Middle Ages were often uneasy about the claims of the Council in legislative and judicial matters, but despite protests the Council did in fact maintain its claims successfully to a considerable extent, so that it is impossible to state with any precision what were the legal limitations on the royal prerogative exercised through the Council in the later Middle Ages and the sixteenth century. The question was not resolved until the very different world of the seventeenth century, with the peaceful revolution of the opening months of the Long Parliament, the ensuing Civil War, and the more constructive period of Restoration Monarchy.

In this book we are more concerned with the claim of the Council to exercise judicial functions outside the course of the common law than with its claim to legislate by proclamation or ordinances without the assent of Parliament. In the former branch of the problem some points are clear. First, the Council never succeeded in hearing appeals from the decisions of the common law courts. In 1366 the Council purported to reverse a judgment of the Court of Common Pleas, but the judges paid no attention to the reversal because the Council was not, in their view, a place where a common law judgment could be reversed. Appeals from the Common Pleas went normally to the King's Bench, and the only court which the judges would recognise as superior to the King's Bench was Parliament itself.[1] After this attempt the Council practically abandoned its claim to act as a court of appeal from the common law. Secondly, there were some matters of such importance that to decide them elsewhere than in the common law courts by the time-honoured method of trial by jury could not be tolerated. Especially it was felt that a man ought not to be deprived of life or land without the verdict of a jury ;

[1] See Chapter 13, below.

and the Council (in response to constant protests by Parliament) eventually abandoned all claim to decide questions of title to land and—more important—to try cases of treason or felony which were punishable with death and a conviction for which entailed the forfeiture or escheat of the accused's land. In consequence of these limitations the Council's heaviest weapons came to be fines and imprisonment.

Outside these accepted limits the jurisdiction of the Council was quite unfixed. There were some types of cases with which it was recognised that the Council was well qualified to deal—cases in which foreign merchants were involved, for instance, which might turn on the law merchant [1] rather than the common law, and which might even raise diplomatic questions fitter to be answered by a body of politicians than a court of law, or cases involving the relations of England and the Papacy under the Statute of Provisors and Præmunire. Further, there were cases which were properly triable at common law but in which for one reason or another the plaintiff could get no remedy in the common law courts. Trial by jury seems to us an eminently fair method of settling issues of fact, but in an age when the power of some individuals was almost unbounded in their own neighbourhood the submission of a case in which they were interested to the verdict of a local jury was often a farce. If, on the other hand, such a man could be brought up to London and the facts of the case heard by the Council, the plaintiff might obtain justice. It is not surprising, therefore, to find many petitions couched in the humblest terms addressed to the Council and asking for its intervention in such cases, and the Council consistently claimed the right to summon the parties before it in cases in which it was credibly informed that for "maintenance and oppression" the common law could not be enforced.

Again, there were cases in which the common law did

[1] See Chapter 14, below.

not give a remedy but the plaintiff felt that a remedy ought to be forthcoming. Eventually, of course, this type of case came to be more and more referred to one particular member of the Council—the Chancellor—and formed the foundation of the jurisdiction of the Court of Chancery.[1] But in the Middle Ages the distinction between the jurisdiction of the Chancellor and that of the Council was not clearly drawn, and just as we find a number of early Chancery petitions which do not ask for a remedy outside the common law but merely state that by reason of maintenance or fraud the plaintiff cannot enforce his common law rights, so we find petitions to the Council asking for its intervention in supplementing the common law by an exercise of the Crown's residuary jurisdiction. It was not often that the Council heard such cases in full itself ; sometimes it remitted them to common law courts with suggestions how effect might be given to the plaintiff's claim ; sometimes it handed the case over to the Chancellor. It must be remembered that the relations between the common law judges and the Council and Chancellor were still close and not altogether uncordial. Both Council and Chancellor often submitted difficult points in cases which came before them to the decision of the judges, either by inviting them to attend at the Council board or by sending the case to a meeting of the judges in the exchequer chamber ; and the Chancellor on occasion even invited some of the judges to sit with him in the Chancery. In this way a certain unity and harmony in the administration of justice were still maintained in the later Middle Ages, which was subsequently lost.

In the fifteenth century the violence and oppression of local magnates which had hampered the administration of the common law in the fourteenth grew more wanton, and the desire of the Council to check such practices grew less. Henry VI's councillors for the most part cared less for the interests of their ineffectual master than

[1] See Chapter 8, below.

for their own interests and those of their friends, and in their hands the government of England deteriorated rapidly. At length a condition of anarchy ensued, in which the Council ceased to have any continuous or stable existence at all and became an ever-shifting body— now composed of Lancastrians and now of Yorkists— which bothered itself very little with the administration of the law. With the Wars of the Roses the days of Stephen seemed to have returned.

Edward IV did something to re-establish the central government in England, but much remained to be done by Henry VII, and in this task he made considerable use of the Council ; but his was not such a Council as the last two centuries had known. The fourteenth century had seen a continuous struggle for the control of the Council, the king endeavouring to retain the sole right of appointment to it, and Parliament, especially the House of Lords, striving to secure a place for its own nominees. Under the House of Lancaster the magnates had succeeded to a large extent in their desire, but the Council controlled by them had brought disaster on England both abroad and at home. Henry VII chose his own councillors (many of them lawyers) who were the instruments and not the framers of his policy.

Henry's Council was a large undivided body of fluctuating attendance which acted both as an executive board and as a court of law. It did the work later covered in Elizabeth's reign by the Privy Council (government business and some cases of special importance to the Crown), the Star Chamber (the trial of criminal cases) and the Court of Requests (the trial of small civil suits). Its judicial functions were at that time predominantly civil— the hearing of suits between private citizens—but it did some work in suppressing violence and keeping down the overmighty subject. In the exercise of these judicial functions the Council often sat in the Star Chamber of the Palace at Westminster. At this date there was not yet a separate Court of Star Chamber—it was merely an aspect of the work of the Council—but this is the origin of Star Chamber, whose development we must now follow.

First, however, it is necessary to mention the famous Act of 1487, the so-called " Star Chamber Act ". This recited that " by unlawful maintenances by giving of liveries and retainders by indentures by untrue demeanings of Sheriffs in making of panels and other false returns by bribery of jurors by great riots and unlawful assemblies the policy and good rule of this realm is almost subdued," and it created a special tribunal to deal with the problem. The Act was in no way the origin of, or indeed in any way connected with, the Court of Star Chamber. The framers of the Act had no idea of giving parliamentary sanction to the work done by the Council in the Star Chamber nor of defining the limits of its jurisdiction or procedure. But at a later date the title " Pro Camera Stellata " was added to the 1487 Act and this assisted the mistaken identification of the Act with the Court of Star Chamber, an identification which was, as we shall see, important in the later attacks on that court. The tribunal established in 1487 did in fact sit during Henry VII's reign but it was an unsuccesful experiment and " the new tribunal with its limited powers gave way to the old court (the Council sitting in the Star Chamber) with its unrestricted jurisdiction."[1]

In the early sixteenth century we find a general distinction growing up between the judicial and the political side of the Council's activity—a distinction between the Council at Westminster or the Council in the Star Chamber, and the " Privy Council " or the Council with the king. With the distinction of function came a distinction of personnel. While it was true that any Privy Councillor could, if he had the inclination or time to tear himself from business of state, sit as a judge in the Star Chamber, and the Chancellor habitually did so sit, the main body of councillors in the Star Chamber

[1] C. G. Bayne, *Select Cases in the Council of Henry VII* (Selden Society, vol. 75), p. lxxii ; this is the best account of the Act of 1487.

were not necessarily Privy Councillors. In particular there were generally one or two common law judges in the Star Chamber, and the judges (as we have seen) had long ceased to be full members of the Royal Council.

In this manner it came about that by the middle of the sixteenth century the Star Chamber had become a court of law closely connected with the Privy Council but yet distinct from it, with its own official style, " the Lords of the Council sitting in the Star Chamber," its own official staff and its own special procedure. Its jurisdiction we may consider under three heads. First there were a number of matters lying outside the scope of the common law involving, for instance, the law merchant or ecclesiastical. It is true that in the sixteenth century there was a tendency for most questions concerning foreign trade and foreign merchants to come before the Court of Admiralty [1] while under a provision of the Act of Supremacy Elizabeth established a committee of councillors—known as the " High Commission " [1]—specially charged with the enforcement of the ecclesiastical settlement against all recusants, Popish or Puritan ; but even so a certain amount of mercantile and ecclesiastical business still came before the Star Chamber.

Secondly, and this was the chief head of its jurisdiction, the Star Chamber dealt with a mass of criminal or quasi-criminal cases affecting the good government of the State and the administration of the law. Felonies, as we saw, the Council never attempted to try. Sometimes, indeed, it inflicted pecuniary punishment for acts which might have formed the subject of an indictment for felony at common law,[2] but no trials for felony as such involving the death penalty were ever held before the Star Chamber. There were, however, many " misdemeanours " (to use the modern phrase which was then only just coming into use) which were not, or were supposed not to be, suffi-

[1] See Chapter 14, below.
[2] *E.g.* it fined Lord Rutland £30,000 for being implicated in the rebellion of the Earl of Essex.

ciently recognised at common law, and which were solely
or chiefly punished in the Star Chamber. Especially
noteworthy among them were the following : riots,
conspiracy, attempts to commit crimes, libels, perjury
and forgery ; and it will not be out of place to say a few
words in connection with each.

1. "The great riots and unlawful assemblies" recited
in the Act of 1487 were no doubt not so frequent in 1600,
but organised disturbance of public order was still common enough, and it is to the Star Chamber that we owe
the foundations of our modern law on the subject. It
was, for instance, in the Star Chamber that it was laid
down that when three or more assemble together to do an
act of unlawful violence, and do it, it is a riot.

2. The most usual types of "conspiracy" to be
punished by the Star Chamber were malicious attempts to
ruin other persons by preferring false charges against them,
and here again our modern law of the abuse of legal
procedure owes something to the activities of that court.

3. "Attempts to commit crimes" were not regarded
as criminal offences by the common law at all, and in
punishing them the Star Chamber rendered an undoubted
service to the criminal law.

4. "Libel" in the Middle Ages had been a subject
of ecclesiastical rather than civil jurisdiction, and though
the common law courts had recently introduced an action
"on the case" giving damages for defamation to the
injured party, the invention of the printing press had made
the question one of public importance and (in view of
the government at least) necessitated the punishment of
libel as a crime. Charges against the authors and
printers of scurrilous or seditious publications were
accordingly brought in the Star Chamber and it is to its
decisions that one must look for the origins of our law
of criminal libel.[1]

5. At common law in the Middle Ages the offences

[1] To-day we tend to consider libel from the standpoint of the law of
torts rather than of the criminal law, but in the seventeenth and eighteenth

of perjury and forgery had a very narrow scope. A jury which gave a false verdict might, as we shall see,[1] be punished by " attaint," but otherwise perjury was purely an ecclesiastical offence. Certain kinds of forgery, *e.g.* of the royal seal or the coin of the realm, were treason, and reliance on a forged document in a court of law was a common law misdemeanour, but apart from these exceptions, forgery went unpunished. In the case of both perjury and forgery the Star Chamber intervened, and by punishing the offences drew men's attention to the state of the law, with the result that in 1562 and 1563 statutes of a fairly comprehensive scope were passed making many forms of each offence statutory misdemeanours, and in the case of forgery making a second conviction punishable as a felony. There were, however, varieties both of perjury and of forgery which did not fall under the statutes, and these continued to be punished in the Star Chamber.

A third head of the Star Chamber's jurisdiction consisted of cases which were really private but which the parties, or one of them, were anxious to have tried in the Star Chamber for the sake of saving of expense or time. It is difficult to state any principle on which the Star Chamber acted in deciding whether to entertain these private causes or not, but it is worth observing that in order to give some excuse for invoking the Star Chamber's jurisdiction the plaintiff often alleged on very slender grounds that the conduct of his opponents amounted to a riot or a conspiracy.[2]

We must now pass from the jurisdiction to the procedure of the court. Its procedure in civil cases was substantially identical with that of the Court of Chancery, which will be described in a later chapter and here we

centuries the criminal aspect predominated. " The publication of a libel," said Lord Eldon, " is a crime."

[1] See p. 186, below.

[2] For instances of the type of private cases heard in the Star Chamber, see Holdsworth, vol. I, pp. 506–507.

will confine ourselves to the Star Chamber procedure in criminal cases. This procedure differed fundamentally from the common law criminal procedure and represented a different conception of the function of the court in a criminal trial. "The Lords of the Council sitting in the Star Chamber" viewed it as their duty in the interest of the good government of England to suppress certain forms of disorder and in performing their duty they proceeded inquisitorially. An assize court, on the other hand, was in theory a forum in which the supposedly injured party instead of taking the law into his own hands accused the wrong-doer before a jury of his neighbours and sought to obtain his conviction from them, while the judge acted as an umpire in the combat.

Instead of the public accusation leading to the presentment of the suspect to the court by the Grand Jury, proceedings in the Star Chamber were commenced by an information filed by the Attorney-General against the defendant based on a charge laid before him by persons whose identity might never be disclosed. To this information the defendant must put in an answer signed by counsel, and in the most serious cases it was not always easy to find a counsel to take the responsibility of signing the answer. Then the defendant was examined by interrogatories based on his answer and was liable to be required to take an oath to speak the truth on the matters objected against him. Meanwhile the evidence of other witnesses was taken by affidavit, with the result that the defendant had no opportunity of cross-examining them. Both defendant and witnesses might (if need be) be examined under torture. All this was in marked contrast to the common law procedure, which did not admit of torture [1] and where such evidence

---

[1] Though torture, which the common law, by one of its finest traditions, had always opposed, was used in preliminary examinations by the Privy Council, it was not, strictly speaking, used by the Star Chamber: "statements to the contrary arise from a total confusion between Star Chamber and Privy Council" (G. R. Elton, *The Tudor Constitution* (1960), p. 169).

as was admissible at all was in general given only at the trial. Finally, in the Star Chamber the whole issue of fact was left to the decision of the court, whereas at common law it was submitted to the jury. At first sight to our modern eyes the procedure of the Star Chamber seems obviously inferior to that of the common law, but before we condemn it there are several considerations to be borne in mind. First, it is only in a country with a settled constitution and free from fear of political convulsion that the government can reasonably be expected in a case of public importance to take the view that it is better for the guilty to escape than for the innocent to be punished. Secondly, trial by jury in the sixteenth century in cases where the accused was strong and the prosecutor weak led only too often to the acquittal of the guilty. Thirdly, in cases in which the Crown was interested the protection of a trial by jury was largely illusory. The state trials for treason were trials by jury, but in most cases the prisoner and witnesses were examined previously before the Council and the " confessions " extorted from them were submitted to a jury which almost automatically found a verdict of " guilty." In short, it is by no means clear that more injustice was done in trials before the Star Chamber than would have been done if the same trials had been held at common law, and it is very probable that justice was often done in the Star Chamber which would not have been done at common law.[1]

So far we have considered the Star Chamber merely as a judicial institution ; but if we are to appreciate the causes and the importance of its abolition in 1641 we must say something of its governmental functions. Bosworth Field is the traditional boundary between mediæval and modern history in this country, and it is to the years 1471–1540 that we owe the foundation of

[1] The best summary account of the Star Chamber is in Elton, *Tudor Constitution*, pp. 158–63, 167–71 ; see also his entertaining and instructive *Star Chamber Stories* (1958).

our modern State. In nothing, perhaps, does the modern state differ from the mediæval more than in possessing a central executive body with sufficient authority to exercise a continuous control and supervision over the organs of local government, and England possessed such a body for the first time in the Tudor Council. There had been strong kings in England before the Tudors. Indeed, in a purely personal sense William the Conqueror and Henry I wielded hardly less authority than Henry VIII, but though they could crush any local rebellion against them they had not sufficient means to control local government effectively. It is true, as we have seen, that our mediæval kings by sending their itinerant justices round the country on circuit were able, at all events before the abolition of the general eyre, to take stock of local administration from time to time and to exact financial penalties for faults of it, but they made little or no attempt to enforce a continuous control. Under the Tudors, however, such a control was enforced by the Council through the justices of the peace.

We have seen that the justices of the peace, who were first appointed in the fourteenth century to assist the sheriff in his work in apprehending suspected criminals, had soon become judges with wide powers of trial of criminal offences at quarter sessions, and had further gradually acquired various administrative functions, so that by the close of the Middle Ages they had practically superseded the old local and manorial courts as the effective local government of the country. They were, of course, appointed by the Crown, and as such were a very suitable medium for the enforcement of the policy of the central government on the countryside. It would be quite outside the scope of this book to go into the details of this policy, but the construction and maintenance of highways and bridges and the provision for the poor under the Elizabethan Poor Law Act are two examples of Tudor government policy enforced locally by the justices under the control of the Council.

Sometimes this control took the form of general orders addressed to the justices, sometimes of advice, and often it was exercised by way of enquiry by the Council into specific cases which had come to its notice through proceedings in the Star Chamber. Obviously it was necessary for the Council to be in constant communication with the justices, and this necessity was probably one of the grounds for the establishment of subordinate branches of the Council in remote and disturbed parts of England, such as the Council of Wales and the Marches, and the Council of the North.[1]   Another channel of communication was through the justices of assize. Though the procedure of the Star Chamber was, as we have seen, in many respects opposed to that of the common law courts, there were still many connecting links between the Council and the common law judicial system. Common law judges habitually sat with the councillors in the Star Chamber, and on their circuits they often carried down with them into the country warnings or directions from the Council to the county justices who would assemble to meet them in the county town.[2]

The natural result of the great increase in governmental activity by the Council and Star Chamber in the

[1] For the history and jurisdiction of these provincial councils, see Holdsworth, vol. I, pp. 502–503 ; Elton, *Tudor Constitution*, pp. 195–200.

[2] The practice, which prevailed down to the extinction of the Grand Jury in 1932, of the panel being drawn from the county magistrates, with the Chairman of Quarter Sessions at their head, may well have been a survival from this time.   It is probable that the use of the judges to voice the views of the Executive ceased when the independence of the Bench was secured by the Bill of Rights.   But the use which the judges made of their charges to the Grand Jury to express views on matters not strictly raised by the calendar in front of them is an unexplored byway of legal history.   Certainly it may have influenced the development of the law, and particularly of the criminal law.   Lord Campbell, for instance, records a campaign which Lord Kenyon waged in his charges for the suppression of gaming houses (*Chief Justices* III, 69), and Lord Ellenborough refers to the cruelty of cock-shies as a regular topic " in the dehortatory charge of judges to grand juries." (*Squires* v. *Whisken*, 3 Camp. 140.)

sixteenth century was to foster the idea that there was a fundamental distinction between the affairs of the government and the affairs of private individuals. A school of thought grew up which considered that while the ordinary rules of property and contract were properly to be established in the common law courts, government was a matter of the royal " prerogative " and the Crown and its servants to some extent outside the scope of the common law. The prevalence of this view tended to enhance the importance of the Court of Star Chamber. It was the " government " court *par excellence* ; a court whose jurisdiction was largely based on the prerogative and which employed an exceptional prerogative procedure ; a court, further, which concerned itself especially with affairs of government and enforced the orders of the Council with which it was so closely connected. But with this increase in importance there came a certain unpopularity, for there was a rival school of thought which was very loth to accept the distinction between " government " and " private " affairs, which considered that (generally speaking, at least) the Crown, or at any rate its officers, was subject to the same common law as the subject of the realm, and that a court which habitually employed an exceptional procedure and habitually enforced as though they had the force of law ordinances of the Royal Council which had not the sanction of Parliament, was an abuse.

In the period from 1629 to 1640 during which Charles I ruled this country by virtue of his prerogative without any recourse to Parliament, the existence of the Court of Star Chamber was vital to the continuance of the royal government. Naturally its unpopularity with

The last such use of the charge which we have been able to trace was after the passing of the Criminal Evidence Act, 1898, which allowed the accused to give evidence on his own behalf. Some County benches began to commit prisoners for perjury on account of their evidence, and a number of judges took occasion in their charges to deprecate the practice, save in extreme cases (*Ex relatione*, Lord Goddard).

the Parliamentary party increased, and to an unpopularity based on political grounds there was added the professional jealousy of the common lawyers and the religious prejudices of the Puritans groaning under the strict discipline of the High Commission. Its enemies began to attack the competence of the court, and it was argued that its only lawful jurisdiction was that conferred by the statute of 1487, and that in so far as it had stepped outside the matters referred to in that statute in pretended reliance on the " prerogative " it was an illegal court. These arguments had not even the support of the best Parliamentary lawyers of the time, and can now be seen clearly to have been false, but they served their turn, and when the edifice of prerogative rule crashed to the ground one of the first acts of the Long Parliament was to pass statutes destroying the Court of Star Chamber and the High Commission.

By these acts of 1641 the Star Chamber, the High Commission, the Council of Wales and the Council of the North were abolished, and it was declared that the Privy Council had no jurisdiction to determine any question concerning the property of any English subject, but that such questions ought to be determined in the ordinary courts of justice and by the ordinary course of the law. Parliament did not, however, enact that the Privy Council was incapable of exercising any judicial functions whatever, and in particular did not take from it the then somewhat unimportant jurisdiction, which it had always exercised, of hearing appeals from the King's Dominions outside England. With the growth of the Empire in the later seventeenth and eighteenth centuries, this jurisdiction grew enormously in importance, and is now exercised by the Judicial Committee of the Privy Council, of which we shall speak in another chapter.

In retrospect we may say that the two most important activities of the Star Chamber were the supplementing of the criminal law by the punishment of various misdemeanours which were either not punished at all, or

inadequately punished at common law, and the foundation of something that can almost be called a system of
administrative law by the control exercised by it over the
justices of the peace and other servants of the Crown.
The fall of the court did not destroy the work which it
had done in the sphere of criminal law, for it had been
obviously useful and the common law was glad to take
it over and to build on the groundwork laid by it.   On
the other hand such control as the common law courts
could exercise on the justices of the peace was, in the
nature of things, much less effective than that which had
been exercised by the Star Chamber and it was not until
the nineteenth century that local government was brought
under the control of the central government.[1]

[1] See pp. 206–209, below.

VIII

THE COURT OF CHANCERY FROM ITS ORIGIN TO THE RESTORATION

IN Chapters 5 and 6 we gave an account of the development of the common law courts and the common law between the issue of the Great Charter and the close of the Middle Ages. In this chapter we propose to discuss the origin and early history of the system of equity administered by the Court of Chancery. It is a subject which has given rise to considerable disagreement and is still provoking research. But, before we turn to its substance, it may be well to begin by saying something of the office of Chancellor in its general aspects, which existed before there was any Court of Chancery in which he was judge. Most of the European rulers of the early Middle Ages had their " Chancellor," the head of their writing office, who supervised the drafting and issue of charters, writs, and diplomatic correspondence and authenticated them by affixing the royal seal. The office was one of great potential, for it is a short enough step from issuing the ruler's letters to influencing the policy expressed in them, and in the thirteenth century both the Pope and the King of France cut the office down as a precautionary measure. In England, though there the office was suspended for part of the reign of Henry III, a single great officer of state remained at the head of the Chancery. (A reason for the survival of the office, into which we cannot go here, may have been the development of other seals and writing-offices—the privy seal and the signet—which interposed between the Chancery and the decision-making heart of government.) But the future development of the office was to lie, not in the general sphere of government, but in the particular field of the administration of justice; there is a wealth of history behind the fact that to-day Germany has an executive head styled " Chancellor " and Britain one styled " Prime Minister."

We have seen that legal proceedings in the royal court were usually initiated by writs directed sometimes to the sheriff of the county in which the dispute arose and sometimes to the feudal lord whose tenants the disputants were, and that the increase in the jurisdiction of the royal court was effected by means of an increase in the variety of forms of writ available, new writs being framed to meet new circumstances of which the royal court desired to take cognisance. These writs were issued out of the Chancery under the Great Seal, and naturally the Chancellor, or his principal clerks, had a great deal to say as to their form. The increase in the business of the Chancery caused by this function of framing and issuing writs is illustrated by the fact that at the close of the twelfth century the Chancery became a department of state quite separate from the Exchequer, which hitherto had been a sort of general government office in which every kind of business was transacted.

In the thirteenth and fourteenth centuries as the courts of common law gradually grew to an independent existence separate from the central government the Chancellor and the Chancery came to occupy a key position midway between them and the Council. On the one hand the Chancellor was one of the king's chief advisers and an important member of the Council, while on the other his writ-making functions kept him in close contact with the work of the common law courts and the development of the common law. Indeed, the Chancellor had even a certain limited common law jurisdiction. First, in accordance with the invariable practice in the Middle Ages, the officials of the Chancery had the privilege of suing and being sued in personal actions before the Chancellor instead of in the common law courts, and secondly, proceedings against the Crown—as, for instance, proceedings by " scire facias " to cancel royal letters patent on the ground that they were made against the law or induced by the misstatements of the patentee, and "petitions of right" asking for the redelivery of the property of a subject of which the king had improperly taken possession—were generally brought before the Chancellor. In exercising this jurisdiction the Chancellor followed the rules of the common law and in later days when trial by jury had become the usual method of trying issues of fact in the common law courts he sent issues of fact arising in such cases for trial by a jury in the King's Bench.

This common law or Latin[1] jurisdiction of the Chancellor is, however, of very little importance compared with his equitable or English jurisdiction, the growth of which we must now attempt to explain. The traditional view has presented the equitable jurisdiction as a response to defects in the common law; but its stress, at least, has been increasingly called into question.[2] It may be that the question we should try to answer is, not "how did equity arise?", but "how did common law cease to be equitable?" In the thirteenth century the king was the source and ultimate guarantor of justice and the law existed to do justice. "Not only was there no equity, as a nascent body of rules different from those of the common law. There was no common law, no body of substantive rules from which equity could be different. There was justice . . ."[3] But in the four-

---

[1] So called because the "record," like the "record" in the common law courts, was in Latin, whereas the proceedings in the later "equitable" jurisdiction were in English.

[2] The traditional view will be found in many works, including (though with substantial modifications) earlier editions of the present book. It will be obvious that the account above owes much to Milsom, *Historical Foundations*, ch. 4, though Professor Milsom is concerned more with doctrine and we are here more concerned with institutions.

[3] Milsom, *Historical Foundations*, p. 76; but it should be noted that in the original the passage appears to the fourteenth, rather than the thirteenth, century and to use "justice" in a slightly different sense from that used above.

teenth century there was (as we have seen) a tendency
for the common law to grow more rigid. Originally it
had been the exceptional justice of the royal court, now
by its victory over the communal and feudal courts it
had become the ordinary law of the land, administered
in courts which, though royal, had lost their original
connection with the fountain head of government, and
by men who were not, like their predecessors, government officers, but professional lawyers. We must not
exaggerate the inadaptability of the common law of the
later Middle Ages—the development of the action of
" case " is sufficient to show that the common law was
very far from static ; but still it is broadly true to say that
if general principles of justice were to remain a pervading
force in our law after the middle of the fourteenth century
they had to be applied from outside the common law
system.

The formal method of setting the royal court in
motion was, as we have seen, to sue out an original writ
from the Chancery. It was not, however, always certain
that there would be a writ forthcoming to suit a given
case. Consequently, when the aggrieved party thought
that his case, though very deserving, was an exceptional
one, he would often adopt the expedient of presenting a
petition to the royal council setting out the facts in his own
words and asking, very humbly, for relief. We must
remember that a large part of the time of the officials of
the central government in the Middle Ages must have
been spent in answering petitions of one sort or another.
When Parliament assembled, for instance, petitions
poured in in shoals : to those of a purely private character (for example, seeking financial concessions) were
added, in the later Middle Ages, those raising matters of
public importance which would be remedied, if at all, by
statute or general ordinances of the Council. Petitions
for a special exercise of the royal power of dispensing
justice were thus only one class of a recognised form of
procedure.

Most commonly, then, if someone needed an exceptional remedy he sent a petition to the king in his council in Parliament; and thousands of petitions have survived to the present day in the Public Record Office. But as Parliament developed as a legislative and deliberative assembly the king and his council referred such matters to special committees. The obvious official to supervise such business was the Chancellor, because he was the official in charge of issuing the letters which must follow upon a favourable decision.

We have already described in the last chapter how, despite the jealousy of Parliament and the common law courts, the Council regularly heard petitions complaining that for one reason or another—bribery, maintenance or the like—the common law could not be enforced in the case in question, and we have traced this jurisdiction of the Council and the history of the Court of Star Chamber to its close. Now we are concerned with petitions which alleged not so much that the common law could not be enforced as that it gave no remedy to the petitioner when it ought to give one, or had given relief to the petitioner's opponent to which in natural justice he was not entitled. At first, no doubt, the line between the two classes of petition was not clearly drawn, but in the fifteenth century we find a tendency for petitions alleging a defect in the law to be entrusted particularly to the Chancellor. As yet, it is true, the Chancellor only acts as the chief member of a committee of the Council ; other councillors assist him in the hearing and the decree is still the decree of the Council. But even before the close of the fourteenth century we find petitioners addressing themselves to the Chancellor direct and by the end of the fifteenth century he is sitting alone at the hearing of the petitions and the decree is made in his name. From this moment we may say that the equitable jurisdiction of the Court of Chancery has come into being.[1]

[1] See *Select Cases in Chancery*, edited for the Selden Society by W. P. Baildon, 1896. The date from which an independent Court of Chancery

We must now discuss quite briefly the class of case in which the Chancellor or Council was prepared to grant special relief in this period, the procedure by which they acted in granting it, and the relation of this exceptional jurisdiction to the common law. The jurisdiction was, of course, still very vaguely defined. The Chancellors, who were almost always bishops, intervened to correct the harshness of the common law on grounds of " conscience." They were thus more concerned with the facts of the individual case than with the laying down of any principles which their successors might follow. Nevertheless, there were certain types of cases in which it came to be recognised that the Chancellor would grant relief, and we will mention the three chief of them.

Most important, was the recognition and protection of " uses." The use was a device employed by those who wished to secure for themselves or for others the beneficial enjoyment of property without the liabilities (e.g. escheat for felony) which the common law attached to the holding of real property. The land was conveyed to " feoffees " (usually two or three) who held it " to the use of " the person or persons who were to have the beneficial enjoyment. In such a case the legal estate in the property was held by A, B and C as feoffees to the use of D, and the Chancellor would give effect to the " equitable " rights of D while fully recognising that the legal right of property (which alone was regarded in the common law courts) was in A, B and C. Secondly, as the Chancellor tended to look behind an act or document to the state of mind of the agent or the circumstances in which the document came into existence he was often ready to give relief in cases of duress or fraud, and even to prohibit persons who had obtained judgments at common law

can be said to exist is much disputed : the arguments are summarised in Holdsworth, vol. I (7th ed., 1956), pp. 53*–57* where S. B. Chrimes regards the view taken above as " still the sound view."

which were tainted with these elements from enforcing them. Thirdly, since he looked to the intent of the parties, the Chancellor took a far broader view of contracts than the mediæval common law could do. He was ready to enforce the obligation of good faith created by the mere fact of mutual agreement, while the common law still demanded either that the obligation should be recorded in a sealed document or that one party to the contract should have performed his side of the bargain before it would interfere, and even then would only grant damages to the injured party while the Chancery would sometimes compel the defendant to carry out his agreement.

The procedure by which the Chancellor exercised his equitable jurisdiction resembled that of the Star Chamber and may well have been one of its chief initial attractions.[1] Besides, the fact that the rules of the common law were fixed by tradition or statute while equity was still largely a manifestation of the ideas of justice entertained by the individual Chancellor, naturally gave a different character to the proceedings in the two jurisdictions. The common law judge was like a referee at a fight. He saw that the rules were observed and awarded points, but he could not make up new rules as the fight developed before him. The Chancellor, on the other hand, had a complete discretion whether to intervene at the instance of the petitioner or not. Relief in equity was a matter of " grace " not of right. Consequently, in order to decide whether to intervene or not, the Chancellor concerned himself actively in the merits of the dispute between the parties. He summoned the defendant before him by the writ of " subpœna " and subjected him to an examination with the

---

[1] " In origin the popularity of the court was due to its superior machinery for the suppression of disorder and to its protection of certain types of contract " : M. E. Avery, " The Equitable Jurisdiction of the Chancery before 1460 " (1969), 42 *Bulletin of the Institute of Historical Research*, pp. 129–44, at p. 135. Miss Avery holds that uses were responsible for the rapid expansion of the jurisdiction.

object of ascertaining the condition of his conscience and purging it, if need be, by the appropriate prescription. This compelling of the defendant to disclose the secrets of his case on oath was something quite unknown to the mediæval common law.

But it would be wrong to think that the relations between common law and equity were in the later Middle Ages as distant as they were later to become. It was not yet considered that equity was a rival system to the common law and one of which the ordinary common lawyer would naturally have no knowledge. On the contrary, the Chancellor frequently consulted the judges not only on points of pure common law arising in a case before him, but also on the principles on which he should give equitable relief.[1] Further, so far as he could he strove to follow the common law, as, for instance, by attaching to the equitable interest of the beneficiary under a use the same incidents and character as were possessed by the corresponding legal estate. There is no doubt, however, that by the end of the fifteenth century the more prescient of the common law judges were beginning to regret that the equitable jurisdiction of the Court of Chancery had ever become necessary. Fairfax, J., in 1481 pointed out that the Chancellor's subpœna would not be called for as often as it was if the common law courts made a freer use of actions on the case,[2] and it is probable that the great extension of the action of assumpsit in the sixteenth century was partly due to a healthy fear on the part of the judges that unless they bestirred themselves the whole law of contract would fall under the ægis of the Chancellor.[3]

In the sixteenth century we find a growing jealousy of

[1] Thus even as late as 1634 Lord Coventry took the opinion of the judges in the case of *Townley* v. *Sherborne* (1634), Bridg. 352, on the question of the liability of a trustee for the acts of his co-trustee.

[2] See Year Books, 21 Edw. IV, 23, quoted by Blackstone, vol. III, p. 52.

[3] See p. 161, below.

the Chancery on the part of the common lawyers. This feeling was accentuated by the conduct of Cardinal Wolsey, who, when Chancellor and in the plenitude of his power, treated the common law judges with the arrogance which was peculiar to him. Injunctions prohibiting parties from proceeding with common law actions, or enforcing the judgments which they had recovered, were so freely granted at this time that their issue formed one of the articles prepared for Wolsey's proposed impeachment after his fall from power. Soon after this the common lawyers were persuaded, after a long struggle, to assist Henry VIII against a reluctant landed gentry in securing the passage of the Statute of Uses through Parliament in 1535.[1] (The development of the system of uses in the later Middle Ages had for various reasons which it would be out of place to describe here made their extinction desirable in the interests of the royal revenue,) and the effect of the statute was, speaking generally, that whenever A was or should thereafter be " seised " of land to the use of B, the legal estate held by A should automatically shift from A to B, so that A disappeared from the scene and B was left with a legal estate which was liable to all the feudal burdens, instead of a " use " or equitable interest which could only be enforced in Chancery.

Since the enforcement of uses was the chief head of the Chancellor's jurisdiction it was reasonable to suppose that this statute would be a very serious blow to the Chancery, but though no doubt it resulted in a considerable loss of work, this was more than made good by newly acquired jurisdiction, and the court continued to be busy. In the first place, of course, there were several forms of " use " which were not caught by the statute. " Uses " of personal property, for instance, and " active uses " where the trustees had duties to perform. Then the

---

[1] For Henry's struggle see Plucknett, *A Concise History of the Common Law* (5th ed.), pp. 584–7 ; and E. W. Ives, " The Genesis of the Statute of Uses " (1967), 82 *E.H.R.* 673–97.

development of the organisation of the court which had been made necessary by the extension of the system of " uses " stood it in good stead.   Often the question at issue between the parties would not be " is the defendant a trustee," but " granted that he is a trustee, has he faithfully performed the trust ? "   In such a case it was obviously necessary to go to a court which had a staff capable of going into the dealings of the parties over a long period and taking an account. The Chancellor from the earliest days had always had his staff of skilled clerks headed by the Masters in Chancery, who in their turn had each of them a staff of clerks under them.   On the first hearing of the case before the Chancellor it might soon appear that some account or enquiry was needed, and the Chancellor, who was far too busy a person for such details, would refer the matter to a Master for investigation in the presence of the parties and for a report on which the Chancellor could subsequently found his decree.   In the sixteenth century the existence of this organisation began to bring to the Chancery two new types of work.   First, mercantile and partnership business where accounts were often required, and secondly, the administration of the estates of deceased persons.   In the Middle Ages the latter business had been in the hands of the ecclesiastical courts, but the Reformation had so weakened them that now they could hardly resist the encroachment of the Chancery.

We may observe at this stage that equity was so popular in the sixteenth century that other courts besides the Chancery began to claim an equitable jurisdiction. We shall see later [1] that in this period the Court of Exchequer succeeded in developing an " equity " side which was quite distinct from the " common law " side of the court and exercised a more or less concurrent jurisdiction with the Chancellor.   Then, too, there was the court known as the "Court of Requests," a civil

[1] See p. 173, below.

court of equitable jurisdiction for the benefit of poor litigants which was an offshoot of the Council.[1]

Meanwhile the common lawyers were growing increasingly restive. The business in their courts naturally suffered under the competition of the various special tribunals—Chancery, Star Chamber, Admiralty and Requests, to mention only a few of them—which administered a law different from the common law and in some cases more attractive to litigants. Then, too, the issuing of injunctions interfering with common law actions, though momentarily checked by Wolsey's fall, had been resumed by his successors and was coming to be looked upon as a normal part of the Chancellor's jurisdiction.[2] It was felt that a stand must be made and the attack was first directed to the newest and weakest of the rivals of the common law, the Court of Requests. In 1590 the Common Pleas granted a prohibition against it, and in 1598 it pronounced it an " illegal " court. The Court of Requests, however, continued to flourish as before quite undeterred by these fulminations. But soon the attack was renewed, and this time against the Chancery itself. On several occasions courts of common law held imprisonments by the Chancellor for disobedience to injunctions issued by him to be unlawful, and entertained applications for writs of habeas corpus for the release of the prisoners. 1616 was a crisis year, in which a clash between Chief Justice Coke and Lord Ellesmere was only one of several constitutional and legal conflicts. The personal element was certainly present in the affair and the author of the most recent detailed study of it has quoted with approval the summing-up afterwards by Lord Bacon, " when the men were gone, the matter was

---

[1] For a sketch of its origins and history see Elton, *The Tudor Constitution*, pp. 184–7.

[2] Such injunctions were coming to be known as " common injunctions " to distinguish them from special injunctions restraining the defendant from some other act than pursuing his remedy at common law.

gone." [1]   A defendant in a common law action, counsel, and others involved in his subsequent successful application for an injunction against a judgment obtained by the grossest fraud found themselves indicted under the Statute of Praemunire at the Middlesex Sessions.   (This statute of 1354 had been aimed at the taking to the Papal court of cases that should have gone to the royal courts, and the attempt was now being made to use it as a weapon against the Chancery, for all that the Chancery was a royal court.)   Though (despite bullying by Coke) the Grand Jury "ignored" (i.e., threw out) the bill, matters had come to a head.   (Neither his contemporary opponents nor later historians ever satisfactorily clarified Coke's precise complicity in the indictments.)

Lord Ellesmere's contention was that the injunctions objected to did not interfere with the common law at all. They did not purport to question the validity of the common law proceedings or the judgment given, but were merely personal orders on the party in question telling him not to proceed or enforce the judgment on pain of going to prison.   This argument evaded the gravamen of Coke's complaint, which was that the issue of injunctions ensured that the principles of equity would always in a case of conflict prevail over the rules of the common law ; but the common law at that date offered so many loopholes for fraud and oppression that the control was really a necessity.   As for precedent, there was the usage of the sixteenth century in favour of the Chancery, but on the other hand a statute of 1403 had enacted that after a common law judgment the parties should not be summoned before the Council but should be " in peace."   After consulting his Attorney-General, Sir Francis Bacon, King James I decided in favour of Lord Ellesmere.   The king was no doubt glad of the opportunity of humbling the Chief Justice, whose inde-

---

[1] J. H. Baker, " The Common Lawyers and the Chancery : 1616 " (1969), 4 *Irish Jurist* 368–92, at 392.

pendence of character was galling to him and whom he
soon afterwards removed from office.

The issue of the dispute has generally been treated as
a victory for the Chancery, but its effects on the legal
system were perhaps less than its immediate political
significance.   Like the Star Chamber, though to a lesser
extent, the Chancery tended to be identified with the
maintenance of prerogative and in consequence came to
be viewed with dislike by the parliamentarian opposition.[1]
Ellesmere himself and his successor, Bacon, were both of
them strong supporters of the prerogative, and in 1640,
on the eve of the conflict, the Great Seal was entrusted
to Sir John Finch, who, as Chief Justice of the Common
Pleas, had given the leading judgment for the Crown in
the case of ship money, and was in consequence a very
unpopular figure in opposition circles.   During his brief
tenure of office a defendant in a suit before him demurred
to the validity of an order of the Royal Council, and
received the answer that " whilst he was keeper of the
seal no man should be so saucy to dispute those orders, but
that the wisdom of that Board should be always ground
enough for him to make a decree in Chancery." [2]   It was
no wonder that men doubted how long the Courts of
Chancery and Requests would survive the fall of the Star
Chamber and the High Commission.

The Court of Requests, in fact, survived only for a few
months longer. In the summer of 1642, on the outbreak
of hostilities, the court suspended its sittings, and though
at the Restoration Masters of Requests were once more
appointed they had no judicial duties.   The Court of
Chancery, for its part, led a troubled life during the
Commonwealth.   After the execution of the king, the
Great Seal was put into commission and held by a
series of commissioners, several of whom were army
officers with no particular knowledge of the law. Mean-

---

[1] It should be remembered that the Chancellor habitually sat in the
Star Chamber as well as the Chancery.

[2] See Clarendon : *History of the Rebellion*, Book I, para. 158.

while the court was subjected to the most violent attacks
in Parliament on the score of its delays and the cost
of proceedings in it.   It was described as a " mystery
of wickedness and a standing cheat," and it was alleged
that " for dilatoriness, chargeableness and a faculty for
bleeding people in the purse vein even to their utter
perishing and undoing, the court might compare with,
if not surpass, any court in the world."   Allowances must,
of course, be made for the rancour of the common
lawyers and the fact that there was no one in the House of
Commons to defend the equitable jurisdiction.   But
even so there was probably only too much ground for
many of the allegations.   The organisation of the court—
as we shall see in the next chapter—lent itself very easily
to abuses of all sorts, and the proceedings against Lord
Bacon had already shown that corruption in it might
extend to the highest places.   Some members were for
abolishing the court altogether, others for reforming it
drastically ;   and several schemes of reform were propounded between 1653 and 1657.   These schemes,
like all the various schemes for law reform propounded
under the Commonwealth, combined many excellent
suggestions which would greatly have improved the
working of this court with some impossible proposals
that would have prevented its working at all.   To none
of them, however, was effect given by statute, and with
the Restoration the Court of Chancery, which had been
under continual sentence of death or mutilation, received
a new lease of life.

IX

THE COURT OF CHANCERY FROM THE RESTORATION TO THE NINETEENTH CENTURY

EQUITY in the eighteenth century differed very much from equity in the sixteenth. The latter had been largely a discretionary jurisdiction based on the moral ideas of the individual chancellors who exercised it. It was viewed chiefly in the light of a corrective of the harshness of the common law and its exercise frequently brought the Chancery into conflict with the rival system. The equity of the eighteenth century, on the other hand, though in theory still to some extent discretionary, was coming in practice to be a system of well-recognised rules evolving in accordance with principles enshrined in reported cases. Further, it was a system which had become as much supplementary to the common law as corrective of it. We have seen that the decision of James I in the conflict between Coke and Ellesmere had established the right of the Chancery in effect to set bounds to the common law by the issue of the so-called " common injunction." Naturally, when once the jurisdiction of the Chancery to issue such injunctions was well settled litigants did not often need to invoke it in practice, and it is probably true to say that in many cases in the eighteenth century when litigants at common law went across Westminster Hall to the Chancery for an injunction they were doing so only with a view to delaying just proceedings, and were actually making an abuse of the intervention of equity. The knowledge that the Chancery had this power of intervention in appropriate cases had a salutary effect on procedure at common law. Blackstone, for example, points out that the great extension in the seventeenth century of the grounds on which the common law courts would order new trials of issues tried at *nisi prius*[1] was a product of the tendency of litigants to seek injunctions in the Chancery against the enforcement of verdicts given after an unsatisfactory trial at law. Moreover, equity, having gained the decisive victory, made a moderate use of it and refused to trench unnecessarily upon the province of the common law. Many of the best-known maxims of equity illustrate its tenderness for the legal rule, as, for instance, the rules that equity will not interfere with a purchaser for value of a legal right without notice of the equities affecting it, that where the equities are equal the law prevails, and that a discretionary equitable remedy will not be granted when the legal remedy is adequate.[2]

The way in which the two systems had settled down to amicable co-operation is well illustrated in the account of equity given by Blackstone, who was himself a common lawyer, in his *Commentaries* written about 1760.[3] He is at great pains to point out that equity in his day made no general claim to correct the harshness of common law rules on vague principles of natural justice, and he even says that equity in the broad sense of the word was as much or as little observed in common law courts as in the Chancery. He obviously felt that it was an anomaly that the two systems should be administered in different courts,[4] and his great contemporary, Lord

---

[1] See p. 187, below.

[2] Radcliffe: *Real Property*, 2nd ed., pp. 72–74.

[3] In the earlier parts of his *Commentaries* Blackstone gives an account of equity more appropriate to the equity of the sixteenth than the eighteenth century, but later, with more knowledge of the Chancery of his day, he largely changed his view. The chapter on equity in his third volume was considered by Bentham to be the best Blackstone wrote.

[4] The arguments in favour of the separate administration are set out by Lord Hardwicke in his famous letter to Lord Kames on the subject of the latter's book on *Equity in Scotland*. See Yorke's *Life of Hardwicke*, vol. II, p. 550.

Mansfield, then Chief Justice of the King's Bench, for whose views Blackstone had the deepest admiration, did in fact go a long way in introducing specifically equitable conceptions into the common law. The action for " money had and received " which he fostered was based on the view that the recipient was a quasi-trustee of the money, and he even went so far as to recognise the existence of an equity of redemption. This attempt to anticipate the Judicature Acts by recognising both sets of rules in the same court was not, however, relished by the contemporary Chancellors [1] or by Mansfield's successor, Lord Kenyon, who became Lord Chief Justice after having been Master of the Rolls and knew too much of the nature of equitable relief not to realise the impossibility of administering a system which derived its materials from searching the conscience of the parties in a court which absolutely refused to allow either party to an action to give evidence. It was only after the rules of evidence at law and in equity had been assimilated that the concurrent administration of the two systems became a possibility.

Passing from the general character of equity to the Chancellors who administered it, we notice a marked change in the type of person who is entrusted with the Great Seal. The practice of appointing an ecclesiastic as Chancellor, which had been invariable in the late Middle Ages, came to an end with Wolsey, and with few exceptions the Chancellors after him were laymen. They were not, however, at first necessarily lawyers. Wriothesley and Sir Christopher Hatton, for instance, were courtiers and politicians. But with the seventeenth century, as equity was becoming gradually a system of rules which a layman, however intelligent, could not be expected to master quickly, there came a tendency to appoint only

[1] Equity lawyers complained that Lord Mansfield and his puisne judges knew very little about the equity which they professed to follow. Thus Lord Thurlow said that Mr. Justice Buller " knew no more equity than a horse."

lawyers as Chancellor. Even after the Restoration we find some Chancellors who were not primarily lawyers. Lord Clarendon, who held the Seal from 1658–1667, had not practised the law since before the civil war, and during most of the time that he was Chancellor was in fact Prime Minister of the country. Then in 1672–1673 the famous Lord Shaftesbury, who was a politician pure and simple, was Chancellor. But Shaftesbury was the last of the non-legal Chancellors ; after him none but eminent lawyers [1] have ever held the office, and there are three of them in our period of whom we may make particular mention : Heneage Finch, Earl of Nottingham, Shaftesbury's immediate successor and Chancellor from 1673 to 1682 ; Philip Yorke, Earl of Hardwicke, Chancellor from 1737 to 1756 ; and John Scott, Earl of Eldon, Chancellor from 1801 to 1806 and from 1807 to 1827.

Lord Nottingham was a member of a great legal family famous in the politics of the seventeenth century, and he combined with a profound knowledge of the law something of the breadth of outlook of the best type of statesman. He saw that the time had come for equity to be to some extent systematised, and more than any other man was responsible for that transformation in its character to which we have referred. He classified its rules and laid down broad principles which could be developed by his successors. For example, the doctrine of " clogs " on the equity of redemption and the modern rule against perpetuities are both derived from following paths which he marked out. He has been called " the father of equity," and the title is deserved.[2]

---

[1] In the nineteenth century the specialisation of work led to barristers being either common lawyers or equity lawyers, but several of the eighteenth-century chancellors had practised in both courts while at the Bar. This in itself gave them a great advantage over their successors.

[2] His contribution is discussed in detail by D. E. C. Yale in Selden Society, vols. 73 and 79 ; cf. Yale, *Lord Nottingham's Manual of Chancery Practice and Prolegomena of Chancery and Equity* (Cambridge, 1965).

Lord Hardwicke was an attorney's son who by his great talents and industry raised himself into the narrow circle of the Whig aristocracy and amassed by legitimate means one of the largest fortunes which has ever been made at the law.   He had few interests or accomplishments outside politics and his profession, and the rapidity of his rise made him enemies.   As a judge he was beyond all praise.   In court he was always courteous, always dignified and displayed consistently a balance and lucidity of intellect which few of our judges have ever equalled, and none surpassed.   His great constructive work was the consolidation of the principles of equity as they had developed since Nottingham's day.[1]

Lord Eldon's father was a prosperous coal merchant of Newcastle who produced two famous sons, William, Lord Stowell, the great Admiralty judge,[2] and John, the future Lord Chancellor.   Lord Stowell was a man of wide culture, but Lord Eldon, though notably tactful and courteous, was more limited in his interests.   His judicial reputation is a curious one.   On the one hand, the Court of Chancery came in his day to be a byword for the most scandalous delays, while on the other his judgments were the final authority to which equity lawyers always had recourse by preference throughout the nineteenth century.   The condition of his court to some extent reflected the nature of his temperament.   He was an extreme conservative, and in addition had a great capacity for self-deception.   In politics, of course, this latter characteristic stood him in good stead, for he was enabled by it to do acts of doubtful propriety with a consciousness of rectitude.[3]   But it excluded all possibility of reform

---

[1] Lord Campbell's unfavourable account of Hardwicke (*Lives of the Lord Chancellors* (4th ed.), pp. 158–304) has been in many respects discredited by Holdsworth (xii.237–96).

[2] See p. 254, below.

[3] But the allegation that, for party reasons, he convinced himself that the standards of mental health to be applied to a Sovereign in his public capacity differed from those applicable to a private individual, and took

in the Chancery, for though he knew the facts of the position better than any man he resolutely refused to draw the natural deductions from them. Further, in spite of—or perhaps because of—his unrivalled knowledge of the law he was very diffident in forming a concluded opinion and would delay judgment in a case for months or even years until he could find time to give it his full consideration.[1] The suitors suffered, but, when the judgment appeared at last, the system of equity was generally a gainer by it. Lord Eldon's judgments have not, indeed, any merits of form—they are often ill-arranged and diffuse; but the meticulous care with which he examined the facts of each case and his complete mastery of the whole range of English jurisprudence, both common law and equity, give them a singular impressiveness. During the many years in which he held the Great Seal a vast variety of cases naturally came before him, and he may be said to have gathered up the various strands of development which had been woven by his predecessors and to have presented the system of equity as a more or less finished product to his successors.

We will now turn to consider the jurisdiction of the Court of Chancery in the eighteenth century. Equity presupposed the existence of the common law and supplemented it in varying degrees in different places. Consequently it is impossible to portray the system of equity as an ordered whole. The common law without equity would have been like a coat with holes in it, while equity without the common law would be just the patches floating in the air. In some branches of the law the patches of equity are applied very thickly—the law of property,

instructions from George III for affixing the Great Seal when the king was clearly not capable of giving instructions for making a will, is difficult to make stick : Campbell, *Lives* (4th ed.), ix.237–41 ; Holdsworth, xiii.603.

[1] Lord Eldon illustrated to perfection the maxim of Sir Edward Coke : " The most learned doubteth most."

for instance, and the law of contracts are overlaid with them ; the law of torts, on the other hand, has been little affected by equity ; and of the criminal law it steered very clear. "Criminal equity" died with the Star Chamber. When equity practitioners found it necessary to adopt some classification of their subject for the purposes of their textbooks they divided equity into " the exclusive jurisdiction," *i.e.* those rights such as trusts which could be enforced only in the Chancery and would be unrecognised at law ; " the concurrent jurisdiction," *i.e.* those rights which could be enforced either at common law or in the Chancery, but in connection with which equity would give a form of relief—such as the order for specific performance of a contract—which the law could not give ; and " the auxiliary jurisdiction," *i.e.* cases in which equity was applied to for auxiliary relief in connection with an action at common law, as, for instance, an application for discovery of documents or for the appointment of a receiver by way of " equitable execution " of property of a judgment debtor in a common law action which could not be reached by any of the common law writs of execution. This traditional classification has, however, been rendered obsolete by the fusion of the common law and equitable jurisdictions under the Judicature Acts, 1873–1875, and it has not such inherent merits as would justify its revival even for the purpose of describing the equity of the eighteenth century. On the whole, perhaps, the best classification that we can adopt is the following :

1. Jurisdiction derived from the recognition in equity of forms of property or methods of dealing with property unknown at common law.
2. Jurisdiction derived from the advantages offered by the procedure and organisation of the Court of Chancery.
3. Jurisdiction derived from the character of the orders made by the Court of Chancery.
4. Various miscellaneous jurisdiction.

1. Under the first head the chief subjects—and the only ones which we can mention in such a book as this—are trusts, the separate property of married women, mortgages and the assignment of contracts. We have seen in the last chapter that the Statute of Uses (1535) which dealt so heavy a blow to the system of trusts of real property was passed in the interests of the royal revenue, which was being robbed of the profitable incidents of feudal overlordships. After the Restoration the Crown ceased to look on its feudal overlordship of land as a source of revenue, and a statute of 1660 abolished tenure en chivalry and its burdensome incidents. Consequently the way was now free for the Chancery openly to reintroduce equity into the land law,[1] and this result was primarily achieved by the limitation of a second use,[2] which was treated as a nullity at law but enforced in equity under the name of a trust.

The conception of a trust and of trusteeship has been said by a great authority [3] to be the most notable contribution made by English law to the science of jurisprudence. In systems derived from the Roman Law which draw a hard-and-fast line between rights of property (jura in rem) and rights of contract or obligation (jura in personam) the trust can find no easy resting place, for it is both forms of right at once.[4] In the early period of equity which we described in the last chapter the " use " was viewed chiefly as giving a personal right against the trustee, but as the Chancery came gradually to enforce the trust not only against the original trustee but against persons to whom the legal estate was transferred from him with knowledge of the trust, or in such

[1] Trusts of personal property had not been touched by the statute.

[2] A. W. B. Simpson, *Introduction to the History of Land Law* (1961), pp. 189–91.

[3] Maitland : *The Unincorporate Body*, in *Collected Papers*, vol. III, p. 272.

[4] On the rare occasions when it is necessary to draw the distinction in our law the position of trusts causes difficulty. See *Baker* v. *Archer Shee*, [1927] A. C. 844 ; and *Archer Shee* v. *Garland*, [1931] A. C. 212.

circumstances that they ought to have known of it if they had made reasonable enquiries, the beneficial interest under the trust came to wear the appearance of a right of property enforceable against all the world save a *bona fide* purchaser for value of the legal estate from the trustee.   Naturally, the question arose of what exactly were the incidents attached to this equitable property. Could it be made subject to the same limitations as property at law ?   Did it descend in the same way on an intestacy ?   Could a widow claim dower out of her husband's equitable interest in land ?   If the beneficiary died without heirs could the lord take the equitable interest by escheat ?   These and many other similar questions were answered one by one by the Chancellors of the seventeenth and eighteenth centuries.

The two most important uses to which the trust was put in this period were perhaps in connection with settlements of landed estates and the safeguarding of the property of wealthy married women from the common law rights of their husbands.   With regard to the strict settlement of land, it is sufficient to say that by the end of the eighteenth century it had become an extremely elaborate transaction providing for the devolution of the estate according to the principles of primogeniture, granting jointures to the landowner's widow and portions to his younger children, and empowering the limited owner for the time being entitled in possession to the estate under the settlement to exercise various powers of sale, leasing, etc., without which the estate could not be properly managed.[1]   Frequently the rights of beneficiaries under such settlements were equitable, and a very great part of the litigation arising from settlements thus found its way into the Court of Chancery.

Again this would not be the place to describe in detail the rights which the common law gave a husband over the real and personal property of his wife.   Suffice it to say that they were so extensive that no wealthy father

[1] For details, see Radcliffe : *Real Property*, 2nd ed., Chapter XIV.

would willingly allow any part of his property to pass to a married daughter under the common law if he could possibly prevent it. Equity allowed him to vest the legal estate in trustees to hold it "for the separate use" of the wife, who thus acquired an equitable interest over which the Chancery would not allow the husband any rights. Indeed, for fear that the wife might be induced by her husband to make over her equitable interest to him, equity invented the clause in restraint of anticipation which protected the married woman against herself by rendering her incapable of dealing with the income of her separate property until it was actually paid into her hands. Eventually, in the nineteenth century, the protection which the Chancery had afforded to women wealthy enough to have a marriage settlement, was extended to all classes by the Married Women's Property Act, 1882, under which all property of a married woman was automatically treated as though it were property settled on her for her separate use, and finally, in 1949, the legal position of married women as regards property and contract was completely assimilated to that of men.[1]

In view of this great extension of the employment of trusts, equity had to consider carefully what duties and liabilities it would attach to the office of trustee. What acts or omissions constitute negligence in a trustee? Can a trustee claim remuneration? These and many other similar questions were gradually answered by a series of decisions in the seventeenth and eighteenth centuries. We may observe before leaving this topic that the fact that the conduct expected of trustees has been fixed by the decisions of judges in the Chancery, and has not been left, like the conduct of other persons, to the verdict of juries in a common law court, has had a curious consequence. The decisions of the judges being re-

[1] Married Women (Restraint upon Anticipation) Act, 1949. The Law Reform (Married Women and Tortfeasors) Act, 1935, had, *inter alia*, forbidden the imposition of restraints on anticipation after 1935 but preserved restraints already existing.

ported inevitably tend to be treated as precedents, and
matters which would remain mere matters of fact in a
court of common law, where the verdict of a jury in an
individual case has no abiding influence, are transmuted
into principles of law in a court of equity. Thus the
conduct of trustees has been hedged round with a number
of fixed rules, and the standard of diligence and honesty
required of them has been set much higher than would
have been the case but for the growth of authorities on
the subject. Another instance of the tendency of equity
decisions to establish principles is to be seen in the law
of wills, where an immense mass of authorities on the interpretation of phrases found in individual wills has ended,
in spite of heroic efforts of judges from time to time to
free themselves from the fetters of precedent, in the question " What did the testator mean by the words he has
used ? " being too often decided against his plain intention
in deference to some established rule of construction.

We must now pass to mortgages.[1] A mortgage in the
seventeenth century took the form of a conveyance of
the property intended as security by the borrower to the
lender, with a stipulation that if the money lent was repaid
with interest on a given day the lender would reconvey
the property to the borrower. If the money was not
repaid the property would, according to the tenor of the
bond, become the lender's. Cases, however, might arise
in which it would be inequitable to hold that the property
was forfeited for non-payment on the fixed day. For
instance, the lender might intentionally evade payment
by hiding or some unexpected accident might prevent
the borrower from having the money ready. In such
cases, since the common law adhered to the letter of the
bond, equity gave relief, provided the money with interest
and any costs which the lender had incurred were paid
within a reasonable time. Gradually it came to be felt
that the true object of the conveyance at law was to give

[1] See Radcliffe : *Real Property*, 2nd ed., Chapter XXV, for a full
account of this topic.

the lender security for repayment of his loan and not to give him the chance of making a profit by forfeiting the estate, and that the lender ought not to be able in any case to claim to retain the security if his money was forthcoming from the borrower within a reasonable time of his demanding it. Thus there grew up the doctrine that although the time fixed at law for redemption was passed the borrower still had in equity a right to redeem which could only be extinguished by the lender's applying to the Chancery to destroy it.[1] The Chancery would then calculate what was due, give the borrower six months to pay, and on his default declare the estate forfeited in equity as well as law to the lender.

The right to redeem a mortgaged estate by application to the Chancery was known as an " equity of redemption " and was viewed by the seventeenth-century Chancellors as an equitable estate in the property remaining in the borrower. This estate could be dealt with by its owner with the same freedom with which a beneficiary could deal with an equitable interest in land held on trust for him by a trustee. Since a very large proportion of the land in the country was either held by trustees or incumbered with mortages a great amount of the litigation regarding real property found its way into the Court of Chancery. This foothold which the Chancery gained in the sphere of the land law in the eighteenth century by reason of its jurisdiction in cases of equitable interests under settlements and over mortgages enabled the court in the nineteenth century, after the Court of Chancery Procedure Act, 1852, gave it power to decide for itself the true construction of legal as opposed to equitable limitations of land without having to submit these questions to the common law courts,[2] gradually to draw nearly the whole land law into its orbit. Thus to-day the branch of the law which was once the special province

---

[1] The technical term is, of course, to " foreclose."
[2] See p. 277, below.

of the common lawyers in the Temple is now the recognised sphere of the equity lawyer in Lincoln's Inn.

Equitable interests in property were freely transferable by their owners.[1] If A held property on trust for B, the Chancery would recognise a transfer of the equitable interest by B to C whether by way of gift or for valuable consideration. In the similar case of legal debts and obligations, however, the common law had in the Middle Ages resolutely set its face against recognising assignment. If A owed money to B or was bound to perform some obligations to him, B's right was at law a purely personal contractual right which he alone could enforce. An assignment of it by B to C was nugatory. It is not hard to see the analogy between the interest under a contract at law and an equitable interest in a trust fund, and to understand why the Court of Chancery came to the assistance of the assignee of a legal debt or obligation. In our period it became well settled that, at all events in cases where the assignee had given value for the transfer,[2] he could apply to the Chancery for an order directing the assignor to allow him to sue in his name at law to recover the debt or enforce the obligation. Thus it came about that it was possible to assign with the aid of equity rights which were unassignable at law.

2. We have seen in the last chapter that the procedure and organisation of the Court of Chancery was well adapted for the taking of accounts and enabled the plaintiff to obtain from the defendant the disclosure of facts on oath. These two advantages were the foundations of several branches of the jurisdiction of the Chancery ; in particular the administration of the estates of deceased persons and of partnerships and that branch of the auxiliary jurisdiction known as " discovery," under which a litigant in an action at common law could compel the discovery by his opponent of documents

[1] The Statute of Frauds required such transfers to be in writing.

[2] Whether an equitable assignment of an existing legal chose in action requires consideration cannot be said to have been clearly decided.

which the latter could not have been compelled to produce under the rules of evidence in the common law courts. The interference of the Court of Chancery in the administration of the estates of deceased persons led naturally to another very important branch of the jurisdiction of the court, namely the construction of the wills of personal property. In this branch of its jurisdiction it borrowed largely from Roman Law. On the other hand the constructions of wills of realty whenever the interest devised to the beneficiary was a legal estate remained until 1852 a matter for the common law courts where it was litigated in the form of an action of ejectment between the devisee and the heir, or on a case submitted by a Chancery judge for the opinion of the common law courts.

The necessity for discovery in the Chancery in aid of an action at law was due to the fact that a plaintiff in a common law action might often be very much in the dark as to the defendant's case. The defendant had, of course, to plead to the declaration against him, but, as we shall see in Chapter 11, his plea did not always tell the plaintiff much.[1] Of course, it is not altogether desirable that a plaintiff should in all cases be enabled to find out his opponent's case before the crucial moment of trial. People with a vague sense of grievance should not be encouraged to bring speculative actions in the hope of scraping together a case by a preliminary interrogation of the defendant. On the other hand it is not desirable that a plaintiff with an apparently good case should be taken by surprise at the trial by the production of some document, the existence of which was unknown to him and an earlier production of which would have caused him to drop his action. It was to meet this sort of case that a party in a common law action was allowed to avail himself of the jurisdiction which the Chancery had to compel persons to make disclosures on oath, in order to secure a sworn statement from his opponent of the docu-

[1] *E.g.* the plea of the " general issue " told him nothing.

ments in his possession relative to the action and sometimes even sworn answers to a number of interrogatories directed to the issues involved. The Chancery had, of course, a discretion in the matter. The person against whom discovery was sought could claim that a given document was, on one ground or another, privileged from inspection by his opponent or that it would be unfair to him to compel him to answer any given interrogatory.

3. A successful plaintiff in a common law action generally recovered by the judgment of the court either the possession of some property which he claimed as his own or damages which in default of payment he could enforce by execution on the property of the defendant. That is to say that the judgment was ultimately directed against property in the defendant's possession and did not seek to compel the defendant personally to any particular line of conduct. The decrees of the Chancery, by contrast, were primarily personal orders on the defendant commanding him to do or to abstain from doing certain acts. Originally these orders were enforced by imprisonment of his person for contempt of the court if he proved recalcitrant. But in the seventeenth century the court added another and a powerful weapon in the writ of sequestration under which the defendant's property was taken and sold to satisfy the plaintiff's claim.[1] It is obvious that there are certain circumstances in which a plaintiff desires a personal order much more than damages. If a man has agreed to sell me a unique picture I may well prefer to have the picture rather than damages for the loss of my bargain. If my neighbour persists in taking a short cut across my garden, I may well prefer to get an order that will stop him once for all, rather than to have to bring repeated actions for damages. These considerations explain the jurisdiction acquired by the Chancery in the cases of specific performance of con-

---

[1] See *Coulston* v. *Gardiner*, 3 Swanston 279, and Radcliffe: *Real Property Law*, 2nd ed., p. 74.

tracts and in applications for injunctions to restrain unlawful acts.

The Chancellors in the period which we are considering gradually decided in what circumstances they would compel defendants to carry out their agreements. We shall see in the next chapter that contracts not under seal were not enforceable at common law unless " consideration " had been given by the plaintiff. In deference to this doctrine equity refused to grant specific performance of voluntary agreements, and, going further than the common law, even maintained the refusal if the voluntary agreement was under seal. Further, equity decided not to enforce contracts for the breach of which damages were an adequate remedy, or contracts of a personal character the performance of which could not easily be supervised by the court. By reason of these limitations on its scope the decree for specific performance came to be chiefly sought in connection with agreements for the sale of land, and in respect of these equity showed a boldness which modern judges may well envy. The Statute of Frauds 1677 required such agreements (among others) to be evidenced by a writing signed by the defendant against whom they were being enforced, but despite the express words of the statute, if the plaintiff had previously to bringing his action done an act which was unequivocally referable to some such contract as had actually been made, equity would enforce it against the defendant in spite of the absence of written evidence.

It would be impossible to set out here the infinite variety of cases in which equity would grant injunctions in restraint of unlawful acts. It is by the exercise of this jurisdiction that equity has made its contribution to the law of torts. For instance, much of the law laying down what constitutes a " nuisance " is to be found in equity cases in which the plaintiff was applying for an injunction to restrain acts which he alleged to be a nuisance while the defendant was denying that they amounted to one. But before we leave the subject of " personal orders," we may observe that they were very useful in cases of fraud or mistake. By reason of the possibility of examining the defendant on oath equity early obtained a jurisdiction (concurrent with the common law) in cases of fraud, and, if fraud was proved, it could order the delivery up of an offending document or its rectification to give effect to the true intention of the parties.

4. The only miscellaneous items of jurisdiction to which we can refer here are cases concerning infants, lunatics and bankrupts.

(a) In the Middle Ages the Crown as feudal overlord exercised a guardianship over the person and estate of its infant tenants-in-chief. This guardianship, which was exceedingly profitable to the guardian, was enforced in the Court of Wards, but on the abolition of that court and of the system of military tenures, at the Restoration, the feudal aspect of this jurisdiction vanished. The Crown, however, did not abandon the infant when it ceased to be able to make a profit out of him. On the contrary, it came to claim as " parens patriæ " protective jurisdiction over all infants in the kingdom, and this jurisdiction was entrusted to the Court of Chancery. It would be impossible to go into the details of the jurisdiction here, but we may notice that the court could appoint guardians of the infant whenever through the death or misconduct of the parents this course was necessary, and even though no guardian was appointed it was possible by taking the appropriate steps to constitute the infant a ward of the court with the result that no important step in connection with his upbringing could be taken without the court's sanction. This jurisdiction in cases of infancy still exists, and is exercised by the Chancery Division of the High Court.[1]

(b) The care of all lunatics was claimed by the Crown

---

[1] It is now (1970) proposed that this jurisdiction be transferred to the new Family Division, which is to take the place of the Probate, Divorce, and Admiralty Division : see p. 295, below, and cf. G. Cross, " Wards of Court " (1967), 83 L.Q.R. 200–14.

at an early date. In the case of congenital idiots this guardianship was originally regarded as a source of profit like the guardianship of infant tenants-in-chief, but in the case of supervening insanity the Crown took nothing for its own use. In time the condition of congenital idiots was assimilated to that of ordinary lunatics, and the Crown took no profit from either. The Chancellor had a double jurisdiction in this field. The issue of writs for the enquiry into the state of mind of alleged lunatics and the conduct of such enquiries took place on the common law side of the Chancery, while the care of those found to be of unsound mind as a result of the enquiry was habitually entrusted to the Chancellor by the Crown, and was administered by him along with the other work on the equitable side of his court. Today this jurisdiction is exercised by the so-called " Court of Protection" consisting of the Lord Chancellor, certain nominated judges of the Chancery Division and the Master, Deputy Master and other officers of the Court. Certain orders can only be made by the judges but the bulk of the work is done by the Master and Deputy Master subject to an appeal to a judge. In 1968 over 25,000 estates were being managed by Receivers appointed and controlled by the Court.

(c) An Act of Henry VIII was the first to make provision for the liquidation and distribution of the assets of insolvents. Originally, only traders were liable to be " made bankrupt," but in time the process came to be extended to all classes. The Court of Chancery as such never had any jurisdiction in bankruptcy, but power was given to the Chancellor to appoint commissioners who could exercise control over the persons and property of bankrupts. Originally the commissioners appear to have applied to the common law courts when any legal difficulty arose, but in the eighteenth century applications came to be made by them to the Chancellor, and he acquired a supervisory jurisdiction in bankruptcy. The whole system of the liquidation of estates of bankrupts in the eighteenth century was very unsatisfactory. The Commissioners and the Chancellor made large profits by it, and the debtors were scandalously harried without much corresponding benefit to the creditors. There was hardly any branch of the law more in need of reform in the nineteenth century.

We must now consider the procedure of the Court of Chancery. A suit in Chancery was not started by any writ or process served on the defendant to give him notice of the claim against him, but by a petition or bill presented by the plaintiff to the court, in which he took the court as it were into his confidence, informed it of the enormities of the defendant's conduct, and prayed that the defendant might be summoned before the Chancellor to answer on oath. Originally these petitions, being appeals for the exercise of the Crown's discretionary jurisdiction, were couched in humble and piteous language, and when they became ordinary steps in the enforcement of recognised rights, they continued to show traces of their ancestry. To this day a petition presented in the Chancery Division is styled a " humble " petition and ends with the curious phrase " and your petitioner will ever pray, etc."—the relic of the promise to pray for the soul of the Chancellor, which was all the return the petitioner could, or was prepared, to give for his lordship's intervention. In early times, too, a bill in Chancery followed no stereotyped precedent, but was couched in such form and language as occurred to the petitioner. Gradually, however, as these documents came to be drawn by counsel they began to exhibit a professional uniformity of style and increased enormously in length. A typical bill of the eighteenth century consisted of a statement of the facts (known as " the stating part "), then a purely formal allegation that the defendant had conspired with others against the plaintiff,[1] then a part (known as " the charging part ") which set out what

---

[1] This was no doubt a relic of the early days when the Council or Chancellor intervened chiefly in cases of fraud or conspiracy.

purported to be the statements which the defendant made
as to the facts of the case, then a plea that the plaintiff
had no remedy at law, then a part (known as " the interrogating part ") which turned the points of the case into a
series of questions which the plaintiff desired that the
defendant might be called upon to answer on oath, and
the answers to which might possibly destroy the matters
of defence which the plaintiff had suggested in the charging part. It will be seen from this brief account that
there was some truth in the statement that a bill in
Chancery set out the facts of the case three times over.
This was because it anticipated the defence in the charging part and put questions in cross-examination of that
defence in the interrogating part.

If the petition disclosed a *prima facie* cause of complaint,
the Chancellor would issue a writ of subpœna against the
defendant calling on him to appear by a given day to
answer the petition. This document, unlike the original
writs at common law, told him nothing of the nature of
the case against him, but informed him that he would be
liable to a penalty if he did not appear. In fact, however,
a defendant in default of appearance could be committed to the Fleet Prison for contempt. Assuming the
defendant to have appeared he could if he chose " demur "
to the bill " for want of equity," *i.e.* say that the allegations even if true did not justify the Chancellor's intervention, or he might put in a " plea " which did not go
into the merits of the petition, but raised some point such
as the want of jurisdiction of the court or the incapacity
of the plaintiff which made it unsustainable. Normally,
however, he put in an " answer " controverting the
allegations in the bill and answering the interrogatories.
We may observe that he could, if he chose, demur to part
of the bill and answer another part. We shall see when
we come to common law actions that such a procedure
was impossible at common law. There a defendant could
not " both demur and plead " to the same declaration.

In early days no doubt the defendant made his answer

and submitted to be interrogated orally before the Chancellor, but long before the period with which we are concerned written answers were allowed.   If the plaintiff required it—as he would in a hostile proceeding [1]—the defendant's answer had to be given on oath. Like the petition it had to be signed by counsel and it had to deal with all the allegations in the petition, either simply confessing or denying them or confessing them and raising fresh matter in justification.   We may observe that a defendant's plea to a common law action was not given on oath and was generally a much less voluminous document than an answer in an equity suit.

If the plaintiff thought that the confessions contained in the answer were sufficient to entitle him to the relief he sought, he might at once proceed to set the case down for hearing.   But in most contested suits there would, of course, be disputed questions of fact apparent on the face of the bill and answer, and in those circumstances the parties would join issue with one another and declare their readiness to prove the facts which they had alleged. At common law, of course, issues of fact of this sort were decided by a jury after hearing oral evidence, but in the Chancery a jury was never employed, and these questions were left to the decision of the judge upon the written depositions of witnesses.   For the purpose of obtaining these depositions a number of questions in writing were framed by the party calling the witnesses, and these questions, and no others, were put to the witness by an examiner appointed by the court.   The answers, given on oath, were recorded and copies of them could be taken by the other side.   Leading questions were not allowed to be put, but it is obvious that the lack of opportunity for cross-examination of the witnesses by the other side must have detracted considerably from the value of their

[1] It must be remembered, of course, that in our period, as to-day, a great many Chancery proceedings would be perfectly friendly.   There would be no dispute of fact, but the assistance of the court would be required to construe some document or administer some property.

evidence. When the depositions or " affidavits," to give them their more common name, had all been taken the case was set down for hearing and eventually would come on in court. The allegations of each side would be explained to the Chancellor (who had copies of the affidavits before him) and counsel would address him on the points of law involved. It was then for the Chancellor to make up his mind on all the issues of law and fact involved in the case and to pronounce a decree. He could take as long as he chose over his decision, and he often took a very long time indeed ; but, quite apart from this source of delay there were various considerations which might postpone the making of any final decree for a considerable period.

In the first place, if any pure questions of common law arose, as for instance the true construction of limitations of a legal estate in real property contained in the will of a testator whose estate was being administered by the Chancery, the Chancellor would not decide these unaided. In early days he would send for the two chief justices of the benches to sit with him as assessors " to inform the conscience of the Court " as the phrase ran, but he was not bound by their views and the ultimate decision remained his. Later, probably in order to avoid upsetting the business of the common law courts, it became the practice of the Chancellor to send the point to be argued in one of the common law courts which then returned him a certificate of its judgment. But again the Chancellor was at liberty to disregard it. We may remark in passing that the converse procedure was unknown. Equitable rights were simply not recognised by the common law courts,[1] and therefore there could be no question of their asking the Chancellor for information as to them.

Quite apart, however, from these references to the common law courts, which were not, of course, necessary

---

[1] See p. 130, above, for Lord Mansfield's abortive attempt to recognise them.

in all Chancery suits, the very nature of proceedings in equity often made it quite impossible for a final decree to be made at once. For instance, in an administration suit the Chancellor would at first merely order that the estate be administered by the court. There would be a reference to a Master to take an account of the debts and legacies, and enquiries might be necessary as to the persons entitled under the will. Any questions that arose as, for example, the true construction of a clause in the will disposing of personal estate would be referred back to the Chancellor for decision. When the master had taken the necessary accounts and enquiries, the case would come on again on further consideration by the Chancellor, who might order sums to be set aside in court to satisfy annuities and other sums to be paid out to legatees. In this way a heavy administration suit might last for years, with numbers of certificates by the Master and hearings by the Chancellor until at last the whole capital had been distributed and the estate was finally wound up. It may, perhaps, be seen from this example that complaints of the length of Chancery proceedings are sometimes unjustified. It was often inherent in their administrative nature that they should be long.

Further, we may notice that a decree of the Chancellor was not " final " in the sense that a judgment of a common law court was final. As we shall see in Chapter 13 the common law did not know of any appeal in the sense of a review of the whole case by a superior court. Proceedings by writ of error were very narrow in their scope and a great deal of the subject matter of a common law action was concluded for ever by judgment. But in a Chancery suit the side against whom a decree was made might petition for a rehearing of the suit before the decree was signed and enrolled by the Chancellor, and in such a case it would be reheard by him. It seems curious that the judge who made the decree objected to should himself rehear the case, but this in fact might be the position.

We must remember, however, that in the eighteenth century the Master of the Rolls had become a judge in the Chancery, and no doubt applications for a rehearing before the Chancellor were more frequent when the decree objected to had been made by the Master of the Rolls than when it had been made by the Chancellor himself. Against a decree finally signed and enrolled by the Chancellor, whether with or without a rehearing, there was an appeal to the House of Lords, of which we will speak in Chapter 13.

Before we leave the subject of equity procedure we may observe that there was still in use until 1947[1] a form of proceeding which in many respects recalled the old bill or petition in Chancery. This was an " English Information " filed by the Attorney-General on the Revenue Side of the King's Bench Division for the recovery of duties claimed by the Crown. The Court of Exchequer, as a Court of Revenue, made use of both common law and equity procedure, and since until recently the various Departments of State invariably resisted any procedural reform touching the prerogatives of the Crown in litigation, the old procedure of the Court of Exchequer was still available in revenue cases. The " English Information " was the proceeding employed on the equity side of the Exchequer. The person on whom it was served read with surprise that he was liable to arrest if he did not put in his answer by a given day. That answer he had to make on oath, and the Crown could administer to him a long string of interrogatories on the subject-matter of the information. If by his answers it appeared to the Crown's advisers that they had not stated their case to the best advantage, they could amend the information, and serve more interrogatories until the defendant's position was completely disclosed and the Crown's case put at its highest.

We must now pass to the organisation of the Court of Chancery, but first it will be as well to say something of

[1] Crown Proceedings Act, 1947, First Schedule

the difference between the organisation of the law courts
in general as it was before the reforms of the nineteenth
century and as it is to-day. In most European countries
the administration of justice is to-day a department of
State like any other with a political chief at the head of it.
In England, as we shall see in detail in Chapter 22, the
legal system is still largely independent of political
control and organised on lines quite different from those
of the ordinary administrative departments. But the
independence and self-sufficiency of our courts was far
greater a hundred and fifty years ago than it is to-day.
Thus, whereas to-day the fees paid by litigants for the
use of the machinery of justice form part of the public
revenues out of which the judges and other officers of
the courts are paid fixed salaries, they used to form the
revenue of the court in question and were at the court's
disposal. Similarly the right to appoint officials of the
court which belonged to the head of the court was looked
upon by him as a valuable piece of property like a patron's
right to appoint a clergyman to a living. In the earlier
part of our period, even the sale of such offices by the
chief of the court was not discountenanced, and until at
least the middle of the nineteenth century it was not considered that in the making of these appointments regard
need be had to anything but the ties of relationship,
dependance or affection.[1] The appointment of the
official staff of the courts is still largely in the hands of
the Chancellor and the Lord Chief Justice, but the fact
that these posts now involve more work and less pay than
of old, coupled with the change of attitude which de-

---

[1] Some of these offices were immensely valuable. That of chief clerk
of the King's Bench was worth £7,000 a year, of which £200 was paid to
the deputy who performed the duties. It is said Lord Ellenborough was
riding in the Park when he heard the news of the death of Mr. Way, who
had been appointed to the office by Lord Mansfield, and that for fear
that he might die himself before he made the next appointment, he dis-
mounted, went into a neighbouring house and then and there appointed
it on trust for himself and his family. Campbell: *Chief Justices*, III,
p. 246.

veloped during the nineteenth century as to the principles on which patronage of all kinds should be exercised, has resulted in the disappearance of the grosser evils to which the system was liable.

We have seen that in early days this self-sufficiency of the courts resulted in a certain competition between them which was not without its advantages to the litigant, but by the eighteenth century this was a thing of the past and only the evils of the system were apparent. The chief of these evils were, perhaps, first that the administrative officials of the court were often under no compulsion to perform their duties in person but entrusted important functions to subordinates of no standing to whom they paid a minute portion of the fees which their offices brought them ; and secondly that the desire of the officials to increase their fees and of their subordinates to add to their pittances by underhand means led to the litigant being put to a vast deal of unnecessary expense in his action. The system from which these evils resulted ruled in the common law courts as well as the Chancery, but in the Chancery the evils made themselves far more felt. This was chiefly because the work done by the administrative as opposed to the judicial staff in the Chancery was relatively far more important than was the case in the common law courts.

Each of the common law courts had from very early days a staff of four judges—a chief and three " puisnes " —but in the Chancery the Chancellor himself was at first the only judge. Obviously, in view of his many other duties and the growing complexity and length of equity suits it was impossible for him to deal personally with each stage of each proceeding, and as early as the six-- teenth century he normally delegated the duty of hearing and reporting to him upon the more detailed parts of the case to one or other of the Masters in Chancery. Even with their assistance, however, it was found impossible for the Chancellor to hear every case, and the custom grew up of issuing a commission to the senior

Master—who was known as the Master of the Rolls—to hear certain cases and make orders in them in the absence of the Chancellor. Gradually, with the increase of business in Chancery, the Master of the Rolls came to act as a subordinate judge of the court who sat more or less continuously, and not only in the Chancellor's absence. In view of some questions which had been raised by the other Masters as to his authority to hold this position a statute was passed in 1729 enacting that all orders made by the Master of the Rolls (with certain exceptions) should be valid subject to the right of the parties to apply to the Chancellor for a re-hearing before the decree was actually entered.

In the eighteenth century, therefore, we may say that there were two judges in the Chancery, but the constant increase of work in the court coupled with the fact that the Chancellor could always be asked to review the decisions of the Master of the Rolls and also his own decisions at first instance, made this judicial staff quite inadequate. Arrears of work began to increase, and in Lord Eldon's time they reached an enormous size. Years might elapse before a case could be heard at all, and more years would pass between the hearings of each step in the suit. The extreme gravity of the position is shown by the fact that Lord Eldon himself became aware of it and consented in 1813 to the appointment of a Vice-Chancellor to assist him, but the value of this measure was much diminished by the provision for an appeal from his decisions to the Chancellor as in the case of the Master of the Rolls. The hopeless inadequacy of the judicial staff was, therefore, one of the two most potent causes of the miserable plight in which the Court of Chancery found itself in the early nineteenth century.[1]

The other cause was the prevalence of the gravest abuses in the administrative staff of the court. The

[1] Vice-Chancellor Shadwell, on being asked by the Commission of Inquiry in 1816 whether the three judges of the Court could do the business replied, " No; not three angels."

senior officials of the court were the Masters, and under them the six clerks and the sixty clerks. The clerks had originally performed the functions which are to-day performed by solicitors, but in course of time the litigants found themselves obliged to pay to one or other clerk the fees which he would have earned had he done the work of the solicitor and also to pay his own solicitor for actually doing the work. The duties of the Masters were of a most responsible character. From time to time a Chancellor would issue a set of " general orders " prescribing (among other matters) the method of procedure to be followed in the prosecution of accounts and enquiries before the Masters, but in the nature of the case he was not able to exercise much control in the matter, and the Masters were in fact given practically a free hand. Meanwhile their office began to become more and more valuable by reason of the increase in business of the court and of the funds paid into court to the credit of the various suits. This money was under the absolute control of the Masters, who were not obliged to account for interest on it. In Charles II's reign masterships were worth about £1000 apiece to the Chancellor, but half a century later they were sold for £5,000 to £6,000. Eventually there was a great scandal. Some of the Masters habitually speculated with the suitors' money and on the bursting of the South Sea Bubble (1725) there was found a deficiency of some £100,000 in the accounts of the court.

As a result of these revelations Lord Macclesfield, the Chancellor, was removed from office, impeached, and fined £30,000, and some reforms were effected. The suitors' money was taken from the control of the Masters and thenceforth placed to the account of the Court of Chancery at the Bank of England, and the practice of selling the masterships was abandoned by subsequent Chancellors. But the office of master continued to be a lucrative one to which the Chancellor felt little scruple in appointing incompetent persons whose fortunes in life he wished to advance, and the Masters were still subject to no proper control in the performance of their duties. As a result the conduct of business in the master's chambers and in the other offices of the court continued to be a scandal. Suitors were compelled to pay for attendances before the Master which never took place, for services on the part of the clerks which were imaginary or valueless, and for copies of interminable documents which they did not want. In these circumstances it is not surprising to learn that a large proportion of suits were compromised by the parties before ever a final decree was given in them.

One may wonder that such a condition of affairs was allowed to continue so long, for though the evils reached their height in the later part of the chancellorship of Lord Eldon there is no doubt that the root causes of them were in existence throughout the seventeenth and eighteenth centuries. The truth is, perhaps, that short of a great public scandal, such as that which led to Lord Macclesfield's impeachment, so complicated and technical a subject as the organisation of the Chancery was singularly difficult to reform. The public knew that things were wrong, but it did not know why, and those who were best acquainted with the true cause of the evil and alone able to propose workable remedies for it, were so wedded to the existing system both by custom and their own interest, that they could hardly be brought to imagine that there could be a reform which would not spell revolution.

X

THE COMMON LAW—FIFTEENTH TO EIGHTEENTH CENTURIES (I)

IN the last two chapters we traced the history of the Court of Chancery down to the beginning of the nineteenth century ; we must now return in the next three chapters to the courts of common law and take up their story where we left it at the close of the Middle Ages. On the civil side of the common law the most important developments in the four centuries in question were (i) the virtual supersession of the real actions by the action of ejectment which was a variety of the action of trespass ; (ii) the extension of the scope of the law by a number of actions on the " case," some of which came practically to supersede most of the older personal actions ; and (iii) the encroachment of the courts of King's Bench and Exchequer on the proper domain of the court of Common Pleas. The result of these developments was that by the beginning of the nineteenth century there was no longer any valid reason for the maintenance of a system of numerous separate forms of action, real and personal, or of three separate courts of common law, and, as we shall see later, the nineteenth century did in fact see the abolition of the forms of action and the fusion of the courts. In this chapter, then, we will deal chiefly with the three topics which we have mentioned, and first with the action of ejectment.

The hearing of the real actions of which we gave an account in an earlier chapter was a monopoly of the court of Common Pleas, and that court was, largely in consequence of this fact, the busiest of the three common law courts in the Middle Ages and the most lucrative for

the judges and pleaders who presided or practised in it.
But by the end of the fourteenth century the real actions
were becoming unpopular with litigants. The very care
with which the writs of entry had been elaborated in the
thirteenth century to cover every possible variety of
flaw increased the danger of choosing the wrong form
of writ, and, further, the procedure in them, though
it was reckoned speedy enough in the thirteenth century,
had become, or seemed to the eye of the fifteenth-century
litigants to be, very technical and dilatory. What was
wanted was some one simple form of action which would
meet most cases, and this desire of the litigants was met
by the judges and pleaders of the Court of King's Bench,
who were jealous of their brethren in the Common Pleas,
through the extension of an action originally framed for
the benefit of lessees for years. Leaseholders under a
term of years, since they held no freehold interest in
land, could not bring the real actions, and indeed were
originally regarded as having only a contractual right
against their landlord entitling them to damages if dispossessed by him. By the end of the fifteenth century,
however, the common law courts had not only given to
leaseholders an action of trespass against any person who
invaded their possession, but had even gone so far as to
allow them what was in effect a " real " remedy in a personal action ; for the successful plaintiff obtained a writ
addressed to the sheriff of the county (known as the writ
"habere facias possessionem") ordering him to put the
lessee back into actual possession of his farm. Landowners
soon realised that here was a means of recovering the
freehold by bringing this action (which was known as
trespass in ejectment or ejectment) in the name of a
tenant.

At first the claimant to the freehold would make an
actual lease to a friend who entered under it and, when
he was ejected, would bring his action for the trespass
involved, but in course of time the whole proceeding
became fictitious. The nominal plaintiff was a non-

existent person called Mr. John Doe, who stated in his declaration that the real plaintiff had granted a lease to him, that he had entered under the lease and had been ejected by another equally fictitious person, Mr. Richard Roe (called " the casual ejector "), who was the nominal defendant.   Having filed his declaration [1] against Roe in the name of Doe, the real plaintiff then served the real defendant in possession of the land with a notice purporting to come from Roe stating that he had been sued and did not propose to defend the action.   The real defendant was then admitted to defend, but only on the terms that he confessed the lease, entry and ouster, and waived the objection that there was no writ or bill. Thus the only question at issue between the parties was whether the real plaintiff had the better title to the land so that it was a trespass to eject his lessee.

The perfection of this fiction by the rule of court which prevented the real defendant from disputing the imaginary activities of Doe and Roe and compelled him to rely solely on his better title to the freehold, is attributed to Chief Justice Rolle, who was Chief Justice of the King's (or Upper) Bench in the period of the Commonwealth. It will be observed that the proper title of an action of ejectment would be *Doe* v. *Roe*, but as the real defendant was invariably substituted for Roe, his name is generally found in the reports instead of Roe's, and further, in order that the name of the real plaintiff might appear, the words " on the demise of . . ." [2] were added to the word Doe.   In the reports, therefore, an action of ejectment by Brown against Jones to try the title to land of which Jones was in possession would appear as " Doe on the demise of Brown *versus* Jones," or, for short, *Doe d. Brown v. Jones.*   Finally, before we leave the action of ejectment we may mention that since it was a variety of

[1] The procedure in ejectment was anomalous : there was no writ or bill and the proceedings started as stated above with the pleadings. *First Report of the Common Law Commissions* 1829, p. 75.

[2] *I.e.* " claiming under a lease by . . ."

trespass it could properly be brought in the King's Bench, but that as its criminal aspect was fictitious, the Common Pleas had no compunction in claiming a concurrent jurisdiction over it. Later, as we shall see, it could also be brought by means of a further fiction in the Court of Exchequer.

Now that we have shown how the action of ejectment supplanted the real actions, we must turn to the action of case and its effect in developing the law and supplanting the older personal actions. But before embarking on this enquiry it is interesting and useful to observe how different is the division which we make to-day in our classes of action from that made in the old forms of action before their abolition. To us, the natural division is into actions of contract and actions of tort, cases in which the plaintiff claims that the defendant has broken his agreement with him and cases in which he alleges that the defendant is guilty of a breach of some duty imposed by the law independently of his consent to be bound. The question whether the property, if any, affected by the contract or tort is real or personal or whether the plaintiff's remedy is restitution or damages seems to us quite immaterial in our division, though, as we have seen, it was fundamental in the old classification of forms of action into real and personal actions. It is true that our modern division is not always free from difficulty. When we pass from express to implied and quasi-contracts, the division between contract and tort comes to wear rather thin, but on the whole it seems to us to work well. Our ancestors, however, knew absolutely nothing of it, and as a matter of history most of our modern law of contract and tort grew from the same root.

A breach of agreement as such did not, generally speaking, give rise to any form of action in the royal courts in early times. Glanvill says expressly that the royal courts took no account of " private agreements ", though in his day remedies for breach of them were available in the communal or ecclesiastical courts. It

is true that the old personal actions of " debt " and
" detinue " look rather as though they were founded
on a promise by the defendant to repay the money lent
or return the chattel bailed ; but in their origin at least
they were really proprietary actions in which the plaintiff
based his case not on agreement, but on the existence in
the hands of the defendant of property which belonged
to him.   Moreover the action of covenant, which did lie
for breach of an unperformed promise, required a sealed
document.   However, we have seen that in the second
half of the fourteenth century there developed actions on
the case [1] : it is to these actions that so much of our
modern law of contract and tort can be traced, and it was
only gradually that what one may call the contractual
actions of case became separated in men's minds from the
tortious actions of case, so that the modern division of
actions could come into being to supersede the old one.
These new actions would lie where there was an indirect
interference with some right or property of the plaintiff.
Gradually as actions on the case grew in number one
class of such actions separated themselves from the rest.
They were cases where the defendant took upon himself
(assumpsit) to do something in relation to the person or
property of the plaintiff and did it badly.   Here we have
the germs of a contractual action, but as yet the emphasis
was not laid on the promise of the defendant, for if he
failed to do anything in pursuance of his undertaking no
action lay, but on the loss suffered by the plaintiff by the
defendant's misfeasance.   Then in the sixteenth century
there was a considerable step forward : assumpsit was
extended from misfeasance to non-feasance[2], and held to
lie for a complete failure on the part of the defendant to do
an act which he had undertaken to do, provided always
that the plaintiff had given some consideration for the

---

[1] See p. 89, above.

[2] The extension to those cases in which the defendant had actually
disabled himself from performance had come earlier.   In general, on the
above topics, see Milsom, *Historical Foundations*, ch. 12.

doing of the act.   Consideration at this time meant little more than " reason for making the agreement," and by the middle of the century it was clear that assumpsit would lie on a purely executory (i.e. unperformed) contract founded on mutual promises.   But it would not lie where debt was available.   The action of debt, in which the defendant could wage his law, was still the only remedy for the recovery of a liquidated sum of money owing to the plaintiff : this covered not only cases where money was owed on a loan or as rent, but also all actions by sellers for the price of goods sold.   At the beginning of the seventeenth century it was finally decided in *Slade's Case* [1] that wherever debt would lie so would assumpsit.[2]   With the disappearance of this limitation assumpsit had achieved the status of a general contractual action.   But, unless the agreement was under seal, the plaintiff had to show consideration, and from being no more than a " reason for making the agreement " this requirement came to mean that the plaintiff must " show that the defendant's promise, upon which he was suing, was part of a bargain to which he himself had con-tributed." [3]   Unilateral promises by the defendant and mutual promises unsupported by consideration were, and still are, unenforceable.

In the course of the seventeenth and eighteenth centuries, the action of assumpsit was still further ex-tended, first to cases of contract to be implied from the conduct of the parties, for example, if A employs B to do any work for him the law will imply an undertaking by A to pay B the reasonable value of the work (quantum meruit) ; and finally to what is termed " quasi-contract," where the element of contract is really quite fictitious,

[1] (1602), 4 Co. Rep. 91 : see A. W. B. Simpson in 74 *L.Q.R.* (1958), p. 381 on this case.

[2] The form of " assumpsit " which took the place of debt was known as " indebitatus assumpsit " as opposed to " special assumpsit " which lay in other cases.

[3] Cheshire and Fifoot, *The Law of Contract* (7th ed.), p. 58, where the history and present law of consideration are discussed.

but the law raises an obligation on one party towards the other from the circumstances of the case. For example, the obligation to repay money paid under a mistake of fact.

Students of Roman Law will notice in this connection the remarkable difference between the history of the growth of the English and Roman Laws of Contract. In the Roman system the prætor framed the " formula " which shaped the issue between the parties. Thus he was able freely to create new forms of action, and we find him taking up one after another of the common transactions of everyday life and making them enforceable at law, so that the Roman law of contract grew up as a law of a number of separate contractual transactions—or " causæ." It was only when the law reached its maturity that the great jurists analysed and stated the elements common to all these contractual transactions. In England, on the other hand, the common law judges had no such control over the issue of original writs as would enable them to frame a number of separate contractual forms of action. Our law of contract developed as a whole out of the action of assumpsit and at a fairly early date suddenly reached a stage at which all agreements became enforceable. The law then, as it were, retraced its steps and restricted the ambit of enforceable contract by reference to the requirement of consideration. This historical difference has left an abiding mark upon the form of the textbooks of the two systems. An English book on contract begins with the elements common to all contracts, e.g. offer and acceptance, capacity of parties, etc., matters which are not gathered together in the Institutes of Justinian, but are dealt with under the heads of different transactions such as the well-known chapter " De Inutilibus Stipulationibus." This is not to say, of course, that English lawyers have given no recognition to obvious distinctions between the various transactions which are the objects of contracts. Pleaders naturally found that many common transactions were frequently the subject of litigation and in course of time some of them came to be recognised as what were termed the " common counts " in "indebitatus assumpsit," viz. actions for money lent, for goods bargained and sold, for goods sold and delivered, for work and labour done, for money had and received to the use of the plaintiff, for money paid to the use of the defendant and on an account stated. These phrases are still used by lawyers to describe the several causes of action in question and have even found their place in Acts of Parliament, for example, the Infants Relief Act, 1874, and the Sale of Goods Act, 1893.

While the modern law of contract was developing out of assumpsit, other actions on the case were coming to cover a variety of injuries independent of contract, *i.e.* torts. It would be beyond the scope of this work to enter in any detail into the difficult question of the gradual development of this branch of our law in these centuries, but there was one variety of the action of case which we might perhaps refer to specifically ; that is the action of " trover " which lay for what is known as the " conversion " of personal property to the defendant's use. The old personal action which lay in cases where the plaintiff sought to recover from the defendant identifiable goods which belonged to him, or their value, was the action of " detinue ", but this action was in early days very limited in its scope, for it seems to have lain only where the goods in question came into the possession of the defendant with the plaintiff's consent, as by a bailment, and were still in his possession when he refused to return them. It would not, therefore, cover an unlawful taking by the defendant, nor, originally, an appropriation by the defendant of goods which he had found, or a sale or destruction by him of the plaintiff's goods lawfully in his possession. An unlawful taking was, of course, met by the writ of trespass " de bonis asportatis," but trespass would not cover any case where the goods came lawfully into the possession of the defendant, and accordingly we are not surprised to find that an action of trespass on the case, known as " trover," was developed to meet the case where in the words of the writ the plaintiff " casually lost the chattel from his hands and possession and afterwards . . . it came to the hands and possession of the defendant by finding who nevertheless put and converted it to his own use." In time, however, the allegations of loss and finding became fictitious and untraversable by the defendant, and the action without any change of form was extended to cover cases of unlawful taking (properly trespass) and unlawful detention (properly detinue), with the result that the plaintiff could obtain damages against the defendant for any dealing with the property which would have been actionable had the defendant in fact casually found it. In trover, of course, there could be no wager of law, but damages were assessed by a jury, and though the scope of detinue was in the fifteenth century considerably extended so as to cover cases of finding, trover remained the normal action for conversion, and Blackstone tells us that in his day detinue was " much disused." [1] We may say, then, that in the seventeenth and eighteenth centuries, real actions were very seldom brought, and that the only common law personal actions in general use were trespass proper, ejectment, case (including assumpsit and trover), debt for a liquidated claim under a deed [2] and covenant, for the performance of other agreements under seal, especially agreements in leases.

It now remains for us to show how, by this time, the three common law courts had come to have a concurrent jurisdiction in all these actions, which, being civil actions between subject and subject, one might have supposed would have been, like the real actions, in the exclusive jurisdiction of the Common Pleas. Up to a point the

[1] Blackstone, vol. III, p. 152.
[2] Where the plaintiff relied on a deed the defendant could not wage his law, and therefore debt continued to be brought in such cases.

answer to this enquiry is plain enough.   We have already
seen [1] that the King's Bench shared with the Common
Pleas jurisdiction over trespass : this inevitably involved
a concurrent jurisdiction over the special trespass which
developed as case (including assumpsit and trover).   But
this does not explain either how the King's Bench came
to have a jurisdiction in the older personal actions such as
debt, covenant or detinue, or how the Exchequer came to
have any jurisdiction at all in personal actions between
subject and subject.   To explain this it is necessary to
describe in some detail the mode of initiating proceedings
in the common law courts and ensuring the appearance of
the defendant.

Nowadays, if the defendant in a civil action is served
with the writ and does not choose to appear to it, it is
so much the worse for him.   Judgment will be given
against him in default of appearance.   But this was by
no means the case in English law before the procedural
reforms of the nineteenth century.   It was, generally
speaking, essential that the defendant should be before
the court, and accordingly what we should consider a
disproportionate amount of law was directed to the
question of how to get him there.   As we have seen,
proceedings in the King's Bench or Common Pleas were
in early days normally started by an original writ obtained
by the plaintiff from the Chancery and directed not to
the defendant but to the sheriff of the county in which
he resided, telling the sheriff to summon the defendant
to be before the court on a certain day to answer the
plaintiff's plea.   This procedure by way of original writ
from the Chancery was, however, only necessary in the
normal case in which the parties to the action were, if we
may use the phrase, strangers to the court in which the
proceedings were being brought.   If either the plaintiff
or defendant had a connection with one of the three
common law courts, then any civil proceedings could,
and indeed should, be brought by or against him as

[1] See p. 88, above.

the case might be in that court by a bill, or as we might say, a statement of claim, presented to the court without the formality of the issue of a writ from the Chancery to set the court in motion.   The connection with the court on the part of plaintiff or defendant which would make proceedings by bill rather than by original writ appropriate might be of various kinds.   The officials of each court, for instance, had the privilege of suing and being sued by bill exhibited by or against them in the court.   Prisoners in the custody of the court were in the same position, and so were persons who would have been prisoners of the court if the court had not allowed them to remain free on giving bail for their appearance.   Finally, in the Court of Exchequer the royal debtors were the peculiar " protégés " of the court and were allowed to prosecute their actions by bill exhibited there.   Indeed, proceedings in the Exchequer were only by a bill filed by the plaintiff and never by original writ out of the Chancery, for originally the court was purely a revenue court whose proceedings were confined to bills to recover money or property for the Crown, and actions in which persons who were admittedly debtors to the Crown were involved.   Strangers to the court had no " locus standi " before it at all, and could not sue out an original writ in the Chancery returnable in the Exchequer.[1]

If in an action in the King's Bench or Common Pleas the defendant failed to appear to the writ after being summoned to do so, the next step under the early common law system was for the court to issue a writ to the sheriff directing him to " attach " the defendant, that is to say, to take some of his goods, which would be forfeited if he continued to fail to put in an appearance, or in the alternative to make him find sureties who would be fined if he did not appear.   If he still failed to appear a series of writs would issue against him under which portions of

[1] In the Middle Ages the Crown sometimes granted the privilege of suing in the Exchequer to favoured individuals. There was no " wager of law " there.

his goods would be successively distrained by the sheriff so that eventually he would be stripped of his substance by these repeated distresses.[1]   In the case, however, of a writ, such as the writ of trespass which charged an injury " with force," the interests of the King's peace would not permit a contumacious but impecunious defendant to evade appearance by submitting to a series of ineffective distraints.   In these cases, on his initial failure to appear to the writ the person of the defendant could be subjected to imprisonment by the writ of " capias " directed to the sheriff by the court in which the writ of trespass was returnable.   Similarly, the Court of Exchequer would order the immediate arrest of a defendant to a bill in that court which, *ex hypothesi*, affected the royal revenue.   In time it was found that this process of arrest was much more satisfactory from the point of view of the plaintiff than the process of attachment, and a number of statutes were passed at various dates between the reigns of Edward I and Henry VII under which the writ of capias was permitted to issue in most personal actions even if no force was alleged.   But before this statutory permission to use the capias had been given plaintiffs in ordinary personal actions had found a way, with the connivance of the courts, of availing themselves of the privilege of arresting the defendant.

The method employed was for the plaintiff to pretend that the action which he was prosecuting involved a breach of the peace or the interests of the royal revenue, as the case might be, and then, when he had secured the enforced appearance of the defendant by this means to drop the pretence and bring forward his real cause of action against him ; while the court, for its part, refused

---

[1] It will be observed that all these writs subsequent to the " original " were " judicial " writs issued by the court not by the Chancery.

Some idea of the incredible dilatoriness of the common law procedure for enforcing the appearance of a defendant can be gathered from the list of writs, ten in all, which issued in an action of debt in the Common Pleas (Blackstone, vol. III, Apdx. III).

to allow the defendant to take exception to the false allegation which had brought him before it but compelled him to plead to the declaration eventually brought against him.   In the Court of King's Bench the form which this fictitious procedure took was not for the plaintiff actually to sue out a writ of trespass from the Chancery but for him to apply directly to the court with a complaint that the defendant had committed a trespass within the county (Middlesex) where the Court had now settled after its earlier peregrinations.[1]   The King's Bench then issued a bill, known as a Bill of Middlesex, to the Sheriff of Middlesex commanding him to take the defendant and have him before the court on such and such a day to answer the plea of trespass.   Being thus in the custody of the court the defendant, as we saw, could be proceeded against by bill on any cause of action, and the plaintiff, dropping the plea of trespass, would file his bill of debt or case against him.   If, as might well be the case, the defendant was not in Middlesex so that the sheriff made the return " non est inventus " to the Bill of Middlesex, the court would issue a writ, known as the " latitat,"[2] to the sheriff of the county in which the defendant resided, which recited the issue of the Bill of Middlesex and the return " non est inventus " to it, and went on to say that the court was informed that the defendant " lurks and runs about " (*latitat et discurrit*) in the county in question, and ordered the sheriff of that county to take him and have him before the Court of King's Bench on a certain day as in the Bill of Middlesex.   In time, by the middle of the sixteenth century in cases where it was known that the defendant did not in fact reside in

[1] The court continued to move about somewhat in the fourteenth century, though even then it was most often at Westminster.

[2] It should be remembered that such fictitious devices had originated in real situations.   The writ of *latitat* had a quite straightforward function in coping with the wrong-doing of casual visitors to London : see M. Blatcher, " Touching the Writ of *latitat*," in *Elizabethan Government and Society* (1961), pp. 188–212.

Middlesex, no Bill of Middlesex was actually issued, and the latitat was the first process, but even so the latitat always contained a recital of an ineffectual Bill of Middlesex though one had never in fact issued.

In the Court of Exchequer the fiction was somewhat less elaborate. We have already seen [1] that as early as the thirteenth century this court, as well as entertaining the bills of the Crown against royal accountants and private debtors to the revenue, also heard complaints by these debtors against other persons who, they said, were indebted or under some liability to them, their failure to pay or satisfy which made it impossible for the complainant to render his due to the Crown. The developed form of writ in such a case alleged that the defendant unjustly refused to satisfy the plaintiff's demand " whereby " the plaintiff " is the less able " (" quo minus sufficiens existit ") to satisfy the claims of the revenue. It was a simple step to allow persons who were not in fact indebted to the Crown to say that they were so indebted for the purpose of having their opponents arrested on a " writ of quominus " issued by the Exchequer, and this step was eventually taken.[2] It is to be noted that the " quominus " was not confined to liquidated money claims, it was also available where the plaintiff's demand was for unliquidated damages for breach of contract or tort, or even for the recovery of property.

These devices of the King's Bench and the Exchequer had the effect of withdrawing a considerable amount of work from the Common Pleas.[3] Indeed, so common had the use of the Bill of Middlesex become in the sixteenth

[1] See p. 57, above.

[2] There is ample ground for suspecting abuse of the privilege of suing in the Exchequer from the thirteenth century onward, but the full establishment of a fiction not open to traverse may not have come until the seventeenth century : see Plucknett, *Concise History* (5th ed.), p. 161.

[3] In the sixteenth century, the *latitat*, at least, may have been a response to a decline in business in the King's Bench : see E. W. Ives, " Common Lawyers in pre-Reformation England " (1968), 18 *Trans. R. Hist. Soc.* (5th ser.), 145–73, at pp. 165–70.

century that the statute of 1585 creating the Court of
Exchequer Chamber [1] as a court of appeal from the
King's Bench, speaks of the old personal actions of Debt,
Detinue and Account as being within the jurisdiction of
the King's Bench, though no original writ in those actions
could have then been issued except to begin an action in
the Common Pleas. To repair, as far as might be, the
damage done to it, the Court of Common Pleas by a
fiction of its own allowed suitors to start proceedings
before it in all cases by a writ of trespass " quare clausum
fregit," on which a capias would issue and then to drop
the trespass and proceed with the true cause of action.
It may be asked why this fiction was considered necessary
by the Common Pleas after legislation had made the
capias available in most personal actions. The answer
apparently is that the writ of trespass " quare clausum
fregit " cost less to issue than the writs which alleged no
force, and it is certainly a fact that just as in most cases
other than genuine trespasses, procedure in the King's
Bench was usually not by original writ but by Bill of
Middlesex, so in the Common Pleas procedure in
cases other than debt (in which procedure was generally
by the appropriate original writ) was normally by a
capias founded on a writ of trespass " quare clausum
fregit."

Hitherto we have spoken as though the defendant in
personal actions in this period was invariably imprisoned
pending trial. This, of course, was not the case. He
was liable to imprisonment, but a statute of 1444,
intended to mitigate the intolerable hardship of actual
imprisonment, enacted that any person in custody by
force of any writ or bill in a personal action should be
released on " reasonable " bail although he still remained
theoretically in the custody of the court, and could therefore be sued there in any cause of action. This enact-
ment was the more desirable in view of the fact that the

[1] See p. 214, below.

charges on which the defendant was liable to imprisonment were often, as we have seen, avowedly fictitious, and merely made for the sake of the superior process and to give jurisdiction to the court. A distinction was, however, established in the two centuries after 1444, between " common " or nominal bail which could be demanded as of right,[1] and " special " or substantial bail which would be required if the plaintiff was prepared to swear that his claim exceeded £10. But since it seemed hard that a defendant should be made to find heavy bail, under penalty of imprisonment, in answer to a document which told him nothing of the claim which was being made against him, a statute of 1661 enacted that in cases where the true cause of action was not expressed in the body of the writ no bail for a greater sum than £40 could be taken. This statute, whether or not it was the intention of those who framed it,[2] constituted a serious threat to the jurisdiction of the King's Bench, for neither the Bill of Middlesex nor latitat set out the true cause of action, and litigants who wanted substantial bail were accordingly thrown back on the appropriate original writs which in all cases could be made returnable in the Common Pleas, and in some cases were properly only returnable there. To meet the danger the Court of King's Bench devised the expedient of adding to the plea of trespass in the Bill of Middlesex and latitat a clause, known as the " ac etiam " clause, which set out the plaintiff's true cause of action. Thus the Bill now ran " to answer A.B. of a plea of trespass *and also* (ac etiam) to a bill of the said A.B. against the said C.D. for £200 of debt " or as the case might be. It was now the turn of the Common

[1] In common bail the sureties for the defendant's future appearance were the two imaginary persons John Doe and Richard Roe, and if the defendant failed to put in common bail the plaintiff could do it for him, and so be enabled to proceed against the defendant in his absence.

[2] Hale, who was a contemporary, speaks of the statute as a design of the Common Pleas; Holdsworth, i.200; but see Milsom, *Historical Foundations*, p. 57.

Pleas to grieve at the statute, for their capias issued on a fictitious trespass " quare clausum fregit " was open to the same objection as the Bill of Middlesex and latitat, but the same remedy was quickly found, and Chief Justice North added an " ac etiam " clause to the capias.

By these devious means the three courts of common law acquired a concurrent jurisdiction in personal actions and made use of processes for securing the defendant's appearance which were in effect identical though different in form in each case.   But partly because the King's Bench was the first court to make the arrest of the defendant a " mesne process " generally available and partly because proceedings in it remained to the end somewhat cheaper than proceedings in the Common Pleas, the Common Pleas in the seventeenth century lost that preponderance of work which it had enjoyed in the Middle Ages and took a second place to the King's Bench.   The Court of Exchequer, despite the fictitious quominus, had at all times substantially less work than the two other courts.   But the Court of Exchequer was not only a court of common law ; it was also a court of equity.   As the court concerned with the collection of the royal revenue it was never at any time tied down to the formal procedure of the common law, but both the Crown and its alleged debtors could raise all kinds of equitable matter in their pleas, while the Crown was at liberty by " English information " to compel the defendant to answer interrogatories directed to extracting an admission of fact which made him liable to account to the Crown for taxes or penalties.   But the history of the equity side of the Exchequer " is by far the most obscure of all the English jurisdictions." [1]   The most plausible view is that it developed on parallel lines to the Chancery and by the sixteenth century was entertaining a general equitable jurisdiction and allowing persons against whom

[1] Plucknett, *Concise History* (5th ed.), p. 185.

the Crown had no financial claims to file bills on the
" equity " side of the court and ask for equitable relief.
It should be noted that the equity side of the Exchequer
became (in theory) a separate court from its common law
side.   The latter, known as the Exchequer of Pleas, was
nominally held before the Treasurer and the Barons,
while the equity side was held before the Treasurer, the
Chancellor of the Exchequer and the Barons.[1]   Its
original functions as a court of revenue remained separate
from both the usurped jurisdictions and involved, as we
have said, both common law and equitable procedure and
remedies.

Before we pass from the development of the common
law in this period it may be useful to sketch very briefly
its relations with the other branches of the legal system
between the fifteenth and nineteenth centuries.   We
have seen that despite the writ of trespass on the case the
common law had not been able in the later Middle Ages
to show itself sufficiently flexible to prevent the development of distinct equitable jurisdictions.   In the sixteenth
century the common law had to face still more rivals,
in particular the Star Chamber and the Admiralty, and
all its rivals had this in common that their procedure was
based on the model then general over most of Europe
which derived ultimately from the Roman law.   On the
Continent, and indeed as near home as Scotland, in
this very period a movement, known as " the Reception,"
was in progress by which the Roman law, as interpreted
and developed by the great Italian jurists of the Middle
Ages, was in many countries being substituted for the
native customary law. Voices were heard in this
country advocating a similar reception of the Roman law
here, but the common law was too strong to be in any real
danger.   Its early dose of " romanism " in the twelfth
and thirteenth centuries had given it a logical form, while

---

[1] Neither the Treasurer nor the Chancellor of the Exchequer generally
sat, but each new Chancellor of the Exchequer continued until the
abolition of the court to attend and hear a few cases " pro forma."

the common lawyers had, under the early Tudors, occupied positions of great influence in the realm.   Besides, clearly distinct Bars had not arisen as between Common Law and Chancery.   Nevertheless it is true to say that in the sixteenth century the common law was to some extent on the defensive against the rival tribunals.   In the seventeenth century its position was very different, for in the struggle between Crown and Parliament the courts such as the Star Chamber, Chancery and Admiralty, which derived their authority from the Council, were all identified in varying degrees with the theory of prerogative government, while the common law courts gained enormously in prestige and jurisdiction by being associated with the winning side.   This phase in the history of the common law is associated with one of its most famous masters, Sir Edward Coke, and it is perhaps desirable that we should say something of his life and work.

Coke was very far from being the ideal figure of an opponent of despotism and defender of the liberties of the subject.   After a successful career in private practice at the bar he became Attorney-General in 1945, and in that position was a firm upholder of the rights of the Crown as he understood them and a ferocious prosecutor in all trials for treason.   He was no advocate of a monarch subject to Parliament, but held that the royal prerogative was defined by law and could not be arbitrarily extended by necessities of state; he might, perhaps, have preferred a vision of the Supreme Court of the United States to one of the developed doctrine of parliamentary sovereignty.   Then in 1606, as a due reward for his services, he was made Chief Justice of the Common Pleas, and in this capacity his finer qualities, his intense reverence for the common law and his absolute fearlessness, soon brought him into conflict with the Crown.   In 1613, as a measure of punishment, he was promoted to the more dignified, but then less lucrative and important, post of Chief Justice of the King's Bench.

His hostility to the Crown remained, however, unaltered. His unsuccessful attack on the Chancery had already been recorded. With somewhat greater success he attacked the High Commission, the king's claim to issue Orders in Council binding the subject, and the habit of asking the judges extra-judicially for their opinions on the rights of the Crown. Eventually, in 1616, he was dismissed from office, and as a private individual put his great abilities and experience at the service of the parliamentary opposition until his death in 1634.

So far we have only spoken of his services to English public law, but his position in the history of our private law, though less well known, is equally important. He was "a mean and untidy man,"[1] he could distort the authorities of the old common law; but he knew them as no one was ever to know them again, and in his various works he handed on that law to future generations in a form intelligible to them. Thus he became the oracle of the lawyers of the seventeenth and eighteenth centuries, and in the sphere of the land law, which until a century ago remained largely unaffected by legislation, his authority has extended up to modern times.

But in the seventeenth and eighteenth centuries the law of real property was gradually ceasing to be the most important part of English law. England was becoming a commercial country and the most important development in the common law between 1650 and 1800 was its adaptation to the needs of commerce. We have seen already how the action of assumpsit expanded in this period into a law of contract, and we shall see later how the specifically commercial law administered hitherto in the Courts Merchant or the Court of Admiralty became incorporated in the common law in the eighteenth century. The name chiefly identified with these developments is that of Lord Mansfield, who was Chief Justice

---

[1] Milsom, *Historical Foundations*, p. 52.

of the King's Bench from 1756 to 1788. In character
and attainments he differed very greatly from Coke,
for he was a cold-hearted and timid man, highly cultivated and possessed of a wide knowledge of contemporary
systems of law. He had a very rational dislike for
forms and technicalities, which found expression both
in his attempt to break down the barrier between
law and equity, and also in his determination to adapt
the common law to the needs of commerce. In the
latter task he was as successful as he was unsuccessful in
the former.

Finally, we may notice that this period saw the growth
of the modern system of law reporting and the theory of
precedent. The Year Books came to an end in the early
sixteenth century, and towards the end of that century
we begin to find fuller reports of cases in the common
law courts made and published by known authors.
Sometimes they were in English, sometimes in Law
French, but by the end of the seventeenth century they
came to be invariably in English. Naturally, their
authority varied to some extent with the professional
reputation of the compiler and of the judges whose
decisions he reported, but by the eighteenth century a
certain uniformity in the method of reporting was
attained. Gradually it came to be felt that a competently
reported decision of one of the common law courts sitting
in banc or of the Exchequer Chamber had more than
a merely persuasive authority, and ought to be binding
on future generations. Towards the end of this period
we even find reporters publishing reports of the
decisions of judges sitting at *nisi prius*. Generally
speaking, such decisions had far less authority than those
of the courts sitting *in banc*, both because they were
the decisions of one judge only and because they took
the form of rulings on questions of law given on the spur
of the moment as opposed to the judgment of the court
in banc, which in difficult cases would be reserved. But
Lord Campbell's reports of the decisions of Lord Ellen-

borough when sitting at the Guildhall have always enjoyed high authority.[1]

---

[1] This may be in part due to judicious pruning carried out by the eminent reporter. Lord Campbell used to boast that he had a drawer full of " bad Ellenborough law " (Atlay : *The Victorian Chancellors*, vol. II, p. 138). (The *nisi prius* trials for the city of London were held at the Guildhall.)

XI

THE COMMON LAW—FIFTEENTH TO EIGHTEENTH CENTURIES (II)

WE have seen from our account of the struggle for jurisdiction between the King's Bench, Common Pleas and Exchequer that by the end of the Middle Ages the original writ had ceased to play that commanding part in a common law action that it had taken in the earlier period. Many actions, *e.g.* actions in the Exchequer and actions started by Bill of Middlesex in the King's Bench, were not founded on any original writ at all, and sometimes when an action was founded on an original writ that writ might not really represent the plaintiff's true cause of action, *e.g.* proceedings in the Common Pleas under a writ of " trespass quare clausum fregit," and might never in fact be issued even if it did represent it. But it must be remembered that the law was still confined within the structure of the forms of action. The plaintiff's cause of action, whatever form of process was used, could only be a cause of action for which a recognised form of original writ could have been framed if the plaintiff had chosen to proceed in that way. Further, the plaintiff could not join in one proceeding causes of action falling within different forms of action. He could not, for instance, join a claim in assumpsit and a claim in debt. The modern facilities for joining separate causes of action in one proceeding only became possible when the old system of separate original writs initiating separate forms of action was abolished.

Assuming the parties are before the court the next step in the proceedings is occupied by the pleading. Originally, the pleadings were conducted orally in open court and entered on the " record " of the case by the clerk.   The plaintiff's counsel began by telling his story, whence the use of the word " count " (from the French *conter*) which remained in use until the Judicature Acts for the various paragraphs in the plaintiff's declaration (now called his statement of claim) and is still in use for the different paragraphs of an indictment.   The plaintiff's " counts " were met by the defendant's " pleas," which still remain oral in criminal proceedings. This system of oral pleading determined the character of the Year Books which are almost entirely devoted to a detailed report of the moves of both sides until finally one or the other was manœuvred into a position by which he had to abide.

Oral pleadings were superseded by the exchange of written pleadings [1] at the end of the mediæval period, but the common law system of pleading still retained, after the change, its outstanding characteristics of a system under which the parties were compelled to frame with great exactness the precise issue which they wished to submit to the adjudication of the court, and all pleadings were bound to end in a single " issue," either of law or of fact, to be decided in the first case by the judgment of the court, and in the second by a verdict of a jury.[2]   The system was excessively rigid and technical, particularly in its requirement that every issue should not only be certain but also single, so that it has been justly said of the old system of pleading that " if my opponent tells two falsehoods and I want to deny them both the law will make me admit one to be true." [3]   If the defendant wished to plead that the plaintiff's case was bad in law

[1] But these written pleadings, which were afterwards incorporated in the " record " of the case, retained the form of a contemporaneous account of proceedings in court.   The reader is advised to look at the forms of a record given in the Appendix to Blackstone, vol. III, and in Sutton : *Personal Actions*, p. 76.

[2] The word " issue " is a corruption of the Latin " exitus " or end, *i.e.* of the pleadings.

[3] *A Dialogue in the Shades on Special Pleading Reform between Baron Surrebutter and Mr. Crogate*, by George Hayes ; reprinted in Holdsworth,

he could not at the same time allege that the counts contained misstatements of fact.   He had to " demur " and by his demurrer, raising the issue of law, he admitted that all the plaintiff's statements of fact were true. Besides a demurrer various other pleas were open to the defendant.   They were generally divided into " dilatory pleas " and " pleas in bar."   The general nature of a dilatory plea is apparent from its name.   It did not go into the merits of the claim, but suggested that on some procedural ground the action as it stood could not be maintained by the plaintiff.   It might, for instance, allege that the court had no jurisdiction to hear the action, or that the plaintiff was under some disability, temporary or permanent, such as infancy or excommunication.

A plea in bar might either take the form of the " general issue " or of a " special plea."   The general issue, to quote Blackstone,[1] " is what traverses, thwarts and denies at once the whole declaration without offering any special matter whereby to evade it."   Each form of action had its own appropriate general issue—*e.g.* in debt it was " nil debet," in assumpsit " non assumpsit," and in trespass " not guilty of the said trespass "—and the effect of pleading it was at once to raise an issue of fact and put the plaintiff to the proof of his case.   Under the original system of pleading as developed in the sixteenth and seventeenth centuries the general issue was generally only pleaded when the defendant was in a position wholly to deny the allegations in the declaration ; if he meant to distinguish them, without totally denying them, he had to put in a " special plea," setting out the special facts on which he relied.   In the eighteenth century the courts, in order to diminish as far as possible the field in which the

vol. IX, at p. 424.   Baron Surrebutter was Baron Parke of the Court of Exchequer, a devotee of the strict rules of pleading.   Crogate was the unsuccessful plaintiff in a famous action before Sir Edward Coke, which he lost by an error on the part of his pleader.

[1] Vol. III, p. 305.

special pleader could exercise his ingenuity, encouraged
the pleading of the " general issue " and allowed special
matter to be given in evidence at the trial which ought
strictly to have been specially pleaded.   The result of this
was, of course, that a great many matters of law might turn
up in the course of the trial at *nisi prius*, and in the nineteenth century there was a reasonable reaction in favour
of cutting down the special circumstances which could be
given in evidence at the trial when the general issue had
been pleaded.   Indeed, under our modern system the
" general issue " is almost unknown.   It exists, of course,
in criminal cases where the prisoner pleads " not guilty "
and throws the whole onus of proof on the prosecution ;
but in a civil case the defendant has always to disclose
his defence in the pleadings.   Special pleas " in bar "
(as opposed to the " general issue ") were very numerous
and varied in accordance with the defendant's case.   We
may instance " son assault demesne " (*i.e.* self defence) in
an action of assault, " justification " in an action for libel,
or a defence by some special statute such as the Statute of
Limitations.

We have so far assumed that the pleadings will be
closed and the parties join issue on the defendant's first
pleas, but in fact they might be prolonged through
several stages before a joinder of issue was reached.
For instance, the defendant's special plea might take
the form of a " confession and avoidance " whereby he
confessed the facts stated by the plaintiff, but avoided the
legal conclusion to be drawn from them by the allegation
of further facts.   The plaintiff, instead of traversing,
i.e. denying, the truth of those facts (when the defendant
would have to join issue on the question of fact so raised),
might demur and by so doing he raised an issue of law,
whether granting the further facts alleged by the defendant were true they did in law dispose of the plaintiff's
case ; or again, he might in his turn confess and avoid
the additional facts alleged by the defendant.   The
various stages which the pleadings might go through in

this way had special names, declaration, plea, replication, rejoinder, surrejoinder, rebutter, surrebutter.

Before we leave the subject of the pleadings and pass to the trial of the issues raised by them, there are one or two general observations to make. The reader may suppose from the very summary account that we have given of it that the art of pleading was a simple one. This is far from being the case. To plead well required considerable natural acuteness fortified by years of experience. Indeed, Coke describes the art as " one of the most honourable, laudable and profitable things in our law," and counsels the student to employ " his courage and care " to master it. The pitfalls which surrounded each step were innumerable, and false steps were irretrievable. The bad points of this system are obvious. Under it it has been well said " truth and justice were sacrificed to the science of artificial statement," and only too often a good case was lost, or a bad case won, on the pleadings alone before they ever came to trial. With our modern liberty of amendment this is scarcely possible to-day, but before we congratulate ourselves unreservedly on the present state of affairs, we shall do well to observe that our modern procedure—which was designed as a compromise between the rigidity of the common law pleadings and the formlessness of those in the Chancery— has developed its own defects. The pleadings now count for very little, the parties are often allowed to amend them at the very last moment, and even sometimes to set up at the trial itself a case which they have never pleaded at all. Consequently it often happens that at the trial a good deal of time is taken before the court and counsel discover what the issues are, and, if there is a jury, it is naturally bewildered. Indeed, if anything like the number of cases which were tried by jury a century ago were tried by jury to-day, the modern laxity in defining the issues before trial would have become intolerable. But even if the trial of civil actions by jury is going soon to be a thing of the past, it must be remembered that judges themselves can fail to grasp the issue—especially if they have not time to re-read the evidence and consider their judgment. Perhaps a perfect compromise between too much and too little rigidity of pleading is unattainable, for ultimately the two systems are founded on different conceptions of the functions of a court of law. Is its function to decide questions over which the parties have found themselves at variance ? Or is it to do justice between the parties ? It is often forgotten that these may be two different things.

The trial of an issue of law on demurrer need not occupy us long. The parties had appeared and pleaded before one of the three courts at Westminster which they had chosen for their action, and a demurrer was argued before the same court and judgment entered by it in accordance with its decision. If the point was a difficult one the court might take time " to advise itself " and this is the origin of the letters, C.A.V. (" curia advisari vult "), which appear in the law reports in a case where judgment is reserved. An issue of fact on the other hand was not tried by the court *in banc* at Westminster, but was sent to be tried at the assizes under the *nisi prius* system which we have described in outline in Chapter VI. The working year of a judge was divided between the " law terms " during which he sat *in banc* with the other judges of his court for the dispatch of legal arguments and the period out of term when he took a circuit and tried issues of fact at *nisi prius*,[1] and we cannot remind ourselves too often that in the latter capacity he was not in any way confined to hearing cases which were pending in his own court at Westminster, but heard all the *nisi prius* cases in the counties which he visited. We must remember, too, that there was in those times no possibility of a trial of an issue of fact at common law by a judge alone, and that, therefore, trial by jury, which was the normal [2] method of trial of facts,

---

[1] As well, of course, as holding the criminal assizes.

[2] Even in the eighteenth century some of the older methods of trial

played a much more important part in civil proceedings than it does to-day.

When the parties joined issue on their pleadings and put themselves " on the country," a writ (called the " venire facias ") was issued to the sheriff of the county in which the action was laid directing him to summon a jury for the trial. Actions were sharply distinguished into " local " actions, such as ejectment or trespass, which had to be laid and tried in the county where the trespass occurred, and " transitory " actions, such as debt or assumpsit, in which the plaintiff could choose which county he liked to lay his action in. The place of trial was called the " venue," a word which survives to-day in the phrase " a change of venue," which can be sanctioned by the court in cases in which, from local feeling or other good cause, a satisfactory trial cannot be expected in the place where the cause of action arose. The course of the trial was not unlike a trial at the assizes to-day, but there are certain points to be noticed in connection with the character of the witnesses and the jury. Originally, as we have seen, the jurors were supposed to be persons able to give the true answer from their own knowledge of the parties and their affairs and from enquiries which they might make themselves. From this presumption two consequences followed : (*a*) that there was no need to call the oral evidence of outside witnesses ; (*b*) that if it could be shown that the jury had given a false verdict they ought to be punished for it as being guilty of something like perjury. By the close of the Middle Ages, however, the jury was becoming more like the jury we know to-day, and from the sixteenth century onwards the giving of oral evidence by witnesses in court was usual. It was, therefore, necessary for the courts to decide both who could give evidence and what sort of evidence they could give. It would be quite outside the scope of this book to deal with the rules of

of facts were in theory possible, *e.g.* an action of debt might lead to " compurgation " or a writ of right to " battle."

evidence which were gradually elaborated in this period, but it is important to observe that the evidence of interested parties—especially, of course, the parties to the action themselves—was rigorously excluded at this time. Further, as a consequence of this change in the character and functions of a jury the criminal proceedings against the jurors by writ of attaint for a false verdict fell into disuse, but the Star Chamber and the judges continued on occasions to fine and imprison jurors who gave verdicts of which the court disapproved, and it was not until *Bushell's Case*, in 1670, that the modern immunity of the jury from punishment for their verdict was established.

It did not follow, of course, that the issue in a trial at *nisi prius* would ever get to the jury at all, for it might be that the plaintiff would be " non-suited " on the ground that he had failed to prove something which was essential to his case or that the case which he had proved was different from that which he had pleaded. Assuming, however, that the case went to the jury, the judge would sum it up, as he does to-day, and give rulings as to the legal effect and admissibility of the evidence which had been tendered. If either party wished to question the correctness of the judge's directions or rulings, he could set out his objections in a document known as a " Bill of Exceptions," which would be sealed by the judge and annexed to the record of the case. We will see in Chapter 13 what was the subsequent procedure on such a bill.

Ordinarily the verdict found by the jury was a general verdict for or against the plaintiff on the issue submitted, but, particularly where the general issue had been pleaded, it was often hard to disentangle questions of law and questions of fact. To avoid the inconvenience of requiring the jury to form an opinion on matters of law, it was possible, if both sides agreed to the procedure, for the facts to be as far as possible separated from the law and left to the jury as an independent question. The

jury then returned what was known as a " special verdict " on those facts and added that they were " ignorant
in point of law on which side they ought upon those facts
to find the issue," but that " if the court thought that the
issue was proved for the plaintiff, then they assessed the
damages at £x." The point of law was not argued
before the judge at *nisi prius*, but was reserved for the
court *in banc*. We shall have more to say of this form
of verdict in connection with the Law Merchant, but at
the moment we need only observe once more that resort
could only be had to it if the parties agreed.

With the verdict of the jury (whether general or
special) the proceedings at *nisi prius* closed, and the case
was sent back to the court at Westminster from which
it issued for judgment, after a statement of the holding
of the trial and of the verdict had been added to the
record. This statement, from the fact that it began with
the Latin word " postea," or " afterwards," was known
as the " postea " and was in fact drafted by the party in
whose favour the verdict had gone, whence the phrase
" postea to the plaintiff " or " the defendant " which is
found in the old reports. In many cases, of course, there
was nothing for the court to do but to complete the
record of the case by entering judgment for the party
for whom the jury had found a verdict, but this was by
no means always so. In the first place, as we have seen,
if the verdict was " special " there would be a question
of law to be argued on the facts found. But even if the
verdict was " general " it by no means followed that the
party in whose favour it was given would get judgment,
for his opponent might apply to the court *in banc* for
a new trial or move there for an arrest of judgment or an
entry of judgment in his favour " non obstante veredicto."

We have seen that proceedings to reverse the verdict
by a writ of attaint had become obsolete by the sixteenth
century, and even in the fourteenth and fifteenth centuries
it was quite common for parties against whom a verdict
had been given, instead of suing out a writ of attaint, to

apply to the court for a new trial on the ground that the
jury had had private communication with the other side
during the trial or that for some other irregularity their
verdict was suspect. But about the middle of the seventeenth century applications for new trials began to be
entertained by the courts on other grounds as well, such
as that the damages were excessive, that the verdict was
against the whole weight of evidence, or that the judge
had misdirected the jury. One reason for this development was that it had by now been established—after the
quarrel between Ellesmere and Coke which we have
described—that the Chancery had power to prohibit
parties who had obtained oppressive verdicts at common
law from enforcing them, and therefore if the common
law courts did not develop a satisfactory procedure of
their own it was quite likely that their trials would come
to be controlled by the Chancery. On an application
for a new trial the court *in banc* had before it the notes
taken by the trial judge and his report on the trial.
The court would not, any more than it will to-day, order
a new trial simply because it did not agree with the
verdict. If there was no misdirection and there was some
evidence on which the verdict could be supported, it
must stand. But on the other hand, if there was a misdirection the court had not the power, which the modern
Court of Appeal has, of saying that even so there had
been no substantial miscarriage of justice. Consequently,
new trials were more frequently ordered than they are
now.

A motion in arrest of judgment [1] could only be made
on the technical ground of an error appearing on the
record. It was not available (like a motion for a new
trial) to correct mistakes in law made by the judge at
nisi prius since directions to the jury and rulings on
points of law formed no part of the " record " which set

---

[1] For the difference between an " arrest of judgment " and an entry
of judgment " non obstante veredicto," see Sutton, *Personal Actions*,
pp. 129–132.

out only the writ, pleadings, issue and verdict. In early days the most trifling errors—such as, for instance, the omission of the words " with force and arms " in a declaration in trespass—were sufficient to support a motion in arrest of judgment, but before the eighteenth century a series of statutes—known as the Statutes of Jeo-fails [1]—enabled the court to overlook most objections which had no substance, and even substantial errors in pleading were sometimes " cured by verdict " though they might have been a good answer for the party raising them if he had made them the subject of a demurrer on the pleadings instead of allowing the case to go to trial at *nisi prius* and then attempting to raise them, after the verdict had gone against him, on a motion in arrest of judgment.

After judgment a plaintiff in whose favour damages had been awarded could issue execution of which there were three forms. The first, " fieri facias levari " (commonly known as " fi. fa.") ordered the sheriff to raise the amount of the judgment by an execution on the defendant's goods and chattels ; the second, the writ of " elegit " by which the process was extended to a moiety of the freehold lands as well as the goods ; and the third a " capias ad satisfaciendum " (commonly called a " ca. sa.") under which an impecunious judgment debtor could be imprisoned.[2]   In substance, the first two forms (which by the Judgments Act, 1838, was extended to the whole of the freehold lands) are still available to the judgment creditor to-day, but imprisonment for debt was, with a few exceptions, abolished by the Debtors Act,

---

[1] A corruption of the Law French " j'ai faillé " (" I have made a mistake ")—the confession of the pleader asking the court to overlook his error.

[2] It will be remembered that Messrs. Dodson and Fogg proceeded by way of ca. sa. against Mr. Pickwick to recover their costs of the action of *Bardell* v. *Pickwick*. As the defendant lived in furnished lodgings fi. fa. or elegit would have been useless, and before 1838 the common law courts had no process of execution which would reach stocks and shares of which Mr. Pickwick's fortune presumably consisted.

1869.[1] If the judgment debtor possessed property, *e.g.* an equity of redemption in land, which could not be reached by fi. fa. or elegit, the creditor could, as we saw, apply to the Chancery for " equitable execution " against it and obtain the appointment of a receiver.

[1] It is now (1970) proposed that imprisonment for debt should be abolished altogether.

XII

THE CRIMINAL COURTS—FIFTEENTH TO NINETEENTH CENTURIES

THE system of criminal justice reached a settled form at a fairly early date, and the changes which we shall have to record in this period are by no means so extensive as those which affected the courts exercising a civil jurisdiction. It will be useful first to recall the main lines which we have traced in Chapter 5. Crimes were among the " Pleas of the Crown "—criminal cases were proceedings in which the Crown had a particular interest by reason of the injury to its peace and dignity caused by the wrong done. Some of the early codes of laws of the Saxon and Norman kings contained lists of specific acts which were pleas of the Crown, but by the thirteenth century the law had passed from the enumeration of particular cases to the generalisation that any act of wrongful violence or breach of the peace was a Plea of the Crown. The most serious of such acts were known as " felonies " ; the less serious as " trespasses." Felonies were prosecuted either by indictment in the name of the king and on the presentation of a grand jury at the criminal assizes or (from the second half of the fourteenth century) quarter sessions, or by the injured party himself by means of an appeal of felony. A conviction for felony generally entailed death, a forfeiture of goods and an escheat of lands. Trespasses, on the other hand, were either prosecuted by writs of trespass in the common law courts which, as we have seen, led to civil proceedings for damages ; or, like felonies, by indictment at assizes or quarter sessions where they were punished by fine and, pending payment, imprisonment ; or they might be punishable by fine or imprisonment in some local court such as the sheriff's tourn or a court leet.

In course of time appeals of felony gradually died out, so that the procedure by indictment became the universal mode of prosecuting felonies. At the same time prosecution by indictment came to be extended to a number of offences which fell short of felony and were known as " misdemeanours." Some of these misdemeanours were acts which in the Middle Ages might have been dealt with as " trespasses " ; others were not recognised by the mediæval common law as crimes at all, and were either made indictable by statute or were first effectually dealt with by the Star Chamber and then on the fall of that court, punished by the common law courts. Meanwhile the old local criminal courts such as the tourn and the leet decayed and their place was largely taken by the jurisdiction of the justices of the peace either sitting in quarter sessions or exercising a summary jurisdiction out of sessions. Thus in the eighteenth century we can think of crimes as divided into indictable offences (whether felonies or misdemeanours) which were normally tried by jury either at the criminal assizes or at quarter sessions, and offences dealt with summarily by justices sitting alone or in groups of two or three. We must also remember that the justices sitting both in and out of quarter sessions had taken over a great many of the administrative functions of the older local courts and also had had many more such functions imposed on them by statute, with the result that in the seventeenth and eighteenth centuries they were the chief organs of local government.

In this chapter we shall, therefore, deal first with the courts which tried indictable offences, secondly with the mode in which such offences were prosecuted, thirdly with the summary jurisdiction of the justices, and fourthly we will say a few words of the administrative functions exercised by them and how their exercise of these functions was controlled by the King's Bench.

I

The principal court of criminal jurisdiction in England was the Court of King's Bench, which exercised such jurisdiction on what was termed the " Crown side " of the court. Any indictment for felony or misdemeanour brought in any county might be removed into the King's Bench by writ of certiorari and tried by that court instead of by commissioners of assize or the county quarter sessions, and further, the King's Attorney-General and the Master of the Crown Office [1] had each a power of filing informations in the King's Bench in any case of misdemeanour, but not of felony, without any indictment brought or presentation made by a grand jury. This power of entertaining criminal informations was largely an inheritance from the Star Chamber for—as Blackstone says—" all that was good and salutary in the jurisdiction of that Court reverted to the King's Bench." Criminal cases brought before the King's Bench, either by information or by the removal there of an indictment, were either tried at the bar of the court at Westminster or, more usually, were sent for trial at *nisi prius* at some assize as though they were civil actions, with the consequence that the record had to be returned into the King's Bench for judgment to be pronounced there, instead of the whole case being dealt with by a commissioner of assize.

But despite its wide jurisdiction, in actual fact the trial of a felony or misdemeanour by the King's Bench was something of a rarity. The great mass of indictable offences were tried either by courts sitting under one or other of the criminal commissions or by the justices of the peace at quarter sessions. There were two such commissions in general use—that of " oyer and ter-miner " and that of " gaol delivery "—which were issued at least twice a year in the case of most counties. Under the first the commissioners had authority to hear

---

[1] *I.e.* the head of the official staff of the Crown side of the King's Bench.

and determine all treasons, felonies and misdemeanours in respect of which the grand jury of the county in question had made a presentment at that particular assize, while under the second they could try all prisoners who were in the county gaol when they arrived in the county whenever or wherever such prisoners had been indicted. The king's commissioners generally included two common law judges, some of the serjeants-at-law and a number of eminent laymen, but the commission could not be executed without the presence of either a judge or a serjeant, and, in fact, the lay members of the commission had ceased to take part in the proceedings by the eighteenth century.[1]

It is important to notice the difference between these two criminal commissions and the commission of assize under which trials at *nisi prius* were held. Trials at *nisi prius* were trials of civil actions started in one or other of the common law courts, and, as we have seen, the judge who presided at the trial under the commission of assize did not enter judgment. The verdict was entered on the record of the case and the subsequent proceedings took place at Westminster before the court in which the action was brought. Trials under the criminal commissions on the other hand were conducted quite independently of the Court of King's Bench, and judgment was pronounced by the judge in court after the trial.

We have spoken in Chapter 5 of the origin of the office of the justice of the peace. By the royal commission of the peace certain persons, headed by the " custos rotulorum," [2] were assigned in each county [3] to keep the

[1] But as late as the beginning of the seventeenth century the lay members of the commission sometimes played an important part, *e.g.* at the trial of Sir Walter Raleigh.

[2] This office came in practice to be united with that of Lord Lieutenant of the county.

[3] Separate commissions of the peace are sometimes issued for parts of the same counties, as, for instance, for the Isle of Ely and the rest of Cambridgeshire, and the three " Ridings " of Yorkshire.

peace and to enquire into, hear and determine felonies
and misdemeanours, with a proviso that difficult cases
were to be reserved for the presence of one of the judges
of assize. Their court—which came early to be known
as " quarter sessions "—was to be held four times a year
before two or more of the justices of the peace of the
county, and the commission contained a clause providing
that one or more of certain specified justices (known as
the " quorum " [1]) should be present. The original
intention seems to have been to secure the presence of
some qualified lawyers, but in course of time all, or
substantially all, the county justices came to be put on
the quorum, with the result that the jurisdiction of quarter
sessions long remained exercisable by courts composed of
persons none of whom were professional lawyers.[2] They
had no jurisdiction over treasons, and by the eighteenth
century it had become customary for them to send to the
assizes all cases that might be capitally punished. Since
in those days nearly all felonies might be so punished, this
custom largely confined their jurisdiction to misdemeanours, and even in that field it was not universal, for they
could not try statutory as opposed to common law misdemeanours unless the statute had empowered them to
do so. The justices of the peace were appointed by the
Crown on the advice of the Chancellor, who in his turn
relied largely in his choice upon the recommendation of
the Lord Lieutenant of the county. In the Middle Ages
the number appointed in each county was quite small,
six or eight at the most, but with the growth of their
administrative duties their numbers rose, and in the
eighteenth century probably a fair proportion of the
county gentry were on the commission of the peace.
By statutes of 1731 and 1744 a property qualification
consisting in the possession of land of the annual value
of £100 was imposed, but in practice only men of wealth

[1] The clause ran " Assignavimus vos et quoslibet duos vel plures
vestrum *quorum* A.B., etc., unum esse volumus."
[2] See p. 337, below.

and position had been appointed even in the days when no qualification was needed.

The county commission of the peace was not, however, the only such commission. In the sixteenth and seventeenth centuries the custom grew up of issuing separate commissions of the peace for some of the boroughs and occasionally of granting the borough the right to hold its own court of quarter sessions to the exclusion of the county justices. The procedure before borough quarter sessions was the same as that before the county quarter sessions, but the borough commission, as well as including the mayor and aldermen, usually included an official known as the " Recorder " of the borough, who was generally a salaried lawyer and came in time to occupy the position of the sole judge of the court.

II

We will now pass to a consideration of the principal steps in the course of the proceedings by which a man was brought to trial on indictment and convicted of a felony or misdemeanour before one or other of the courts which we have mentioned. There were six such steps : arrest, committal for trial, accusation, arraignment, plea and issue, trial and verdict, and judgment, and we will deal with them in that order.

1. In primitive times, as we said in Chapter 1, there was no distinction between the criminal and the civil law : the exaction of punishment for a violent injury and the recovery of a loan were equally the concern of no one but the injured party or maybe his kin. Gradually, however, the interest of the community, or at least of the sovereign, in the suppression of what we should call grave crimes of violence became apparent. Such acts came to entail a very heavy penalty for the doer of them, and the " frankpledge " system offered some prospect that his neighbours would surrender him to justice for fear of the penalties which would fall on them if they did

not. Further, the Assize of Clarendon (1166) laid it down that juries representative of each hundred in the county should present to the royal commissioners, when they came to the county for the trial of felonies under the assize, those whom they suspected of such crimes either by their own knowledge or by the testimony of others given at the " sheriff's tourn " when the operation of the frankpledge system was reviewed.

But it is only a comparatively simple state of society that can rely for the apprehension of criminals on the action of the wrongdoer's neighbours. As society grows more complex a system like the " frankpledge " becomes unworkable and something more like a police force is required. In this country the frankpledge system died out in the fourteenth century, but it was not until the nineteenth that we had an efficient professional police force, and the lack of it in the intervening period was one of the most serious blots on our legal system. Quite early, however, we can see the germs of the modern idea. By the end of the Middle Ages it had become the law that every parish should have a " constable," who was generally elected by the local court leet or hundred court, but was sometimes appointed by the local justices of the peace. The primary duty of the constable was to keep the king's peace in his district, and for that purpose he had conferred on him considerably larger powers of arresting persons whom he suspected of crime than were enjoyed by the ordinary private individual. Constables were drawn from a humble class in society, and Blackstone remarks that it was probably a good thing that they were generally ignorant of the extent of their powers. The characters of Dogberry and Verges in *Much Ado about Nothing* give one an idea of the light in which the Elizabethan public viewed its constables. Meanwhile, as we saw in Chapter 5, the control of the administration of criminal justice was passing more and more from the sheriff and his officers to the justices of the peace. Gradually the constables came more and more

under the control of the justices, while the justices themselves built up the practice of issuing warrants to the
constables for the arrest of persons who were suspected
of felony on the evidence of a person laying a complaint
before them.

2. A person arrested on suspicion of felony, either
under a warrant or by a constable or private individual on
his own initiative, was next brought before one or more
local justices for a preliminary enquiry to determine
whether or not he should be admitted to bail. The conduct of this preliminary enquiry was regulated by two
statutes of 1554 and 1555. The justices of the peace
were directed to examine the prisoner and his accusers, to
put the evidence against the prisoner into writing, and to
send it to the court before which the prisoner was to be
tried. No doubt this preliminary examination in its early
days was not the impartial enquiry into the probable guilt
or innocence of the accused which it is to-day,[1] but was far
more inquisitorial and was used for getting up a case for
the prosecution as the enquiry of the " juge d'instruction "
in France still is to-day. It is to be observed that these
statutes of Philip and Mary were the first provision made
in the history of the common law for the examination of
persons accused of crime. The general principle that
the accused could not be questioned and his offence
wrung out of him but that the crime must be proved by
other evidence, was very deep seated in English law, and
at the trial itself the accused was not competent to give
evidence until the Criminal Evidence Act, 1898. But
the preliminary examination instituted in the sixteenth
century did a great deal to deprive the accused of the
advantages of this bar while leaving him its disadvantages.
A number of statutes laid down the cases in which bail
could not or must be allowed, and the writ of habeas
corpus was available to any person who was refused bail
in a case in which he was entitled to it.

3. The next step in the course of the criminal pro-

[1] See p. 341, below.

ceedings was the formal accusation of the suspect before the court which was to try him. We have seen already that in cases of misdemeanours the Attorney-General and the Master of the Crown Office had a certain power of lodging informations against suspects and so bringing them to trial without any formal accusation by a grand jury, but apart from this possibility a presentment of the suspect by the grand jury was essential. The grand jury of the county summoned on the occasion of the commissions of assize or of quarter sessions consisted of twenty-three freeholders of the county. In practice gentlemen of substantial fortune were chosen by the sheriff for the service. The grand jury was, of course, the descendant of the jurors of hundreds instituted by the Assize of Clarendon with the difference that instead of a number of separate juries representing each hundred being summoned, there was now one jury representing the county. In early days the hundred jurors had frequently presented suspects of their own knowledge, and to the end the grand jury retained the right to do so, but in practice by the end of the sixteenth century the great majority of persons suspected of felony who were presented by the grand jury had been previously brought before a justice of the peace in the manner which we described above. However, accusations of felony might be, and charges of misdemeanour frequently were, first made before the grand jury by the prosecutor. After being charged [1] by the presiding judge or chairman of quarter sessions the grand jury retired to hear the accusations or " indictments," to use the technical term. They heard only the case for the prosecution, and upon it they either threw out the bill (by writing " ignoramus " on the back—hence the phrase " ignoring the bill ") on the

[1] It was improper for counsel attending the assizes to be present in court when the grand jury was being charged. This rule, which lasted until the abolition of grand juries, was a curious survival of the jealousy with which the courts had viewed the intervention of counsel in criminal cases.

ground that no prima facie case had been made out, or—
and this, of course, was far more frequent—they expressed
themselves satisfied with the propriety of the case going
to trial by endorsing the words " true bill " on the
indictment. The indictment was then said to have been
" found " and was brought into court by the foreman of
the grand jury and two other jurors.

4. When the indictment had been found the next
step was to arraign the prisoner upon it. In many cases,
of course, the prisoner would already be in custody,
having been committed to prison by a justice of the
peace ; in others he would surrender to his bail ; in
others again it might be necessary to arrest him, and
even to proceed to outlaw him if he evaded arrest. On
his appearance at the bar of the court the indictment
would be read to him and he would be asked whether
he was guilty or not guilty. If he pleaded guilty judgment was at once passed. If he refused to answer, the
court ordered an enquiry whether he stood mute of
malice or by the visitation of God. If the latter was the
case, the court proceeded to trial as though the prisoner
had pleaded not guilty. If, however, it was found that
the prisoner stood mute of malice, this finding in cases
of treason or of misdemeanour was equivalent to a plea
of guilty, but in cases of felony entailed the process of the
"peine forte et dure" which we have described in Chapter
5.[1] It may be remembered that this state of the law was
not amended until 1772, when standing mute of malice
in cases of felony was made equivalent to a plea of guilty.
Finally, in 1827 it was enacted that if a prisoner stood
mute from whatever cause a plea of not guilty should be
entered in all cases.

Assuming, however, that the prisoner neither pleaded
guilty nor stood mute, he would plead to the indictment.
The most usual plea was, of course, the general issue of
not guilty, but there were a variety of other pleas which he

---

[1] See p. 68, above.

might set up. In the Middle Ages he might plead his clergy—but, as we have seen, by the close of that period benefit of clergy had come to be invoked not as a bar to the proceedings, but as a mitigation of the penalty if the prisoner was convicted. Examples of other pleas which might be set up are : a plea to the jurisdiction of the court, a demurrer to the indictment on the ground that assuming the facts stated to be true no offence is disclosed by it ; a pardon ; or the fact that he had been previously convicted or acquitted of the identical charge now brought against him a second time.[1] To the plea of not guilty the clerk of the court on behalf of the Crown replied that the prisoner was guilty and that he was ready to prove him so. Issue was thus joined between the Crown and the prisoner, and the latter was then asked by what mode of trial he would prove his innocence. As we showed in Chapter 5, after the abolition of the ordeal, there was no method of trial for felony other than trial by jury, which the prisoner claimed by the words " By God and my country."

5. A few of the chief differences between such a trial in those days and to-day should be noted. In the first place the prisoner, except in cases of treason, had no copies of the indictment supplied to him before his arraignment; secondly, in cases of treason and felony, he was allowed no counsel to speak for him in matters of fact as opposed to matters of law, a state of affairs which in the eighteenth century was coming to be regarded as a hardship ; thirdly, as we have said, the prisoner could not give any evidence on his own behalf, and before the seventeenth century it was doubtful whether a man charged with felony could even call any witnesses on his behalf against the Crown. It will be seen from this brief statement that the prisoner in those days laboured under great disadvantages, and though it was to some extent considered the duty of the judge to

[1] The technical name for these pleas is " autrefois convict " and "autrefois acquit."

give him what assistance he could in his defence, and to sum up fairly to the jury, many judges right down to the end of the seventeenth century were prepared, in political cases at least, to take advantage of the defenceless condition of the prisoner to subject him to all sorts of abuse and ridicule.

6. Assuming the jury to have returned a verdict of guilty it was the business of the court to pass judgment, and here we may once more emphasize the distinction between criminal trials at the assizes and at quarter sessions and civil trials at *nisi prius*. In the former the court which heard the case passed judgment ; in the latter the record was sent up to Westminster for judgment to be given by the appropriate court *in banc*. On his conviction for felony the prisoner, if it was his first offence, might be able to escape the death penalty by pleading his clergy. Broadly speaking, however, benefit of clergy was only available in the case of common law as opposed to statutory felonies, for the statute creating a new felony normally provided that it should be without benefit of clergy, and further, the privilege had been expressly taken away from several grave common law felonies. Thus by the eighteenth century a large number of felonies were " unclergyable," and for this reason, even in the case of first offenders, a conviction for felony— and a very large number of crimes were felonies at that time—normally entailed the death sentence. For misdemeanours, on the other hand, the punishment was, as it is to-day, imprisonment or fine, or both. In cases of felony juries would sometimes be encouraged by the court to return verdicts in defiance of the evidence in order that the necessity of passing the death sentence might be avoided in trivial cases. Thus in cases of larceny it was by no means uncommon for articles of value to be held by the jury to have been worth less than twelve pence, the sum which marked the boundary line between larceny, which was punishable with death, and petty larceny, which was not. But the chief mitigation

of the atrocious severity of the criminal law was afforded
by the practice—started soon after the Restoration—of
granting pardons after sentence, conditional upon transportation for life or a long term of years to the American
—or later the Australian—colonies.[1]   This practice
involved a constant use of the royal prerogative of mercy,
which was then exercised by the sovereign personally,
so far as concerned cases tried at the Old Bailey, after
consultation with the trial judge.[2]   Since the accession
of Queen Victoria this branch of the prerogative has been
exercised through the Home Secretary.

III

We saw that in the Middle Ages minor offences were
punished in the local courts ; that is to say either at the
sheriff's tourn in the hundred court, or in the court
leet of a franchise holder.   The presiding judge, whether
sheriff or steward, placed the " articles of the tourn " or
" leet " before the jurors of the court, and the latter presented those who were in their view guilty of the offences
specified.   The offenders were then fined or imprisoned
by the judge.   But at the close of the Middle Ages we
find this power of punishing small offences passing
gradually into the hands of the justices of the peace.   Just
as they had obtained the power of arresting and examining those charged with serious offences, so in the sixteenth century statutes begin to confer sometimes on one
sometimes on two justices sitting out of quarter session
a power of trying specified minor offences summarily

---

[1] The number of executions at the end of the eighteenth century seems
to have varied from a fifth to a ninth of the death sentences passed, see
L. Stephen: *The English Utilitarians*, 1, p. 26.

[2] On one occasion King George IV held up the administration of
justice by refusing to see Mr. Denman, then Common Serjeant of London,
when he was to come to Windsor with the report on those sentenced to
death at the Old Bailey, on the ground that as counsel for Queen Caroline
at her trial he had used language grossly insulting to his sovereign. See
Greville's Diary, vol. I, pp. 156, 250.

without the intervention of a jury and of punishing those whom they convicted. It is quite impossible here to give any comprehensive list of the offences which were thus made punishable summarily under statutes of the sixteenth, seventeenth and eighteenth centuries, but we may instance swearing, drunkenness, and vagrancy. The effect of this extension of the jurisdiction of the justices was, of course, to lessen the importance of the old local courts. The trial of serious crimes and the greater part of its old civil jurisdiction the county court had long since lost to the royal court, and now the smaller local courts were fast losing their petty criminal jurisdiction to the justices.

There are several points in connection with the summary jurisdiction exercised by the justices in this period which we may notice before we pass to consider the administrative functions of the county magistracy. First there was no uniformity in the proceedings before the magistrates in those cases. Some statutes required the presence of one justice only for the summary trial of the offences with which they dealt ; others required two ; and the method of procedure differed in many cases. It was only at the beginning of the nineteenth century that the familiar expression " petty sessions " came to be used as a general description of all their sittings out of quarter sessions, and it was not until 1848 that at long last a statute was passed regulating the procedure at petty sessions generally and giving these sessions all the attributes of an ordinary court of law.[1]

Secondly, in the exercise of this summary jurisdiction, as in the exercise of their jurisdiction at quarter sessions, the justices were under the control of the King's Bench. By means of the writs of mandamus and certiorari that court could both compel the justices to act when they ought to act but refused to do so, and could quash their convictions if they had been given without jurisdiction or irregularly.

Thirdly, the enormous increase in the power of one

[1] See p. 357, below.

or two justices sitting out of quarter sessions both with respect to the preliminary stages of prosecutions and the summary trial of petty offences was by no means without its dangers.   In his capacity as " J.P." the local squire was in a position to use the authority of the state to further personal and class interests.   " They played ducks and drakes with the law when it suited them, breaking with impunity what they were supposed to maintain." [1]   This was especially the case after 1688, and the Game Laws, which flourished from 1706 to 1831, showed the justices at their worst.   On the other hand, there is no doubt that very many of them did their work well.

The dangers were of a graver kind in the disordered large towns of late pre-industrial England and the early Industrial Revolution.   Many borough justices were not only quite unfitted for their work but used their powers as a means of earning a disreputable livelihood. The inefficiency of the constables and the corruption of the local magistracy combined to make the enforcement of the criminal law in London and other large cities extremely unsatisfactory in this period, and eventually produced a demand for the modern system of qualified and salaried police magistrates.   Indeed, as early as the end of the seventeenth century, the government found it necessary to have at least one magistrate in the metropolis who should be a man of capacity and honesty in the confidence of the Secretaries of State.   This magistrate, who was paid to some extent out of government funds, had his office at Bow Street and controlled a small body of reasonably efficient constables, known as the " Bow Street Runners."   The post of Bow Street magistrate was held from 1747 to 1751 by the novelist, Henry Fielding, and many passages in his works give us an insight into the deplorable fashion in which the criminal law was administered in the metropolis in the eighteenth century.[2]

[1] J. H. Plumb, *The Growth of Political Stability in England* (1967), p. 21.

[2] *E.g.* the opening chapters of *Amelia*.

IV

In the Middle Ages the local government authorities in England were the old communal courts and courts leet, of which we spoke in the earlier chapters of this book. As well as trying such cases, civil and criminal, as the encroachment of royal justice allowed them to entertain, these courts were responsible for the general good order of the district—as, for instance, for the repair of roads and bridges and the maintenance of the police system. The method of procedure in them was generally by the presentment by a local jury of persons charged with neglect of their obligations ; the immediate control of the system was largely in the hands of the sheriff and his officers and the stewards of the feudal lords ; such central control as was exercised at all was exercised periodically at the General Eyre when every district appeared by representatives before the justices in eyre to answer for its conduct during the last seven years.

In the fifteenth and sixteenth centuries the justices of the peace came gradually to replace the local courts as the chief organs of local government, and the parish came to take the place of the manor or the hundred as the administrative unit.[1] We pointed out in Chapter 7 that the Tudors were the first English sovereigns who were in a position to enforce a uniform system of local government throughout England. Their highway and poor law legislation was enforced locally by the officers of the parish—constables, overseers and churchwardens —under the control of the justices of the peace either in or out of quarter sessions. Until 1641 central control was exercised over the justices through the Star Chamber

---

[1] The chief reasons for the emergence of the " parish " as the lowest unit of civil government were probably that in the Middle Ages the Church had been largely responsible for the care of the poor and that the Poor Law was the most important function of local government after the Reformation. The State adopted the unit of the Church.

or the provincial councils of Wales and the north, but after the fall of the Star Chamber effective central control came largely to an end.

The period from 1650 to 1830 is the great era of the justices of the peace. In it they were the real governors of the English countryside. Their principal functions they exercised collectively at quarter sessions, where they met for judicial and administrative business, but very wide powers of the most varied description were given to one or more justices sitting out of sessions. We have mentioned in the last section some of the summary judicial powers given to justices out of session ; here we may mention two of their many administrative functions, the licensing of alehouses and the appointment of overseers of the poor. Originally the administrative functions of the justices in quarter sessions were exercised in exactly the same way as their judicial functions : that is to say they proceeded upon presentment by a local jury. But in time this procedure was found to be exceedingly inconvenient for the dispatch of administrative business, and the justices came to be given power to take independent action on their own initiative or on the information of single officials in matters such as rating, the poor law and the maintenance of bridges and gaols. Gradually the judicial business of sessions came to be a thing quite separate from the " county business," which was also transacted there, and in this latter sphere the justices in the eighteenth century appointed county officials such as the county treasurer and the county surveyor to assist them.

The justices of the peace—in or out of sessions and whether performing administrative or purely judicial functions—were, of course, at all times judicial officers, and their courts were subject to the control of the King's Bench exercised by means of the prerogative writs. This mode of control was, indeed, almost the only control to which the justices were subject in this period, for, as we have said, the central executive government hardly attempted to exert much pressure on local government after the fall of the Star Chamber. But judicial control through the prerogative writs was in the nature of the case not very effective. The judges of the King's Bench would not move to enforce a duty by mandamus or to quash an order by certiorari unless some aggrieved person applied to them, and, even when applied to, their powers did not extend beyond the enforcement of positive duties and the quashing of orders made irregularly or without jurisdiction. When the justices had a discretion the King's Bench could not put any pressure on them to exercise it in any particular way.

Towards the end of the eighteenth century and the beginning of the nineteenth, the local government of England by the justices of the peace showed some signs of breaking down. The industrial revolution with the consequent movements of population and the great distress caused by the Napoleonic wars raised problems which could only be met by some comprehensive national policy. The weakest spot was the administration of the poor law. With a mobile population in the overcrowded cities, the parish ceased to be a realistic and effective unit of administration. In 1834 the Poor Law Act vested the poor law powers of the justices in local boards of guardians under the close control of a body of Poor Law Commissioners in London, and at the same time extended the unit of administration from the parish to the poor law unions consisting of groups of parishes. Greater economy and efficiency was secured by the measure, but the introduction of the workhouse system and the abolition of the " Speenhamland " expedient of subsidising wages out of the rates caused temporarily at least considerable hardship. This Act was the first of a number of statutes which in the course of the nineteenth century stripped the justices of nearly all their administrative powers and gave them to elected local authorities more or less under the control of departments of the central government.

To-day quarter and petty sessions are predominantly courts of law, while it is county and borough and district councils that administer the various services—public assistance, roads, education, public health and the rest— that our modern society demands.

The details of the modern law of local government and administration lie, of course, outside the scope of this book, but it is important for us to remember that the King's Bench, which exercised a control over the administrative functions of the justices by means of the prerogative writs has continued to exercise such control over their successors, the modern local and central government authorities.   By mandamus, certiorari and prohibition the King's Bench controlled the activity of inferior " courts," but a body or an individual may be a " court " for the purpose of these writs though it is far from being a court of law in any true sense of the word. The justices in quarter sessions sitting for " county business " were hardly a law court, but the writs lay against them, and so now can on appropriate occasions be issued against such bodies as the Greater London Council or the Ministry of Health.   " Wherever any body of persons, having legal authority to determine the rights of subjects and having the duty to act judicially act in excess of their legal authority they are subject to the controlling jurisdiction of the King's Bench Division exercised in these writs."[1]

---

[1] Atkin, L. J., in *R. v. Electricity Commissioners*, [1924] 1 K. B. 205. E. G. Henderson, *Foundations of English Administrative Law* (1963), explains the seventeenth-century beginnings of the use of the prerogative writs for these purposes.

XIII

COURTS OF APPEAL : THE EXCHEQUER CHAMBER AND THE HOUSE OF LORDS

IN this chapter we are to deal with proceedings by way of appeal. It will be convenient to divide the subject into three parts. In the first we will describe the methods by which the judgment of a common law court in a civil proceeding could be questioned on appeal and give an account of the various courts in which such appeals were brought. The second will deal with appeals in criminal cases, and the third with the jurisdiction of the House of Lords, which still remains the highest court of appeal in the land.

I

Nowadays an appeal brought before the Court of Appeal from a judgment of the High Court is technically a rehearing of the whole case, but with the onus on the appellant, whether plaintiff or defendant below.[1] The Court of Appeal does not indeed in practice rehear oral evidence given in the court below, but is satisfied with such account of it as appears in the transcript of the shorthand note of the case, or, if no such note was taken, then with the judge's note of the evidence. Moreover, the Court of Appeal is always reluctant to differ from the opinion of the judge below as to the credibility of any witness whom he has had the advantage of seeing in the box and will not upset the verdict of a jury merely because it disagrees with it provided there was material on which it could be founded by reasonable men. Subject to these

[1] The Court of Appeal has power to hear fresh evidence not heard below, but this power is very sparingly exercised.

limitations, however, the whole case comes at large before the Court of Appeal. This was the system followed in the Court of Chancery in the old days. The Chancellor reviewed all the material which had been before the Master of the Rolls—or even before himself at an earlier stage[1]—and came to a decision on the case as a whole. In the common law courts, however, before the reforms of the nineteenth century, no appeal by way of rehearing was possible at all.

With the judgment given by the court *in banc* an action at common law came to an end, and it could not be reheard. But there was a permanent memorial of the action in the form of the record entered on the roll of the court, and either party could, if he chose, impeach this record before the appropriate superior court by showing that the conclusion of it, *i.e.* the judgment given, did not flow from the premises, *i.e.* the antecedent statement of the pleadings, issue and verdict. To do this he initiated an entirely fresh proceeding by suing out from the Chancery a " writ of error " directed to the chief justice of the court whose record he was impeaching, calling upon him to produce the record of the case before a superior court, so that it might consider the errors in the record alleged by the appellant, who was known as the " plaintiff in error." Two facts will illustrate that a writ of error was an entirely distinct proceeding from the original action. The defendant in error had to be summoned afresh by the sheriff to appear before the higher court, while a man who had defaulted in the court below could nevertheless sue out a writ of error to impeach the record of the judgment so obtained against him.[2]

On the hearing of the proceedings in error all that that superior court could consider was the bare record of the case ; how the record had come to take the form it had was immaterial ; the record, the whole record and

---

[1] See p. 150, above.
[2] See Sutton, *Personal Actions at Common Law*, pp. 120, 144.

nothing but the record was before it.   It is important, therefore, in this connection to recall exactly what the record contained.   It contained a note of the writ or bill by which the proceedings were started ; the pleadings between the parties and the issue arrived at between them ; if the issue was one of fact, a note of the writ of " venire facias " bidding the sheriff summon the jury for the *nisi prius* trial and a note, known as the postea, recording the appearance of the parties at the trial, the empanelling of the jury and their verdict ; and, finally, whether the issue was one of law or fact, the judgment of the court given either upon demurrer or, after the *nisi prius* trial, with or without an application in arrest of judgment.

To confine the court of error to the record, and at the same time to attach a mystical importance to every word of it, meant that the appellant was given at once too much and too little latitude.   On the one hand, the most trifling errors, the omission of a word or a mistake in a name, originally gave ground for a writ of error, though this injustice was largely a thing of the past in the eighteenth century by reason of the various Statutes of Jeofails to which we have referred.[1]   On the other hand, the confining of the errors alleged to errors on the record meant that appeals were in effect confined to matters of law.   A party could appeal against a judgment against him on demurrer or after a motion in arrest of judgment, for a consideration of the record enabled the superior court to say whether on the pleadings, issue and verdict, the defendant in error could or could not be entitled to his judgment.   But one could not bring a writ of error for matters which had occurred at the trial, such as the admissibility of evidence, defects of summing up, or that the verdict was against the evidence, for the record contained no account of the proceedings at *nisi prius* beyond the empanelling of the jury and their verdict.   For the same reason one could not appeal

[1] See p. 189, above.

against a refusal of the court *in banc* to grant a new trial, for only the bare judgment appeared on the record and not the reasons given by the judges for their refusal.

There was, however, an important exception to the rule that matters arising at the trial could not come before the court in error, and that was the proceeding by way of a Bill of Exceptions. If a party at the trial considered that the judge had given a wrong ruling, say on a question of evidence, he had two courses open to him. He could, if he liked, wait and apply to the court *in banc* for a new trial on the ground of the misreception of evidence—and, as we have said, if the court *in banc* refused a new trial that was the end of the matter— or he could formulate his objections at the trial in the manner which we described in the last chapter [1] and take the Bill of Exceptions straight to the superior court by a writ of error. The Bill of Exceptions was annexed to the record and formed part of it, and so could be made the ground of proceedings by way of appeal.

It remains for us to say what were the appropriate courts of error from the several courts of common law. Error from the Common Pleas was brought in the King's Bench, but the Court of Exchequer contended that it stood on a different footing from the Common Pleas and refused to send up its record to the King's Bench. Accordingly, by a statute of 1358, a special court, known as the Court of Exchequer Chamber, was set up to hear error from the Exchequer of Pleas. Under the Act the court was to consist of the Treasurer and the Chancellor,[2] who were to call to assist them " the justices " (of the other two courts) " and other sage persons as to them seemeth." This arrangement proved unsatisfactory, for

---

[1] See p. 186, above.

[2] Not the Chancellor of the Exchequer. He only sat on the equity side of the Exchequer from which there was an appeal to the House of Lords.

it was difficult for two such great personages as the Treasurer and Chancellor to be present at each stage of every appeal, and if either were absent the appeal " discontinued." Provision was, therefore, made by statute for either or both being absent at some stage, though both had to be present to give judgment.[1] The judges were merely assessors, and accordingly, after the office of Treasurer was put into commission in the seventeenth century, the Chancellor was the sole judge. From the King's Bench, whether as a court of first instance or sitting in error from the Common Pleas, and from the Exchequer Chamber, a writ of error could be brought before the House of Lords.

This was the original system, but the increase in the work of the King's Bench and the infrequency of the sessions of Parliament in the sixteenth century led to statutes being passed in 1585 and 1589 which set up a second Court of Exchequer Chamber to hear error from the King's Bench sitting as a court of first instance. This court consisted of the justices of the Common Pleas and the Barons of the Exchequer, or any six of them, and from its judgment a further appeal could be taken to the House of Lords. The statute, however, only referred to actions " of debt, detinue or covenant, account, case, ejectment, or trespass if first begun in the King's Bench," and these qualifying words were interpreted to confine the jurisdiction of this Court of Exchequer Chamber to actions started by bill, since actions started by original writ strictly began in the Chancery and not in the King's Bench. Further, the appellant could if he chose go straight to the House of Lords. This rather complicated state of affairs obtained until 1830, when a statute was passed abolishing both courts of Exchequer Chamber, taking away from the King's Bench its jurisdiction to hear error from the Common Pleas, and setting up as a new Court of Exchequer Chamber to hear error from

---

[1] " It is the practice for the two chief justices alone to sit in this court of error "; Blackstone's *Commentaries*, vol. III, p. 410.

all three courts. This court was composed of the judges of the two courts, other than the one from which error was being brought in any case, and from its judgment error could be brought in the House of Lords.

Before we pass to the system of appeals in criminal as opposed to civil cases, there is one other Court of Exchequer Chamber to which it is convenient to refer here, although it was not strictly a court of appeal. In the Middle Ages it was the custom of the common law judges if any point of exceptional difficulty arose in a case coming before a court *in banc* to adjourn it to be further argued in the Exchequer Chamber before a meeting of the judges of all the courts.[1] Sometimes, too, the Chancellor or the Council would refer some question of law in a case before them to such a meeting of the judges. Strictly speaking these meetings were informal ; after all the judges in the Exchequer Chamber had discussed the point and arrived at a decision, the case went back to the court from which it had been adjourned and it was that court that gave judgment. In theory, of course, such a judgment was no more sacrosanct than any other, and could be made the subject of a writ of error, but in practice great authority attached to it by reason of the fact that it had the approval of all the judges of England. Some of the most famous cases in English legal history were argued in this way before the twelve judges in the Exchequer Chamber—the case of Ship Money, for instance, and *Godden* v. *Hales*, the great case on the dispensing power. This system of adjourning cases into the Exchequer Chamber died out in the early eighteenth century.

II

After what we have said of appeals in civil cases it will not be necessary to deal at great length with the system of criminal appeals, since the principles on which both

[1] Until 1579 this meant the King's Bench and Common Pleas ; after that the Barons of the Exchequer were also present.

rested were fundamentally identical.   A writ of error
against a conviction at quarter sessions or the criminal
assizes was limited like the writ of error in civil cases to
errors appearing on the record which set out in full the
commission under which the court sat : the arraignment,
the plea and the issue, and finally the verdict and judgment, but said no word of the course of the trial, the
evidence or the summing up.   These omissions were
even more serious in criminal than in civil cases, since
facts as opposed to law play a larger part in the former
than the latter.   Down to 1705 [1] writs of error in criminal
cases were not issued as of right, but as a matter of favour
on the fiat of the Attorney-General.   After that date they
came never to be refused, but in view of the limitations
on their scope they were very seldom applied for.[2]   The
court which heard them was, of course, the King's Bench,
and from it there was a further appeal to the House of
Lords.   Applications for a new trial were also far more
restricted in criminal than in civil cases.   In cases of
felony no new trial could be ordered at all, and in cases
of misdemeanour a new trial could not be awarded after
a trial at quarter sessions or the criminal assizes, but only
after a trial before the King's Bench in the exercise of its
original jurisdiction.   As we saw in the last chapter it
was only relatively rarely that this jurisdiction was
exercised, and cases removed from the ordinary tribunals
to the King's Bench by certiorari.

Some efforts were made by the judges to remedy these
defects.   In the first place the jury might be asked to find
a special verdict on the facts, leaving a question of law,
whether on those facts the prisoner was guilty or not, to
the judge.   Secondly, when points of difficulty in law
arose at a trial at the assizes the judges developed the
custom of postponing judgment after conviction and
causing the question of law to be argued in London before

[1] *R.* v. *Paty* (1705), 2 Salk. 503.
[2] Strictly speaking, *Paty's Case* was limited to misdemeanours : for
details see Holdsworth, vol. I, p. 215.

the other judges. This was a quite informal proceeding, and was not available if the case was tried at quarter sessions, but in 1848 this informal tribunal of the judges was erected into a court known as the Court for Crown Cases Reserved, which consisted of all the common law judges, with a quorum of five. Any judge or chairman of quarter sessions might state a case for the opinion of the court as to any questions of law which had arisen at the trial, but it was absolutely at his discretion whether he would do so or not. We may say then that even as late as the nineteenth century there was practically no possibility of appealing on the facts in criminal cases, and only a limited opportunity of appealing on the law. A pardon was in many cases the only remedy for an unsatisfactory conviction. This state of affairs was eventually remedied in 1907 by the creation of the Court of Criminal Appeal, now the Criminal Division of the Court of Appeal, of which we will speak in a later chapter.[1]

III

We have seen in Chapter 4 how in the course of the fourteenth century the Court of King's Bench separated itself from the Royal Council and from those occasional reinforced meetings of the Council which were known as Parliaments. We have also seen in Chapter 7 that the common law courts would not admit that the Council had any power to correct errors in their judgments. They were quite prepared, however, to admit that the Court of Parliament—the highest court in the land—had this power, and accordingly writs of error went to the King's Bench and the Exchequer Chamber calling on those courts to send up their records to be reviewed in Parliament. Now in this same century there was growing up in Parliament a distinction between the Lords who received an individual writ of summons and Commons who appeared by representatives. The Commons were beginning to deliberate separately from

[1] See p. 353, below.

the Lords under the chairmanship of their Speaker. But it must not be supposed that this separate deliberation meant that (in theory at least) the unity of Parliament was in any way destroyed. " Parliament " was the meeting in the Parliament Chamber where the king's throne was, round which his councillors stood, and in front of which his judges sat, while the Lords were ranged on benches down each side and the Commons stood at the Bar at the bottom.[1] It would have been ludicrous to suggest that the House of Commons formed a " Parliament " which could hear a writ of error, but what does require a little explanation is the fact that these appeals came to be heard only by the Lords in the Parliament Chamber and not by the Lords and Commons assembled there together.

Even as late as the end of the seventeenth century Chief Justice Holt contended that in theory the judgment of Parliament in appeals was the judgment of King and Commons as well as of the Lords,[2] but in practice since the fifteenth century the judicial power was exercised by the Lords alone. If we remember that the Commons were coming to spend more and more of their time during the sessions of Parliament in private deliberation in their own chamber, and only to appear in the Parliament Chamber on important occasions, to hear messages from the Crown and the like, it should not surprise us very much to find that the hearing of appeals in the Parliament Chamber fell into the hands of the Peers, who were always there. If the Commons had been eager to share in the jurisdiction they might have prevented this result, but, in fact, they were far from eager to share in it. Cases which came before Parliament—and in the Middle Ages Parliament sometimes heard important cases as a court of first instance and not only as a court of appeal—were often

---

[1] Pollard : *Evolution of Parliament* contains several reproductions of pictures of " Parliament " at various dates which illustrate the development of the seating arrangements.

[2] See Holdsworth, vol. I, p. 362, n. 8.

cases of a political cast involving the fortunes of great
men. This was not the sort of case with which a knight
of the shire or a burgess would want to have anything to
do. The Commons were insistent on their rights in the
matter of taxation or legislation which would affect
them personally, but they had no wish to meddle in the
quarrels of the nobility. For these reasons the judicial
powers of Parliament came in practice to be exercised by
the House of Lords in the later Middle Ages. In the
sixteenth century, when Parliaments were infrequent and
somewhat overshadowed by the Council, we hear little
of their judicial powers, but in the seventeenth century
they were revived and their scope definitely defined. On
the one hand it was established in 1666, after a long controversy in the case of *Skinner* v. *The East India Company*,
that the Lords had no jurisdiction to hear civil actions at
first instance,[1] and, on the other hand, the case of *Shirley*
v. *Fagg* (1675) decided that the Lords could hear appeals
from the decrees of the Chancellor made in exercise of
his equitable jurisdiction, as well as from the courts of
common law. The Lords had before this established
their right to hear appeals from the common law side of the
Chancery and the equity side of the Exchequer. After
the Act of Union with Scotland in 1707 had united the
Scottish and English Parliaments, the Lords became the
Court of Appeal from the Court of Session at Edinburgh,
and by the Act of Union of 1800 they regained a right
to hear appeals from the Irish courts which they had
previously exercised but had abandoned in 1782.

We must next consider how the Lords exercised their
judicial powers. We have seen that in the fourteenth
and fifteenth centuries the growth of the doctrine of
" peerage " excluded from full membership of the House
of Lords most of those persons who attended it who were
not properly speaking " peers," so that the royal judges

[1] There was one practical—though not theoretic—exception to this
position in the jurisdiction exercised by both Houses in considering
divorce bills. See p. 235, below.

and counsellors who had formed the core of Parliament in the reign of Edward I came to be present only as expert assistants unless they happened to be actually peers. Common Law judges—even the Chief Justices—were very seldom peers, and the only peers with legal qualifications tended to be the Chancellor of the day and any of his predecessors who chose to attend. Consequently there was a tendency for the judicial functions of the House to be exercised by the Chancellor with or without the advice of the judges who were summoned to attend the hearing. It must not be thought, however, that in the seventeenth and eighteenth centuries the judicial sittings of the House were regarded as a thing apart from its sittings as a branch of the legislature or that the lay peers considered themselves disqualified from taking part in them. When Sir Bartholomew Shower, in 1698, attempted the laudable task of publishing some reports of the decisions of the highest court of judicature in the land, his book was treated exactly as though it had been a report of the ordinary debates in the House, and was consequently held to be a breach of privilege for which the author and printer were reprimanded.[1] On the same principles the lay peers voted on appeals when they chose to do so, and as late as 1783 the judgments of the Common Pleas and King's Bench, and the opinion of seven of the eight judges summoned to advise the Lords, were overruled by nineteen votes to eighteen in a House made up almost exclusively of bishops and lay peers.[2]

In the early part of the nineteenth century, however, it began to be felt that the House in exercising its functions as a court of appeal ought to be regarded in the same light as other courts. Regular reports of its judicial proceedings were published and the intervention of the lay peers began to be discountenanced. The decisive moment came with the appeal of the Irish leader

---

[1] It must be remembered that at this date the publication of debates in Parliament was not authorised.

[2] *Bishop of London* v. *Ffytche*, Lords Journals, vol. 36, p. 687.

O'Connell in 1844 from conviction in Dublin.   In the House of Lords some Tory peers were anxious to vote with Lords Brougham and Lyndhurst in support of the conviction against Lords Cottenham, Denman and Campbell, who were for quashing it.   Lord Wharncliffe, the President of the Council, advised them not to do so, remarking that "if noble lords unlearned in the law should interfere to decide such questions by their votes instead of leaving them to the decision of the law lords the authority of this House as a court of justice would be greatly impaired." [1]   His advice was followed then and thereafter, so that by a convention of the constitution lay peers take no part in the hearing of appeals.[2]

The House accordingly consisted, for judicial business, of the Lord Chancellor and such ex-Lord Chancellors or other peers who had held judicial office as chose to attend. In the early 1850's, owing to the death of Lords Cottenham and Denman, the great age of Lord Lyndhurst and the promotion of Lord Campbell to be Chief Justice of the King's Bench, the House generally consisted of Lords Cranworth, St. Leonards and Brougham.   The two first were very eminent lawyers, but unfortunately found it almost impossible to agree on any difficult point, while the profession had little confidence in the casting vote thus left to Lord Brougham.   Soon complaints began to be heard.   Sir Richard Bethell (Lord Westbury) declared in the House of Commons that the House of Lords "was inferior to the lowest tribunal in what ought to be the accompaniments of a court of justice," [3] and the government felt that the judicial personnel of the House must be strengthened.   It was not desired, however, to set the practice of creating hereditary peer-

---

[1] O'Connell v. The Queen, 11 C. & F., at p. 421.

[2] Even after O'Connell's Case, however, lay peers might be called upon to make up a silent quorum : R. F. V. Heuston, " Who was the Third Lord in Rylands v. Fletcher? " (1970), 86 L.Q.R. 160–5, and added note by D. E. C. Yale, ibid., 311–12.

[3] Hansard, 139, p. 2120.

ages for this purpose, and the expedient was adopted of granting a life peerage by letters patent to Baron Parke, the greatest common lawyer of the day, under the title of Lord Wensleydale. It is, however, a privilege of the Lords to decide on the validity or effect of any newly created peerage, and on this occasion Lords Brougham and Lyndhurst induced them to decide that the prerogative of the Crown did not extend to creating a non-hereditary peerage with a right to sit in the Lords. Consequently Lord Wensleydale had to be given a hereditary peerage, but he lived to enjoy it only a short time, and the composition of the House continued to be somewhat unsatisfactory. At last it was decided to abolish its appellate functions altogether, and the Judicature Act of 1873 contained a clause to that effect.

The Act, however, was not to come into operation until 1875, and in 1874 Mr. Disraeli and Lord Cairns succeeded Mr. Gladstone and Lord Selborne. The new government decided to retain the appeal to the Lords, but to make provisions by statute for the creation of salaried life-peers to assist the Lord Chancellor and ex-Lord Chancellors. This was done by the Appellate Jurisdiction Act, 1876, the provisions of which have been extended by subsequent Acts with the result that there are now ten such Lords of Appeal in Ordinary. In view of the fact that the House hears appeals from the Court of Session it is customary for two of them to be Scottish lawyers, and until the Irish Union was in effect repealed in 1922 there was generally one Irish law lord. When the Irish Free State became a Dominion the House of Lords ceased to hear appeals from Dublin, but appeals from the Court of Appeal in Northern Ireland are still brought before it. Its chief judicial function is, however, the hearing of appeals in civil matters from the Court of Appeal in England, established by the Judicature Act. The Administration of Justice (Appeals) Act, 1934, provided that such an appeal can only be brought with the leave either of the Court of Appeal or the House of Lords. The House has also a power of hearing appeals, whether by the defendant or the prosecutor from the Criminal Division of the Court of Appeal and from any decision of a Divisional Court of the Queen's Bench Division in a criminal matter provided that the Court in question certifies that a point of law of general public importance is involved and that either the Court in question or the House of Lords gives leave to appeal.[1] Finally, we may observe that though since the Second World War the arguments in appeals are heard in a Committee Room, the decision of the House is still given in the Chamber and observes the forms of a sitting. A quorum of three is essential. The judgments, though in fact written, are couched in the form of speeches addressed to the House, and the Chancellor, or the senior law lord present, puts the matter formally to the vote of the House.[2]

We must now mention quite briefly the two cases in which the House used to exercise a jurisdiction at first instance, in both of which the lay peers took a part. These were (*a*) impeachments; and (*b*) the trial of peers for felony.

(*a*) By an impeachment the House of Commons can bring any man—peer or commoner—to trial before the House of Lords on a criminal charge. In this proceeding the House of Commons is, as it were, the grand jury not of a single county, but of the whole of England, while the Lords are the full Curia Regis in its original feudal form, and are at once both judges and jury. There are several instances of impeachments in the later Middle Ages, but none in the sixteenth century, when Acts of Attainder were preferred as a means of removing persons of whom the Tudor sovereigns desired to be rid. The great era of impeachments came in the seventeenth century, when they were used by the Commons on their

---

[1] Administration of Justice Act, 1960, s. 1.

[2] In 1968 the House of Lords disposed of 40 appeals, 4 of which were from Scotland.

own initiative as a means of making ministers, over whose choice they had as yet no control, responsible to law. From this point of view the rule established in the impeachment of Lord Danby, and re-approved in the Act of Settlement (1701), that the Crown cannot block an impeachment by pardoning the accused in advance was of considerable importance.

As a method of controlling ministries an impeachment suffered from the defect that in theory at least it was necessary in it to prove an offence known to the criminal law, which it might be difficult to do. As the Grand Remonstrance puts it : " There be grounds of diffidence that lie not in proof." In joining in an act of attainder, on the other hand, the Lords acted as legislators and not as judges, and consequently peers who would have refused to find Lord Strafford guilty of treason on his impeachment by reason of the manifest lack of legal proof, were prepared to vote in favour of the Bill of Attainder which the Commons substituted for it, since they were—or professed to be—satisfied in their conscience that the Earl was guilty. With the establishment of Parliamentary control over the choice of ministers the chief *raison d'être* of the impeachment disappeared. It was used in a few instances in the eighteenth century as a means of trying high officials on charges of misconduct in their posts, but it has not been employed since the impeachment of Lord Melville in 1806 for malversation in the Admiralty.

(*b*) The 39th clause of the Great Charter enunciated the principle that a man was entitled to " the judgment of his peers "—"judicium parium suorum." We have already considered what was the meaning of this phrase.[1] The old mode of trial—that which had obtained universally in the communal and manorial courts and in the royal court when a charge was brought against a tenant-in-chief—was that the members or suitors of the court,

------

[1] See p. 50, above.

who would be the "equals" in station of the accused,
should decide on his fate. The encroachments of the
royal court, with its distinction between the verdict of the
jury and the judgment given by the royal judge, constituted a serious threat to this principle, and the baronage
were determined that, as far at least as they were concerned, the old system should prevail. The lower ranks
of society were not able to maintain their right to the
judgment of their peers. Trial by jury—which was the
negation of the old principle—became the established
mode of trial, and though in the thirteenth century it was
felt that a knight should only be tried by a jury of knights
even this faint memory of the old principle soon vanished.
The baronage, however, maintained their right to a trial
by their "peers," and owe their designation as "peers"
to this fact. In the fourteenth century this privilege
of trial by peers was a powerful weapon in the hands of
the baronage in their struggle to exclude the royal counsellors from effective membership of Parliament. The
"peerage," they argued, formed a class apart, and only
those who were "peers" could sit and vote in the House
of Lords. In the fifteenth century the boundaries of
the privilege came to be more exactly defined. It was
established that it only applied to treason and felonies,
not to mere misdemeanours or, of course, to civil proceedings. It was further established that it applied to
the wives of peers, but not to the bishops. The bishops,
indeed, fell between two stools. They claimed that they
ought to be tried only by the ecclesiastical courts, and in
fact they were tried by jury like commoners.

In the days when charges of treason and felony—sometimes well and sometimes ill founded—were frequently
brought against peers at the instance of the Crown, the
privilege of being tried by their fellow peers rather than
by a jury directed by a royal judge was no doubt a valuable
one ; but it long outlived its usefulness. A jury of
peers was not likely to be more lenient than a jury of
commoners—even if it were desirable that it should be

so—and the division between felony and misdemeanour, which was once based to some extent upon the degree of wickedness involved in the offence, had become quite arbitrary.   The privilege, however, such as it was, could not be waived, and accordingly there were a few instances of these "trials by peers" in modern times.   Earl Russell was convicted of bigamy by his peers in 1901, and Lord de Clifford was acquitted of manslaughter by them in 1935.   We may notice a distinction in the mode of trial in these cases depending on whether Parliament was in session or not.   In either case the court was presided over by the Lord High Steward.[1]   Just as the lord's steward presided in the manorial court, so the king's steward presided over the king's tenants-in-chief. But if Parliament was in session his functions were merely those of a chairman.   The peers were judges and jury all in one, deciding both law and fact by a majority. Whereas if Parliament was out of session the Lord High Steward was the judge and tried the accused with a jury of peers whom he directed on the law and who had to give a unanimous verdict.   It will be seen, therefore, that it was only in the former case that the true "judicium parium" was preserved.

Privilege of peerage in cases of treason and felony was at long last abolished by the Criminal Justice Act, 1948, s. 30.

----

[1] This office was called out of abeyance for the purpose of a trial, and the Chancellor appointed to it.

XIV

COURTS OF SPECIAL JURISDICTION

FROM Chapter 4 onwards we have been speaking almost entirely of courts which could trace their descent back to the Curia Regis of Norman times, but though these royal courts were by far the most important tribunals in the land, we must not suppose that they had a complete monopoly of jurisdiction over all topics. Not to speak of the old local and feudal courts of which we said something in the early chapters of this book and which lived on in a somewhat decayed condition even after the close of the Middle Ages, there were a number of other courts which stood to a greater or lesser degree outside the system of royal justice. In many cases these courts (though their history is interesting enough) had little influence on the development of our legal system, but two of these "special jurisdictions," the courts of the Church and the Courts Merchant and Maritime, were of considerable general importance.[1]

A. The Ecclesiastical Courts

In the Middle Ages the Church in this country was an integral part of the Western Church. Throughout the whole of Western Europe the Church maintained a system of courts administering a law—the so-called

---

[1] Examples of other " special jurisdictions " have been the courts of the Palatinates of Durham and Chester, the Forest Courts, the Courts of the Stannaries, and the University Courts. Members of the armed forces of the Crown also become liable to special Naval, Military and Air Force Courts, known as courts martial, which derive their jurisdiction from special Acts of Parliament. This liability does not exempt them from the jurisdiction of the ordinary courts. For the constitution and jurisdiction of courts martial see Wade and Phillips : *Constitutional Law*, 7th ed. pp. 396–9.

" Canon Law "—which, though often varying in details
in the different countries, was fundamentally the same
in all.   At the head of the system stood the Papal Court
at Rome.   The Pope was the supreme legislator and
judge of the Church, and his supremacy ensured a certain
coherence throughout the elaborate structure.   It is not
easy to define exactly the limits of the jurisdiction exercised by the Church courts, for their claims were perhaps
nowhere admitted in full by the temporal power, and the
extent to which effect was given to them in practice varied
very much in different countries at different times in
their history.   Put at their highest we may perhaps say
that the claims of the Church extended to a monopoly of
jurisdiction over clergymen in all their affairs and a
jurisdiction over laymen in all matters which affected
their spiritual health or were connected with any phase
of their lives, such as marriage or death, which called for
the ministration of the Church.

Mediæval princes were not in a position to demand—
and indeed never thought of claiming—that exclusive
control over the lives of their subjects which is aimed at
by some modern states, but a complete acceptance of
the claims of an international Church was hardly com-
patible with even the modest degree of control which
they could hope to achieve.   As a result, we find that in
most European countries there was at one time or
another friction between the ecclesiastical and temporal
powers which was ended, or sought to be ended, by
legislation defining the boundaries of the two spheres
at a point which was generally substantially below the
highest claims of the Church, though considerably above
what most modern states would regard as the proper limit
of ecclesiastical influence.   In this country the most
important of such arrangements were the Constitutions of
Clarendon (1164), of which we have already said something in Chapter 3, and a statute of 1315, known as the
" Articuli cleri."   These general enactments did not,
however, suffice to settle all questions of jurisdiction

between the lay and spiritual courts, and throughout the Middle Ages we find the royal courts making frequent use of the prerogative writ of prohibition as a means of preventing the ecclesiastical courts from entertaining particular suits which the common law judges considered to be outside their competence. The issue of these writs often evoked protest from the bishops in Parliament, but in the long run the control thus exercised by the common law courts was acquiesced in.

We may perhaps divide the generally admitted jurisdiction of the ecclesiastical courts in this country in the Middle Ages into four categories : (*a*) a professional jurisdiction over clergymen and ecclesiastical affairs ; (*b*) a corrective jurisdiction over all persons in questions of faith and morals ; (*c*) a jurisdiction over questions arising out of the status of matrimony ; and (*d*) a jurisdiction over the personal property of deceased persons. We will say a few words of each before passing to describe the system of ecclesiastical courts and the changes produced by the Reformation in their position in this country.

(*a*) Civil suits to which clergymen were parties and charges of misdemeanour against clergymen were tried in the lay courts, but, as we have seen in Chapter 5, a cleric accused of felony was tried and punished by the ecclesiastical courts. Further, of course, any charge of professional misconduct brought against him would be investigated by the Church courts. We may also put under this head the jurisdiction exercised by the ecclesiastical courts over the fabric of churches and consecrated soil, and the enforcement of the payment of tithes where the title to the tithe was not in dispute. Questions of title to tithe, like questions of title to advowsons, were tried in the lay courts.

(*b*) The corrective jurisdiction exercised over clergy and laity alike was very extensive. Under it fell all offences against religion, such as heresy or blasphemy, and a large number of lesser offences of a moral or quasi-moral character, such as incontinence, swearing, drunkenness, usury and slander, some of which are now punished in the lay courts while others go altogether unpunished. The ecclesiastical courts necessarily had to rely to a large extent on private denunciations for the exercise of this branch of their jurisdiction, and this fact with the increase of the system of money payments for indulgences towards the close of the Middle Ages combined to make it extremely unpopular.

(c) Whether a marriage was valid or invalid was a matter for the Church courts, and as a natural consequence the question of the legitimacy or illegitimacy of the offspring was often decided by the canon law. In some cases, however, the common law courts refused to be bound by the rules of the canon law as to legitimacy.[1] As well as pronouncing decrees of nullity when a marriage was void, the Church courts could grant a judicial separation—a so-called divorce " a mensa et thoro "—when either spouse could show good cause for not continuing to cohabit with the other, and a decree for restitution of conjugal rights in cases of unjustified desertion. A divorce in the modern sense, i.e. a divorce " a vinculo matrimonii," by which a marriage which was valid when contracted is dissolved, was unknown to the canon law.

(d) In the Middle Ages any real property which a man held for an estate not ceasing on his death descended on his death to the appropriate heir, in accordance with rules established by the common law courts. It was not until 1540 that there was any general power of disposing of land by will, and down to the middle of the nineteenth century, the validity and construction of a will so far as it disposed of realty could only be decided in the common law courts by means of an action of ejectment brought by the devisee against the heir. Personal property, on

---

[1] E.g. the common law refused to recognise the canon law doctrine of legitimation " per subsequens matrimonium " which was at length introduced into English law by the Legitimacy Act, 1926.

the other hand, stood on quite a different footing. From early times a man could make a will of his personal property, and even if he died intestate such property did not descend to his heir at common law but was distributed amongst his next of kin. As early as the reign of Henry II the ecclesiastical courts succeeded in asserting an exclusive jurisdiction over questions as to the validity of wills of personalty and came to grant " probate " of the will to the executor appointed by the deceased and to control him in his duties. Similarly the ecclesiastical courts made good a claim to superintend the distribution of the goods of an intestate by his relatives and eventually to carry out the distribution themselves. It was found, however, that a distribution by the Church authorities themselves led to many abuses, and by a statute of 1357 the Church court was obliged to grant administration in such cases to one of the relatives of the deceased.[1]

We must now pass from the jurisdiction of the ecclesiastical courts to the courts themselves. Many ecclesiastical corporations, such as deans and chapters, had courts of their own (known as " Peculiars "), but normally the lowest ecclesiastical tribunal was the court of the archdeacon. Above the courts of the archdeaconries were the diocesan courts of the bishops, known as the " consistory " courts, which were the courts in which most important business was started, and in which probate was granted of wills of testators whose goods lay within the diocese. From the consistory courts there was an appeal to the provincial courts of the two archbishops who also had so-called " prerogative " courts for testamentary business which were much used for proving the wills of testators of substance who had goods (" bona notabilia ") in more than one diocese. At the head of the whole system stood the Papal Curia at

---

[1] In connexion with this " testamentary " jurisdiction we should note the surprising number of suits for debts, often by executors, which the ecclesiastical courts handled in the fourteenth and fifteenth centuries: see Holdsworth, vol. I (7th ed., 1956), pp. 73*–74*.

Rome. The Pope possessed not only an appellate but also an original jurisdiction, and at any stage either party might call him in to decide the suit, which he might do either by calling the parties to Rome or by delegating the hearing to papal legates, who superseded the ordinary courts. Obviously it was only in important cases that the Papal Curia would be called in, but such cases were by no means rare. The judges in the diocesan and provincial courts in England were not the bishops themselves but officials appointed by them. These judges, who were generally styled " Chancellors," [1] were clerics expert in the canon and civil laws. The procedure in cases before them was far more akin to that of the Chancery than to common law procedure. In particular, the litigation was initiated by a so-called " libel " equivalent to a bill in Chancery, the parties were liable to examination, and there was no jury.

The Reformation in the sixteenth century affected the structure of the Church in a curious and typically English fashion. On the one hand the provincial and diocesan organisation was left untouched, and in this sense the mediæval constitution of the Church of England has suffered less change than that of most of the other Churches of Western Europe. On the other hand, a profound change was effected at the top by the transfer of the legislative and judicial power of the Pope to the Crown, which exercised the former through Parliament and the Convocations of the clergy, and the latter through Royal Delegates and Commissioners. It would be beyond the scope of this book to embark on the subject of ecclesiastical legislation in this country since the sixteenth century, the parts played in it by the Crown, Parliament and the Convocations respectively, or the position of the modern Church Assembly. We

[1] The judge of the Provincial Court of Canterbury bore, and bears, the title of Dean of the Arches from the Church of St. Mary-le-Bow (Sancta Maria de Arcubus, the steeple of which was supported on arches) in which he used to hold his court.

must confine ourselves to the judicial sphere and speak first of the two new ecclesiastical courts which came into being at the Reformation—the Court of Delegates and the High Commission.

The Court of Delegates was established by a statute of 1534 to take the place of the Papal Curia as a court of appeal from the archbishops' courts.[1] The court was composed of commissioners appointed by the Crown to hear the case in question, and accordingly was differently constituted for each case. In the sixteenth century some of the commissioners were often bishops, but in the seventeenth and eighteenth centuries the custom grew up of appointing three common law judges and three "civilian" lawyers practising in Doctors' Commons to form the court. As the common law judges knew no civil or canon law and the salary of a guinea a day only tempted the more junior and inexperienced civilians to offer their services, the court came to be by no means a satisfactory one. In 1832 it was abolished, and its jurisdiction over ecclesiastical and admiralty appeals transferred to the Privy Council.

The High Commission was at first rather an administrative board than a court of law. Henry VIII and Edward VI each of them issued commissions to various persons to exercise the powers over the Church vested by the Reformation in the Crown, and Elizabeth's Act of Supremacy (1559) gave statutory recognition to the issuing of such commissions. The chief duty of the Commission was to enforce the Acts of Supremacy and Uniformity against all recusants and dissenters, whether Roman Catholic or Protestant, and gradually it came to be more and more a judicial body with a fixed procedure supplementing the activities and making good the defects of the ordinary ecclesiastical courts in much the same way as the Star Chamber made good the defects in the organisation of criminal justice. Its extreme unpopu-

---

[1] Appeals from the Court of Admiralty were heard by a similar court of royal delegates.

larity with the Puritans led to the abolition of the High
Commission in 1641, and it dragged with it to destruc-
tion the whole system of ecclesiastical courts. At the
Restoration the ordinary ecclesiastical courts and the
Court of Delegates were re-established, but the High
Commission, like the Star Chamber, had been too
detested to be revived.

Passing from the Church courts to the law administered in them we may observe that no new system of
ecclesiastical law was promulgated at the Reformation.
Such portions of the canon law as were not inconsistent
with the changed position of the Church in the country
continued in force, and together with the statutes and
canons of the English Church passed by Parliament
and the Convocations since the Reformation form the
modern English ecclesiastical law.[1] To practise or preside in the ecclesiastical courts a man required to have a
knowledge of the canon and civil law. Such knowledge
would also qualify him for practice in the Court of
Admiralty and might get him very profitable employment as a diplomat, since he would be able to negotiate
with foreigners whose laws were directly derived from
Rome with far greater success than a man trained in
the " common law " at the Inns of Court could possibly
do. The Universities of Oxford and Cambridge had
from the earliest times offered instruction in the civil
and canon law, and though the study of the latter was
discouraged after the Reformation, Henry VIII encouraged the teaching of Roman law by establishing
Regius Professors in it at both Universities. In time
the degree of Doctor of Civil Law taken at one or other
University became a condition precedent to admission
by the Archbishop of Canterbury to practise as an
advocate in the ecclesiastical and admiralty courts, and

---

[1] Of course additions made to the Canon Law of the Roman Church
since the Reformation, e.g. the decrees of the Council of Trent, form no
part of the ecclesiastical law in this country. The canons of the English
Church passed since the Reformation do not per se bind the laity.

the doctors so admitted formed themselves into a society with its headquarters at " Doctors' Commons," a group of buildings in what is now Queen Victoria Street, where the Court of Arches and the Court of Admiralty sat. In the Middle Ages the practitioners and judges in the ecclesiastical courts had been clerics, but this requirement was abandoned at the Reformation.

The Reformation had no immediate effect on the jurisdiction of the ecclesiastical courts, but after the Restoration the growth in the later seventeenth and eighteenth centuries of the principles of religious toleration led to the gradual disappearance of the corrective jurisdiction over the laity in questions of faith and morals. This jurisdiction has never been expressly abolished, and in theory a layman might still be punished " pro salute animæ " by an ecclesiastical court for heresy or immorality. In fact, of course, the jurisdiction is quite obsolete. We may notice, however, that some of the offences cognisable by the Church courts in the Middle Ages became the subject of proceedings in the ordinary courts, e.g. defamation, perjury and unnatural vice. At the beginning of the nineteenth century, therefore, the effective jurisdiction of the Church courts fell under three heads: the purely ecclesiastical jurisdiction including the discipline of the clergy, the matrimonial, and the testamentary jurisdiction. In 1857 these two latter jurisdictions were transferred to newly formed civil tribunals. But before we come to the statutes by which these changes were effected, we must say something of the history of these two jurisdictions since the Reformation.

The Church courts continued in the seventeenth and eighteenth centuries to be under the same inability as they had been in the Middle Ages to grant divorces " a vinculo matrimonii," but after the Restoration Parliament assumed a jurisdiction to dissolve the " vinculum matrimonii " by a private Act. The first instance was the Act obtained by Lord de Roos in 1669, and his example was followed by a considerable number of wealthy persons in the following two centuries. It must not be supposed, however, that such bills were passed on slender grounds or as a matter of course. As a condition precedent to introducing the Bill in Parliament it was necessary for the promoter both to have obtained a judicial separation in the ecclesiastical courts and also to have brought a common law action for " criminal conversation " against the adulterer.[1] Obviously the whole proceeding was extremely expensive and made " divorce " a luxury for the very rich. In 1857 the Matrimonial Causes Act, which established a new civil court known as the Divorce Court, to which was transferred the old jurisdiction of the ecclesiastical courts in matrimonial matters, and which was given a new power to pronounce a divorce " a vinculo matrimonii " for the grounds on which Parliament would have passed a divorce Act. At the same time the common law action for criminal conversation was abolished and the new court was given power to award damages against the corespondent. The judges of the Divorce Court (as originally established) were the Lord Chancellor, the Chief Justice and Senior Puisne of each common law court and the judge of the newly formed Probate Court, of which we shall say something in the next paragraph. Normally the latter judge sat alone, but in some cases there was an appeal to a full court consisting of three judges. But despite the creation of a Divorce Court the number of divorces in the late nineteenth and earlier twentieth centuries remained comparatively small. It was only after the first World War that they began to grow apace.

[1] The first divorce Act passed at the instance of an injured wife was passed in 1801. A woman could not bring an action for " criminal conversation," but she had to prove not merely adultery on the part of her husband but cruelty or some aggravating circumstance, such as incest, as well. It was not until the Matrimonial Causes Act, 1923, that the sexes were put on a footing of equality as to grounds for divorce.

We have already pointed out in speaking of the work of the Court of Chancery that such jurisdiction over the administration of the estates of deceased persons or the construction of wills of personalty as had been possessed by the Church courts in the Middle Ages passed to the Chancery in the seventeenth and eighteenth centuries. The ecclesiastical courts, however, still pronounced upon the validity of wills of personal property and made grants of probate or of letters of administration. In 1857 the Court of Probate Act gave this jurisdiction to a newly formed Probate Court, from which an appeal lay to the House of Lords, and provided that the decision of the court as to the validity of a will whether of personalty or realty should be binding on all jurisdictions. The two Acts of 1857 meant the end of Doctors' Commons. A common lawyer, Sir Cresswell Cresswell, was made the first judge of the Probate and Divorce Courts, and the courts themselves, together with the Court of Admiralty, moved to Westminster Hall. The existing doctors and proctors continued to practise in the new courts, but the society itself was dissolved. In 1875 the Probate, Divorce and Admiralty Courts were incorporated in the new Supreme Court of Judicature.[1]

Since 1857, therefore, the ecclesiastical courts have been in effect professional courts entrusted with the task of enforcing the discipline of the clergy in matters of conduct and doctrine, maintaining the order established by law in the public worship of the Church and exercising control over the fabric of churches and over churchyards. It must not be supposed, however, that the Church of England and its courts are in contemplation of law on the same footing as voluntary religious associations such as the Roman Catholics. Such bodies, some of which maintain domestic tribunals for the regulation of their internal affairs, are legally on the same footing as companies or clubs formed for secular purposes, and the trusts on which their property is held, and the

[1] See p. 288, below.

rights *inter se* of the members of the sect may have in case of dispute to be determined by the civil courts. The constitution and law of the Established Church, on the other hand, are part of the public law of the country, of which the ordinary courts take judicial notice, and the courts of the Church have the status of public courts of limited but, within their own sphere, exclusive jurisdiction.

The system of ecclesiastical courts which existed for more than a century after 1857 comprised consistory courts in each diocese from which appeal lay to the provincial courts of Canterbury and York ; at the head of the system stood the Judicial Committee of the Privy Council. The bishop or archbishop appointed the judges of the consistory or provincial courts, and the Privy Council was assisted by bishops acting as assessors. The three main heads of jurisdiction in these courts were the discipline of clergy, the regulation of public worship and the hearing of applications for " faculties " to sanction some addition to, alteration in, or removal from a church or churchyard. Some of this jurisdiction can well be, and was, exercised by laymen, but they are not always well fitted to deal with questions involving doctrine, ritual or ceremonial. Growing discontent with the system, and especially with the primacy of the Privy Council, led to the Ecclesiastical Jurisdiction Measure of 1963 which radically altered the position. Only a bare outline can be given here.

Consistory courts have jurisdiction principally in faculty cases and over offences by priests and deacons not involving doctrine, ritual or ceremonial. Appeal from these courts lies to provincial courts (the Court of the Arches in Canterbury and the Chancery Court in York) but in faculty cases only where doctrine, ritual or ceremonial is not involved. The sole jurisdiction of the Privy Council is to hear appeals from the two provincial courts in the last-named type of faculty case.

The above hierarchy has, with the exception of first instance jurisdiction over faculty cases, no power to deal with cases involving doctrine, ritual or ceremonial. For such cases a new Court of Ecclesiastical Causes Reserved exists with first instance jurisdiction over offences by archbishops, bishops, priests and deacons involving doctrine, ritual or ceremonial ; the Court also has appellate jurisdiction from consistory courts in faculty cases involving doctrine, ritual or ceremonial. The judges are two communicants who hold or have held high judicial office and three persons who are or have been diocesan bishops.   From this Court an appeal lies to a Commission of Review appointed *ad hoc* by the Crown and consisting of three communicant Lords of Appeal and two of the bishops who have seats in the House of Lords.   A Commission of Review can also be appointed to hear appeals in cases of offences by archbishops or bishops not involving doctrine, ritual or ceremonial, such cases being heard at first instance by a commission of the appropriate Upper House of Convocation.

The break with the past is emphasised by a provision that the Court of Ecclesiastical Causes Reserved and a Commission of Review shall not be bound by any decision of the Judicial Committee of the Privy Council in relation to any matters of doctrine, ritual or ceremonial.   Moreover, to ensure that such cases are as far as possible removed from the atmosphere of criminal proceedings, it is provided that where an accused is found guilty of an offence involving matter of doctrine, ritual or ceremonial, no censure more severe than monition (*i.e.* an order to do or refrain from doing a specified act) shall be imposed unless the Court is satisfied that the accused has already been admonished on a previous occasion in respect of another offence of the same or substantially the same nature.

B. The Courts Merchant and Maritime

In the Middle Ages the ordinary Englishman lived on the land and filled one or other of the rungs on the feudal ladder which stretched upwards from the great mass of " villeins " to the small group of " tenants-in-chief." It was therefore to the needs of the landowner that the common law was directed. What he chiefly required of it was that it should protect him from violence and secure him in possession of his land holding, and consequently we find that the bulk of the mediæval common law is made up of the criminal law and the land law. The common law of contracts, before the development of the action of assumpsit in the fifteenth and sixteenth century, was rudimentary by comparison with the intricate technicalities of the real actions designed to meet any and every variety of " disseisin " of a freehold interest in land.

But there were classes in the community which stood to some extent outside the ordinary social system. We have already spoken of the Church and its courts. As great landowners the bishops and cathedral chapters were, of course, involved in the feudal system and with the common law of real property, but in many important respects the lives of the clergy were regulated by the law of the Church. So it was, too, with the merchant. As a landowner, if he was one, he was subject to the common law, and if he suffered or was guilty of illegal violence, the ordinary criminal law would apply to his case as well as to any one else's ; but in his business transactions, the buying and selling of commodities, he availed himself of a law and of courts of his own. Before we pass to discuss this law (the so-called " Law Merchant ") we may observe that the wealthier merchants in this country in the Middle Ages were often foreigners, Italians or Flemings, for commercially England was a backward country compared with the mercantile communities of Italy and the Low Countries.[1] The smaller transactions of inland trade were indeed often in the hands of Englishmen, but the export and import trade (and England had

[1] A more optimistic view of English commerce and an interesting account of the work of borough, fair and staple courts is given by C. H. S. Fifoot, *History and Sources of the Common Law*, pp. 289–98.

a large foreign trade even at an early date) was largely controlled by foreigners. This fact accentuated the separation between the commercial and the common law, for it meant that commercial disputes might lead to diplomatic complications with which the Royal Council would not allow the ordinary courts to deal. Further, it led to a close connection between maritime law and commercial law, and to the dependence of both on foreign customs of an international character.

As a starting point in our enquiry into the character of the law merchant and its courts in the Middle Ages, we may call attention to a difference in the organisation of commerce in those days and its organisation to-day. Nowadays, buying and selling, lending and borrowing, go on day in and day out all over the country. In the Middle Ages, on the other hand, a considerable part of such business was carried on only in special places and at special times, that is to say, in markets and fairs held at intervals. Sometimes such fairs were held in boroughs which had a certain permanent commercial importance apart from the occasional concourse of traders attracted by the fair, but some of the largest of them—the fair of St. Ives, in Huntingdonshire, for instance—were held in places which were mere villages at normal times. The right to hold such a market or fair and to charge " tolls " on the sales effected in it was a valuable proprietary right —a franchise—which was the subject of a grant from the king. Many borough charters conferred this franchise on the corporation of the borough, but sometimes other persons or corporations enjoyed it. Thus, the Abbot of Ramsey took the profits of the fair at St. Ives.

In connection with a market or fair there was normally a special court held for the settling of disputes arising between those resorting to it. Many boroughs, of course, possessed under their charters a right to hold courts of their own exercising a civil [1] jurisdiction over the bur-

---

[1] See p. 278, below. Similarly, of course, many boroughs had their own commission of the peace, see p. 196, above.

gesses to the exclusion of the sheriff's courts, and in such cases the court of the fair or market would be only a special session of the local borough court,[1] but in other cases the court would spring into existence for the duration of the fair and then remain in abeyance until fair-time came round again. These market courts were private courts, the profits of which went to the owner of the franchise, and they were known as courts of " pie-powder " or " dusty feet." Coke says that this was because justice was administered in them as speedily as the dust could fall from the feet of the litigants, but some modern authorities prefer to explain it as a reference to the dust on the clothes and boots of the itinerant merchants who used the court.

The business coming before " pie-powder " courts related mainly to internal trade. Foreign trade in the Middle Ages was largely regulated by what was known as the " staple " system. Various statutes—notably one passed in 1353—named certain towns (known as the " staple " towns) as the only places in which dealings in some of the most important objects of export, such as wool and tin, could take place. In every " staple " town there was a court established with exclusive jurisdiction over the merchants who came there in all cases save those involving title to land or felony, and as many of the litigants would normally be aliens it was provided that their cases should be tried by a jury partly composed of foreigners. General control over the system was exercised not by the common law courts but by the Royal Council.

In their procedure and the law which they administered, the " pie-powder " courts and the courts of the staple were not governed by the principles of the common law but rather by the accepted customs of merchants prevailing over a large part of Western Europe. The common law courts in this period accepted the position that this " law merchant " was a system independent of their own and made no serious attempt to claim to administer

[1] See Veale, *Journal of Society of Public Teachers of Law* (1936), p. 20.

it. Indeed, the rules as to " venue " which made it necessary for the cause of every action in a common law case to be " laid " in one or other English county presented an obvious difficulty in the way of bringing before the common law courts, actions founded on transactions entered into abroad, and many of the more important " law merchant " cases might easily contain a " foreign " element. In procedure the courts merchant were no doubt far less technical than the common law courts. The laws of evidence were less strict and justice was administered far more quickly. Further, the rules of the law merchant which were designed to facilitate mercantile transactions were in many cases widely different from those of the common law. To take the most famous example of this divergence : by the rules of the common law a contract by A to pay money to B was personal to them, so that its benefit could not be made to attach to any one other than B, while the law merchant recognised that a document executed by A might if properly framed create an obligation enforceable against him by anyone who was from time to time in possession of it. A negotiable instrument payable to bearer was known in the courts merchant several centuries before it was recognised by the common law.

If the law merchant was " international " in character the maritime law was naturally much more so. Seafaring men of all nations necessarily mingle together in the course of their profession, and inevitably a certain uniformity in the rules observed in it must grow up. Thus at a very early date there appears to have been a sort of " common law " of the sea in the Mediterranean which came to be embodied in the maritime code—the Consolato del mare—of the great port of Barcelona. The origin of our maritime law is to be found in the sea-laws promulgated by Eleanor of Aquitaine at the castle on the isle of Oleron in the Bay of Biscay, in the late twelfth century. If one remembers that the Angevin kings were rulers of Guienne and that there was a lively trade—especially in wine—between Bordeaux and this country it is not surprising that the " judgments of Oleron" were adopted in most of the English ports. They were, for instance, the foundation of the famous " Red Book " of Bristol, and later they came to be the basis of our maritime law as it was administered by the Court of Admiralty.

But in the Middle Ages there was yet no central court exercising a general jurisdiction over maritime cases. The chief ports—above all, of course, Bristol and the " Cinque Ports "—had their own maritime courts in which speedy justice was administered in cases of collision, salvage, charterparties, and the like. Indeed, these local maritime courts sometimes exercised a criminal jurisdiction ; for it was the general view that the ordinary criminal assizes had no jurisdiction over crimes committed on the high seas out of the bounds of any English county, and consequently out of the knowledge of an English jury. Generally, therefore, such cases had to be tried in the maritime courts according to the maritime law, and not by the common law with its strict rules of evidence and its jury system.

By the end of the Middle Ages we find that the system by which the law merchant and maritime was administered in a number of local courts—courts of pie-powder, courts of the staple, and local maritime courts—was beginning to crumble before encroachment from two sides : on the one side from the common law and on the other from the Court of Admiralty. It would be beyond the scope of this book to trace the decline of these local courts in any detail. Suffice it to say that by the nineteenth century the courts of the fair and the market were quite obsolete, while the court of the Lord Warden of the Cinque Ports was the only local maritime court with any real jurisdiction. We must now turn to consider how their work was absorbed by the common law and Admiralty courts, and first to say something of the origin of this latter tribunal.

The use of the word " admiral " in this country to designate the commander of a fleet dates from about 1300, but it was not until the middle of the fourteenth century that the various " admirals " began to be entrusted with any jurisdiction in maritime matters beyond the enforcement of discipline in their fleets. At first, this jurisdiction seems to have been largely criminal. Crimes—piracy, murder, robbery and the like committed at sea—which previously had either been dealt with in the local maritime courts or occasionally under special commissions by the judges of oyer and terminer, came regularly to be tried by the admirals in their courts according to the law maritime, and they began to claim a civil jurisdiction as well in maritime matters. Complaints of their encroachment began to be heard both from the local maritime courts and from the ordinary common law tribunals, so that in 1389 and 1391 statutes were passed with the purpose of defining the admirals' jurisdiction. That of 1391, for instance, provided that " of all manner of contracts pleas and quarrels and all things rising within the bodies of the counties as well by land as by water and also of wreck of the sea the Admirals' court shall have no manner of cognisance power or jurisdiction " but " of the death of a man and of mayhem done in great ships being and hovering in the main stream of great rivers only beneath the bridges of the same rivers nigh to the sea and in none other places of the same rivers the Admiral shall have cognisance." Soon after this date it became customary in place of several admirals to appoint one " Lord High Admiral " of England, and from the early fifteenth century therefore we can begin to talk of a single Court of Admiralty. The Admiral himself was often an important political figure with no particular knowledge of maritime law, and the work of his court was generally done by his deputy, who came to be known as the judge of the Court of Admiralty. The earliest extant patent appointing such a judge is dated 1482.

In the fifteenth century the jealousy of Parliament and

the disturbed state of the country seem to have combined
to prevent any great extension of the Admiralty jurisdiction beyond the bounds admitted in the fourteenth, but
during the Tudor Period the court increased very greatly
in importance and became almost as dangerous a rival of
the common law courts as were the courts of Chancery
and Star Chamber.   The Admiral, like the Chancellor,
was normally an important member of the Council, and
his court naturally benefited from its close connection
with that body in the period when the Council was so
powerful.   It was, however, only as a court of civil jurisdiction that the Admiralty was a rival of the common law
courts, for a statute of 1536 brought the exercise of its
criminal jurisdiction under the control of common
lawyers.   The procedure of the " civil " law, which was
in use in the Court of Admiralty, required either that the
accused should confess his crime or that it should be
proved against him by witnesses.   Confessions were
hard to extract without torture, and witnesses, even supposing there to have been any, were generally seamen
who " because of their often voyages and passages in the
seas depart without long tarrying."   It was decided
therefore to replace the civil law procedure by trial by
jury, which would allow the accused to be convicted on
circumstantial evidence without torture and accordingly
the statute in question enacted that crimes committed
within the Admirals' jurisdiction should be enquired into
and tried by royal commissioners as if the offence had
been committed on land.   The commissioners under the
Act came invariably to include judges of the common law
courts as well as the judge of the Court of Admiralty, so
that in effect there came to be no distinction in the mode
of trial of crimes committed on the high seas and crimes
committed on land.   At length, in the early nineteenth
century, the necessity for special commissions under the
Act of 1536 was itself abolished.   In 1834 the Central
Criminal Court [1] was given the jurisdiction of the com-

[1] See p. 347, below.

missioners, and in 1844 the jurisdiction was extended to all commissioners of oyer and terminer.

But if the criminal jurisdiction of the Court of Admiralty was brought under the ægis of the common law, its civil jurisdiction remained quite independent of it and threatened to embrace all commercial litigation of importance. Starting from cases the cause of action in which arose abroad or on the high seas and which in consequence were outside the jurisdiction of the common law courts, the Court of Admiralty began in the sixteenth century to take cognisance of commercial causes, arising within England, which had any relation to shipping or foreign trade. It was not surprising that this should be so. The methods and customs of English commerce were based on foreign models, and the practitioners in the Court of Admiralty, who studied the civil law and the continental writers on the law merchant, were far better equipped to deal with commercial cases than the common lawyers. Insurance policies, negotiable instruments, and bills of lading were of everyday occurrence in the Court of Admiralty, while they were still largely unknown in the common law courts. It is in the sixteenth century that we begin to know something of the organisation of the court. We have its records from 1524 onwards, and we know that at that time the court sat at Orton Key near London Bridge. Later it moved to " Doctors' Commons " and established a close connection with the ecclesiastical courts. The doctors of civil law practised alike in both tribunals ; sometimes the same person was both Dean of the Arches and Judge of the Court of Admiralty ; and the Court of Delegates was a court of appeal in admiralty as well as in ecclesiastical cases.[1]

But while the Court of Admiralty was absorbing the jurisdiction of the local maritime courts and building up a general jurisdiction in commercial matters, especially in those which involved some " foreign element," the common law courts were becoming more fit to entertain com-

---

[1] For Doctors' Commons, see p. 235, above.

mercial cases. In the action of assumpsit which (as we saw) was rapidly developed in the later fifteenth and early sixteenth centuries, the common law had a general contractual action of great flexibility, and in the action of trover it had an action by which all cases of title to goods could readily be tried. Gradually much of the business which in the Middle Ages had been transacted in the courts of the fairs and the staple, or in the borough courts, came to flow into the common law courts, and as they became more used to commercial business the common lawyers came to eye with jealousy the commercial jurisdiction of the Court of Admiralty. The rules as to venue formed a difficult obstacle in the way of the common law courts entertaining actions in respect of transactions which took place abroad, but in the sixteenth century a way was discovered of circumventing this difficulty. Already as early as the fourteenth century a distinction had grown up between " local " and " transitory " actions, *i.e.* between those in which the facts relied on by the plaintiff were essentially connected with a particular locality, as, for instance, in a case of trespass to land, and those in which the locality of the event was immaterial. In local actions the plaintiff had to lay the venue in the proper county, while in the case of transitory actions he might lay it in any county he pleased. In the sixteenth century it occurred to ingenious pleaders that this possibility of laying the venue in transitory actions in a county other than the county in which the cause of action arose offered a ready means of bringing in the common law courts actions which were based on acts which took place out of the jurisdiction altogether. If one was allowed to say without contradiction that an act took place in a county in which it did not take place, why should one not say that the place in which it happened was situated in a county in which it was not situated ? So if a contract was made in Bordeaux the pleader would allege boldly that it was made " in Bordeaux to wit in the parish of St. Mary-le-Bow in the Ward of Cheap," and if the action was not in its nature a local action the court would not allow the defendant to take exception to this false geography. It must, of course, be remembered that there was at this time, and indeed down to 1852, no possibility of serving the writ in any action out of the jurisdiction. If the defendant could not be served in England the device of stating that the contract had been made, or the tort in question committed, within the jurisdiction was largely useless. But even with this limitation it gave the common law courts a powerful weapon in the struggle which soon broke out between them and the Admiralty.

We have seen that in the later part of the sixteenth century the common law courts were becoming uneasy at the growing jurisdiction of the Chancery and the Star Chamber, but that these two courts were too powerful to be directly attacked. With regard, however, to the Court of Admiralty, the common law courts stood in a stronger position, for they had both plausible grounds for contending that it was usurping a jurisdiction which did not belong to it and, what was more important, a weapon with which to deprive it of what it was usurping. The Statutes of Richard II, which we have mentioned, appeared definitely to exclude from the Admiralty jurisdiction any matter arising within the borders of an English county and were interpreted by the common lawyers as confining it to matters arising on the high seas —" super altum mare." Torts committed at sea—such as collisions of ships—and contracts made and to be performed at sea, were on this view the proper subjects of admiralty suits, but not so contracts entered into or to be performed abroad. The weapon which the common law courts used to enforce this doctrine was the prerogative writ of prohibition by which the royal court could forbid an inferior court from proceeding with any given case on the ground that it lay outside its jurisdiction. The Court of Admiralty, according to Sir Edward Coke, was an inferior court within the scope of the

writ of prohibition, like the feudal or communal courts
or the ecclesiastical courts. As a badge of its inferiority
he alleged that it was not a " court of record," and had
in consequence (according to Coke) no power to fine or
imprison. In fact, of course, neither the Chancery nor
the Star Chamber was a court of record in the narrow sense
which Coke gave to this word, but they freely sent
men to prison, and even Coke would not have dared to
issue a prohibition against them.[1] The truth is that the
Admiralty was weaker than the Chancery or the Star
Chamber, and that the common law courts could venture to attack it when they could not attack their stronger
rivals.

But the Court of Admiralty was not prepared to
acquiesce tamely in the issue of prohibitions by the
common law courts. Again and again the judges of the
court complained to the Crown, and on several occasions
attempts were made to arrive at some compromise on the
question of the Admiralty's jurisdiction. Thus in 1632
it was agreed that the Admiralty should have at least a
concurrent jurisdiction in cases of contracts made or
torts committed both on and beyond the seas, in suits on
charter-parties for voyages to be made beyond the seas
even though the charter-party was itself made within the
realm, and in suits arising out of contracts for the construction, repair and victualling of ships even though
made within the realm. But the agreement was not
acted on for long, for the victory of the Parliament in
the Civil War was disastrous to the Court of Admiralty,
which was closely allied with the Council and the Star
Chamber. After the Restoration neither the eloquence
of Sir Leoline Jenkins, the judge of the court, nor the
prayers of the merchants of London, who were well aware
how much more efficiently their business was handled
in the Admiralty than it would be in Westminster Hall,

[1] In the struggle over injunctions Coke proceeded against the
individuals who applied for them. He did not venture to prohibit the
Chancery from hearing the applications, see p. 125, above.

availed to induce Parliament to pass a Bill settling the jurisdiction of the court on the lines of the agreement of 1632, and in the later seventeenth and early eighteenth centuries its civil jurisdiction was practically confined to torts committed and contracts made and to be performed on the high seas and suits for mariners' wages. Charter-parties, bills of lading, policies of marine insurance and commercial contracts entered into abroad all fell to the share of the common law courts.

The victory of the common law courts was by no means a blessing for the merchant litigants of the seventeenth century, for the common lawyers were for the most part profoundly ignorant of commercial practice. Pepys remarks on a case on a policy of marine insurance which he heard argued in the Court of King's Bench that " to hear how the counsel and judge would speak as to the terms necessary in the matter would make one laugh." Every mercantile usage which differed from the common law rules had to be specially pleaded as a mercantile custom and proved as such by the evidence of merchants to the satisfaction of the jury, and since the jury were merely directed by the judge to find a general verdict for or against the plaintiff on the evidence given, no general principles emerged from individual cases, but the same custom tended to be proved again and again in successive cases. In consequence of the inefficiency and expense of the common law courts the custom of submitting mercantile disputes to arbitration which had always prevailed among members of the trade guilds *inter se*,[1] became general, and the first Arbitration Act (1698) may be regarded as a mark of this tendency. But already by this date a new attitude to commercial problems is evident in the work of Sir John Holt who was Chief Justice of the King's Bench from 1689 to 1710 : he was prepared to accept evidence of mercantile custom and he

---

[1] It was almost common form for the regulations of the London Guilds to provide for internal arbitration in disputes between members by " probi homines " of the Guild.

consulted merchants in many cases.[1] Finally, in Lord Mansfield (C.J.K.B. from 1756 to 1788), Westminster Hall saw a judge who could look beyond the particular to the general and lay down principles of commercial law. Mansfield, unlike his predecessors on the bench, had studied the works of foreign jurists, in which alone at that time the principles on which our commercial customs were ultimately based could be found. He would, however, have been unable to put his knowledge to the best use if he had allowed the cases which came before him to be decided by general verdicts given by ignorant jurymen. He took pains to see that the jury in important commercial cases tried before him at the Guildhall should be composed of commercial men of experience. Moreover, instead, as had been the practice in the past, of leaving any mercantile question to be determined by a general verdict of the jury according to their own notions of what was fair, with the result that the decision of the case constituted no precedent, he tried as often as possible to secure that they should be asked to give a special verdict on specific questions put to them. Then on the facts so found Mansfield himself could pronounce a judgment laying down or illustrating principles of commercial law, which constituted a precedent in all future cases, and where the case turned on a custom of merchants established that custom as part of the common law, which did not have to be alleged and proved again in subsequent cases. It would be hard to exaggerate the value of the services rendered by Lord Mansfield to this branch of the law. In conclusion we may say, in the words of Lord Birkenhead, that " Coke captured the law merchant for the common law ; Holt retained it ; Mansfield formally incorporated it into our system."

[1] For Holt's career see Plucknett, *A Concise History of the Common Law* (5th ed.), pp. 245–8 : for the view that Holt was responsible for some of the developments traditionally associated with Lord Mansfield see J. M. Holden in 67 *L.Q.R.* 230, where he discusses bills of exchange.

Before we bring this chapter to an end we must say something of the later history of the Court of Admiralty. In 1832 the hearing of Admiralty appeals was transferred from the Court of Delegates to the Privy Council and in the next thirty years the court recovered something of the position which it had lost in the seventeenth century; in particular it gained the status of a court of record [1] and was given jurisdiction in cases of salvage and of the building, equipping and repairing of ships. When Doctors' Commons was dissolved after the transference of the matrimonial and testamentary jurisdiction of the ecclesiastical courts to the new Divorce and Probate Courts, the Court of Admiralty moved to Westminster Hall, where it was accommodated in the " Cock-loft." In 1875 it came to form a branch of the Probate, Divorce and Admiralty Division of the new High Court of Justice, and the various heads of its jurisdiction are defined in the Judicature Act.[2]   The most important branch of it consists of cases of collision at sea.   Since 1868 certain of the county courts have had a limited admiralty jurisdiction which generally does not exceed £1,000.   When, as is now (1970) proposed, the Probate, Divorce, and Admiralty Division is abolished the Admiralty work will be transferred to the Queen's Bench Division and dealt with together with the commercial work.

But as well as the ordinary, or " instance," jurisdiction of the court of which we have spoken hitherto, the admiralty judge exercised a " prize " jurisdiction in time of war which became of great importance during the wars with France at the end of the eighteenth and the beginning of the nineteenth centuries.   When, in the course of a war between maritime nations, ships or goods are captured at sea by the ships of war of one of the belligerent powers the question may easily arise, especially in the case of ships or goods belonging to neutrals— whether according to the usage of civilised nations the ships or goods ought in the circumstances of the par-

[1] See p. 86, above.   [2] Judicature Act, 1925, s. 22.

ticular capture to be condemned as prize and forfeited to the captors, or released to their owners. For the solution of such questions each belligerent power sets up a " Prize Court," and in England the commission to hear such cases was habitually issued to the Admiral from early times, but before the Napoleonic wars there was very little prize law settled and established by the decisions of the court.   Prize law, as we have said, is (in theory at least) an international rather than a national law, and in principle the same law ought to be applied by the prize courts of all nations.   But obviously the practice of the greater maritime powers must play a great part in the formation of any universally accepted body of prize law, and at the time of the Napoleonic wars England was fortunate in possessing in Lord Stowell, the brother of Lord Eldon, an Admiralty judge of exceptional learning and ability who, like Lord Mansfield in another sphere, founded his judgments on principles and gave us what no other country possessed, a body of prize law based not on theory but on decided cases.   Lord Stowell had worthy successors in Dr. Lushington, who was the Admiralty judge during the Crimean War, and later in Sir Samuel Evans, the President of the Probate, Divorce and Admiralty Division during the War of 1914–18, who applied the decisions of his predecessors to the problems arising out of the blockade of Germany. From the decisions of the prize court there is—and always has been—an appeal to the Privy Council.

XV

THE SUPERIOR COURTS OF LAW AND EQUITY 1825–1875

WE have now brought our account of the courts of common law and equity down to the beginning of the nineteenth century, that is to say, to the threshold of the period of reform, in which the labours of Jeremy Bentham and his school bore fruit in legislation which affected most of our institutions. Legal reform began as early as the 1820's, but it was, of course, immensely accelerated by the Reform Act of 1832. In company with the Church, the municipal corporations, the Universities, and much else besides, the legal system of the country became in the half century from 1825 to 1875 the subject of commissions of enquiry, reports and legislation, and underwent in that period more visible change than it had known in the past two hundred years. After 1875 there followed half a century of relative quiescence, but in recent years, as we shall see later, reform has begun to rear its head once more. Before we pass to the details of the earlier changes it will be as well to say something in general of their historical background.

The law and procedure in the courts of common law and equity at the end of the eighteenth century was for the most part the product of centuries of judicial decision and experiment. Parliament had never made any attempt to deal comprehensively with the subject of the law or its administration. Occasionally an isolated statute was passed, the Statutes of Uses and Frauds, for instance, in the sphere of substantive law, and the Statutes of Jeofails in that of procedure ; but, on the whole, it was left to the judges and practitioners to adapt what they found to the needs of their generation. It is important to bear in mind the limitations incident to such a course of development. A legislator has a free hand. He can fashion his new house as he chooses. But a judge has not a free hand. He is confined to the existing materials, and if he is to achieve any progress he may often have to make them serve purposes for which they were never intended. Every such expedient or fiction adds to the complexity and artificiality of the whole, and the inelegance remains long after men have forgotten why it was necessary. Fines and Recoveries,[1] John Doe and Richard Roe, and the Bill of Middlesex were all three of them clever devices for achieving desirable ends which in the absence of legislation could not be attained by direct means, but by the nineteenth century men took it for granted that entails could be barred, that ejectment could be brought by the tenant of the freehold, and that the King's Bench should have a concurrent jurisdiction with the Common Pleas, and only wondered why such simple matters were involved in so tortuous and expensive a procedure. Nowadays, of course, the necessity of progressing by way of fiction has largely disappeared, for Parliament is usually prepared to give legislative sanction to desirable changes in the law and has given the judges very wide statutory powers of making changes in procedure.

By the end of the eighteenth century, however, the limits of possible development on a large scale by the judges alone without the aid of Parliament had already been reached. Lord Mansfield had indeed incorporated the law merchant in the common law, but many of his innovations in other spheres were not accepted by his successors, and opposition to his attempt to give recognition to equitable rights in common law courts was at least partly based on the sound feeling that a fundamental question such as the relation of law to equity could not be solved without far-going changes, particularly in the

[1] Fines and Recoveries were fictitious actions in the Court of Common Pleas used for the purpose of barring estates tail and alienating the lands of a married woman. For details see Holdsworth, vol. III (2nd ed.), pp. 111-20.

common law rules of evidence, such as no judge, however eminent, could possibly effect himself. Lord Mansfield really lived two centuries too late. By his day only Parliament could bring about sweeping reforms. In fact, of course, it was not until nearly fifty years after Lord Mansfield's retirement that Parliament began to address itself to the reform of the legal system, and nearly fifty years more elapsed before the Judicature Acts were passed, but this delay was to some extent the result of external events. The French Revolution made a far-reaching reform of any English institution temporarily impossible, for it drove moderate reformers, such as Mr. Pitt himself, into the arms of the extreme Tories, and it placed all ardent reformers under the suspicion of aiming at the subversion of Church and State. Reform was accordingly condemned to wait for longer than might otherwise have been the case, but in its years of opposition it found a spiritual leader and a coherent doctrine.

Jeremy Bentham (1748–1832), after an education at Westminster and Queen's College, Oxford, was called to the Bar by Lincoln's Inn in 1769. His father was a solicitor with a considerable practice, and accordingly young Jeremy " found a cause or two at nurse for him." These—if he is to be believed—" he did his best to put to death " by inducing the parties to settle, and after a few years he retired from the Bar to live on his private means and devote himself to the critical study of our institutions. The prevailing attitude of educated men of that day to the English constitution and legal system was one of considerable complacency, which receives its classical expression in Blackstone's *Commentaries on the Laws of England*, first published in 1765. Blackstone was indeed by no means as blind to the defects of the existing state of the law as those who have not read him are apt to suppose, but he was filled with a deep reverence for a system which had its roots so far back in our history and under which England had maintained her freedom and grown great in the world. The defects which he admitted he tended to regard as caused by deviations from the wisdom of our ancestors which a little pruning would remove, and he would certainly have rejected the idea that any far-reaching reconstruction was called for. This attitude was wholly antipathetic to Bentham, whose mind was of a strictly logical and mathematical cast, viewing everything as it was, without regard to its antecedents. He heard Blackstone's lectures as an undergraduate at Oxford and afterwards claimed that even then he detected the fallacies on which the judge's praises of the English constitution were based. His first published work, *A Fragment on Government* (1776), was a very able criticism of Blackstone, which almost at once gained its author a name in the world, and in the course of the next fifty years he poured out a flood of literature which formed the armoury of legal, political and social reformers throughout Europe. " Toujours pillé," said Talleyrand, " il est toujours riche." [1]

The test to which Bentham subjected every institution or rule was its utility as a means of conducing to " the greatest happiness of the greatest number," and if it failed in the test it stood condemned, however venerable. He believed that men were always actuated by motives of self interest, the force of which could be more or less exactly calculated, and apparently, also, that there was no divergence between the particular interest of each individual and the general interests of society. It may seem to us to-day that he over-simplified the problems of government, and certainly some of the methods which he advocated for improving the condition of humanity were curious enough.[2] But, when all that can be said against

[1] See Leslie Stephen : *The English Utilitarians*, vol. I, p. 319, for a list of his works.

[2] Thus he anticipated that immense benefits would accrue to society from the erection of a species of penitentiary which he called the " panopticon," and described as " a mill to grind rogues honest and idle men industrious." The inmates, he thought, would labour with enthusiasm in separate cells under the supervision of a single warder stationed at a central post of vantage from which he could observe them all.

Benthamism and its founder has been said, it remains true that the value of the service which they have rendered to legal and social science can hardly be overestimated. As a principle of ethics the utilitarian theory has considerable limitations, but as a common sense principle of legislation it is far less open to objection, and there was a great deal in the English legal system at the time which could not stand the scrutiny of common sense for a moment. Besides the advantages of a private income which enabled him to devote himself entirely to his writings, and of a long life which gave him time to enforce the same lesson again and again, Bentham had several unusual merits as a law reformer. He was entirely free from professional or class prejudice ; he was well acquainted with the system which he was criticising ; and he had a great inventive faculty which enabled him to suggest remedies as well as to point out abuses. He took no active part in politics himself, but he trained up a school of disciples who formed the core of the radical wing of the Whig party, and just at the moment of his death his life's work began to bear its fruit. The whole course of English legislation for thirty years after 1830 was determined by the ideas which he had popularised, and affords a notable illustration of the truth that a man may live his life in his study and yet influence the course of affairs as powerfully as the greatest men of action.

Here we can only mention two of those who sought to implement Bentham's teaching—Sir Samuel Romilly and Henry Brougham, first Lord Brougham and Vaux. Romilly (1757–1818) was a leader of the Chancery Bar, but the branch of law to the reform of which he devoted himself was the criminal law.[1] In 1800 there were some 160 capital crimes and only about one in eight of the death sentences passed was executed. Year after year Romilly introduced Bills in Parliament to remedy this state of affairs by abolishing the death penalty for crimes in respect of which it was in practice almost always com-

[1] See the *Life of Romilly*, by Patrick Medd (Collins, 1968).

muted, and year after year his Bills (with a very few exceptions) were thrown out by the opposition of Lords Eldon and Ellenborough.   He died in 1818 without seeing the result of his labours, but within ten years of his death Sir Robert Peel began to give effect to his ideas, and within twenty years of it the English criminal law had been transformed.

Henry Brougham (1778–1868) was a leading advocate in the common law courts in the early years of the nineteenth century, and one of the greatest parliamentary orators of his age.   In 1828 he delivered to " a thin and exhausted House of Commons " a six-hour speech on law reform, in which he passed in review the organisation and procedure of most of the existing courts of justice, pointed out the deficiencies in them, and made suggestions for their reform.   Largely as a result of his efforts several " commissions of enquiry " into various branches of the law were appointed, and, on the Whig victory in 1830, he became Lord Chancellor.   His unbounded energy which led him to interfere, even behind the backs of his colleagues, with every department of government, and the self-assurance which rendered him impervious to any rebuke, made him an impossible Cabinet Minister, and after 1834 he never held office again ; but through the rest of his long life he was an active initiator and supporter in the House of Lords of proposals for the reform of the law.   It is by no means easy to estimate how much of the reform which was carried out between 1830 and 1860 was due to Brougham, since he himself claimed credit for nearly all of it, and his enemies—who were many—denied him any credit at all.   The truth obviously lies between the two extremes.   The reform of the Privy Council, the taking away of the bankruptcy work from the Chancellor, the original scheme for the county courts and the reform in the law of evidence which allowed the parties to civil proceedings to be witnesses, were all directly due to him, and these measures alone form a sufficient title to fame.

Much of the detail of the reforms, which we are to describe in outline, was in fact worked out by commissions of lawyers who were appointed to enquire into various branches of the law. The period from 1830 to 1860 was, indeed, the great age of commissions of enquiry into every department of government. " The whole of creation," said Sydney Smith, " has been put into commission and handed over to barristers of seven years' standing." In the field of law reform a burst of energy in the 'thirties was followed by a period of calm in the 'forties, and it was not until the decade between 1850 and 1860 that the systems of common law and equity were really put on a modern footing. After this had been done it was possible to consider how the two systems so reformed might be made one, and to plan the Judicature Acts by which this end was achieved. In this chapter we shall describe separately the chief reforms in the common law and Chancery systems between 1830 and 1875, and in the three following chapters we shall treat successively of the modern county court system, the Supreme Court of Judicature, and the criminal courts.

I. THE COMMON LAW COURTS

The first important common law reform was the Uniformity of Process Act, 1832. We described in Chapter 9 how the competition for business between the three common law courts, coupled with the desire of litigants to avail themselves of a form of process which would ensure the appearance of the defendant, had led to the growth of a number of different modes of starting personal actions in each of the three courts. The whole matter was a maze of intricate fictions. In the King's Bench and Common Pleas, personal actions could be started either by original writ or by bill based on the constructive presence of the defendant before the court, and in proceedings by writ, the writ might or might not in fact actually be issued. In practice, whichever form was chosen, proceedings generally started by some variety

of " capias " under which the defendant could be made
to give bail for his appearance, but though the result was
the same there were, according to the Common Law Commissioners, no less than twenty ways of bringing it about.[1]
This state of affairs was ended by the Act which established one uniform form of writ of summons as the first
step in an ordinary personal action in either of the three
courts. It was not issued, like the old original writs, out
of the Chancery, but by the court in which the action was
started and, like a modern writ, it was not addressed to
the sheriff commanding him to summon the defendant,
but to the defendant himself calling on him to appear.
If service of the writ could not be effected, or the defendant failed to appear, and distraint by the sheriff's
officers proved ineffectual to secure his attendance,
the plaintiff was allowed to enter appearance for him
and go on with the action instead of proceeding to outlawry. It is to be observed that the formal appearance
of the defendant was still considered necessary, even
though it was only entered by the plaintiff on his adversary's behalf. Judgment in default of appearance was
still to come. But after this Act arrest or the giving
of bail on mesne process in civil actions became in
nearly all cases a thing of the past, and resort to outlawry only remained necessary if the defendant was out
of the jurisdiction. Finally, we must notice that this Act
did not in any way affect the system of separate forms of
action. Though the form of writ in personal actions
became uniform, the plaintiff had to state in it the nature
of the action which he was bringing, and if it subsequently
turned out that he had chosen the wrong one, he failed
just as completely as before the Act was passed.

The Uniformity of Process Act, as we have said,
applied only to personal actions. Real actions were dealt
with by the Real Property Limitation Act, 1833, which,
besides making a number of important changes in the
law as to the time limit for bringing actions for the

---

[1] See Holdsworth, vol. IX, p. 249.

recovery of interests in land, made what was in theory a great simplification in the system of real actions by abolishing some sixty of them and leaving only three— two forms of action for the recovery of dower and the action of " quare impedit " by which the questions as to advowsons were tried.   In practice, of course, grand and possessory assizes and writs of entry had long given place to the action of ejectment as a method of trying title to land, and this action was not touched by the Act at all. Doe and Roe continued as before.   Since the Uniformity of Process Act applied only to personal actions the three surviving real actions continued to be started, as real actions always had been started, by original writs out of the Chancery returnable in the Common Pleas, until, by s. 26 of the Common Law Procedure Act, 1860, the ordinary form of writ of summons then used in personal actions was made applicable to them. Dower, of course, is now a thing of the past, but actions in the nature of the old " quare impedit " are still occasionally brought, and the law on the subject was discussed as recently as 1930.[1]   In it we have the last traces of the great actions of the Middle Ages.

Most of the changes in the law introduced by the Civil Procedure Act, 1833, lie outside the scope of this book, but we may notice that by it trial by compurgation or wager of law was abolished and that provision was made by it enabling a defendant to pay money into court in satisfaction of the plaintiff's claim.   More important, however, for our purpose was the power given to the judges by s. 1 of the Act and exercised by them in 1834 to produce a set of rules for the regulation of pleadings in actions at law with a view to diminishing delay, formalities and expense.   The system of pleading, of which we gave some account in Chapter 10, suffered at this time from defects of two quite different orders.   On the one hand it was overlaid with technicalities, and in particular the science of special pleading—*i.e.* of pleading

[1] *Notley* v. *Bishop of Birmingham*, [1930] W. N. 114.

matters of defence in detail—gave many opportunities to expert pleaders of confounding the true issues in the action. On the other hand enlightened judges in the eighteenth century, anxious to confine special pleading within the narrowest limits, had encouraged the habit of pleading the general issue, *i.e.* of totally and succinctly denying the entire claim in the declaration, even in cases where the defendant was really not in a position to deny many of the facts there stated, and at the trial would rely on some special ground of defence. Bentham summed up the matter perfectly in the phrase, " General pleading conveys no information, but there's an end of it. If any information is conveyed by pleading it is by special pleading, but there's no end to it." The problem before the reformers of 1833 was on the one hand to compel pleaders to plead specially, and not to leave the matter at large by pleading the general issue when they were really going to rely on some special and limited line of defence, and on the other hand to make the rules of special pleading as simple and informal as possible. They succeeded in the first task but not in the second. The ambit of the general issue was drastically limited. It could still be pleaded, but the lines of defence which it left open were much reduced. On the other hand, the Civil Procedure Commissioners under the influence of Serjeant Stephen, who had recently published his masterly *Treatise on the Principles of Pleading*, were convinced that special pleading ought to be a logically consistent system bound down by strict rules. Thus, though the rules of 1834 abolished a great many archaic survivals and illogicalities in pleading they preserved and even intensified its formality. If all barristers had had the mental powers of Stephen or Parke no harm might have been done, but the average pleader was often uncertain what he ought to say in his special plea now that he could not raise particular defences under the general issue, and equally uncertain what to reply to a special plea under the new rules when it was pleaded by his opponent. It has been calculated that one out of every four reported cases in the 1840's turns on points of pleading under the new rules, and it was eventually found necessary to jettison them altogether and to make pleadings the informal easily amended documents which they are to-day.

Meanwhile the official staff of the courts was being reformed. The abuses in connection with it were the same as those existing in the Court of Chancery—that is to say that the officials were paid by fees, and not by fixed salaries, that many offices were sinecures and that important duties were often performed by deputy. The evils of this system caused less public inconvenience in the case of the common law courts than in the Chancery, since the official staff was relatively less important in the former than in the latter, but its days were numbered in both alike. In 1837 forty-six high offices were abolished and five masters were established in each of the three courts with a fixed salary to do the work of the vanished officials, and in 1852 the clerical and subordinate staff of the common law courts underwent a similar process of retrenchment and reform.

So far the reforms introduced into the common law system had been of a piecemeal character, but the Common Law Procedure Acts, 1852, 1854 and 1860, which were based respectively on the first, second and third reports of the Commissioners appointed in 1850 to enquire into the " Process, Practice and System of pleading of the Superior Courts of Law at Westminster " were really comprehensive measures. In the 236 sections of the Act of 1852 all the ordinary steps in an action at law from the issue of the writ to the judgment of the Exchequer Chamber were passed in review and subjected to sweeping changes tending to greater simplicity, cheapness and expedition, while the Acts of 1854 and 1860 introduced a number of additional reforms of importance. In this book we can only attempt the barest outline of the results of this legislation, but any one who takes the trouble to look at Day's *Common Law Procedure Acts* will see for himself that a great deal of our modern procedure contained in the Rules of Court made under the Judicature Acts is in fact based on the earlier Common Law Procedure Acts.

First, in the department of process, the requirement that the writ of summons should name the form of action which was being brought was abolished. The old classification of forms of action—debt, detinue, assumpsit, trover, case, etc.—had in fact long outlived its usefulness, and the Act of 1852 definitely accepted the modern classification into actions based on contract and actions based on wrongs independent of contract.[1] If any defendant failed to enter an appearance to a writ with which he had been served, provision was made for judgment being given in favour of the plaintiff " in default of the defendant's appearance " without the formal necessity for appearance being entered for him by the plaintiff. It was further provided that if the writ claimed payment of a liquidated debt it might be "specially endorsed " with the particulars of the claim, and that if the defendant in such a case did not appear the plaintiff might obtain summary judgment for his claim with interest and costs without pleadings. The student will see here the origin of Order 13. Now, too, for the first time service of the writ out of the jurisdiction by leave of the court was allowed in certain cases where the defendant was abroad. Hitherto, all that a plaintiff could do in such a case was to outlaw the defendant. The defendant might then take steps to get the outlawry reversed and only be allowed to do so on terms of entering an appearance in the action. But since 1852 outlawry has become a thing of the past, and in the provisions as to the circumstances in which service out of the jurisdiction could be allowed we have the origin of the modern system embodied in Order 11.

[1] Readers of Professor Winfield's *Province of the Law of Tort* will realise that the modern classification is not nearly so simple a matter as it looks at first sight.

Reforms of the greatest importance were also introduced with regard to the joinder of parties and of causes
of action.   Under the old system the failure to join as
plaintiffs or defendants persons who ought to have been
joined, or the mis-joinder of persons who ought not to
have been joined, might lead to a demurrer or a plea
in abatement which might be fatal to the whole action.
Now provision was made for the addition of necessary,
and the removal of unnecessary, parties by application
made during the course of the proceedings, and the
student will see the origin of Order 15, Rule 6.
Similarly under the old system it was, generally speaking,
impossible to join together in one proceeding causes of
action which fell under the heads of two separate forms
of action, *e.g.* breach of a covenant to repair a house let
by lease under seal (covenant) could not be joined with
breach of an agreement to repair contained in a tenancy
not under seal (assumpsit). . But now that the old
categories were falling into the background it was
provided that, with some limited exceptions, any causes
of action against the same defendant might be joined in
one action.

Next various archaic survivals which were untouched
by the Acts of 1832 and 1833 now disappeared. Thus
the fictitious allegations of loss and finding in the
action of trover and the statement that acts of trespass
were done by " force and arms against the peace of our
Lady the Queen " were now declared unnecessary, and
Doe and Roe were at last abolished. The action of
ejectment was replaced by an action for the recovery
of the possession of land, which substituted for the
fictitious lease entry and ouster a simple form of writ by
which the actual claimant of the land called on the persons
in possession to appear and defend the action.

We have seen that the attempt made in 1834 to reform
the old system of special pleading had led to most unsatisfactory results. The Common Law Procedure Act,
1852, recognised this fact, and as well as definitely

relaxing the strictness of the older rules in many particulars introduced a wide power of allowing " all such
amendments as may be necessary for determining in the
existing suit the real question in controversy between the
parties." Here, for good or ill, we breathe the modern
atmosphere so far as pleadings are concerned, and Mr.
Day was no doubt right in saying that it was difficult to
exaggerate the importance of this power of allowing
amendments.

But great as were the innovations made by it, the Act
of 1852 did not attempt to deal with the cases in which
courts of law and equity applied different rules to the
same subject-matter. For centuries now past there had
been grounds of defence, such as mistake, accident and
certain types of fraud, which were recognised in equity
but not at common law, so that a defendant could not
plead them in bar to an action at law, though he could
use them to obtain an injunction from the Chancery
restraining the plaintiff at law from enforcing his judgment. The Common Law Procedure Act, 1854, took a
great step towards the joint administration of the two
systems, which was finally achieved by the Judicature
Acts, by enacting that a defendant at law could make use
of equitable defences in any case in which he would be
entitled to relief in equity against the judgment. In
fact, however, this reform was more important for the
recognition implicit in it of the necessity for the joint
administration of law and equity than for any immediate
benefit which it conferred, for it was really only useful
when the equitable defence was so complete that it would
have formed grounds for a final and perpetual injunction.
In such cases the common law court could bring about
the same result by simply dismissing the plaintiff's
action. But in the more usual cases of an equitable
defence in respect of which the Court of Chancery would
have granted a temporary or conditional injunction which
might be dissolved or might be made perpetual in the
light of the subsequent conduct of the parties, the com-

mon law courts were without machinery to give effect to
equitable pleas. They could give judgment for the
plaintiff or for the defendant, but the elaborate decrees
of the Court of Chancery were entirely alien to the whole
spirit of a common law action.

Just as the common law courts could not entertain
equitable defences prior to 1854 so they could not give
the plaintiff the equitable remedy of an injunction in lieu of,
or in substitution for, the common law remedy of damages.
This defect, too, was partially remedied by the Act of
1854, which allowed a successful plaintiff at law to obtain
an injunction in the common law court against the continuance or repetition of the breach of contract or wrong
in question. But it is to be observed that the injunction
could only be granted after the plaintiff's right had been
actually violated. The power of courts of equity to intervene to prevent threatened or apprehended injuries by
" quia timet " actions was not extended to the common
law courts. Another extension of the powers of courts
of equity to the common law courts contained in the Act
of 1854 was the power to compel discovery of documents in the possession of a party to the action and
to administer interrogatories. Hitherto discovery and
interrogatories could only be obtained in a common law
action by appealing to the auxiliary jurisdiction of the
Chancery and filing a bill there for the purpose. Now
they could be obtained far more cheaply and quickly in
the action itself at common law.

Hitherto, with the exception of archaic modes of trial
such as compurgation or battle, the one method of deciding issues of fact in common law actions had been by
trial by jury. The Common Law Procedure Act, 1854,
recognised that this mode of trial might be unsuitable
in some classes of case, and marked the beginning of
the decline of trial by jury in civil cases which has
gathered such momentum of recent years. Provision
was made by it for the trial of issues of fact by a judge
sitting without a jury with the consent of the parties, and

it also empowered a judge at any time after the issue of the writ in an action in which the matter in dispute consisted wholly or in part of matters of account for which trial by jury was quite unsuitable to refer such issues to an arbitrator. In this connection we may mention that the Act of 1854 made considerable amendments in the law of arbitration itself, and in particular empowered the courts to stay proceedings before them on the application of the defendant in cases where it appeared that the parties had previously agreed to submit the matters in dispute between them to arbitration.

The Common Law Procedure Acts did not make any changes of importance in the method of trial by jury, but we must mention at this point the great reform in the law of evidence brought about by Lord Brougham's Acts, 1851–53, under which the parties to an action at law and their husbands and wives were made competent and compellable witnesses on either side in an action. Finally, before we leave the common law system and pass to Chancery reform, we may observe that proceedings by writ of error were abolished by the Act of 1852 and their place taken by a so-called " Memorandum of Error," which was not the initiation of a new proceeding as the writ of error had been, but a mere step in the action like a modern notice of appeal. No change, however, was made in the scope of common law appeals. They were still confined to matter appearing on the record, and were not rehearings of the action.

II. The Court of Chancery

The condition of the Court of Chancery in the latter part of Lord Eldon's Chancellorship was so scandalous that the necessity for its reform was recognised in principle by all parties. Even the Duke of Wellington consoled himself for the Whig victory in 1830 with the reflection that Lord Brougham as Chancellor would " reform that damned court " if any one could.[1] The

---

[1] Atlay : *The Victorian Chancellors*, vol. I, p. 294.

arrears of business in it were such that it was only many years after a case was set down that it could hope to come on for its first hearing, and, as an ordinary administration action entailed several hearings at different stages after the intermediate taking of accounts and making of enquiries, it was by no means unusual for the legatees to be still unpaid twenty years after the death of their testator.[1]   Lord Eldon's dilatory habits no doubt contributed to this lamentable state of affairs, but the chief reasons for it lay deeper.   They were three in number.

First, the inadequacy of the judicial staff.   In spite of the great increase in the business of the court, caused by the growth in the population and wealth of the country, the Chancellor and the Master of the Rolls remained until 1813 the only judges of the court.   Nor were either of them whole-time judges.   The Chancellor, quite apart from his political work, was increasingly occupied with hearing appeals in the House of Lords, which had steadily grown in number since the Union with Scotland in 1707, and the Master of the Rolls was only permitted to hear certain classes of case, all of which could be, and often were, taken before the Chancellor for rehearing on appeal.   In 1813, a whole-time Vice-Chancellor was appointed, but his decisions again were all subject to appeal to the Chancellor.

The second great defect was the lack of any effective control by the judicial over the official staff.   As the judges were so few and the time which the Chancellor, at least, could give to the work of the court so limited, it necessarily followed that the detailed, and often very important, administrative business which was transacted in chambers was left entirely to the Masters and clerks of the court, of whose manner of conducting it we have said something in Chapter 9.   It was, of course, possible to take steps to bring the decisions of the Masters up for review by the court, but, in view of the additional delay and expense which such a course entailed,

[1] Holdsworth, vol. I, pp. 438-9.

there was not much temptation to embark on it. What was needed was a close co-operation between judges and officials, and without more judges that was impossible.

The third defect, and though it is less obvious it was almost as great as the other two, was that there was in general no procedure allowing for the decisions of isolated points of administration or construction without a full-fledged bill of complaint and a general order for administration with full accounts and enquiries which might take years and cost many hundreds or even thousands of pounds. An executor or trustee in order to obtain the assistance of the court on some particular point might be compelled to throw the whole trust estate into Chancery, from which it would emerge substantially diminished some twenty years later.

A commission of enquiry into the state of the Court of Chancery was appointed as early as 1825, and though no extensive measure of reform was proposed by it, a matter which need cause no surprise if one remembers that Lord Eldon himself presided over it, its report led to the partial remedy of one abuse by the passing in 1830 of an Act amending the law with regard to committals for contempt. Readers of *Bleak House* will remember the pathetic figure of the trustee languishing in the Fleet for some contempt, the nature of which he does not understand, appearing from time to time before the Chancellor to " purge his contempt," and being again and again remanded back to prison. There were two main grounds on which a man might find himself in prison for contempt. In the first place the Chancery, like the courts of common law, felt great difficulty in proceeding in default of the appearance of the defendant, and insisted on the plaintiff making every effort to seize the person of the defendant for the contempt which he had committed in neglecting the subpœna before it would allow the allegations in the bill to be taken as admitted (" pro confesso "). But the defendant, if apprehended, might remain in prison indefinitely even if he put in an answer, for he might have no means of securing his discharge by paying the plaintiff the costs occasioned by his attachment. Further, one might be committed to prison for failure to comply with some order of the court. The procedure of the Court of Chancery was essentially *in personam*. The defendant was often ordered to do some act, to pay money into court or to execute some document, etc., and on failure to do so he was liable to imprisonment, as indeed he is to-day. The Act of 1830 laid it down that the Masters of the Court should visit the Fleet regularly to examine the case of every prisoner, and made provision for the payment out of unclaimed funds in court of the costs of the discharge of those whose further imprisonment could benefit no one. The Act further empowered the court compulsorily to discharge those who could obtain their discharge if they wished but refused to apply for it. Lord St. Leonards (who was largely responsible for the whole measure) asserts that he knew of several prisoners who occupied lucrative offices, such as that of cook, in the Fleet, and hoped to spend their lives in undisturbed possession of them.[1]

In 1830 Lord Brougham became Chancellor, and set himself at once to work off the arrears of business in the court. How far he was successful it is hard to say, for he and his friends produced figures which indicated that he had dispatched in a few months the accumulation of years, while his enemies asserted that the figures were grossly misleading, and that in any case he had displayed an ignorance of equity and an inattention to the details of the cases before him which constituted a graver abuse than Lord Eldon's dilatoriness. There can, however, be no question that the Act which he caused to be passed in 1831 for the separation of the bankruptcy business from the Chancery, and the

[1] Atlay: *The Victorian Chancellors*, vol. II, pp. 15–16. Those committed to prison for "contempt of court" are now sent to Brixton. The functions imposed on the Masters by the Act of 1830 are now performed by the Official Solicitor.

establishment of an independent Court of Bankruptcy, was a reform of the greatest value which relieved the Chancellor of a mass of work which he had no time properly to discharge.[1]   Further, in 1833, another of his Acts enacted that the Master of the Rolls should sit continually and deal with all types of cases, and provided for the payment of the Masters by fixed salary instead of fees, the lowering of the court fees payable by suitors and the reduction of the Six Clerks from six to two.[2]   On the whole one may safely say that Lord Brougham's immense, if sometimes misdirected, energy must have done a good deal to clear the air of the court and produce an atmosphere conducive to further reform.

In 1841 the equity side of the Court of Exchequer was abolished and its business transferred to the Chancery, and at the same time two more Vice-Chancellors were appointed.   There were thus now four whole-time judges in the court besides the Chancellor, and it became possible to relieve the Chancellor of the burden of sitting at first instance, and to confine him to appellate work. This end was finally achieved by an Act of 1851, which established a court of appeal from the Master of the Rolls and the Vice-Chancellors, consisting of the Chancellor and two Lords Justices in Chancery. The two Lords Justices could form a court without the Chancellor, and he, if he chose, could sit alone with the same powers of hearing appeals as they possessed.   After 1851 the Chancellor practically ceased to sit at first instance.[3]

The increase in the number of judges of first instance also made it possible for the whole system of Chancery chambers to be reorganised and for the business con-

---

[1] Holdsworth, vol. I, pp. 470–473.

[2] The Six Clerks were abolished altogether in 1842.

[3] The bitter tongue which made Lord Westbury so many enemies was well illustrated by the answer (entirely, it may be said, unjustified) he gave to the question : " Why does Lord Chancellor Cranworth sit so often with the Lord Justices ? "   " I suppose it's because he's afraid of being alone in the dark."

ducted in them to be brought under the immediate direction and control of the judges. By an Act of 1852 the office of Master in Chancery was abolished, and the Master of the Rolls and the three Vice-Chancellors began each to sit at chambers as well as in court, and to supervise their chamber business themselves in conjunction with their court work. Power was given to them to direct what class of work should be transacted in chambers and what in court, and to adjourn individual matters out of chambers into court when they thought a hearing in open court desirable, and from court into chambers when it seemed that it could be more conveniently dealt with there. Two chief clerks and a subordinate staff, all paid by fixed salary, were attached to each of the four judges for the conduct of the business of their chambers, and naturally many matters in chambers were disposed of in the first instance at least by a chief clerk, but it was provided that any suitor should always have the right to bring any point decided by the chief clerk before the judge in person. The reader may be tempted to think that this reform meant no more than the substitution of the chief clerks for the old Masters, but this is very far from being the case. The Masters in Chancery had been for practical purposes independent of the judges, while the chief clerks were under their direct control, and though in 1897 the chief clerks were allowed to assume the title of " Masters," the modern Master of the Chancery Division occupies quite a different position from the old Masters of the Court of Chancery.

Besides the Act for the abolition of the Masters a number of other Acts were passed in the decade from 1850 to 1860 for the reform of the organisation and procedure of the Court of Chancery which are the counterpart of the Common Law Procedure Acts, and tended, as well as simplifying the procedure of the court, to assimilate it to the new procedure of the common law courts and so to pave the way for the Judicature Act.

First the Court of Chancery Act, 1850,[1] " to diminish the delay and expense of proceedings in the High Court of Chancery," provided, *inter alia*, for the stating of special cases to the court for the determination of isolated points of construction in wills, deeds and other documents, and also enabled executors who might be in doubt whether their testators had left any debts of which they were unaware, and dared not proceed to distribution until they knew, to obtain an order for an account of outstanding liabilities without the expense of a suit for administration.

Then the Court of Chancery Procedure Act, 1852, abolished the writ of subpœna and provided that its place should be taken by a printed copy of plaintiff's bill served on the defendant. The form of the bill itself underwent changes which brought it into line with a declaration in a common law action. It was no longer to contain a charging part or end with a list of interrogatories converting all the preceding allegations of fact into questions for the defendant to answer, but was to be a concise narrative of the material facts on which the plaintiff relied divided into numbered paragraphs and ending with a prayer for the relief to which the plaintiff conceived himself entitled. If the plaintiff desired to administer interrogatories they were to be filed separately, and thus were no longer a necessary concomitant of every Chancery suit. Similarly the defendant's answer, instead of being as heretofore, primarily an answer to the plaintiff's interrogatories, took on the form of a modern defence in which the defendant set out the facts material to his own case. The same Act made great innovations in the mode of taking evidence in Chancery suits. By it provision was made for the first time for evidence to be given orally if either party so desired it, though such evidence was normally to be given out of court before an examiner, who was to record the statement of the witness and his answers to

---

[1] Commonly called Sir G. Turner's Act after Lord Justice Turner, who was mainly responsible for it.

the questions put to him in cross-examination, and prepare them for the use of the judge.   Furthermore, even
if the usual affidavit evidence was used, either party could
claim the right to cross-examine his opponent's witnesses
before an examiner on the statements made by them in
their affidavits.   If one remembers that Lord Brougham's
Acts were at this moment enabling the common law
courts to hear the evidence of the parties to the action,
who had always been subject to examination in Chancery
suits, one will see that only very slight changes were now
needed in order completely to assimilate the practice of
the two jurisdictions in regard to evidence.   It has
already been pointed out that this assimilation was an
essential pre-requisite to any fusion of the two systems.[1]

Finally, there are two provisions touching the relations
of the Chancery to the common law courts which should
be mentioned here.   The Act of 1852 abolished the
practice of stating cases for the opinions of the courts of
common law and empowered the Court of Chancery to
decide for itself all matters of law arising in any case
before it and the Chancery Amendment Act of 1858
(known as Lord Cairns' Act) empowered the Court of
Chancery in all cases in which it had jurisdiction to
entertain an application for an injunction to restrain a
breach of contract or a tort, or for specific performance
of a contract, to grant damages either in addition to, or in
lieu of, the injunction or decree of specific performance,
and provided that in such cases the issues of fact should
be decided and the damages assessed either by a jury or
the judge.   In practice the power to summon a jury was
hardly ever exercised, but the power given to the court
to award damages as well as its old remedies of specific
performance or injunction resulted in a great many
actions of contract or tort which otherwise would have
been tried at common law being tried in Chancery.

[1] See p. 130, above.

XVI

THE MODERN COUNTY COURTS

IN the Middle Ages England was well supplied with
local courts with a jurisdiction over both criminal and
civil cases. Besides the sheriffs' courts of the county
and hundred, and the manorial courts and courts leet
of the feudal lords, most boroughs had under their
charters the right to hold a court with a jurisdiction of
varying extent over cases arising within their boundaries.
These local courts were all of them " popular " in the
sense that there was no professional legal element in
their composition. The presiding officer in them was a
layman and the proceedings were conducted by him
and the suitors who owed " suit " to the court. We have
seen, in Chapter 6, that these local tribunals tended to
decay in the later Middle Ages and to lose their jurisdiction to courts which derived their authority immediately from the Crown. A great part of English criminal
justice continued, it is true, to be administered locally
by the justices of the peace, who, though royal officials,
were generally laymen, but the trial of the gravest crimes
and of nearly all important civil business came into the
hands of the justices of the royal court and was held
before them partly on assize and partly in one or other
of the three common law courts at Westminster.

Naturally all these local courts did not decay equally
rapidly. In particular the borough courts, especially in
the larger towns, possessed a greater vitality than the
sheriffs' courts or the manorial courts, and though any
criminal jurisdiction which they had possessed passed
into the hands of the borough justices of the peace and
the Recorder, many of them continued in possession of
a fairly important civil jurisdiction, which was in practice
usually exercised by the mayor and other corporation

officers. At the time of the Municipal Corporation Act, 1835, there were more than 200 of these borough courts nominally in existence and some 170 of them survive. Probably the great majority of these are for practical purposes dead, but there are some borough courts, such as the Tolsey Court at Bristol and the Court of Passage at Liverpool, which are still fairly busy courts. Their jurisdiction is limited in space, but unlimited in amount, as far as personal actions are concerned, and the judges in them—who are sometimes the local Recorders —are nowadays always lawyers.[1]

The concentration of nearly all civil litigation in the courts of common law and its handling there by barristers-at-law, who alone had a right of audience in them, had the advantage of habituating Englishmen to one system of common law and to a uniform method of trial of issues of fact by jury. But by the seventeenth and eighteenth centuries these advantages had already been definitely and permanently secured, and only the disadvantages arising from this extreme centralisation were apparent. It is true that the actual trial of issues of fact in actions at law took place at *nisi prius*, but quite apart from the fact that even the assize town might well be some considerable distance from the place of residence of the parties, an action had to be started in London and the pleadings were drawn and arguments of law heard in London, so that, as well as the country solicitor, a London agent had to be employed and, of course, a barrister too, to come round on circuit to argue the case at *nisi prius*. The expense entailed in all this might well be out of all proportion to the sum in dispute, and it is not surprising to hear as early as the seventeenth century complaints of the

[1] See Halsbury: *Laws of England*, 3rd ed., IX, " Courts ", pp. 496–572.

The Beeching Commission (Cmnd. 1969, 4153) recommended that these local courts should be abolished and the Courts Act, 1971 contains provisions to that affect.

absence of an efficient local tribunal for the dispatch of small civil causes, and in particular for the everyday matter of collecting small debts.

To meet this need various towns obtained private Acts of Parliament in the course of the eighteenth century to establish so-called " Courts of Requests " for the recovery of small debts. These tribunals were generally composed of a board of five or six local worthies who sat once or twice a week to decide cases summarily without a jury on the evidence of the parties and other witnesses. Blackstone, while admitting the necessity for some local tribunal, disapproved of these courts of requests on the ground that the judges were irresponsible laymen and their procedure quite contrary to that of the common law courts. But he favoured the extension to the rest of England of a statute passed in 1749 for the revival of the County Court of Middlesex under which a special session of the court was to be held at least once a month in every hundred of the county under the presidency of the county clerk (who would normally be a barrister or attorney), assisted by twelve freeholders of the hundred summoned by rotation, for the trial of all causes not exceeding 40s. The members of the court were to decide the cases themselves after hearing the parties and witnesses, and their decision was to be final and not subject to any appeal to the common law courts. This device of a rejuvenated county court presided over by a trained lawyer was the one eventually introduced generally by the legislature, but it was not for many years after Blackstone's death that the modern county courts came into being.

To establish a system of local courts for small civil disputes was one of Lord Brougham's favourite projects, and he devoted a passage in his famous Law Reform speech in 1828 to pointing out the crying need for them. Statistics showed that of the average of 90,000 causes entered annually in the three common law courts between 1822 and 1827, no less than 30,000 were for amounts not exceeding £20, and it was calculated that the costs of trying these cases out to judgment if they were defended would amount to four times the aggregate amount in dispute. No doubt a large number of these cases were undefended, and the issue of the writ must often have led to payment by the defendant, but the mere cost of initiating an action in the courts at Westminster was not negligible, and Brougham was certainly right in saying that as things were a small debt could not be recovered from an obstinate debtor without an expenditure by the creditor in costs far larger than the debt itself. In 1830 when he became Chancellor, he introduced in the House of Lords a Bill for the establishment of local district courts, with a jurisdiction of £100 in debt, of £50 in actions for personal injuries, and a wide jurisdiction in bankruptcy, but the Bill was lost on its third reading owing to the skilful opposition of Lord Lyndhurst, who voiced the fears of the legal profession at the probable effect of the measure on the volume of business tried at *nisi prius*.

Within a few years, however, Lyndhurst himself was a convert to the necessity of some such Act, and as Chancellor in 1846 he introduced a measure closely modelled on Lord Brougham's Bill, which eventually became law as the County Courts Act, 1846. But before the Bill passed Sir Robert Peel gave place to Lord John Russell, and the great harvest of patronage arising out of its provisions—the appointment of sixty new county court judges—fell neither to Brougham nor Lyndhurst, but to the incoming Whig Chancellor, Lord Cottenham, who had played no part in the earlier struggle at all.[1] Under the Act some 500 " county courts " were set up, grouped into sixty circuits, each of which had its own judge, who was to preside in the courts in his district. The judges were to be barristers of at least seven years' standing, appointed by the Chancellor and removable by

[1] Naturally the Tories complained of his exercise of it ; see Atlay : *The Victorian Chancellors*, vol. I, p. 410.

him for incapacity or misbehaviour. The county court was to be a court of record and to have jurisdiction over all personal actions with a few exceptions, (of which ejectment, libel, and breach of promise were the most important), where the debt or damage claimed did not exceed £20. Proceedings were not to be started by writ, but by a simple summons. There were to be no formal pleadings, though notice had to be given to the other side when a party intended to rely upon one of those pleas, such as the Statute of Frauds or infancy, which had to be expressly pleaded in cases in the Common Law Courts. Otherwise the action was to be disposed of in a summary way under rules of procedure to be framed for the purpose. If the claim exceeded five pounds either side could demand a jury of five to try any questions of fact, but normally the judge was to decide all the issues both of law and fact, and the parties were competent to give evidence. If the defendant did not appear judgment could be given in his absence, and the judge was given jurisdiction to order the payment of judgment debts by instalments. The immense volume of business which flowed at once into the new courts was the most convincing proof of the want which they supplied. The yearly average of cases tried in them in the first five years of their existence was 433,000, compared with the 100,000 which had been the average in the common law courts in the years before 1846. As early as 1850 it was thought wise to extend their jurisdiction from £20 to £50, and to give them a power of hearing certain actions beyond their jurisdiction by the consent of the parties. The same Act also provided for an appeal from the county courts on questions of law or the reception of evidence to two judges of one of the common law courts, and in 1856 power was given to the judges of the superior courts to remit to the county court actions of contract started at Westminster for sums not exceeding £50. There is no doubt that this rapid success of the new courts, which began to constitute a real threat to the old

courts at Westminster, had an influence on the course
of common law reform at this period.

It would be tedious to follow out in detail the steps by
which the jurisdiction of the county courts was gradually
extended. The limit of £50 in those actions of contract
and tort in which the Court had jurisdiction was extended to £100 in 1903, to £200 in 1937 and to £400 in
1959. Under the legislation now in force the most
important ordinary jurisdiction of the county court is as
follows [1]:

(1) Actions founded on contract or tort (other than
libel, slander, seduction or breach of promise) where
the debt or damages claimed is not more than £750.
A plaintiff who has a cause of action for more than £750
can, if he wishes, abandon his claim to the excess in
order to give the court jurisdiction.

(2) Actions for the recovery of land where the net
annual value of the land for rating purposes does not
exceed £400.

(3) An equity jurisdiction up to £5,000, e.g. in cases
of administration, foreclosure and specific performance,
where the amount of the estate, mortgage or purchase price, as the case may be, does not exceed
£5,000.

By the agreement of the parties most proceedings which
could have been started in the High Court can be determined in a county court notwithstanding that the sum in
dispute exceeds the statutory maximum. Actions which
ought in the opinion of the court to have been commenced
in the county court and not in the High Court may be
transferred by the High Court to the county court, and if
an action which could have been started in the county
court is fought out in the High Court, and the plaintiff
recovers less than certain specified amounts in different
classes of action, he may though successful either recover

[1] The County Court Act, 1959, as amended by the County Court
Jurisdiction Act, 1969. The Beeching Commission has recommended
an increase from £750 to £1,000 in actions of contract and tort.

no costs at all or at best only costs on the County court scale.

But the ordinary jurisdiction which we have outlined above accounts for only a portion of the volume of business which comes before the county courts, for Parliament by a number of Acts has entrusted these courts with a special jurisdiction in a great variety of matters. Thus, immediately after the Act of 1846 the Bankruptcy Act, 1847, entrusted a certain number of county courts with jurisdiction in bankruptcy to an unlimited amount, and, outside London, bankruptcy jurisdiction is to-day exercised exclusively by the county courts. Then, to mention only a few out of many other branches of jurisdiction, proceedings under the Agricultural Holdings Acts, the Rent Acts and the Hire Purchase Acts are brought in the county court. Under the Matrimonial Causes Act, 1967, all matrimonial proceedings are started in the county court and if they are undefended are tried there. Defended proceedings are transferred to the High Court.

Some 1,500,000 proceedings—four-fifths for sums less than £100—were started in the county court in 1968. The great majority of these were, of course, undisputed claims which were settled before trial or on which the plaintiff obtained judgment on the defendant's default, but some 140,000 cases were determined after a hearing before the judge or the registrar. The proceedings have always maintained the simplicity which was their distinguishing mark in 1846. There need be no pleadings; the parties can be and usually are represented by their solicitors, and not by counsel; and there is hardly ever a jury.[1] In most cases an appeal lies on questions of law or the admission or rejection of evidence and in some cases—notably where the debt or damages claimed exceeds £200—on questions of fact as well.[2] Under the Judicature Acts such appeals came before divisional

[1] In 1968 only two cases were tried by jury.
[2] See County Courts Act, 1959, ss. 108–109, for the details.

courts of the High Court, and from them there might be further appeals with leave to the Court of Appeal and the House of Lords. But some of the statutes which gave special jurisdiction to the county courts provided for appeal direct to the Court of Appeal, and eventually in 1934 this principle was applied to all the ordinary jurisdiction of the county court.[1] The Court of Appeal can enter judgment for either party as it thinks fit or order a newtrial. In 1846 Parliament recognised that the small debtor might be unable to pay the judgment debt at once and gave the county court a power, not possessed by the Superior Courts, to order payment by instalments with a stay of execution so long as payments are kept up. The usual methods of enforcement are either by warrant of execution against goods or a judgment summons under Section 5 of the Debtors Act, 1869, which may result in the debtor being committed to prison if the court is satisfied that he has or has had since the date of judgment means to pay and is contumaciously refusing to pay. The number of judgment debtors who are actually imprisoned is comparatively small—only 2,789 in 1968.[2]

County court judges of whom there are now about 100 are appointed by the Lord Chancellor from among barristers of at least seven years' standing. Normally, of course, they have practised at the Bar for far longer than that. They are removable for incompetence or misbehaviour and retire at 72. Their salary is now £5,700 a year. In addition to their civil work many county court judges do a substantial amount of criminal work as chairmen or deputy chairmen of their local quarter sessions. Under the proposals of the Beeching Commission, quarter sessions will be abolished but all county court

---

[1] But bankruptcy appeals still come before a Divisional Court of the Chancery Division, see p. 299, below.

[2] Under Part II of the Administration of Justice Act, 1970, the remedy by way of attachment of the debtor's earnings introduced by the Maintenance Orders Act, 1958, is to be extended to all civil debts and with

judges will become also circuit judges in the Crown
Court and as such try lower and middle band criminal
cases.   As well as its judge each county court has its
registrar who is a solicitor of at least seven years' standing
also appointed and removable by the Chancellor.   In
busy courts he is precluded from private practice.   The
registrar, who has a staff of assistants under him, acts as
clerk of the court, entering all the plaints and recording
and executing the judgments.   Further, he is empowered
to enter up judgments in many undefended cases himself
and to try small cases as deputy for the judge.   In 1968
over 100,000 cases—mostly for amounts of less than £30
—were determined by Registrars.[1]   In addition to their
duties in connection with the county court, many county
court registrars are also district registrars of the High
Court, and have the powers of a Master of the Supreme
Court in the early stages of actions in the High Court
started in the district registry.[2]

some exceptions—*e.g.* maintenance orders and debts to the Revenue—
imprisonment for debt will be abolished.

   [1] The Beeching Commission has recommended that the Registrar
should be given jurisdiction to try cases involving up to £100 even without
the consent of the parties.

   [2] See p. 303, below.

XVII

THE SUPREME COURT OF JUDICATURE

WE saw in Chapter 15 that the reforms made in the organisation of, and the conduct of business in, the courts of common law and equity between 1830 and 1860 tended to bring the two systems closer together and so to pave the way for the setting up of a single court in which both law and equity should be administered concurrently. In 1867 a commission was appointed to enquire, among other things, into the operation and effect of the separation and division of business between the various superior courts of law and equity, and on its first report, presented in 1869, the Judicature Act, 1873, was based. This measure, which was introduced into Parliament by Lord Chancellor Selborne, was originally intended to come into operation on November 2nd, 1874, but it was found that the new system contemplated by it could not be conveniently introduced without longer preparation, and further that a number of amendments were necessary. Accordingly, the date for the commencement of the Act was postponed until November 1st, 1875, and on that day the original Act and an amending Act, the Judicature Act, 1875, came into effect together. The three chief results of the Judicature Acts, 1873–1875, were the establishment of a single Supreme Court (1) in which the jurisdiction of the various existing superior courts was concentrated (2) the concurrent administration in this new court of the rules of law and of equity (3) and lastly, the framing of a uniform code of procedure applicable to most civil proceedings in the new court. In this chapter we will deal with each of these topics separately. Between 1875 and 1925 a number of subsidiary Judicature Acts were passed supplementing and amending the original Acts, and in 1925 the whole series of Acts was consolidated in the Judicature Act, 1925. There have, of course, been many further changes in the last 45 years but basically the system introduced in 1875 still subsists.

I. The Supreme Court of Judicature

Under the Judicature Acts the Court of Chancery, the Courts of Queen's Bench, Common Pleas and Exchequer, the Court of Probate, the Court for Divorce and Matrimonial Causes, the Court of Admiralty and the London Court of Bankruptcy were consolidated and united together in one Supreme Court of Judicature, which was divided into two parts, the High Court of Justice and the Court of Appeal.[1] To the High Court was assigned the jurisdiction formerly exercised by the Court of Chancery, both on its common law and equity side ; by the Courts of Queen's Bench and Common Pleas; by the Court of Exchequer—both as a revenue court and as a common law court ; by the Courts of Common Pleas at Lancaster and Durham; by the Courts of Admiralty and of Probate, and the Court for Divorce and Matrimonial Causes; by the London Court of Bankruptcy, and by the courts created by the commissions of assize, oyer and terminer and gaol delivery.[2] To the Court of Appeal was assigned the jurisdiction formerly exercised by the Lord Chancellor and the Court of Appeal in Chancery, by the Exchequer Chamber, by the Privy Council in respect of appeals from the Lord Chancellor in

[1] Judicature Act, 1873, ss. 3 and 4. The Judicature Act, 1875, s. 9, excluded the London Court of Bankruptcy from the Supreme Court and continued its separate existence, but it was soon afterwards incorporated in it by the Bankruptcy Act, 1883, ss. 92–93. The bankruptcy jurisdiction outside London is exercised by the county courts, see p. 284, above.

[2] Judicature Act, 1873, s. 16. The jurisdiction of the Chancery Courts of the Palatinates of Lancaster and Durham was untouched by the Act. See p. 294, below.

lunacy matters [1] and from the "instance," but not the "prize" jurisdiction of the Court of Admiralty, by the Court of Appeal from the Chancery Court of Lancaster and by the Court of the Lord Warden of the Stannaries.[2]

The High Court was composed of the Lord Chancellor, the Chief Justices of the Courts of Queen's Bench and Common Pleas and the Chief Baron of the Exchequer, the Master of the Rolls and the three Vice-Chancellors, the puisne judges and barons of the three common law courts, the judge of the Court of Probate and of the Court for Divorce and Matrimonial Causes (who was the same person) and the judge of the Court of Admiralty.[3]   For convenience in transacting business the High Court was divided into five divisions,[4] the Chancery Division, consisting of the Lord Chancellor, the Master of the Rolls and the Vice-Chancellors; the Queen's Bench Division, consisting of the Chief Justice of the Queen's Bench and his puisnes ; the Common Pleas Division, consisting of the Chief Justice of the Common Pleas and his puisnes ; the Exchequer Division, consisting of the Chief Baron of the Exchequer and the junior barons, and the Probate, Divorce and Admiralty Division, consisting of the judge of the Court of Probate and of the Court for Divorce and Matrimonial Causes and of the judge of the Court of Admiralty.   These divisions, however, were in no sense separate "courts."   A judge of one division might be required by the Chancellor to sit in another, and no injunction or prohibition was to issue from one part of the Supreme Court restraining or prohibiting proceedings in another.

The general principle regulating the distribution of business among the several divisions of the High Court was that business which had been within the exclusive jurisdiction of one of the old courts should be assigned to the division which now represented that court, but

---

[1] See p. 144, above.
[2] Judicature Act, 1875, s. 18.
[3] Judicature Act, 1873, s. 5.
[4] *Ibid.*, s. 31.

that in the case of business not assigned to any particular division a litigant should be at liberty to bring his action in whatever division he chose. Provision was, however, made for the transference from one division to another of actions brought in the wrong division, and for the redistribution of business between the divisions. Further, the number of divisions might itself be increased or reduced by Order in Council.[1]

It was contemplated in 1875 that there might be no necessity for retaining permanently three separate common law divisions, and, after the deaths in 1880 of Sir Alexander Cockburn and Sir Fitzroy Kelly, who had been Chief Justice of the Queen's Bench and Chief Baron of the Exchequer respectively at the date of the passing of the Acts, it was decided that the offices of Chief Justice of the Common Pleas and Chief Baron of the Exchequer should be abolished, that Lord Coleridge, the Chief Justice of the Common Pleas, should become Lord Chief Justice of England,[2] and that the Common Pleas and Exchequer Divisions should be merged in the Queen's Bench Division. This merger was effected by Order in Council dated December 16th, 1880, and from that date the common law side of the High Court has consisted of one division, now the Queen's Bench Division, presided over by the Lord Chief Justice of England, the successor of the Chief Justices of the King's Bench.

We will now consider the work done by the judges of each of the three divisions of the High Court noting the chief changes which have occurred in the character of their work since 1875. Although the Chancery Division is the senior, it will be convenient to start with the Queen's Bench Division. The working life of a Queen's Bench judge is divided, as it was in 1875, between the

---

[1] Judicature Act, 1873, ss. 32–36.
[2] Since the days of Sir Edward Coke the Chief Justice of the King's Bench had habitually used the title Lord Chief Justice of England, but it was not until the abolition of the Chief Justiceship of the Common Pleas that the title was strictly appropriate.

time which he spends in London and the time which he spends on circuit and between civil and criminal work. But the great increase in crime in recent years has led not only to a great increase in the number of Queen's Bench judges but also to their spending more than half their time on circuit and more than half of their time on circuit in trying criminal cases.[1] The civil actions which he tries, whether in London or on circuit as a Commissioner of Assize, are mainly claims for damages for breach of contract or tort, and to-day the great majority are claims for damages for personal injuries caused by accidents on the road or in factories. The great change which has taken place here in the last 95 years is that whereas in 1875 nearly all common law actions were tried by jury, to-day nearly all are tried by a judge alone.[2] The only civil actions which are at all often tried by jury are actions for defamation. As we have said, during the greater part of his time on circuit he will be doing criminal work as a commissioner of " oyer and terminer " and " gaol delivery." In London the only first instance criminal work which he will do will be when he takes his turn as the High Court judge at the Old Bailey, the seat of the criminal assizes for the metropolitan area, where in addition to the dozen or so regular judges of the court there is generally one High Court judge sitting to deal with the most serious cases.[3] But when in London a Queen's Bench judge is called upon from time to time to sit in the Criminal Division of the Court of Appeal.[4] The court will be presided over by the Lord Chief Justice or a Lord Justice of Appeal and sometimes a second Lord Justice will be sitting; but the court of three almost invariably includes one and often two Queen's Bench

[1] In 1938 some 10,000 persons were tried on indictment; in 1967 some 30,000. In 1881 there were 14 puisne judges of the Q.B.D.; in 1938, 17; and to-day 39.

[2] In 1968 of 1,001 actions tried in the Queen's Bench Division in London 975 were tried by a judge alone.

[3] For the " Old Bailey " see p. 347, below.

[4] See p. 301, below.

judges.   A further task which a Queen's Bench judge may be called upon to perform when in London is to sit with another Queen's Bench judge under the presidency of the Lord Chief Justice in the Divisional Court which hears cases stated on points of law by magistrates and by some other inferior tribunals and also " prerogative " proceedings.   So if one takes a day at random—19th October, 1970—one finds that of thirteen Queen's Bench judges then in London one was sitting in the Criminal Division of the Court of Appeal, two in the Divisional Court, and one at the Old Bailey. Eight were trying ordinary civil actions, one who had been a commercial lawyer at the Bar was taking the " Commercial " list [1] and one was sitting as the judge in chambers hearing applications for interlocutory injunctions and appeals from Queen's Bench masters in interlocutory matters.

Section 56 of the Judicature Act, 1925 (replacing Section 34 of the 1873 Act), lists a number of types of work which are assigned to the Chancery Division exclusively.[2]   But whatever may have been the position a century ago, only quite a small part of the work done by Chancery judges to-day is work assigned to the Division by the Judicature Act.   In the first place, a great deal of work has been assigned to the Division from time to time by other Statutes or by order.   Thus to

[1] See p. 323, below, for the " Commercial " court.

[2] (1) The administration of the estates of deceased persons.

(2) The dissolution of partnerships and the taking of partnership accounts.

(3) The redemption or foreclosure of mortgages.

(4) The raising of portions or other charges on land.

(5) The sale and distribution of the proceeds of any property subject to a lien or charge.

(6) The execution of trusts charitable or private.

(7) The rectification or setting aside or cancellation of deeds or other written instruments.

(8) The specific performance of contracts between vendors and purchasers of real estate, including contracts for leases.

(9) The partition or sale of real estates.

(10) The wardship of infants and the case of infants' estates.

mention two recent Statutes, work under the Variation of Trusts Act, 1958, and the Mental Health Act, 1959, is so assigned. Again all High Court work under the Companies Act and the Bankruptcy Act is assigned to the Chancery division and so since 1950 has been the hearing of Revenue Cases.

But the reader must beware of supposing that the jurisdiction of the Chancery Division is limited to these specially assigned matters. The Court of Chancery had a wide " concurrent " jurisdiction under which it entertained actions which might have been brought at common law but in which the plaintiffs were seeking some peculiar equitable remedy such as an injunction or specific performance, and, as we have seen, Lord Cairns' Act (1858), which allowed the Chancery to grant damages as well as or instead of these particular remedies added greatly to the number of actions of contract or tort brought there. The Judicature Acts did not alter this position at all, and consequently there are a great many cases in which a plaintiff can choose whether to proceed on the common law or the chancery side. Of course, if he desires a jury he must bring his case in the Queen's Bench Division and actions for damages for personal injuries which constitute the bulk of the work of the Queen's Bench Division are in practice never brought in the Chancery Division. But it is true to say that there are many actions tried in the Chancery Division which might equally well be tried before a judge of the Queen's Bench Division and conversely many non-jury actions in the Queen's Bench Division which might equally well be tried in the Chancery Division. Which Division is chosen often depends on whether the plaintiff's solicitor sends the papers to Mr. X in Lincoln's Inn or to Mr. Y in the Temple.

There have not been many changes made in the organisation of the Chancery Division since 1875. In 1881 the Master of the Rolls ceased to sit at first instance and came to sit permanently in the Court of Appeal, and a fourth ordinary judge of the Chancery Division was appointed to take his place. To-day the number of judges of the Division is ten, of whom the senior has recently received the title of Vice-Chancellor and two of whom are Patent experts who deal primarily with the Patent work all of which is assigned to the Chancery Division. Before leaving the Chancery Division, we may observe that a co-extensive jurisdiction is exercised locally by the Chancery Courts of Lancaster and Durham.[1]

The most notable change which has taken place in the Probate, Divorce and Admiralty Division since the Judicature Act lies in the vast increase in Divorce work. In 1875 divorce cases were comparatively rare and it may almost be said that the ordinary man was as little likely to be involved in matrimonial proceedings as in a contested probate action or a salvage case. But while the Probate and Admiralty work has remained quite small,[2] over 53,000 divorce petitions were filed in 1968 and the number of judges of the division is now 18. The future of the division is somewhat uncertain. In 1968, as we have seen, the hearing of undefended divorce cases (which account for some seven-eighths of the total) was transferred to the county court, and with the introduction of the concept of " breakdown of marriage " in place of " matrimonial offence " the number of defended divorce cases which is already declining will probably become quite small. In the future in most cases in which there is any conflict it will be only over maintenance and the custody of children and will generally be determined in the county court. The only reason for lumping together such diverse subjects as probate, divorce and admiralty

---

[1] The Court of the Vice-Chancellor of the County Palatine of Lancaster is a fairly busy court. In 1968, 461 proceedings were started in it. In the same year 65 proceedings were brought in the Chancery Court of Durham. In accordance with recommendations of the Beeching Commission the Courts Act, 1971 provides that these local Chancery Courts shall be merged in the High Court.

[2] In 1968, 100 probate writs were issued and 50 actions tried. In the same year 427 admiralty writs were issued and 24 actions tried.

in one division was, of course, that they had all been dealt with up to 1858 by the advocates and proctors in Doctor's Commons and not by common or equity Lawyers. They are now to be separated,[1] the contested Probate work being given to the Chancery Division and the Admiralty work to the Queen's Bench Division, where it will be dealt with together with the Commercial work. The division will be renamed the Family Division and have transferred to it the wardship jurisdiction at present exercised by the Chancery Division. It is unlikely that under the new arrangement there will be enough family work for as many as 18 High Court judges. For some years, divorce judges, when they go on circuit to try divorce cases, have been helping the Queen's Bench judges with their work and it is by no means unusual to see two or three divorce judges in London trying civil actions as additional judges of the Queen's Bench Division.[2] Recently, too, they have begun to help in the work of the Criminal Division of the Court of Appeal by dealing as single judges with applications for leave to appeal. It seems possible that in the not very distant future the distinction between Queen's Bench judges and Family Division judges will disappear.

The Judicature Acts made changes both in the composition of the individual tribunals for the trial of some types of case and also in the circuit system. In the Court of Chancery the trial of a suit at first instance had always been before a single judge, and this had also been the case in the admiralty and ecclesiastical courts, though in many classes of admiralty proceedings the judge was assisted—as he still is to-day—by the advice on nautical matters of two of the Elder Brethren of Trinity House [3]

---

[1] Under the Administration of Justice Act, 1970.

[2] Two were in fact doing so on 19 October, 1970.

[3] Trinity House was incorporated by charter in 1516 as an association of mariners. The duties of the corporation are discharged by 13 Elder Brethren, of whom 2 are drawn from the Royal Navy and 11 from the merchant service.

sitting with him as assessors. In the common law courts, on the other hand, judgment had been given by the court as a whole sitting *in banc*. It is true, of course, that jury trials for the decision of issues of fact under the *nisi prius* system were held before a single commissioner of assize, but, as we have pointed out in earlier chapters, a civil commissioner of assize (unlike a commissioner sitting under one of the criminal commissions) had no power to enter judgment. Arguments of law, whether on an issue of law raised by demurrer or against entry of judgment in accordance with the verdict at *nisi prius*, took place before the court *in banc*, as also did motions for new trials and appeals from inferior courts. The method adopted by the Judicature Acts for harmonising this divergence of practice between the various courts which were being consolidated into the Supreme Court was to lay down as a general principle that the trial of actions at first instance should be before a single judge,[1] but to provide for so-called "Divisional Courts," consisting of two or three judges of one division sitting together, to take the place of the old sittings of the common law courts *in banc* so far as, having regard to the changes made by the Acts in the trial of civil actions, such a tribunal was still necessary.

It may be remembered that we described the working life of a common law judge in the old days as divided between the terms which he spent sitting *in banc* at Westminster with the other judges of his court, and the time out of term that he spent on circuit as a commissioner of assize or of one of the criminal commissions. By the Judicature Act the old division of the legal year into short terms for sittings *in banc* and periods out of term for circuit work was finally abolished, and was

---

[1] The general acceptance of this principle in England since 1875 is one of the chief differences between the legal systems of England and continental countries. In France and Germany cases of importance are almost invariably heard, even at first instance, by several judges. This, it must be remembered, was the old practice in the English courts of common law.

replaced by the modern division of the working year into much longer terms during which the assizes are held concurrently with the sittings in London.[1]   At the same time a step was taken towards reducing the number of civil actions tried on assize by providing that courts should sit continuously in London throughout the sittings for the trial of civil actions, and that notwithstanding the old rules as to venue all actions should be tried in London wherever the cause of action arose unless the plaintiff preferred that it should be tried elsewhere, and the court agreed to this course.[2]   Further, it was provided that the courts of the commissioners of assize should constitute " courts " of the High Court of Justice in as full a sense as the court of a judge sitting in the courts of justice in London, so that henceforth an action tried on circuit could be disposed of completely there without the old necessity of recourse to the court *in banc* for entry of judgment.[3]   Under the modern system, therefore, instead of all the common law judges proceeding together to their various circuits on the close of the legal term in London some of them are sent out to hold the various assizes while the others are sitting in the Royal Courts of Justice.   For some years now judges of the Probate, Divorce and Admiralty Division have been sent on circuit to try divorce cases; but, as we have seen, when they are there they often help the Queen's Bench judges with their work.   The Beeching Commission suggests that Chancery judges should be sent on circuit to try Chancery cases.   In view of what has happened in the case of the Divorce judges, some Chancery judges view this proposal with some apprehension.   It must be remembered that though the courts of the commissioners of assize and of oyer and terminer and gaol delivery are courts of the High Court of Justice, the presiding officer in them sits by virtue of his commission and that

---

1 Judicature Act, 1873, ss. 26, 27.
2 Judicature Act, 1875, schedule 1, order 36.
3 Judicature Act, 1873, s. 29.

the commission can still be issued to persons who are not judges of the High Court.   In the old days the serjeants-at-law often acted as commissioners, and to-day Queen's counsel are sometimes sent on assize as paid commissioners when there is a shortage of judges.

Before we return to the organisation of the Supreme Court in London it will be convenient to speak here of the modern position of the circuit system.   The establishment of the county courts in 1846 deprived the assizes of a great many small actions, while the fact that any action can be tried in London, now that the rules of venue have been abolished, has resulted in most of the heavier civil work coming to London.   In consequence there has been a decline in the importance of the civil side of the assizes.   Down to the end of the last century the leaders of the common law bar habitually went on one or other of the circuits, but now this is no longer the case.   It must not be supposed that the volume of civil work done on circuit is inconsiderable.   Over 1,700 Queen's Bench actions were tried on assize in 1968.   But to-day with the increase of crime it is the criminal work which predominates, and as criminal work is given priority it often happens that the civil list at an assize town cannot be finished in the time available and that many cases have to stand over to the next assize.   In order to improve the position the Beeching Commission (whose recommendations with regard to the criminal work we will discuss in the next chapter) has recommended that civil and criminal work should no longer be taken together on circuit by the same judges but should be kept quite separate.   " Civil work should only be taken in a few large centres on each circuit and the High Court judge sent down to deal with it should have power, at his discretion, to enlist the assistance of one or other of the local county court judges to deal with the lighter cases, if necessary, in order to clear the list."

Now that we have said something of the modern system of trial of actions at first instance in London and on circuit, we are in a position to return to the divisional courts which were to take the place of the old courts *in banc*.   Since a single judge of the Queen's Bench Division or a commissioner of assize now constituted a court of the High Court of Justice capable of dealing with the whole case which came before him, whether in London or on assize, there was no need for the new divisional courts to hear arguments of law on demurrer or to enter judgment after the verdict of the jury as the courts *in banc* had done.   Issues of law could now be decided by the single judge before whom the case came, issues of fact would be decided by him if the trial was without a jury, and by the jury if there was one, and in every case the trial judge could enter judgment himself.   There were, however, two important functions of the courts *in banc* which it was thought could not well be performed by a single judge—the hearing of motions for a new trial and of appeals from inferior courts, such as the county courts and the courts of the justices of the peace. These matters, together with certain other business, were entrusted to divisional courts, and from their decisions there was generally a further appeal to the Court of Appeal with the leave either of the divisional court or the Court of Appeal.   In time, however, it came to be seen that now that there was a permanent court of appeal an intermediate tribunal was not really necessary in all these cases.   Accordingly, it was enacted in 1890 that applications for a new trial should be made to the Court of Appeal instead of to a divisional court, in the first instance, and some of the Acts which entrusted special jurisdiction to the county courts, such, for instance, as the Workmen's Compensation Acts, provided for an appeal direct to the Court of Appeal instead of to a divisional court.   Eventually, as we have seen, it was laid down in 1934 that appeals from the ordinary jurisdiction of the county court should go straight to the Court of Appeal. The chief function left to divisional courts of the Queen's Bench Division is the hearing of appeals by way of " case stated " on points of law from quarter and petty sessions, and from tribunals established under various Acts of Parliament such as the Redundancy Payments Act, 1965, and the Selective Employment Payments Act, 1966, and also the hearing of applications in prerogative proceedings.[1]   If the matter is criminal—as it normally is where cases are stated by justices—there is an appeal direct to the House of Lords with leave.   In civil cases there is an appeal with leave to the Civil Division of the Court of Appeal.   As there had been no sittings *in banc* in the old court of Chancery or in the ecclesiastical or admiralty courts, divisional courts have always been a rarity in the Chancery and Probate, Divorce and Admiralty Divisions. There are, however, examples of them in each.   A divisional court of the Chancery division hears bankruptcy appeals from the county courts, and a divisional court of the Probate, Divorce and Admiralty Division hears appeals from the exercise by the justices of the peace of the matrimonial jurisdiction conferred on them by the Summary Jurisdiction (Separation and Maintenance) Acts 1895–1949.

We must now pass from the High Court to the Court of Appeal.   The Lord Chancellor, the Lord Chief Justice, the Master of the Rolls, the President of the Probate, Divorce and Admiralty Division, and the Lords of Appeal in Ordinary are *ex-officio* members of this court, but the Master of the Rolls is the only one of them who habitually sits there to-day.   In addition there are thirteen permanent Lord Justices of Appeal,[2] and the court

---

[1] In 1968 the Divisional Court heard 123 cases stated by courts of summary jurisdiction and over 90 cases stated by other bodies. There were 95 applications for leave to apply for some form of prerogative order. In 72 cases leave to apply was granted " ex parte " but only in 25 cases was the order issued after hearing both sides.

[2] Judicature Act, 1925, s. 6.   It is to be observed that in 1875 the new Court of Appeal was constituted on the model of the Court of Appeal in Chancery, and not on that of the Exchequer Chamber.   It is composed of permanent judges of appeal and not of judges of first instance sitting to hear appeals " pro hac vice."

generally sits in four divisions of three judges, one presided over by the Master of the Rolls and the others by the three senior Lord Justices. We have already mentioned the courts whose jurisdiction was vested in the Court of Appeal in 1875. With certain exceptions it hears appeals in all matters from all the divisions of the High Court and from the assize courts, as well as hearing nearly all appeals from the county courts. It was provided by the Judicature Act that the Court should not hear any appeal in a criminal matter. As we shall see in the next chapter, the jurisdiction of the Court for Crown Cases Reserved and the jurisdiction of the King's Bench to hear writs of error in criminal cases was in 1907 vested in a separate court, the Court of Criminal Appeal, composed of the Lord Chief Justice and the judges of the Queen's Bench Division. With the increase in the number of criminal appeals the court had often to sit in two divisions and it came to be thought unsuitable that the Court to hear appeals from a Queen's Bench judge on assize should be composed exclusively of his fellow puisne judges. So in 1968 the functions of the Court of Criminal Appeal were transferred to the so-called Criminal Division of the Court of Appeal. The Queen's Bench judges can be required to sit in the Court. Normally two Lords Justices are available at any given time for criminal work so that a division of the Court is almost invariably presided over either by the Lord Chief Justice or a Lord Justice of Appeal, but always one and often two Queen's Bench judges will be sitting in it. From the Court of Appeal there is a further appeal to the House of Lords. We have seen already how the Judicature Act, 1873, provided for the abolition of the second appeal and how it was preserved by the Acts of 1875 and 1876. But since 1934 such an appeal can only be brought with the leave either of the Court of Appeal or of the House of Lords and in the case of criminal appeals " if " the Court certifies that a point of law of public importance is involved.

The establishment of one Supreme Court of Judicature was accompanied by the erection of a suitable building to house it. Hitherto the superior courts of law and equity had been scattered in many places, but now they were brought together and the Royal Courts of Justice in the Strand were opened by Queen Victoria on December 4th, 1882.[1] As well as courts for the judges the new building contained accommodation for some of the official staffs of the old courts which were themselves the subject of a certain measure of consolidation. The various Masters of the common law courts (first appointed in 1837) became Masters of the Supreme Court (Queen's Bench Division). Of these the senior is Master of the Crown Office and, as such, has charge of the work of the Criminal Division of the Court of Appeal. One of the functions of the Masters of the Queen's Bench Division is to supervise and control the central office of the Supreme Court (established in 1879), in which writs are issued, appearances entered, judgments registered, etc. Another of their functions is to sit in chambers in the Queen's Bench Division and to deal there (subject to an appeal to a judge) with the various preliminary stages in an action of which we shall have something to say later. The Masters of the Queen's Bench Division are barristers, and with the exception of the Master of the Crown Office, who is appointed by the Lord Chief Justice, are appointed in rotation by the Lord Chancellor, the Lord Chief Justice and the Master of the Rolls. As well as the eight Masters of the Queen's Bench Division there are seven Masters of the Chancery Division who until 1897 were styled Chief Clerks, and are

---

[1] For many years there were too few courts in the building to accommodate all the judges sitting in London, but recently a number of additional Courts have been built and the old-fashioned administrative block is to be replaced by a new building. It is to be hoped that the central Hall will be spared. It is hardly ever used—except by young people playing Badminton in the evening—but it is a magnificent specimen of Victorian Gothic.

solicitors appointed to their office by the Lord Chancellor. It is their function both to deal with the preliminary stages of proceedings in the Chancery Division and also to take and make the various accounts and enquiries which such proceedings sometimes entail.   It is to be observed, however, that the Masters of the Chancery Division have not the independent jurisdiction possessed by the Masters of the Queen's Bench Division.   The orders they make are made in the name of the judge, and any party can claim to bring any point before the judge himself not by way of appeal but by way of adjournment.   Then there are several other classes of official, as, for instance, the taxing masters, whose duty it is to tax the costs of all proceedings in the Queen's Bench and Chancery Divisions, and the registrars of the Chancery Division, who sit with the judges in Court and draw up the orders made in Chancery proceedings.

But we must not think of the whole official staff of the Supreme Court as concentrated in the Law Courts. Scattered over England there are 89 district registries of the Supreme Court where writs can be issued, and proceedings carried on, down to the stage of entry for trial and where the district registrar (usually the registrar of the local county court) has the authority and jurisdiction of a Master of the Supreme Court.[1]   The headquarters of the official staffs of the Probate and Divorce sides of the Probate, Divorce and Admiralty Division are at Somerset House, and there are also district probate registries in different parts of the country where wills can be proved provided probate is not disputed.   These local registries were established in cathedral cities, where the bishops' probate courts had sat, and wills proved in those courts before 1857 are preserved in them.   Similarly wills proved in the Canterbury Prerogative Court are to be found at Somerset House.   The Admiralty Registry is

---

[1] About three out of eight proceedings in the Queen's Bench Division are started in district registries.

housed in the Courts of Justice, but its work is highly specialised and its registrar is as independent of the Central Office as are the probate and divorce registrars in Somerset House.

Our legal system hinges to-day on the occupants of three high offices: the Lord Chancellor, the Lord Chief Justice and the Master of the Rolls, and we will conclude this section by considering how their work has changed in the course of the last century. The Lord Chancellor, who presides over the House of Lords, is a member of the Cabinet and sits on occasion as a judge, performs legislative, executive and judicial functions. His judicial functions, however, loom far less large to-day than they used to do. Up to 1851 he sat at first instance in his High Court of Chancery. From 1851 to 1875 he sat regularly in the Court of Appeal in Chancery and under the original scheme of the Judicature Act whereby the judicial functions of the House of Lords were to be abolished and the Supreme Court was to be a Supreme Court in reality he would have presided over the newly created Court of Appeal. But as the jurisdiction of the House of Lords was preserved he sat but rarely in the Court of Appeal and soon confined himself to sitting on appeals in the House of Lords and the Privy Council. Until the end of the second war, however, successive Lord Chancellors presided on a substantial number of such appeals including most of those which raised important issues. But in the last 25 years the occupants of the Woolsack have largely given up sitting on appeals. This is partly because to-day the House of Lords is itself often sitting while the Appeal Committee is hearing an appeal; but largely because the Lord Chancellor is now responsible for the working of a legal system of increasing complexity and has not the time also to sit as a judge. In 1938 the senior staff of the Lord Chancellor' office numbered only four or five. To-day it numbers over 20 and is still too small for the work now falling on it. This development may have consequences which some people at least would deplore. Some Lord Chancellors have been much better lawyers than others; but hitherto no one has been able to become Lord Chancellor unless he has had a successful career at the Bar. But if the Lord Chancellor does not sit as a judge what need is there that he should have been a successful barrister or indeed a lawyer at all ? Would it not be a " good thing," some people might say, to have a Minister of Justice who was not embued with the traditions of the Bar but came to his office with an open mind ?

The great difference between the position of Lord Coleridge in 1881 and of Lord Parker in 1970 is that as a result of the great increase in crime the Lord Chief Justice has practically—if not entirely—ceased to try civil cases at first instance. He goes on circuit for a few weeks each term to try criminal cases at first instance but otherwise his time is spent in presiding in the Criminal Division of the Court of Appeal and the Divisional Court. Owing to the pressure of work most of the judgments of these courts have to be given " off the cuff " and most of them are in fact given by the President of the Court. In addition to this heavy burden of judicial work the Lord Chief Justice has a great deal of work to do out of court. He must of necessity be in constant contact with the Home Office as the authority responsible for the police and the prisons and he has hitherto had to cope with a mass of administrative work in connection with the assizes. The Beeching Commission recommends that the Lord Chancellor's office should take over the less important of these latter responsibilities. As they say (paragraph 310) it cannot be right that the Lord Chief Justice should have personally to concern himself with such matters as the availability of judges' lodgings for a particular assize.

Before the Judicature Act the Master of the Rolls was the senior judge (under the Lord Chancellor) of the Court of Chancery and the intention of the Act was that he should be the working head of the Chancery Division as the Lord Chief Justice was of the Queen's Bench Division and the President of the Probate, Divorce and Admiralty Division. But the retention of the final appeal to the House of Lords meant that the Lord Chancellor could not preside in the Court of Appeal. So in 1881 Sir George Jessel moved from sitting at first instance in the Chancery Division to sitting in the Court of Appeal and since that date successive Masters of the Rolls have been the effective presidents of the Civil Court of Appeal, since neither the Lord Chancellor nor the Lord Chief Justice sits in it. Although several of the Masters of the Rolls appointed since the death of Sir George Jessel have been Chancery lawyers, the office has ceased since 1881 to have any particular connection with the Chancery Division. The Civil Division of the Court of Appeal—like the Criminal Division—works under ever mounting pressure. In 1968 there were 1,273 appeals for hearing of which 893 were heard as against 1,034 in 1967 of which 909 were heard. Not as many judgments are reserved as ideally should be reserved and the pressure of deliving extemporary judgments day in and day out without a break falls ever more heavily on the Master of the Rolls than on the Lords Justices presiding in the other divisions of the Court since the most interesting—and therefore often the most difficult—cases seem to find their way into his Court.

II. LAW AND EQUITY

We saw in Chapter 15 that one of the chief objects aimed at by the reforms introduced in the half-century before 1875 was the bringing together of the systems of law and equity by, for instance, enabling courts of law to entertain some equitable defences and to give some equitable remedies, and courts of equity to decide questions of law and to award damages. The final step in this process of assimilation was taken by the union under the Judicature Acts of the former courts of law and equity in one court, in every branch of which law and equity were to be concurrently administered. " This Court," said Lord Cairns of the new Supreme Court, " is now not a court of law nor a court of equity but a court of complete jurisdiction." We have indeed seen that much of the business which in the old days was within the exclusive jurisdiction of the Court of Chancery was assigned to the Chancery Division, but this fact does not mean that that division has any monopoly of equity. Broadly speaking it is true to say that any right which could have been asserted and protected in the Court of Chancery can now be enforced in a case brought in any division of the High Court.

Sections 24 and 25 of the Act of 1873[1] laid down the principles upon which law and equity were to be concurrently administered. In any action brought in the High Court in which the plaintiff claims to be entitled to any equitable right or relief against the defendant or the defendant relies on any equitable defence to the plaintiff's claim, the court is directed to give the same effect to the claim or defence in question as the Court of Chancery would have done had the matter in question been raised before it in the old days. Further, if any equitable title or right or liability appears incidentally in the course of any action in the High Court the court is to take notice of it in the like manner as the Court of Chancery would have done. As a natural consequence of these provisions the common injunction by which the Court of Chancery had in appropriate cases restrained on equitable grounds the further prosecution of an action at law disappeared. No injunction can be granted by one division of the High Court to restrain proceedings in another. The defendant can either rely on the matters which in the old days would have formed ground for a common injunction as a defence to the action brought against him, or in some cases can apply to the court which is hearing the action for an order that further proceedings

[1] Now Judicature Act, 1925, ss. 36–44.

in it may be stayed.   One of the chief objects of the Act was to avoid the multiplicity of proceedings which had been among the chief defects of the old system.   Now that the same court can give effect to both legal and equitable rights the parties can have all matters in controversy between them completely and finally determined in one action.

It may be asked " How are two separate systems of law which in the past had often been in conflict with one another, and the rules of which were often at variance, harmoniously administered in one court ? "   If we are to understand the answer to this question we must remind ourselves of the nature of equity.   To a great extent it was supplementary to, not contradictory of, the common law, and to this extent the joint administration of law and equity could raise no difficulties.   Take the example of a trust.   The common law says A is the owner of the property ; equity supplements the law by saying, " Yes, A is the legal owner of the property but he holds it on trust for B."   Obviously these two sets of rights, legal and equitable, can be as conveniently administered in one court as in two.   Similarly there was no difficulty in allowing the same court to give all or any of the different varieties of remedies which formerly had been given only by one or other of the old courts.   In some cases, of course, the rule of equity had been not so much supplementary of the common law rule as in conflict with it. Those were, broadly speaking, the cases where equity recognised some right to relief or defence which the law did not recognise and would, in effect, nullify the legal rule by the use of its injunctions.   In such cases if the party entitled to the equitable relief in question applied to the Chancery the rule of equity could be made to prevail over the rule of law and in the new court the continuance of this prevalence was secured by the general provisions which we have mentioned allowing all equities to be raised and given effect to in any action.

But it was felt that in certain well-known cases of

variance between the legal and equitable rule a general provision of this sort might not be sufficient to avoid conflict, and accordingly section 25 of the Act of 1873 expressly directed that effect should be given to the equitable and not the legal rule in a number of specific cases, and ended with the well-known sub-section (11), " Generally in all matters not hereinbefore particularly mentioned in which there is any conflict or variance between the rules of equity and the rules of the common law with reference to the same matter the rules of equity shall prevail." [1] But in truth so much of equity was supplementary of the common law and so much of what was conflicting fitted harmoniously into the general scheme when it was allowed to be pleaded together with matters of law in the same action, that it has very seldom been found necessary to decide a conflict between the two systems by reference to this sub-section.

It must not, of course, be supposed that the Judicature Acts by abolishing the separate courts of law and equity and providing for the concurrent administration of the two systems in one court have abolished the distinction between law and equity. It is indeed true that some old common law rules, the application of which could have been nullified in the old days by an application to the Chancery, disappeared entirely when the systems were administered in one court, and it is also true that in the realm of procedure—with which we will deal in the next section—a new code derived partly from one and partly from the other took the place of the old distinct chancery and common law procedures. But in the main the distinction between legal and equitable rights was unaffected. Legal and equitable estates in property continued to exist side by side after 1875 as well as before it, and the fact that both could be considered in the same court did not mean that the possession of one was equivalent to the possession of the other. Indeed, this continued distinction between legal and equitable estates

[1] Now Judicature Act, 1925, s. 44.

was laid hold of by the Legislature in 1925 and made the basis of the modern law of real property. Before January 1st, 1926, any interest in land might be either legal or equitable. Since that date some interests can only exist in equity. It is no longer possible to conceive of the law of real property as a common law system with an equitable supplement. It is a unified system compounded of both legal and equitable interests, each of which is a necessary part of the whole.

It cannot, however, be said that in all branches of the law common law and equity have settled down side by side as harmoniously as in the law of real property. In the law of contract in particular there are still a number of inelegancies and uncertainties which are ultimately referable to the divergence between the common law and equity point of view. To the common lawyer a contract consists of obligations to be performed by one person to another person. Equity, on the other hand, looking upon what ought to be done as done, always projects itself into the future and tries to give effect in advance to the changes which will ensue at law when the contract is carried out. The different results to which these different views lead is well illustrated by the case of a contract by which A undertakes with B to pay money to C. Here the common law saw only an obligation of A to B which B could enforce, but C could not, while equity, perceiving that C would benefit if the contract was duly performed, often held that C had from the first an equitable interest in the property which he might eventually receive and that B was a trustee of the benefit of the contract for him. No principle has yet been evolved to which one can refer the question whether any given agreement does or does not create a trust for a third party, and consequently one finds merely a number of particular cases decided in one way or the other which are in truth irreconcilable on any grounds of principle.[1]

[1] For a recent discussion of the topic see *Beswick* v. *Beswick*, [1968] A.C. 58.

III. Procedure

Down to the nineteenth century the course of procedure in the various courts of common law and equity was regulated by orders issued from time to time by the judges of the courts or the Chancellor, not under any statutory authority but in virtue of an inherent right to control proceedings before them, which they had claimed and exercised for centuries. The reforming statutes of the nineteenth century tended to supersede this prerogative jurisdiction of the judges by express statutory powers given to them to make rules or orders for carrying into effect the procedural reforms initiated by the legislation in question. Further, it was one of the objects of the Common Law Procedure Acts and the Chancery Amendment Acts to assimilate to one another the procedure of the courts of law and equity. The Judicature Acts completed this process by establishing a single code of procedure for most proceedings in the new Supreme Court which purported to adopt the best features of the several existing systems. The foundation of this new code of procedure was contained in sixty-three orders, each containing a number of separate rules which were scheduled to the Judicature Act, 1875, and by Section 17 of that Act power was given to the judges of the Supreme Court to make new rules of procedure from time to time which should be laid before Parliament and become law if not disallowed by that body. To-day, this rule-making power is exercised by the " Rule Committee," consisting of the Lord Chancellor, the Lord Chief Justice, the Master of the Rolls, the President of the Probate, Divorce and Admiralty Division, together with four judges of the Supreme Court, two members of the General Council of the Bar and two practising solicitors selected by the Chancellor.[1]

The orders and rules scheduled to the Judicature Act,

---

[1] Judicature Act, 1925, s. 99.

1875, have been, of course, substantially amended and extended since then. Every few years there appears a new edition of the Supreme Court Practice (the White Book), which contains the orders and rules brought up to date, with copious notes on the interpretation which the courts have put on them in the past. Recently—in response to a recommendation of the " Evershed Committee " [1]—a complete revision was undertaken and the rules have been rearranged in a more logical form. It is to be observed that these rules of procedure do not cover all proceedings in the Supreme Court. The practice of the Probate, Divorce and Admiralty Division is of a special character and is largely the subject of separate rules. In this book we must confine ourselves to a very brief outline of the course of procedure in ordinary civil cases in the Queen's Bench and Chancery Divisions.

The most common form of proceeding (in the Queen's Bench Division at least) is an action commenced by writ, and we will first deal with the various steps in such an action before passing to proceedings initiated in other ways. We have seen already that the Uniformity of Process Act, 1832, established a common form of writ of summons for use in all personal actions at common law, and the modern writ of summons for use in all divisions of the High Court is in much the same form. It is a command from the Queen to the defendant to enter an appearance to the action within eight days of its service on him, but instead of being witnessed, like the writs of summons at common law from 1833 to 1875, by the Chief Justice of the court, it is nominally witnessed (like the old original writs) by the Chancellor. In fact, printed forms with blanks are sold by law stationers, and the blanks are filled in by the plaintiff's solicitor, who takes the form to the central office of the Supreme Court or one of the district registries, where it is issued by being sealed by the proper officer on payment of the

---

[1] See p. 327, below.

appropriate fee. The writ specifies the division of the High Court to which the plaintiff has assigned the action, and on its back it is endorsed with a statement of the plaintiff's claim or if a separate statement of claim is going to be delivered—which will be the case in complicated matters—with a concise statement of the general nature of the claim made.

We have seen that before 1852 the plaintiff had to choose one or other of the various forms of action and to cast his claim into the mould appropriate to his choice. The Common Law Procedure Act, 1852, however, did away with that necessity, and since then the plaintiff has been at liberty to state his claim in his own words without reference to any particular form of action. This reform was, of course, in its origin a mere reform of procedure and not of substantive law. Though the plaintiff did not have to formulate his claim under the rubric of one of the forms of action it was not intended that he should be thereby enabled to advance claims which could not have been brought under any form of action, and there are not wanting quite modern cases in which the success or failure of the plaintiff has depended on whether or not his claim could have been stated in the form of one of the old actions.[1] Nevertheless there is no doubt that the disappearance of the forms of action has been one of the several factors which has helped of recent years to give much greater elasticity to the common law, in particular to the law of tort. Instead of a fixed number of classes of remedy we now have general principles of tortious liability.[2]

As well as allowing the plaintiff complete freedom to state his cause of action as he pleases the rules of court permit almost all causes of action to be joined together in one proceeding and give a wide liberty for several

[1] See, *e.g.*, the discussion of the scope of the action for " money had and received " in *Sinclair* v. *Brougham*, [1915] A. C. 398.

[2] See, *e.g.*, the great " Ginger Beer Bottle " case, *Donoghue* v. *Stevenson* [1932] A. C. 562.

parties to be joined as plaintiffs or defendants in one action. Speaking generally, all persons may be joined in one action as plaintiffs in whom any right to relief is alleged to arise out of the same transaction or series of transactions either jointly, severally or in the alternative where if such persons brought separate actions any common question of law or fact would arise, and all persons may be joined as defendants against whom the right to any relief is alleged to exist whether jointly, severally or in the alternative. Further, under the Judicature Acts the practice of the Court of Chancery in allowing so-called " representative " proceedings has been extended to every division of the Supreme Court. Thus where numerous people have the same interest in a single cause or matter one or more of them may be allowed to sue or be sued on behalf of them all.

When the writ has been issued the next step is to serve it on the defendant. In most cases where the defendant is represented by a solicitor his solicitor undertakes to accept service on his behalf and to enter an appearance for him so that personal service on the defendant is unnecessary. Otherwise the writ must be served personally, or if this can be shown to be impossible an order for so-called " substituted " service must be obtained which allows the writ to be sent by post or advertised. If the defendant is out of the jurisdiction when the writ is issued he can only be served by the leave of a judge. The rules by which the judges exercise their discretion to allow service out of the jurisdiction are complicated, but speaking generally the plaintiff must show either that the defendant is domiciled or ordinarily resident within the jurisdiction or that the cause of action is by reason of the situation of the property which is its subject-matter, or of the circumstances in which the liability which is being enforced arose, an " English " cause of action.

If the defendant proposes to contest the plaintiff's claim he or his solicitor must enter an appearance to the action by delivery to the proper officer at the central

office or district registry of a memorandum in writing in
the prescribed form. Of course, in a very large number
of cases no appearance is entered by the defendant at all.
In many cases no doubt the mere issue of the writ secures
compliance with the demand, but if it does not the plaintiff
can take steps to obtain judgment on the failure of
the defendant to enter an appearance within the prescribed time.[1] The nature of those steps and the speed
with which judgment in default can be obtained depend
on the character of the plaintiff's demand. Thus if it is
a demand for a liquidated sum of money final judgment
for the amount claimed can be obtained forthwith, while
if the claim is for unliquidated damages a judgment conclusive as to the plaintiff's right to the damages may be
obtained speedily, leaving their amount to be assessed by
a subsequent enquiry. In more complicated cases, on
the other hand, the plaintiff may be obliged notwithstanding the defendant's default to deliver a statement
of claim setting out his case with more particularity than
the endorsement on his writ before he can obtain judgment. In all cases the defendant may still appear at any
time before the entry of judgment notwithstanding his
initial default.

Even if the defendant enters an appearance it does
not follow that the plaintiff will be put to the expense of
prosecuting the action in the ordinary way. Often a man
who has no real defence puts in an appearance merely
in order to gain time, and a plaintiff who is confident that
there is no arguable ground of defence to his claim can
in many cases compel the defendant to satisfy the court
that he has a possible defence before he will be allowed
to defend the action. The procedure to be pursued for
this purpose is regulated by Order 14 of the Rules
of Court. It is applicable to every class of action other

---

[1] In 1968 over 75,000 writs were issued in the Central office in
Queen's Bench proceedings and some 32,000 judgments " in default "
were entered.

than actions for libel, slander, seduction, false imprisonment, malicious prosecution or breach of promise, or
actions in which a charge of fraud is made against the
defendant,[1] but to bring it into play the plaintiff must have
served a statement of claim on the defendant either by
endorsing it on the writ or delivering it separately.
Then on the defendant entering an appearance to the writ
the plaintiff can take out a summons supported by an
affidavit stating that he believes the defendant to have no
defence and asking for judgment. The defendant must
then either satisfy the court by affidavit that he has some
ground of defence or allow judgment to go against him.
It is for the Master before whom the summons is heard to
say, subject to appeal to the judge, whether the defence
disclosed is so obviously hopeless that the plaintiff
ought to have judgment at once or whether the defendant ought to be given leave to defend in the ordinary
way. Procedure under Order 14 is naturally most
common in the case of liquidated money claims, and
in 1961 some 2,500 judgments under it were entered
in proceedings assigned to the Queen's Bench Division.

Assuming that the plaintiff does not obtain judgment
under Order 14, the next step after the statement of claim
is the delivery of the defence. The object of the pleadings is, of course, to bring the parties to an issue by
defining the questions of fact or law in dispute between
them so that there may be no doubt what is to be proved
or decided at the trial. The rules of pleading laid down
after the Judicature Acts were intended to be a compromise between the old common law and equity systems.
Bills and answers in Chancery were prolix and somewhat
formless, while declarations and pleas in common law
actions, even after the reforms of 1833 and 1852, tended
to be either too uninformative or too technical. The
general principle of modern pleading is laid down in the

---

[1] In all these actions the defendant's character is in issue. In such
cases it is obviously proper that the defendant should have complete
liberty to defend the action, however hopeless the task may seem.

following words : " Every pleading shall contain and contain only a statement in a summary form of the material facts on which the party pleading relies for his claim or defence as the case may be, but not the evidence by which they are to be proved." [1] An adherence to this rule should secure that pleadings shall be at once brief and informative, but if they are to play their proper part in an action it is obvious that the parties must be bound by them and must not be allowed to raise unpleaded claims and defences at the trial. Modern judges in fear of being thought technical are perhaps too apt to listen at the trial to a case which has never been raised on the pleadings. The pleadings begin with the plaintiff's statement of claim which, in default of agreement between the parties or the leave of the court, must be delivered within fourteen days of the defendant's appearance. The statement of claim, which is signed by the plaintiff's junior counsel, [2] sets out in numbered paragraphs the material facts on which the plaintiff relies as giving him a cause of action and states specifically at the end the relief or alternative reliefs to which the plaintiff considers himself entitled. As an ordinary indorsement on the writ is only intended to give the defendant general notice of the nature of the plaintiff's claim, the statement of claim if not endorsed on the writ can modify or extend the relief asked for by it provided that it does not completely change the cause of action indicated. The defendant in default of agreement, or the leave of the court, must deliver his defence within fourteen days of the delivery of the statement of claim or the time limited for appearance, whichever is later. It must be signed by his junior counsel and must deal separately with the various allegations in the statement of claim. What he does not deny or refuse to admit he is taken to have admitted, but he can, of course, " confess and avoid "—*i.e.* admit certain allegations and allege

[1] Order 18, rule 7.
[2] See p. 394, for the distinction between Queen's Counsel and juniors.

fresh matters in justification which may put a different complexion on the facts which he admits.

We have seen that under the old system of pleading the issue in the action had to be either one of law or of fact, and that a party, if he chose to raise an issue of law would demur to his opponent's pleading, thereby admitting for the purposes of the action that the facts pleaded by his opponent were true but contending that even on that assumption his opponent would show no right in law to the relief which he claimed. Under the modern system demurrers have been abolished and points of law arising on the facts pleaded are normally not themselves raised on the pleadings at all but are argued at the trial. Any party may, however, if he chooses, raise a point of law on his pleading and with the consent of his opponent or the leave of the court get it set down for hearing and disposed of before the trial of the action. In such a case the judge may, if he thinks that the decision of the point of law has substantially disposed of the whole action, dismiss the action or make such order in it as he thinks fit. It is interesting to observe that while in England proceedings in lieu of demurrer are very rare, in Scotland it is still quite common for the equivalent of the English demurrer, termed a plea of irrelevancy, to be argued and decided before proof of the facts.

At any time after putting in an appearance the defendant may, in an action for debt or damages, and subject to various rules, pay money into court in satisfaction of the plaintiff's claim, which he is taken to admit to the extent of the amount paid in. The object of this step is, of course, to secure that the plaintiff will have to bear the costs if he does not take out the money but proceeds with the action and recovers no more than he was offered. Further, the plaintiff's claim may be the subject either of a set-off or of a counterclaim by the defendant. A set-off can only be pleaded by the defendant when the plaintiff is claiming a liquidated sum and the defendant claims that there was another liquidated sum due to him from the plaintiff at the date of the issue of the writ. If so he can claim by his defence to set one off against the other. But a set-off is only a shield, not a sword. If the debt which the defendant claims to set-off exceeds in amount the debt claimed by the plaintiff the defendant, even if successful in establishing his set-off, cannot get judgment against the plaintiff for the excess. A counterclaim, on the other hand, is a sword. If the defendant has any claim against the plaintiff which he might make the subject of an independent action against him, he can (subject to a few exceptions and the discretion of the court) raise it by way of counterclaim in the plaintiff's action. If the defendant has raised new matter in his defence the plaintiff may, if he chooses, deliver a reply to it, and if the defendant has a counterclaim the plaintiff must deliver a defence to it together with his reply. In theory it is possible for the defendant to put in a rejoinder to the reply which may be followed by a surrejoinder from the plaintiff, a rebutter from the defendant and a final surrebutter from the plaintiff, but in the vast majority of cases the statement of claim, the defence (with or without a counterclaim) and the reply and defence to counterclaim (if any) are the only pleadings in the action.

Between the service of the writ and the trial there are a variety of applications some of which must be, and all of which can be, made to the court in connection with the action. These applications are in most cases made in the first place to the Master to whom the action has been assigned or, if the action is proceeding in a district registry, to the district registrar, but his decision is not final, and the matters can always be taken before a judge. After the close of the pleadings a summons for directions must be taken out by the plaintiff, and when this has been done subsequent applications are generally made under it, but before the summons for directions has been issued the application will normally be by an ordinary

summons in the action.   Here we have only space to
mention the most usual of these applications.

First there may be applications for leave to amend the
writ or the pleadings, or to add or strike out parties, and
either side may apply for " further and better particulars " of one or more allegations in his opponent's pleadings which in his view are not stated with sufficient detail
for him to know exactly what case he will have to meet
at the trial.   Then each side is certain to require some
measure of discovery from his opponent.   Discovery
takes two forms.   The party against whom it is ordered
may be obliged to answer on oath formal questions known
as interrogatories directed to some matter in dispute in
the action, and further may be obliged to disclose documents in his possession relating to it.   The fundamental
rule of discovery is that what is called " fishing " is not
allowed.   That is to say that discovery is not to be
granted simply in order to help a party to see if he has a
case, but only in order to help him to support the case
which he has pleaded, by obtaining information or admissions which will make the burden of proving it lighter.
Leave to deliver interrogatories is by no means always
applied for, nor, if applied for, are the suggested interrogatories always allowed.   If the cases have been fairly
pleaded there is often no real need for them.   Discovery
of documents, on the other hand, is always allowed.[1]   Each
side is ordered to file an affidavit setting out all the
relevant documents which are or have been in his possession and specifying those which on any ground he
objects to produce for inspection.   In this way it is usually
possible for the documentary evidence which is to be
adduced at the trial to be agreed between the parties
beforehand.   Among other possible applications are
applications by the defendant that the plaintiff be ordered
to give security for the costs of the action on the ground,

[1] Under the new rules there is not in most cases any need for an order
for discovery.   On the close of pleadings each side is automatically bound
to disclose all relevant documents in his possession or power.

for instance, of his residence out of the jurisdiction, or that the action be remitted to the county court on the ground that the claim falls within the county court jurisdiction and ought to have been brought there.

But besides the various applications which are concerned with the procedure to be adopted in the action, it may be necessary to apply to the court for some order touching the actual subject-matter of the action pending the trial. Thus, if the defendant is pursuing some course of conduct which the plaintiff complains is injuring him, it may be proper provisionally to restrain the defendant from continuing it pending the determination of the rights of the parties, and if the ownership of property is in dispute it may be advisable to appoint an independent receiver of it who will protect and manage it pending the decision. In the Queen's Bench Division such applications are made by summons in chambers, but in the Chancery Division, where they are naturally particularly common as the jurisdiction to issue injunctions and appoint receivers is derived from the practice of the Court of Chancery, they are made to the judge in open court by a motion asking for the provisional or, to use the technical term, " interlocutory " relief in question. The evidence for and against the motion is by affidavit ; and if the judge decides to make an order on the motion the party at whose instance it is made will have to undertake to indemnify his opponent against any damages which he may suffer by reason of the order if it turns out at the trial that he was in the right. Motions may be made at any stage in the proceedings on notice to the other side, but it is usual for them to be made at the commencement of the action before the pleadings, and notice of motion is often served with the writ. In many cases, of course, the whole position between the parties is so clarified by the affidavits read on the motion and the discussion in court that the whole action can be disposed of there and then without the necessity for pleadings or trial.[1]

[1] In 1968 some 1,600 writs assigned to the Chancery Division were

A great many actions are, of course, settled at some stage in the proceedings prior to trial. Assuming, however, that the action is going to be fought it is necessary to decide where it is to be tried and how it is to be tried. The old rules of venue have all been abolished and the place of trial is now entirely in the discretion of the court which, in deciding on it, is to have regard to the convenience of the parties and their witnesses. We have seen already that the old *nisi prius* system has been radically altered and that there are now judges sitting in London continuously throughout the term for the trial of civil actions at the Courts of Justice. Nearly half the Queen's Bench actions are tried in London and so are substantially all Chancery actions even though the parties and their witnesses reside in the country. In 1968 about 1,700 Queen's Bench actions were heard on assize. The majority of these were, of course, proceedings in which the writ had been issued and the earlier proceedings taken in the local district registry.

Actions tried in the Chancery Division are tried by a judge without a jury. In actions tried in the Queen's Bench Division trial by jury has been on the wane for the last fifty years. The present position is that in cases of libel, slander, malicious prosecution, false imprisonment, seduction or breach of promise a jury must be granted on the application of either side, and in cases in which fraud is alleged on the application of the party against whom it is alleged, unless the court thinks the trial will involve a prolonged investigation of documents or accounts, or scientific or local investigation, such as cannot conveniently be made with a jury. Cases of fraud often involve such prolonged investigation, but none of the other six named actions is ever likely to do so. Apart, however, from these special provisions it is now entirely

issued in the Central Office. In the same year over 1,000 motions were heard and only some 150 actions tried. These figures show that a high proportion of Chancery writs are followed by " motions " and that many of them go no further.

within the discretion of the court whether the trial will
be with or without a jury.   In fact it is very seldom
asked for in cases outside the specified class and by no
means always in cases within it.   In 1968 only 26 actions
tried in London and 10 actions tried on assize were tried
by jury.   Until 1949 the jury might be either a common
jury or a special jury composed of persons with higher
property qualifications and, therefore, supposedly of
higher education.   Special juries were, however, for
practical purposes abolished by the Juries Act, 1949,
s. 18.[1]

Finally, the action must be entered for trial.   In the
Queen's Bench Division there is a special list for commercial actions, *e.g.* actions involving the construction of
mercantile documents, bills of lading, policies of insurance, etc., which are heard by a special judge assigned to
take that list.   The chief objects of this arrangement are
to secure that such cases should be heard by a judge
specially conversant with commercial law and with a
minimum of expense and delay.   The judge of the commercial court has power to make such order as he may
think fit for the speedy determination of the questions
between the parties, dispensing, if necessary, with formal
pleadings and the technical rules of evidence.[2]

We have now brought our action down to the moment
of trial.   Counsel for the plaintiff opens his case at

---

[1] The reasons for the decline of trial by jury in civil actions are discussed by Lord Devlin in his *Trial by Jury* (Hamlyn Lecture, 1956).
He thinks that the basic reason is that in the most common type of action
—claims for damages for negligence—the litigants wish to be able to
predict the result and that the award of a judge, being influenced by his
knowledge of what he and other judges have awarded in similar cases, is
far more predictable than that of a jury.

[2] The commercial court was not established under the authority of
the Rules Committee, but rests simply upon a practice agreed upon by
the judges of the Q.B.D. in 1895, at the instance of Mr. Justice, later
Lord Justice, Mathew, a great commercial lawyer.   See *per* Scrutton,
L.J., in *Butcher* v. *Norman*, [1934] 1 K.B. 475, at p. 477.   Despite its
introduction the commercial community still shows a preference for
arbitration.

length, stating the facts on which he relies and referring to the relevant documents. After the opening speech the plaintiff's witnesses are called to prove those facts alleged in the opening which are not admitted by the defendant or proved by the documentary evidence. It is, of course, most improper for the plaintiff's counsel to make any statement in his opening which he does not believe that he will be able to prove. Each witness is examined, cross-examined by the defendant's counsel and then re-examined by the plaintiff's counsel. The next step in the trial depends on whether the defendant proposes to call witnesses or not. If he does not the plaintiff's counsel addresses the court a second time in order to sum up the evidence, and the defendant's counsel answers the whole case without the plaintiff's counsel having any right of reply. If on the other hand the defendant calls witnesses the plaintiff's counsel makes no second speech at the close of his evidence, but allows the defendant's counsel to open his case and call his witnesses. After the defendant's witnesses have been examined, cross-examined and re-examined his counsel addresses the court for a second time to sum up the evidence, and the plaintiff's counsel has a right of reply. If the trial is by jury the judge will then sum up the facts to them, giving them any necessary directions as to the law applicable to the case. As we have mentioned before, the jury may be asked to give either a general verdict for one or other side, or, in complicated cases, a special verdict on particular questions of fact left to them by the judge. On the verdict being returned the judge has to give judgment. Often the verdict really concludes the case, but sometimes, especially if it is a special verdict, it may raise legal questions of difficulty which have to be argued before judgment. If the trial is without a jury the proceedings are substantially the same save that there is no summing up, and the judge finds both facts and law in his judgment.

After judgment has been given either party may in most cases apply to the Court of Appeal either for the reversal of the judgment or for a new trial. As we explained at the beginning of Chapter 13 all appeals in civil matters are now by way of a rehearing, not by way of error on the record. When an appeal is from a judge sitting alone—as is nearly always the case to-day—the Court of Appeal has a far freer hand than it would have had if the case had been tried by jury. This is because a judge, unlike a jury, gives reasons for the conclusions of fact at which he arrives. He has, of course, seen the witnesses and if the reason for his decision is that he believed A and not B the Court of Appeal is very unlikely to interfere with it. But generally the conclusion at which he arrives—and the amount of damages which he awards—depends on inferences which he draws by a train of reasoning from the so-called " primary " facts. In such cases the Court of Appeal does not hesitate to disagree with his conclusions. On the other hand as it does not know the process of reasoning adopted by the jury it will only interfere with its verdict if it thinks that no acceptable process of reasoning could possibly have led to the result.[1] From the judgment of the Court of Appeal an appeal lies, with leave, to the House of Lords.[2]

Actions started by writ of summons form the most numerous and important class of proceedings in the High Court. Some proceedings, however, are initiated in other ways, and even in a book of this size we must say something of the Originating Summons. Among the reforms contained in the Court of Chancery Procedure Act, 1852, was one which permitted an order for the administration of the estate of a deceased person to be made in chambers on a summons, supported by affidavits

---

[1] See Devlin, *Trial by Jury*, pp. 133–141. In 1968 of 399 appeals from the Q.B.D. heard by the Court of Appeal the judgment below was reversed in 114 cases and varied in 14. Probably in only 2 or 3 of the 399 cases were the trials by jury. If they had all been it is difficult to imagine that anything like a third of the verdicts would have been upset.

[2] See p. 222, above.

setting out the facts, without the necessity for the usual order in court made after the filing of pleadings in a formal suit. Gradually this speedy and inexpensive procedure was applied to other matters assigned to the Chancery Division, such as applications under the Trustee Acts and the Settled Land Acts, and applications for the foreclosure of mortgages, so that to-day a large proportion of proceedings in that division are begun [1] by summons. Further, under Order 5, rule 4, an originating summons is the normal method in any division of the High Court for obtaining a decision on the construction of any written instrument where no dispute of fact is involved. The chief ways in which procedure by originating summons differs from procedure by writ are (*a*) that there are no pleadings in it ; (*b*) that the evidence in support of it is given in the first instance on affidavit and not orally, though any deponent is liable to cross-examination on his affidavit ; and (*c*) that it first comes on and may be finally disposed of in chambers. In practice, however, in the Chancery Division a distinction is drawn between those originating summonses which involve the exercise of a judicial discretion and those which raise questions of law, and while the former are heard privately in chambers, either by a Master if the point is simple or by the judge if it is of substance, the latter are adjourned by the Master into court for argument before the judge.

It remains for us to say something of the problem of the costs of litigation. Generally speaking, a judgment in favour of one or other of the parties to an action includes an order that the successful party be paid by the unsuccessful his " taxed costs " of the action—*i.e.* such of the expenses incurred by the successful party as a taxing master of the Court after hearing the solicitors for both parties considers were reasonably incurred by him in

---

[1] This is the meaning of the adjective " originating," *cf.* the " original " writs. Summonses which are issued in proceedings which have already been commenced are known as " ordinary " summonses.

bringing or defending the action. Taxing masters take a strict view of what costs were really necessary to be incurred by a litigant. Normally they exclude expenses to which the party is put before he commences his action, and restrict what is subsequently incurred to a minimum. In all actions there therefore is a substantial difference between the costs which the successful party will have to pay to his own solicitor (solicitor and own client costs) and the costs (party and party costs) which he will recover from the loser. Therefore any prospective litigant knows that even if he is successful he will not recover all his expenses from the other side and that if he fails he will have to pay the taxed costs of his opponent as well as all his own costs. This fact obviously gives a wealthy litigant a great advantage over a poor one, and of recent years efforts have been made to lessen this advantage in two different ways: (*a*) by reducing the costs of litigation in the High Court and (*b*) by providing free legal aid for poor litigants.

A committee under the Chairmanship of Lord Evershed which reported in 1953 (Cmnd. 8878) considered every step in procedure in an ordinary action in the High Court in great detail and made a number of suggestions for improvement to many of which effect has been given. But it is now becoming clear that a far more drastic change than any envisaged by the Committee is required if any real impression is to be made on the problem of the length and cost of civil litigation. Lord Devlin has recently pointed out [1] that there are two features in our procedure which add very much to the cost. The first is that under our system—the so-called " adversary system "—each side prepares his case in secret giving away as little as possible to his opponent in preparation for the day of battle when each will meet the other face to face before the judge. The second is that on the day of battle each side presents his case orally through his representative and supports it by the oral evidence of witnesses

[1] What is wrong with the Law?" *B.B.C. 1970*, pp. 75–77.

who are examined, cross-examined and re-examined even though often their testimony can add little to what is apparent from the documents which are themselves read aloud to the Court. In cases where the facts are complex it may well be that oral presentation of the opposing contentions by counsel and oral examination of at least the principal witnesses—slow and expensive though such a procedure necessarily is—is better calculated than any other mode of trial to lead the court to the correct result. But to apply it indiscriminately to all cases means that the only persons who can face civil litigation in the High Court with equanimity are wealthy corporations and people poor enough to get legal aid. Lord Devlin goes so far as to suggest that even the procedure of the county court is too elaborate for many cases and that simple cases could be decided by the judge with the aid of an enquiry officer on written submissions without any professional advocacy at all. In other cases he suggests that the judge should have a complete discretion to decide at an early stage what form the trial should take and in particular what, if any, oral evidence or oral submissions by lawyers should be permitted.

We turn finally to the subject of legal aid. The rules of Court long provided facilities for persons to sue and be sued " in forma pauperis " and to have counsel assigned to them, and for many years a vast amount of free legal aid was given to poor persons by members of the bar, solicitors, legal aid societies and trade unions. But by the Legal Aid and Advice Act, 1949, legal aid has been made generally available at the expense of the state to numbers of people who are not in the ordinary sense of the word poor. The Act does not apply to proceedings for defamation, breach of promise, seduction, enticement or damages for rape. With these exceptions, it now applies to all proceedings in the County Court, High Court, Court of Appeal and House of Lords and to domestic proceedings in the Magistrates Courts. Any person who wishes to receive legal aid in the prosecution or defence of any such proceeding can apply to one of the 112 local legal aid committees, set up under the Act (consisting of barristers and solicitors) for a legal aid certificate.   To obtain a certificate the applicant has to show that he has a prima facie case and that his means are within the prescribed limits.   The upper limit is a " disposable income " (*i.e.* a net income after payment of income tax, rent and certain other deductions such as payments to dependants) of not more than £700.   This would normally mean a gross income of some £1,000. There is no fixed upper limit for capital, but an applicant with more than £500 free capital will not normally be granted legal aid.   An applicant with a " disposable income " of less than £250 and less than £125 free capital cannot be called upon to make any contribution towards the costs of his case.   But other applicants may be required to contribute an amount which is not to exceed one third of the excess of their " disposable income " over £250 or the whole of the excess of their free capital over £125. On being granted a certificate the legally aided litigant selects a solicitor and counsel from the panel of solicitors and counsel who have agreed to take legally aided cases, which in fact includes the majority of both professions. Whatever the result of the proceedings the costs of the legally aided litigant are taxed in the normal way as between solicitor and client and his solicitor and counsel are paid out of the legal aid fund 90 per cent. of the amount allowed each of them respectively on the taxation. If the legally aided litigant is successful and an order for costs is made in his favour, such costs are paid into the fund in relief of the state.   If the legally aided litigant loses the Court can order him to pay his successful opponent such costs as it considers to be reasonable in the circumstances.   In nearly all cases the legally aided litigant is too poor for such an order to be made; but under the Legal Aid Act, 1964, the Court has power to order payment out of public funds of the costs of an unassisted litigant who has successfully defended proceedings brought against him by a legally aided litigant if the Court is satisfied that he would suffer " serious hardship " is no such order was made.   In 1968 some 90,000 parties to civil proceedings had legal aid certificates and nearly half of them made no contribution whatever to their cost.   The great majority—some 76,000—of the certificates were granted in respect of matrimonial disputes, some 35,000 in matrimonial proceedings in the High Court and some 41,000 in proceedings for maintenance or for custody of children in the magistrates' courts.   There were in addition some 5,800 certificates in county court proceedings, 5,500 in Queen's Bench proceedings, 590 in Chancery proceedings (probably mostly in wardship cases) and 184 in the Court of Appeal.   Many proceedings are, of course, settled without a hearing.   The overall ratio of success to failure is somewhat misleading because so many certificates are given to petitioners in undefended divorce cases where failure is virtually impossible.   But if one confines oneself to contested proceedings in the Court of Appeal and the Queen's Bench and Chancery Divisions, one finds that there are substantially more successes than failures, though the proportion of failures is by no means negligible.   The Legal Aid Scheme suffers from several defects.   In the first place it does little to help people who cannot afford to pay for the advice of a solicitor to get advice as to their rights in cases where there is no need to take legal proceedings.   Secondly there is no reason why an unassisted litigant who has successfully resisted proceedings by an assisted litigant should have to prove that he will suffer " serious hardship " before he can recover his costs from the State which has subsidised the bringing of the action.   Thirdly, with the steady fall in the value of money the financial limit for the granting of legal aid has dropped below the ceiling which was envisaged.   But the scheme as it stands costs some £8,500,000 a year and it is not surprising that the Government should be chary of introducing amendments

which will add to the cost.   There is a further defect
which is inherent in the scheme and could not be cured
by expenditure of money.   When once the ball has been
set rolling there is little or nothing to induce a legally
aided litigant (who in most cases will have had to pay
nothing or only a small sum himself) to act in a reasonable spirit.   He is " sitting pretty " and can always hope
that his opponent will be forced to buy him off rather than
face the bill for costs.   In such cases the scheme has to
rely on the assisted persons legal advisers having a
sufficient sense of their duty to the public to decline to
act further for their client and to procure the discharge of
his certificate if it turns out that he has really no case.

Before we leave the subject of the cost of litigation and
legal aid in civil cases, some general reflections may not
be out of place.   Everyone would agree that the cost of
litigation should be as low as is consistent with the proper
presentation of the case for the plaintiff and the defendant.
Again most people would probably agree that if anyone
has a clear and meritorious case for relief at law but is
unable through lack of means to bring an action, the community should subsidise his action to the extent that he
needs the subsidy.   But unfortunately not everyone who
feels a grievance has a clear and meritorious case for
relief at law.   His case may be fairly clear but not at all
meritorious.   Again his case may be meritorious but far
from clear.   Yet again he may, possibly in good faith,
present the facts to his ad visers in a form which turns out
to be, after a good deal of time and money have been spent,
most misleading. These various possibilities—which are
very real possibilities—inevitably prompt the question :
" What is the ideal which we would like to achieve if
money were no object?"   Is it that everyone who has
what a competent and honest lawyer would regard as a
reasonable chance of asserting or resisting some claim at
law should be enabled to assert or resist it at the public
expense in so far as his own means are insufficient to
enable him to do so, without inconvenience to himself,

until either he has won or the House of Lords has decided against him or his lawyer has come to recognise that he has no case ? A state in which such an ideal was realised would certainly be a paradise for lawyers ; but it is permissible to doubt whether its achievement would increase the happiness of the community as a whole.   But if that is not the ideal at which we are aiming, what are we aiming at? Perhaps simply to achieve some sort of logically unjustifiable half-way house between too much injustice through actions not being brought or defended and too much litigation through actions being brought and defended ? If our ideal is no higher than this the position which we have achieved, namely that poor people and rich people can indulge in litigation which may prove to be unjustified with comparative impunity but that those of moderate means cannot indulge even in justifiable litigation may be as good a compromise as another.

XVIII
THE MODERN CRIMINAL COURTS

IN the last three chapters we have been speaking chiefly of courts exercising a civil jurisdiction, but the reforming movement of the nineteenth century affected the criminal as well as the civil law, and, though the criminal courts themselves were not subjected to any changes as drastic as those which the Judicature Acts effected in the system of civil tribunals, their working to-day differs substantially from their working in the eighteenth century. In describing their history in the last century and their present position, it will be convenient to start with the police force—the foundation of any efficient system of criminal justice.

At the end of the eighteenth century there was still no organised system of disciplined police in this country. Each parish had its constable appointed and controlled by the local justices of the peace, but as often as not he was a decrepit old man appointed to his office in order to keep him off the poor rate.[1] A few boroughs had attempted on their own initiative to make more efficient provision for the preservation of order within their boundaries, but as a whole it is not untrue to say that the community was at the mercy of the criminal classes, a fact which goes some way to explain the continued ferocity of the criminal law. Such thieves as were caught were liable to be hanged. The position was, of course, far worse in the towns than in country districts, and worst of all in London. The necessity for some more efficient police than the local constables and the Bow Street runners was emphasised by the Gordon Riots in 1780, when a large part of the capital was for several days in the hands of a mob which, among other excesses, broke open Newgate Gaol and burnt Lord Mansfield's house in Bloomsbury Square.

---

[1] The constables were not paid by salary but were entitled to certain fees, and sometimes had strips in the common fields attached to their office.

It was not, however, until 1829 that a comprehensive measure of reform was introduced. In that year Sir Robert Peel, acting to some extent on the plans of Lord Sidmouth, who had been Home Secretary from 1813 to 1824,[1] promoted the Act creating the Metropolitan Police Force, a disciplined and salaried body of constables charged with the preservation of the peace in the capital (outside the City of London [2]) and under the direct control of the Home Secretary. The Municipal Corporations Act, 1835, provided for the establishment in municipal boroughs of a salaried and disciplined force of constables appointed by, and to some extent under the authority of, a " Watch Committee " of the borough council, and in 1856 the establishment of a similar force in each county was at last made obligatory on the county justices. In 1888 the control of the county police was taken out of the sole hands of the justices and confided to a " Standing Joint Committee " made up in part of representatives of quarter sessions and in part of representatives of the newly formed county councils. The position to-day is that where a county or a county borough has its own police force the police authority is a committee two-thirds of whose members are members of the county council or county borough council and one-third are magistrates appointed by Quarter Sessions or the borough magistrates as the case may be. But the Police Act, 1964, contains provisions for schemes of amalgamation under which larger police areas embracing more than one county or county borough can be created in the interest of efficiency. The Home Secretary has no immediate control over the county and borough police forces, such as he has over the Metropolitan Police, but his indirect control over them is considerable, since half the cost of their maintenance is met by grants from the central government, which may be withheld if the standard of

---

[1] See Maitland : *Justice and Police*, p. 108, for earlier stages in the creation of the Metropolitan Police Force between 1792 and 1829.

[2] The City has its own police force, dating from 1839.

efficiency required by the Home Office is not attained. Further, he has power to make regulations ensuring uniformity in pay and conditions of service in all police forces. There are now some 90,000 members of the police force in England and Wales—some 3,500 of whom are women—that is about one to every 500 of the population. There is, however, no doubt that there are not enough of them to cope with the great increase in crime which has taken place in recent years.

Some criminals are caught red handed ; but in most cases the police have to decide whom, if anyone, to charge by interrogating suspected persons. Broadly speaking no one is obliged to answer questions put to him by the police nor have the police any power to detain a suspect unless and until they arrest and charge him. But unless he is an " old hand " he may well not realise this. In practice, therefore, suspects are at a disadvantage in their encounters with the police and there is always a danger that confessions or admissions which they make may not be free and voluntary. In order to lessen this danger the judges of the Queen's Bench Division have formulated rules, the so-called " Judges' Rules," for the guidance of police officers in interrogating suspects. The salient feature of these rules is that whenever a police officer has grounds for suspecting that a person whom he is questioning or proposes to question has committed a crime he must " caution " him, *i.e.* tell him that he need say nothing but that anything which he does say will be recorded and may be used in evidence. Questioning can continue after the caution so long as no charge is made but a record must be kept of the time and place at which it began and ended and of the persons present. As soon as anyone is charged with an offence a further caution must be given and after it questions in relation to the offence can only be put in certain specified cases, as for instance to clear up ambiguities in any statement which the accused chooses to make.[1]

[1] See generally Lord Devlin, *The Criminal Prosecution in England*, published, however, before the latest revision of the rules.

From the police who interrogate, charge, and arrest suspects we pass to the judges before whom the accused is brought.   The administration of criminal justice is still largely in the hands of the justices of the peace, as it has been for the last five hundred years, and the royal commissions of the peace for counties, and for boroughs which have commissions of their own, still issue in much the same form as they did in the eighteenth century.[1]   There has, however, been a considerable change in the type of person appointed to the office in country districts.   In the eighteenth century the ownership of land of an annual value of £100 was a necessary qualification for inclusion in the county commission, and accordingly no one below the rank of a substantial country gentleman was a county J.P.   In the nineteenth century the fall in the value of money may have slightly diminished the importance of this qualification, but in practice the county justices continued to be appointed almost exclusively from the squirearchy until 1906, when the property qualification was removed.   For borough justices there has not, generally speaking, ever been any property qualification at all.   Justices are appointed by the Lord Chancellor.[2] In selecting county justices the Chancellor usually follows the recommendation of the Lord Lieutenant of the county, who in his turn is assisted by a committee of selection, and in selecting borough justices he receives recommendations from the advisory committee of the Borough.   It has been the aim of recent Chancellors to maintain as far as possible an even balance between the various political parties in the composition of the magistracy and nowadays J.P.'s in both counties and boroughs are drawn from many different classes.   It cannot be said, however, that the present position is in all respects satisfactory, since as they are not paid for their services

[1] *The English Magistracy*, by Sir Frank Milton—the senior Metropolitan magistrate (O.U.P., 1967), gives an admirable sketch of the history of the J.P.'s and a vivid account of their work to-day.

[2] In Lancashire, by the Chancellor of the Duchy.

it is difficult to find young, or young middle aged, persons of any walk of life who can find time to be magistrates. The number of justices is now very large. There are nearly 19,000 of them on the active list. The retiring age for lay magistrates is 70.

A magistrate is not required to know anything about the job which he is going to do before he is appointed and until recently he was not required to learn anything about it otherwise than by experience. But since 1966 those appointed give an undertaking that they will complete a prescribed course of training—partly before they sit for the first time and partly in their first year of office. In some cases both at quarter sessions and petty sessions provision is made for the exercise of the judicial functions of the magistracy by qualified lawyers to the exclusion or partial exclusion of the lay magistrates. Thus at borough quarter sessions in the boroughs which have a separate court of quarter sessions [1] the Recorder of the borough is the sole judge. He is a practising barrister of at least five years' standing appointed by the Crown on the advice of the Lord Chancellor. He is paid a small salary out of the borough funds and visits the borough (of which he is *ex-officio* a justice of the peace) several times a year to hold its quarter sessions. At county quarter sessions, on the other hand, all the magistrates on the commission are qualified to act as judges whether or not they are trained lawyers, though the number who may sit at one time is restricted to nine by the rules made under the Justices of the Peace Act, 1949, s. 13. Naturally, however, they always had to choose one of their number to preside at the trial, take notes of the evidence and sum up to the jury and though until comparatively recently it was not unusual for the presiding magistrate at quarter sessions to be a layman now all chairmen and most deputy chairmen of quarter sessions are lawyers. In a few cases, as for instance in the County of London, on

[1] Some 120 of the boroughs with separate commissions of the peace have their own quarter sessions as well as their own petty sessions.

account of the amount and importance of the work to be done, express provision is made by statute for a salaried and legally qualified chairman of quarter sessions. In other places some of the part-time chairmen and deputy chairmen who sit with fair regularity are paid while others —such as the local county court judge, or High Court judges or barristers who live in the district and are prepared to " help out " when needed give their services for nothing. But, though the presiding magistrate is now almost invariably a lawyer, when it comes to sentencing— if the accused pleads guilty or is convicted by the jury— all the magistrates present have an equal vote and the decision is by a majority.

The jurisdiction of the justices out of quarter sessions is in some urban districts exercised by legally qualified and salaried magistrates known as " stipendiaries." In speaking of them we must distinguish between London and other towns. In the eighteenth century the local magistracy in London was almost as defective as the police force, and in 1792 the first of a series of Acts was passed which established paid magistrates with a legal training to exercise the summary jurisdiction of the justices and to conduct preliminary enquiries in the cases of indictable offences throughout the metropolis. To-day there are 14 stipendiary courts in the metropolis staffed by some 30 magistrates, who must be barristers or solicitors of seven years' standing, each of whom sits alone and possesses the powers exercisable elsewhere by two lay justices sitting together. The system which obtains in London has not been compulsorily extended to any other part of England, but any borough with a separate commission of the peace, which is willing to pay his salary may obtain the appointment by the Crown of a barrister or solicitor of at least seven years' standing to act as stipendiary for the district. Surprisingly few places have availed themselves of this right, and there are less than 20 stipendiaries outside the metropolis. The shortcomings of the London magistrates at the end of the eighteenth century were so great that Parliament deprived them of their judicial functions altogether in favour of the stipendiaries. Elsewhere, however, it was rather the shortage of suitable lay magistrates in the new centres of population which emerged from the industrial revolution than their shortcomings that called for the appointment of stipendiaries. So though like the London stipendiary magistrates the provincial stipendiary has the powers of two justices and can sit alone, he is not the sole judge of the court. If one of the local justices chooses to sit with him each has an equal vote.[1]

Crimes in English law are divisible into indictable offences and non-indictable offences. The more serious indictable offences must be tried on indictment and the less serious non-indictable offences must be tried summarily; but many of the less serious indictable offences may be tried summarily (but usually only with the consent of the accused) while conversely the accused can in the case of some of the graver non-indictable offences claim to be tried by jury.[2] In fact most indictable offences are tried summarily. Thus in 1968 of some 193,000 persons over the age of 17 who were found guilty of indictable offences some 166,000 were tried summarily. It is worth observing—because it is often overlooked—that over 80 per cent. of the persons convicted of indictable offences were guilty either of theft or breaking and entering or receiving. Though the increase in crimes of violence is alarming, it is the number of cases of dishonesty unaccompanied by violence which is the core of the crime problem.[3]

The first step in the prosecution of all offences, whether indictable or non-indictable, will be, broadly speaking,

[1] In " domestic " proceedings and the " juvenile " court both in London and the provinces lay magistrates and stipendiaries sit together.

[2] See Milton, pp. 58/59, for illustrations of the working of this very complicated system.

[3] In 1968 over 200,000 were found guilty of crimes of dishonesty— some 16,000 on indictment, some 125,000 over 17 before ordinary magistrates' courts and some 58,000 under 17 before juvenile courts.

either the laying of an information before a magistrate by some person (not necessarily the injured party) who is acquainted with the facts, or the arrest of the accused by a constable or private person without any preliminary information followed by a charge against him when in custody. On the original information being laid before him the magistrate usually only issues a summons requiring the accused to attend, but if the charge is a grave one and made under oath he may issue a warrant to a constable for the arrest of the accused. As we have said, a large number of persons are taken into custody without any preliminary information or warrant. If an " arrestable "[1] offence has been committed any person whether a constable or not may arrest without warrant anyone who is or whom he with reasonable causes suspects to be guilty of it. Further if a constable with reasonable cause suspects that an arrestable offence has been committed he can arrest without warrant anyone whom he suspects with reasonable cause to be guilty of it. Of those accused of indictable offences some 3c per cent. appear in answer to a summons and some 70 per cent. are brought up before the magistrates in custody, of whom about 10 per cent. have been arrested under warrants, while about 90 per cent. have been arrested (nearly always by constables) without any preliminary information or warrant. In the case of non-indictable offences, attendance is, of course, far more frequently enforced by a mere summons than in the case of indictable offences. In the old days the rules of venue in criminal cases were very strict and, generally speaking, the accused had to be tried in the county in which the crime was alleged to have been committed, but (as in civil cases) these rules have been gradually whittled away, and now the accused can be tried in the county or place in which he is in custody.

[1] An arrestable offence is—broadly speaking—one for which a person may by statute be sentenced to imprisonment for 5 years or more. Plainly, unless it is abundantly clear that a serious offence—e.g. theft or unlawful wounding—has been committed, a private individual runs some risk in arresting a suspected offender.

When the accused is brought before the magistrates the subsequent proceedings will differ fundamentally according to whether he is to be tried summarily or by a jury, since in the latter case the magistrates can only conduct a preliminary examination into his case and not dispose of it finally. In our account we will first follow the course of a case tried by jury through all its possible stages up to the House of Lords and return later to consider the exercise by the magistrates of their summary jurisdiction. For the moment, therefore, we will assume that our prisoner has been charged with an indictable offence which cannot be tried summarily, or, if it could be tried summarily, either he or the prosecution or the magistrates have not been willing that it should be so tried.

The preliminary examination into cases to be tried by jury at the criminal assizes or at quarter sessions can be conducted by a single justice of the peace, but nowadays, save in cases brought before London police magistrates or provincial stipendiaries, at least two justices are almost invariably present. In the seventeenth and eighteenth centuries the magisterial enquiry in cases of indictable offences was hardly a judicial proceeding at all. The examining magistrate's duty was originally conceived to be not so much to see if the prosecutor, whether constable or private individual, could make out a prima facie case against the accused, as to enquire himself whether such a case could be made. Consequently, it was not thought essential that the accused should be present when the possible witnesses against him were making their statements, or, if present, should be given any opportunity of cross-examining them. Further the magistrate himself interrogated the accused. But with the establishment of an adequate police force it became possible to relieve the magistrate of the function of inquisitor and to give the preliminary examination a more judicial form. The modern practise originated in the Indictable Offences Act, 1848 (one of the Acts known as the Sir John Jervis's Acts), and is now regulated by the Magistrates Courts Act, 1952, as amended by the Criminal Justice Act, 1967. It is, of course, most important that the accused should know in advance of the trial the nature of the case which the prosecution is seeking to make and the evidence by which it proposes to prove it, and also that he should have an opportunity if he wishes to cross-examine the prosecution witnesses at the preliminary examination with a view to inducing the magistrates to dismiss the case out of hand on the ground that even if the prosecution's evidence be accepted no reasonable jury would convict. But in the great majority of cases the accused does not seek to contend that there is not—on the prosecution's evidence—a *prima facie* case against him nor does he wish to disclose his defence in advance of the trial. Nevertheless until the 1967 Act was passed it was necessary in every case for the prosecution witnesses to give their evidence orally and for it to be recorded—in long hand at dictation speed—in the form of " depositions " which were read over to them and signed by them. Now under the Criminal Justice Act, 1967, if a copy is delivered in advance to the other party and he raises no objection a written statement is admissible at the preliminary examination to the like extent as oral evidence to the same effect provided that it is signed by its maker who declares that it is true to the best of his knowledge and belief and that he made it knowing that if it is tendered in evidence he will be liable to be prosecuted if he wilfully states in it anything which he knows to be untrue. Further, in a case where all the evidence before the magistrates consists of such written statements and the defendant is legally represented and does not wish to make a submission of " no case to answer " the magistrates can commit for trial without themselves considering the evidence. If, on the other hand, the defendant wishes to examine the prosecution witnesses the prosecutor [1] opens his case and calls his witnesses, who

[1] The prosecutor will be either the private individual who laid the

are examined, cross-examined and re-examined. Their
evidence, which has been taken down by the clerk to the
justices, is signed by them and read over to the accused.
The magistrates then explain to the accused the nature of
the charge against him, telling him that he can call witnesses and give evidence himself if he wishes, and asking
him if he desires to make a statement, with the warning
that anything he says will be taken down and may be
given in evidence at the trial. Any statement which he
makes is taken down and signed by the magistrates, and
then his witnesses, if he calls any, including himself if he
gives evidence, are examined in the same way as those for
the prosecution, and their evidence recorded and signed.
Further, the solicitor or counsel representing the accused
can address the court on his behalf.

If the defendant is committed for trial either because
he does not submit that there is no case for him to
answer or because such a submission is overruled, the
magistrates have to decide whether he shall be tried at the
assizes or quarter sessions, whether he should be allowed
bail or kept in prison pending trial, and if he asks for it
whether he should have legal aid. All indictable offences
can be tried at the assizes and some can only be tried
there, but the general rule, where both tribunals have
jurisdiction, is that offences which can be tried by quarter
sessions are to be sent for trial at quarter sessions rather
than the assizes, unless there is some special reason to the
contrary. In granting or withholding bail the justices
have a complete discretion. The grounds on which the
police oppose " bail "—if they do—are generally either
the likelihood that the defendant will not appear at the
trial and allow his bail to be forfeited or that he will seek
to interfere with the witnesses for the prosecution or if he
admits his guilt that he may commit further offences
before he is sentenced. In practice some 50 per cent. of

information or, if as is, of course, nearly always the case it is a prosecution
initiated by the police, a police officer. In either case the prosecutor
often appears by solicitor or counsel.

those committed for trial are let out on bail pending the hearing of the case and if bail is refused by the justices an application for it may still be made to a judge of the Queen's Bench Division.[1] Legal aid in criminal proceedings is now granted far more readily than was the case even a few years ago. It is indeed now comparatively rare for anyone—even if he pleads guilty—to be unrepresented at his trial. Of some 6,700 persons tried at the assizes or quarter sessions between 1st October and 31st December, 1968, only 214 were unrepresented. If the magistrates refuse legal aid it can, of course, be granted by assizes or quarter sessions. The magistrates have also power to grant legal aid even on the preliminary examination if the charge is very serious or seems likely to raise difficult issues.

Two criticisms of the procedure at the preliminary examination which used often to be made have been met or partially met by the Criminal Justice Act, 1967. The first related to publicity. It was said—with force—that for the details of the evidence given at the preliminary examination to be made public might be very hard on the accused in cases which aroused public interest since the jurors might go into the box with their minds half made up. It is now provided that unless the defendant requests that the restriction shall not apply then if the magistrates commit for trial no written or broadcast report of the committal proceedings may be published going beyond a statement of the names and descriptions of the parties and their witnesses, of the offences with which they are charged, the decision to commit and whether bail or legal aid was granted. The second criticism is that it is unreasonable that while the prosecution is forced to disclose its case in advance the defendant even after he has received legal aid is under no corresponding obligation to disclose his defence but can at

[1] In about 7 per cent of the applications made to them the judges overrule the decision of the magistrate and grant bail in opposition to the wishes of the police.

the trial spring on the prosecution some totally unexpected line of defence. There is still no general obligation on a defendant to disclose his defence but it is now
provided that at the trial a defendant shall not without
the leave of the Court adduce evidence in support of an
" alibi " unless he furnishes the prosecution with particulars of the " alibi " within 7 days from the end of the
committal proceedings. The magistrates before committing him for trial must warn him of this provision.

After the accused has been committed for trial the
next step is the preferment of a bill of indictment against
him by the prosecutor. The issue in an indictment is,
of course, between the Crown and the prisoner. The
case is *Regina* v. *B.*, not *A.* v. *B.*, and Her Majesty's
Attorney-General has an absolute right to stop any prosecution at any stage by entering a " Nolle prosequi."
Nevertheless in this country the prosecution, though in
the name of the Queen, is not normally carried on by
agents of the central government but either by private individuals who have been injured or much more frequently
by local chief constables. In 1879 an official known as
the Director of Public Prosecutions was appointed for
the purpose both of giving advice to private prosecutors
and chief constables of the conduct of cases, and also
of himself undertaking the prosecution of important cases
on behalf of the state. The number of prosecutions
undertaken by the Director of Public Prosecutions is,
however, relatively small, *e.g.* in 1968 of some 32,000
persons tried on indictment only about 2,000 were
prosecuted by him. Whoever prosecutes must cause a
bill of indictment to be framed setting out the charges
against the accused. The old forms remained in force in
criminal proceedings longer than in civil, and right down
to this century an indictment was a very verbose and
technical document. Now, however, the Indictments
Act, 1915, has substituted simple forms for the old ones.

Until 1933 it was necessary for each bill of indictment
to go before the grand jury assembled for quarter sessions

or the assizes and to be found a true bill by them before it was presented to the court as an indictment ; but the Administration of Justice Act, 1933, abolished the grand jury for most crimes, and it was totally abolished by the Criminal Justice Act, 1948. Now, when a bill of indictment has been prepared, the mere signature of the clerk of the assize or the clerk of the peace, as the case may be, converts it into an indictment which the court can try. While the grand jury was with us it was in theory possible for them to present a man for trial of their own knowledge without any preliminary examination, and similarly a private individual might prefer a bill to them against a man who had not been committed for trial. Such bills were, of course, very rare, and are now impossible. There are now very few cases in which a bill of indictment can be preferred against anyone who has not been committed for trial by examining magistrates.[1] Further, the power of the Attorney-General and of the Master of the Crown Office to file criminal informations for misdemeanour in the Queen's Bench Division has been abolished.

Indictments are almost invariably tried either at quarter sessions or the assizes. Though the Queen's Bench Division still has power to order the trial of any indictment before itself, this power has not been exercised for many years. It is significant that whereas Lynch in 1903 and Casement in 1916 were tried for treason " at bar " before three judges of the King's Bench Division, Joyce in 1945 was tried at the Central Criminal Court. The tendency throughout the nineteenth century has been to enlarge the jurisdiction of quarter sessions over indictable offences, and to-day it is to a great extent concurrent with that of the assizes, but there are still a few

---

[1] One exception is that a person may be committed for trial without appearing before examining magistrates where a coroner's jury has returned a verdict of murder, manslaughter or infanticide against a named person.—See Cross and Jones Introduction to Criminal Law, 6th ed., pp. 291, and also 295 for other exceptions.

offences which quarter sessions cannot try. Broadly speaking, they are offences punishable on a first conviction by imprisonment for life, and certain offences, such as bigamy, which may raise difficult questions of law. Of about 27,000 persons found guilty on indictment in 1968 some 19,000 were tried at quarter sessions.

We have already spoken of the constitution of quarter sessions. The courts of the commissioners of assize have, as we have seen, been made courts of the High Court of Justice, but in the case of the criminal commissions this change has been purely nominal. The assizes are still held as of old under the time-honoured commissions of oyer and terminer and gaol delivery. The commissioners always include judges of the High Court, and as in the case of the civil side of the assizes, Queen's Counsel practising on the circuit are named as commissioners with them and sometimes take some of the cases. Each county is visited several times a year by the commissioners, and for London and its suburbs almost continuous sittings are held at the Central Criminal Court (the " Old Bailey "), which was established in 1834 as the seat of the criminal assizes for the metropolitan area. In this case the Recorder and Common Serjeant of London and the other permanent judges of the Court are on the commission as well as the judges of the High Court, and often as many as twelve courts are sitting simultaneously for the trial of indictments. In 1956 it was found necessary, in view of the increase in crime, to extend the " Old Bailey " system to Liverpool and Manchester. So called " Crown Courts " were set up in these cities which are more or less continuously in session and take the place of the criminal assizes and quarter sessions there. The Recorders of Liverpool and Manchester are the ordinary judges of these courts but they may postpone the hearing of any case to enable it to be tried before a judge of the High Court. In 1968 some 3,700 persons were found guilty at the ordinary criminal assizes; some 2,100 at the " Old Bailey "; and some 1,800 at the Lancashire Crown Courts.

About ten years ago the steady increase in crime, the increase, due to legal aid, in the number of those who plead " not guilty," and the consequent increase in the length of criminal trials began to lead to serious and increasing delays between the committal and trial of those accused of criminal offences and also, since criminal is given priority over civil work, to very serious delays in the hearing of civil cases both in London and on assize. One way of coping with the problem was to increase the number of judges and as we have seen whereas there were only 17 judges of the Queen's Bench Division in 1938 there are 39 to-day. But it was thought that a considerable saving of judge time might be effected by an overhaul of the arrangements for the trial of cases at assizes and quarter sessions. In 1966 a Committee under the Chairmanship of Lord Beeching was appointed to look into the problem and in its report made in 1969 (Cmnd. 4153) it made a number of recommendations to which effect is being given so far as legislation is needed by the Courts Act, 1971. We will, therefore, summarise them here. (1) The Assize Courts including the " Old Bailey," the Lancashire Crown Courts and the Courts of Quarter Sessions will all cease to exist as separate Courts. (2) A new Court—to be called the " Crown Court "—will be set up to exercise all criminal jurisdiction above the level of petty sessions. The Crown Court will be a branch of the Supreme Court and the High Court will henceforth be confined to civil work. (3) The judges of the Crown Court will be (*a*) the judges of the High Court, (*b*) judges to be called " Circuit Judges " the first of whom will be the existing county court judges and the existing full-time judges exercising criminal jurisdiction above the petty sessional level, other than High Court judges— *e.g.* the judges of the Central Criminal Court, of the existing Crown Courts and full-time Chairmen of Quarter Sessions, and (*c*) a limited number of part-time judges

to be called " Recorders." [1] (4) Offences will be divided
into three categories : (*a*) " upper band " offences which
can only be tried by a High Court judge, (*b*) " middle
band " offences which may be tried either by a High
Court judge or a circuit judge, (*c*) " lower band " offences
such as are now triable at quarter sessions which will
normally be tried by a circuit judge.   (5) The country
will be divided into six circuits—instead of seven as now
—in each of which there will be a few large centres at
which there will be sittings both of the High Court for
civil work and of the Crown Court for criminal work and
a number of centres at which there will be sittings of the
Crown Court only.   A large number of places which are
at present visited by judges on assize or have courts of
quarter sessions will cease to have any sittings for civil
or criminal work above the level of the county court and
petty sessions.   (6) In each circuit there will be two
High Court judges—known as Presiding Judges—who
will take it in turn to spend most of their time there in
order to ensure—in consultation with the Lord Chief
Justice—that the use of High Court judge power is
adjusted to the current needs of criminal and civil work
in the circuit and to allocate the circuit judges in the
circuit to various duties.   Further, there will be in each
circuit a " circuit administrator " to work in close conjunction with the Presiding Judge and be responsible for
the various aspects of the Court service on the circuit
other than the provision of judge power.

An indicted defendant is arraigned at the bar of the
court which is to try him and pleads to the indictment
in the manner which we have recounted in Chapter 12.
The majority, about two-thirds, plead guilty.   If the
plea is " not guilty," the jury is empanelled and sworn,
and the trial begins.   The whole course of the trial
is now more favourable to the accused than it was in

[1] The scheme will involve the reduction of part-time criminal judges
from about 300 to about 120.   Consequently about 40 new appointments to the Circuit Bench will have to be made.

the eighteenth century.   In the first place the rule that
in cases of felony he was not allowed the assistance of
counsel to examine the witnesses or sum up the evidence
was finally removed in 1836.   Since then any prisoner
who can afford to employ counsel has been able to have
his assistance at any stage, and as we have said legal aid
for those unable to pay or to pay fully for their own
defence is freely granted.   It has been well established
for the last hundred years that it is not the duty of a prosecuting counsel to strive to secure a conviction, but merely
to see that the case is put fairly before the court.   Thus
he may not try to discredit one of his own witnesses if he
proves unexpectedly favourable to the prisoner.   Then
again, the prisoner knows in advance from the evidence
given at the preliminary enquiry what case he will have
to meet.   After opening the case prosecuting counsel
calls his witnesses one after another for examination,
cross examination and re-examination.   Next comes the
prisoner's defence.   Until 1898 the accused and his or
her wife or husband were unable to give evidence at the
trial, but, by the Criminal Evidence Act, 1898, they were
made competent, though not compellable, witnesses.
Counsel for the prosecution is not allowed in any reply he
makes to comment on the fact that the prisoner has not
chosen to submit himself to cross-examination, but the
judge may, and frequently does, do so in his summing up.
Probably, therefore, the Act has made it harder for
a guilty person to escape by being given the benefit of
the doubt than it was before.   No reference may be made
by the prosecution to the fact that the accused has been
previously convicted of similar offences unless he himself
gives or calls evidence of his good character or attacks the
character of witnesses for the prosecution.   If the defence
calls no witnesses, then after the prisoner has given
evidence himself, if he chooses to give it, and counsel for
the prosecution has summed up his case if he wishes to do
so counsel for the defence sums up his case.   If the
prisoner calls witnesses, then he or his counsel opens his

case, his witnesses (including himself if he gives evidence) are examined, cross-examined and re-examined, counsel for the prosecution sums up his case and counsel for the defence makes a second speech summing up the defendant's case.   After the evidence has been completed and the speeches of counsel made, the judge or chairman sums up and the jury retire to consider their verdict.   Until 1967 the verdict had to be unanimous but now by s. 13 of the Criminal Justice Act, 1967, if the jury cannot reach a unanimous verdict after deliberating for at least 2 hours but at least 10 of them are agreed either for conviction or acquittal a majority verdict may be accepted.   If the jury cannot reach even a majority verdict they are discharged and the prisoner remanded for a new trial—though, of course, the Attorney-General may enter a " nolle prosequi."

Assuming that the accused is found guilty—as about four-fifths of them are—we must next consider the judgment passed on him.   We saw that in the eighteenth century the ferocity of the criminal law was somewhat mitigated by the continued possibility of pleading clergy in the case of a first conviction for some felonies and by the practice of granting pardons conditional on transportation.   Benefit of clergy was finally abolished in 1827, and transportation in 1853.   On the other hand, a series of Acts passed in the decade 1827 to 1837 implemented the reforms advocated by Sir Samuel Romilly by abolishing the death sentence in the case of a great number of felonies, and in 1870 the forfeiture of the felon's property on convction was also abolished.   For many years murder was the only offence of frequent occurrence for which sentence of death was passed and now the death penalty has been for practical purposes abolished.   The reforms of the early Victorican period left on the hands of the authorities numbers of persons who previously would have been hanged or transported and necessitated the building of a number of new prisons.   But to-day, despite the anxiety of all concerned to avoid immediate sentences of imprisonment whenever possible, the great increase in crime has led to our prisons being seriously overcrowded.[1] The sentence of the Court may or may not involve " custodial treatment." Such treatment for adults means imprisonment. Offenders between the ages of 17 and 21 can be sent to prison but will only be so dealt with in exceptional cases. Normally they will be sent either to a " detention centre " (maximum 6 months) or to " Borstal training " (average 18 months). Offenders under 17 cannot be sent to prison but if over 14 can be sent to a " detention centre." Under the Criminal Justice Act, 1967, the court in passing a sentence of imprisonment may in certain circumstances and in certain other circumstances must suspend its operation for a period not exceeding 3 years.[2] If the offender commits a fresh offence during that period the suspended sentence will normally be brought into operation consecutively to any sentence imposed for the fresh offence. The common forms of " non-custodial " treatment are conditional discharge, probation, or fines. In considering what sentence to impose the Court normally has before it as well as the offender's police record a social enquiry report prepared by a probation officer who has seen him and where necessary a medical report. Of some 18,000 persons over 21 found guilty on indictment in 1968 some 13,000 were sentenced to terms of imprisonment—the sentences being suspended in some 4,000 cases—some 2,400 were conditionally discharged or placed on probation and some 2,500 fined. Of some 9,000 persons under 21 found guilty on indictment 736 were given immediate and 421 suspended sentences. Some 1,200 were sent to detention centres and some 1,300 to Borstal training.[3]

We saw in Chapter 12 that under the old common law

[1] The prison population is now about 40,000.

[2] See the Home Office pamphlet, " The Sentence of the Court," for the details.

[3] Of course only relatively few juvenile offenders are tried on indictment.

system the chances of obtaining the reversal of a judgment were even less in criminal than in civil cases. New trials after a conviction were practically unknown, and though writs of error could be brought from the assizes or quarter sessions to the King's Bench, and thence to the House of Lords, they were hardly ever used in practice since the only errors which could be relied on were errors apparent on the record of the case, which contained no account of the course of proceedings at the trial. It is true that in the eighteenth century a practice had grown up of the trial judge reserving difficult questions of law for consideration with his colleagues in London, and in 1848 a special court, the Court for Crown Cases Reserved, was set up for the hearing of points, reserved for it by judges of assize and chairmen of quarter sessions. The jurisdiction of this court was vested in the Queen's Bench Division in 1875, but only points of law could be so reserved. There was no opportunity of appealing to the court on questions of fact. This unsatisfactory system continued until 1907, when writs of error in criminal cases were abolished, and the Court of Criminal Appeal consisting of the Lord Chief Justice of England and the judges of the Queen's Bench Division, was established in place of the Court for Crown Cases Reserved.

With the growth of crime the court often sat in two divisions and it came to be thought in some quarters unsuitable that criticisms of the summing up or of the sentence passed by a Queen's Bench judge should be addressed to a court which might consist exclusively of judges of no higher rank than his own. Consequently by the Criminal Appeal Act, 1966, the jurisdiction of the Court of Criminal Appeal was transferred to a newly-created Criminal Division of the Court of Appeal; but the judges of the Queen's Bench Division may be required to sit on it and invariably one and often two of them sit under the presidency either of the Lord Chief Justice or a Lord Justice. The jurisdiction of the Court

is now governed by the Criminal Appeal Act, 1968.   It
has no jurisdiction to hear any appeal from petty sessions
or any appeal by the Crown against an acquittal.   But
every person convicted on indictment has a right of
appeal to the Court on any question of law and a right
with the leave of the trial judge or the Court to appeal on
any question of fact or of mixed law and fact.   The
Court has power which is very seldom exercised to hear
fresh evidence and if it allows an appeal simply by reason
of such evidence it may order a re-trial.   Otherwise the
Court has no power to order a re-trial unless the first
trial was a nullity.   The Court is not bound to allow an
appeal against conviction even if the appellant is technically right on some point which he raises if it is satisfied
that no miscarriage of justice has actually occurred.
With the leave of the Court any person convicted on
indictment can appeal against the sentence passed on him
unless it has one fixed by law.

The number of applications for leave to appeal against
conviction and sentence has increased enormously of
recent years.   In 1961 there were some 2,600 applications.   They are now running at the rate of over 12,000
a year.   Indeed, it may almost be said to be normal
practice for a man sentenced to immediate imprisonment
to send in an application for leave to appeal as soon as
he arrives in prison.   This huge volume of applications
—80 per cent. of which are without any merit—creates a
serious administrative problem.   In every case a transcript of the parts of the proceedings relevant to the
application has to be obtained and summaries prepared
by the staff of the Registrar for the use of the Court.
If—as is usually the case—the grounds of the application
have not been prepared and signed by counsel the application goes in the first instance to a single judge.   If he
refuses it the application can be renewed to the full Court.
In the past the Court of Criminal Appeal had power to
increase the sentence if it considered the appeal to be
frivolous but the Court no longer has that power and the

only deterrent available is a power to direct on refusing the application that the time—or part of the time—during which the applicant has been in custody pending the determination of his application shall not count towards his sentence.   The best way out of the difficulty would, perhaps, be to provide that counsel who appeared for the defence at the trial should be asked to advise on the prospect of an appeal either against conviction or sentence, if the defendant so wished and if he thought that an appeal would not be hopeless should himself prepare and sign the grounds of appeal.   This would—or should—mean that frivolous appeals would not be brought unless the defendant chose to apply himself after his counsel had told him that an appeal would be hopeless. In such cases there would seem to be no reason why the Court should not have power to direct a loss of time or even in the case of appeals against sentence to increase it.

As we have said, an appeal lies to the House of Lords at the instance either of the prosecution or the defendant, but only if the Court of Appeal certifies that a point of law of importance is involved and either the Court or the House of Lords gives leave.   The establishment of the Court of Criminal Appeal reduced the necessity for the use of the prerogative of mercy, but it must not be supposed that this branch of the prerogative which is exercised on the advice of the Home Secretary is obsolete. Every year a few free pardons are granted and a number of sentences mitigated.   Finally, we may mention here that under s. 60 of the Criminal Justice Act, 1967, prisoners may be released on " parole " on the recommendation of a Board which includes among others members of the judiciary and members of the prison service.   In 1969, 7,278 cases of prisoners serving sentences for fixed periods were considered and 1,835 were recommended as suitable for parole.   In the same year licences were revoked in 90 cases for breach of condition.

We must now turn back to the work done by the jus-

tices in petty sessions other than the conduct of preliminary enquiries into offences to be tried on indictment,
and we must emphasise that though the great bulk of
this work consists in the summary trial of criminal
offences a good deal of it cannot be called " criminal "
justice at all. We have already seen that before the nineteenth century a great part of local government was in
the hands of the justices, and though most of such work
is now conducted by elected councils, some administrative functions, such as licensing, are still exercised by
the magistracy. Moreover, some proceedings taken
before justices of the peace are definitely civil proceedings, *e.g.* so-called " domestic proceedings "—that is to
say applications for custody and maintenance orders or
affiliation orders, and others, *e.g.* infractions of local bye-
laws and minor traffic offences, are matters which,
though technically the subject of criminal proceedings,
would not be generally looked on as crimes. The
volume of the work done by justices at petty sessions
is enormous, and only to be appreciated by statistics.
In 1968 some 1,576,000 persons were found guilty of
offences in all the English criminal courts. Of these
some 257,000 were found guilty of indictable offences,
and some 1,320,000 of non-indictable offences. Of the
257,000 found guilty of indictable offences some 64,000
boys and girls under 17 and 166,000 persons over 17 had
been tried summarily by the justices in petty sessions,
or the juvenile court, while only about 27,000 were
found guilty on trial by indictment. The 1,320,000
persons found guilty of non-indictable of offences were,
of course, found guilty on a summary trial at petty sessions.
Of the 166,000 persons over 21 found guilty of indictable
offences on a summary trial, over 100,000 were found
guilty of theft, some 20,000 of breaking and entering,
12,000 of violence, 10,000 of receiving, 7,000 of fraud,
and 3,000 of sexual offences. Of the 1,320,000 found
guilty of non-indictable offences, traffic offences accounted for over 1,000,000, drunkenness for 75,000,

revenue offences for 67,000, railway offences for 17,000, malicious damage for 17,000, and disorderly conduct for 11,000.

The summary jurisdiction of the justices has grown up in a haphazard fashion from the sixteenth century onwards. Statute after statute created new offences triable summarily without a jury before one justice, or more often two, and at last, in the nineteenth century, the procedure in these summary trials was regulated by statute. The phrase " petty sessions," which came into use at the beginning of the nineteenth century to designate sittings of the justices out of quarter sessions, was eventually adopted by the Legislature. Every county was divided into a number of petty sessional divisions, often co-terminous with the old hundreds and their only practical survival, each provided with a petty sessional court house, sitting in which two justices or a stipendiary constitute a petty sessional court. Similarly the metropolis, as we have seen, was divided into a number of police court districts. There are now over 800 Petty Sessional Divisions. In some rural areas the magistrates may sit only once a fortnight—or even less frequently—whereas in Birmingham eight magistrates courts are in session nearly every day.

Procedure in petty sessions, first regulated by an Act of 1848 (another of Sir John Jervis's Acts), is now governed by the Magistrates' Courts Act, 1952. The procedure is very simple and the same both in cases of non-indictable offences and of indictable offences tried summarily. Attendance is enforced by summons or arrest with or without warrant. There are no formal pleadings, and after hearing each side and its witnesses the magistrates give their decision. The prosecution is sometimes conducted by a solicitor or by a counsel instructed by the police, but often simply by a police officer. The proportion of defendants who plead guilty is even higher in the magistrates' courts than at quarter sessions or the assizes—perhaps as high as 80 per cent.—but even so justices have to decide in some 250,000 cases a year after hearing the parties and their witnesses whether the prosecution has proved its case. Since 1848 the accused has had a right to be represented by a lawyer, and in some cases—especially where questions of law arise—legal aid is granted. On questions of law lay justices have, of necessity, to rely on the advice of their clerk who is nowadays always a qualified lawyer. His position is obviously one of some difficulty. If he fails to intervene, his magistrates may go wrong. If, on the other hand, he intervenes frequently he may appear to be usurping the position of the judges. In selecting types of sentence, magistrates have broadly the same alternatives open to them as judges in the higher courts. Generally they have not power to imprison for longer than 6 months ; but if the offence is an indictable offence which is being tried summarily, and the offender is over 17 and they consider on hearing his antecedents that he should be given a more severe sentence than they can impose, they can commit him to quarter sessions for sentence. In sentencing, magistrates have the assistance of probation officers and social enquiry reports in the same way as the higher courts. When dealing summarily with indictable offences, magistrates in 1968 imposed fines in some 88,000 cases, made orders of conditional discharge or probation orders in some 38,000 cases, sentenced some 28,000 people to imprisonment—the sentences being suspended in some 18,000 cases—and committed some 8,000 to quarter sessions for sentence. Of the 1,320,000 persons who committed non-indictable offences the great majority, some 1,253,000, were fined, only 15,000 were sentenced to imprisonment, and in 8,000 cases sentence was suspended.

There are two forms of appeal from petty sessions, one to quarter sessions, the other to the Queen's Bench Division. Any person aggrieved by the conviction of a court of summary jurisdiction may appeal against it to quarter sessions unless he admitted his guilt, and even then he can appeal against his sentence. The appeal is heard by quarter sessions, or, in the case of boroughs, by the Recorder, sitting in each case without a jury, and it involves a complete rehearing. The prosecutor has to open his case and prove it all over again, and new witnesses not heard at petty sessions may be called. Compared with the number of convictions at petty sessions, the number of appeals to quarter sessions is small,[1] though larger than it was before poor persons received legal assistance to prosecute them. Appeals to the Queen's Bench Division, unlike those to quarter sessions, are confined to errors of law. The jurisdiction of the Queen's Bench Division may be invoked in one of two ways, either it may be asked to issue a writ of certiorari to the magistrates to bring up the conviction so that it may be quashed for defect of law or excess of jurisdiction, or a case may be stated by the magistrates at the instance of either party raising a point of law for decision. In either case the case is heard before a divisional court. If the matter is a criminal matter and not part of the civil jurisdiction of the justices there is no further appeal to the Court of Appeal, but there is now an appeal to the House of Lords subject to the same provisions as govern appeals from the Criminal Division of the Court of Appeal. This controlling jurisdiction of the Queen's Bench Division is exercised not only over the magistrates in petty sessions but also over quarter sessions when it is hearing appeals from petty sessions.[2]

It remains for us to say something of offences committed by " juveniles," *i.e.* either by " children " between the ages of 10 (below which there is no criminal responsibility) and 14 or by " young persons " between the

---

[1] In 1968 there were about 8,500 appeals to Quarter Sessions, in 944 of which the conviction was quashed, and in 2,500 of which the sentence was reduced.

[2] In 1968 123 cases stated by courts of summary jurisdiction and 15 cases stated by quarter sessions were heard by the Divisional Court. Appeals were allowed in 76 cases.

ages of 14 and 17. The law on the subject will be substantially changed when the provisions of the Childrens and Young Persons Act, 1969, have been put fully into force, but at the moment we are in a transitional stage. In a book of this sort all that we can do is to give a short account of the position as it was and of the main lines of the changes envisaged. Special courts for the trial of juveniles were set up under the Children and Young Persons Act, 1935. Juvenile courts must be held at a different time and place from the ordinary magistrates' court. The justices constituting the court are drawn from a panel of specially qualified magistrates. Not more than three justices sit at a time, of whom one is generally a woman. The court is not open to the general public, though representatives of the press are admitted, and the parents or guardians of the juvenile must attend. Under the system prevailing hitherto if a child was charged with any indictable offence (other than homicide) he had to be tried summarily unless charged jointly with someone not a child who was committed for trial. If a young person was charged with any indictable offence (other than homicide) he could be tried summarily if he consented to be so tried. In fact of some 64,000 juveniles found guilty of indictable offences in 1968 only about 1,000 were found guilty at assizes or quarter sessions after a trial on indictment. The rest and also some 50,000 juveniles found guilty of non-indictable offences were tried summarily. If the juvenile was found guilty of the offence with which he was charged, the magistrates could discharge him either absolutely or conditionally or put him on probation. If they took none of these courses they could impose a fine (which they could order to be paid by the parents) or send the juvenile to an approved school or a detention centre or commit him to the care of a " fit " person. They could not send him to prison. The chief objects of the Act of 1969 appear to be (1) to secure so far as possible that juveniles who commit criminal offences shall not be prosecuted but shall be brought before the juvenile court in its civil jurisdiction as a juvenile in need of care and protection, and (2) to ensure as far as may be that the treatment which such juveniles receive shall not be of a punitive character. The first object is to be secured by providing (*a*) that "children," *i.e.* juveniles under 14, shall not be charged with any offence other than homicide, (*b*) that no "young person," *i.e.* a juvenile between 14 and 17, shall be prosecuted except at the instance of a qualified informant, normally a police officer, who has satisfied himself that the case cannot be properly dealt with in any other way, and (*c*) that if the juvenile court is satisfied that a juvenile has committed a criminal offence (other than homicide) they may make an order committing him to the care of the local children's authority if they think that he is in need of care or control which he is unlikely to receive unless such an order is made. The second object is sought to be secured by abolishing in the case of juveniles attendance centres detention centres, and fit person and approved school orders and by substituting for probation orders which will place children and may place young persons under the supervision of the children's authority rather than the probation service.

A hundred years ago the future of the lay justices of the peace looked gloomy enough. They had lost most of their administrative functions; they had lost all their judicial functions in London; and it seemed to be only a matter of time before they were replaced throughout the country by professionals. Maitland writing in the 1880's said of the lay J.P.: "He is cheap; he is pure; he is capable; but he is doomed; he is to be sacrificed to a theory on the altar of the spirit of the age." [1] In fact, however, he has survived, and in the last 50 years or so his power has been increasing. It is true that in quarter sessions the presiding magistrate is now always a professional; but in county quarter sessions the lay magistrates still have a voice in sentencing. In petty sessions

[1] Quoted by Milton (op. cit.), p. 17.

the number of stipendiaries outside London is no greater to-day than it was 100 years ago and even where there are stipendiaries the lay justices take part on equal terms with them in the domestic and juvenile work which has become so important in recent years. Further, in the course of the last 100 years the great majority of indictable offences have come in fact to be tried summarily by magistrates, whether lay or professional, and the proportion is constantly moving in favour of summary trial. In 1961 of some 117,000 indictable offences, 86,000 were tried summarily, and some 31,000 on indictment. In 1968 of some 193,000 indictable offences some 166,000 were tried summarily and only some 27,000 on indictment.[1] Trial by jury in civil cases is almost extinct. The same cannot yet be said of trial by jury in criminal cases; but there is no doubt that it is on the wane.

[1] It may well be that the 27,000 in 1968 took longer to try than the 31,000 in 1961 for probably in many more of these there was a plea of "not guilty," and with legal aid the average length of trial has increased considerably.

XIX

THE PRIVY COUNCIL

SIR Edward Hyde, in exile from his country, began in 1646 to write his *History of the Rebellion,* and in it comments in the following terms on the Act abolishing the Star Chamber. " Thus fell that high Court, a great branch of the prerogative ; having been rather extended and confirmed, than founded by the statute of King Henry the Seventh ; for, no doubt, it had both a being and a jurisdiction before that time, though vulgarly it received date from thence ; and whilst it was gravely and moderately governed was an excellent expedient to preserve the dignity of the King, the honour of his council and the peace and security of the kingdom. But the taking it away was an act very popular ; which it may be, was not then more politic, than the reviving it may be thought hereafter, when the present distempers shall be expired." [1] " The distempers " in question " expired " fourteen years later, and Sir Edward Hyde, soon to become Lord Clarendon, returned to England in 1660 as the chief Minister of King Charles II. The revival of the Star Chamber did not, however, form part of the Restoration Settlement—the memories of it were no doubt too bitter—and the Royal Council (then coming to be known exclusively as the Privy Council) [2] never again tried to assert a right to hear any case, civil or criminal, within the jurisdiction of the ordinary courts of law and equity.

There were, however, a few cases outside the jurisdiction of the ordinary courts which used to

[1] Clarendon : *History of the Rebellion* (1826), vol. 1, p. 500. The so-called " Star Chamber Act " had even less importance in the history of the Court than Clarendon thought ; see pp. 102–3, above.

[2] We saw in Chapter 7 that before the fall of the Star Chamber a distinction had grown up between the Council and the Privy Council, see p. 103.

come before the Council and which were not affected by
the abolition of the Star Chamber. In particular there
were petitions to the Crown against the judgments of
courts which were outside the control of the courts at
Westminster, such as the courts in the overseas posses-
sions of the Crown. In the sixteenth century, for
instance, petitions from the Channel Islands came before
the Council, and after the Restoration such petitions,
together with petitions from the colonies in America and
the West Indies, continued to be brought there. The
Privy Council at this time was coming to do its work
by means of a system of committees which were in some
cases the ancestors of the present government offices, and
one such committee was that for " trade and the foreign
plantations." It was to this committee that the business
of hearing these petitions was assigned, and the hearings
appear usually to have been before a small sub-committee
of five or six persons, one or two of whom might be
lawyers while the rest were lay members of the Privy
Council.

It is a principle of English law that a man has no
right to appeal from the decision of a court unless
the right has been specially conferred upon him. Consequently the appeals which came before the Privy Council
in those times were entertained as a matter of grace.
The Privy Council might refuse to hear any given
petition. In the course of the eighteenth century,
however, as the British Empire expanded and British
courts were set up in various parts of the world, such as
Canada and India, it became usual to make provision in
the charters or enactments establishing them for an
appeal from their decisions to His Majesty's Privy
Council, sometimes with, and sometimes without, the
leave of the Colonial Court. The express right of appeal
so granted did not, however, in any way affect the power
of the Privy Council to hear any petition it chose, and so
one finds two forms of appeal to the Privy Council which
should be carefully distinguished, appeals brought as of

right and appeals brought with the leave of the Council where the colonial constitution made no provision for an appeal or (if it did) leave to bring it had been refused by the colonial courts.

With the growth of the Empire the business coming before the Privy Council naturally increased, and complaints began to be heard of its method of conducting it. The committees which heard appeals had no permanent existence but were collected together from time to time to deal with a batch of petitions. If possible a legal privy councillor was put on the committee—the Master of the Rolls seems often to have been a member of it at the close of the eighteenth century—but the majority often consisted of men with little acquaintance with the law. Further, all the members had other work to do and disposed of important appeals with the most indecent dispatch. It is hardly surprising in these circumstances that their decisions were often treated with very little respect by the colonial courts which were supposed to carry them out. In 1828 Lord Brougham devoted a long passage in his famous speech on law reform to the state of the hearing of appeals by the Privy Council, and when he became Lord Chancellor in 1830 he determined to introduce a bill on the subject. The matter, meanwhile, became more pressing by reason of the transference of the hearing of ecclesiastical and admiralty appeals to the Privy Council in 1832 on the abolition of the Court of Delegates.[1]

The Act passed in 1833, "for the better administration of justice in His Majesty's Privy Council," constituted a committee of the Privy Council to be known as the "Judicial Committee" which was to consist of those Privy Councillors who were or had been in high judicial office,[2] while the Crown was to have power to appoint two other Privy Councillors members of the committee.

---

[1] See Chapter 14, p. 233, above.
[2] The Lord President and ex-Lord Presidents, who are usually laymen, are also members, but they do not attend.

The composition of the committee has subsequently been extended to include Privy Councillors who are or have been chief justices or judges of the Superior Courts of countries which are members of the British Commonwealth. The Lords of Appeal in Ordinary, established by the Appellate Jurisdiction Act, 1876, are all of them members of the Privy Council, and form the nucleus of the Judicial Committee,[1] but until 1947 there were always at least two persons with experience of Indian law and procedure available to take part in the hearing of Indian appeals, and Commonwealth members of the committee who happen from time to time to be in London sometimes form part of the board. Further judges of the English High Court and the Scottish Court of Session are often made Privy Councillors on their retirement from the bench and voluntarily give their services when required as members of the Committee. A quorum of three is essential.

Under the Act of 1833 and a subsequent Act of 1844 the Judicial Committee took on the aspect of an ordinary court of justice. There were provisions regulating its procedure and the cost of appeals, and it was enacted that the grounds of each decision should be read in open court. Already for some years reports of the more important cases before the Council had been published, and now the practice of reporting its decisions became regular. There are, however, even to-day some traces of the fact that the Judicial Committee is in theory the committee of an executive council and not a court of law. Thus the decision of the board does not take the form of a judgment but of a report tendering advice to Her Majesty, and though in practice the Crown always allows or dismisses the appeal in question in accordance with the

---

[1] The Judicature Act, 1873, which, as we saw, provided for the abolition of the appellate jurisdiction of the House of Lords in English cases, also provided for the transfer of the Privy Council's jurisdiction to the new Court of Appeal, but both jurisdictions were restored by the Act of 1875 before their abolition took effect.

advice given, the report of the Judicial Committee is strictly of no effect until confirmed by Her Majesty at an ordinary meeting of the Privy Council. Further, as logical consequences of the advisory character of its pronouncements, the committee does not consider itself bound by its previous decisions [1] and until recently it never took note in its report of any dissentient opinion among its members. Now, however, one or more members of the committee may subscribe to a single dissenting opinion.

We have seen that there were two forms of appeal to the Privy Council; an appeal brought as of right under the provisions of the constitution of the colony or dominion in question, and an appeal brought by the special leave of the Judicial Committee, either in the absence of any right to appeal given by the colonial legislation, or on the refusal of the colonial court to give leave to appeal from its decision in cases where the colonial legislation makes such leave a condition precedent to the right to appeal. Naturally, the Committee has formulated principles on which it exercises its discretion to give leave to appeal. Thus it will not give such leave in criminal cases unless it appears prima facie that the trial has been conducted with such a disregard of the forms of legal process or the principles of natural justice as to involve a substantial and grave injustice to the accused. Similarly in civil cases it will only grant leave to appeal in cases of public importance or where either the legal issues or the property involved are substantial.

With the growth of responsible government in the Dominions towards the close of the last century the propriety of the decisions of their courts being subject to review by a court which, though in theory an Imperial

[1] Normally, of course, the Judicial Committee will follow a previous decision of its own, and without being in any way bound to do so it naturally tends to accept the judgments of the House of Lords on questions of English law. In the same way the English courts, though not bound by Privy Council decisions, attach considerable importance to them.

court, was in practice largely staffed by English judges began to be canvassed. Despite the fact that the Judicial Committee was called upon to administer a variety of different systems of law with some of which none of its members are conversant, there was very little criticism of the quality of its decisions.[1] The question was rather one of prestige. So far as concerned appeals brought as of right the matter could be settled by the Dominion Parliaments, for any such right was conferred by Dominion legislation and could be taken away by it, but before 1931 the right to petition the Crown for special leave to appeal could only be taken away or abridged by an Act of the Imperial Parliament,[2] since Dominion legislation had no effect outside its own territories and, further, by the Colonial Laws Validity Act, 1865, had to yield to any Imperial legislation with which it was inconsistent. In 1931, however, the Statute of Westminster was passed repealing the Colonial Laws Validity Act, so far as the Dominions were concerned, and giving extra-territorial effect to Dominion legislation. In 1933 the Parliament of the Irish Free State, in reliance on it, purported to abolish all appeals from their courts to the Privy Council, while the Canadian Parliament purported to abolish all such appeals in criminal cases. The question whether this legislation was effective to prevent the Crown from exercising its prerogative right to grant leave to appeal, notwithstanding that no Imperial Act had taken it away, came before the Privy Council in 1935, and it was decided that the Free State and Canadian Acts had had this effect.[3] Other self-governing members of the

---

[1] It is worth noticing, as a sign of the complete independence which Commonwealth Courts have now achieved, that the High Court of Australia has refused to follow a decision of the House of Lords.

[2] It was, in fact, so abridged in cases raising the question of the constitutional powers of the Commonwealth and States of Australia *inter se* by the Commonwealth Act, 1900.

[3] *Moore* v. *A.-G. for the Irish Free State*, [1935] A. C. 484; and *British Coal Corporation* v. *The King*, [1935] A. C. 500.

Commonwealth have passed similar legislation ; but some of them, *e.g.* Australia, New Zealand and Malaysia still permit appeals to the Privy Council. The position of appeals from parts of the Commonwealth which are not yet self-governing remains the same. The Privy Council heard 29 appeals in 1968.

The hearing of appeals from Commonwealth courts is by far the most important part of the work of the Judicial Committee, but it has also a few other functions. Its position as a court of appeal in ecclesiastical and prize cases has been dealt with in Chapter 14, but we may notice here that it hears appeals by registered medical practitioners whose names have been struck off the register by the Disciplinary Committee of the General Medical Council. Again, the Crown may specially refer to the Judicial Committee any matter which it thinks fit for such a reference, and has from time to time referred to it various disputed questions which were capable of legal as opposed to political treatment.[1]

[1] For a list of such references, see Halsbury, *Laws of England,* 3rd ed., vol. 9., para. 883.

XX

CASE LAW AND STATUTE LAW

THE subject of this book is the English legal system past and present. It deals with the organs through which, and the methods by which, justice has been and is now administered in this country rather than with the subject-matter of the law itself. It is, of course, impossible to maintain a rigid division between the two topics, for the history of the various courts cannot be told without some reference to the character of the rights which they would enforce, and in our earlier chapters we have touched, sometimes at some length, on the growth of the law of property, contract and tort. The substance of the modern law lies entirely outside our field, but it belongs to a work on the legal system, rather than to a work on any branch of the law itself, to describe where the law is found and how it is declared, and accordingly we propose in this chapter to deal quite briefly with the chief sources of modern English law.

First, however, it is as well to emphasise, what is often in danger of being forgotten, that the finding and declaring of the law is only a small part of the work of the judges of this country. In every case which comes before the courts the facts have first to be established. Sometimes they are undisputed. If there is a dispute as to them it has to be resolved either by the finding of the judge or the verdict of a jury. On the facts so found a decision has to be given by the judge, but he does not always, or even generally, arrive at his decision by applying principles of law to the facts and working out the result as he might a mathematical calculation. In very many cases he has, to a great or lesser degree, a discretion in the exercise of which he is as free from the fetters of the law as an administrator in a government office. In criminal cases, for instance, the two questions to be decided in the great majority of cases are (*a*) has the accused done the act on which the charge against him is based—a question of fact; and (*b*) if so, what sentence is he to receive—a matter largely of discretion. It is true, of course, that every criminal case involves the question of law whether the facts alleged against the accused, if proved, constitute a crime, but in the great majority of cases there is no doubt as to this. If there was, the administration of so much of our criminal justice by laymen would be less defensible than it is. Turning to the civil law the jurisdiction of the courts over the persons of lunatics and infants and over property subject to trusts involves the exercise of discretion far more than the application of law. Ought the ward of court to live with his father or his mother? Ought the trustees to be allowed to invest all the trust fund in ordinary shares? These are not questions of law. In answering them the judge must make up his mind what would be expedient in the particular case by applying his common sense to the facts proved in just the same way as the civil servant applies his common sense to the report of the Ministry's inspector when the Minister is asked to confirm a slum clearance order.

But assuming that the case in question is one which involves the application of a principle of law to the facts, where is the principle to be found? Historically, law developed from custom, and in the old communal courts of Anglo-Saxon England the principle of law applied was a reflection of the usages of the community in question, and was declared by the freemen of the community, who were the judges of the court. But as communities grow in size and in civilisation, custom comes to play a smaller and smaller part in their law. Speaking generally one finds that in civilised states the law flows from one or more of three sources. It may be deduced from principles laid down in codes enacted by bodies having legislative

authority, as is the case in most European states to-day ;
it may be inferred from the records of previous decisions
of the courts which are called upon to declare it, as is still
largely the case in England to-day ; and finally it may
be sought in the writings and opinions of professional
experts as was largely the case in the great period of
Roman legal history. It must not, of course, be supposed that these sources of law are in any way mutually
exclusive. The judges in countries whose law is codified
do not reject all aid from decided cases and often rely on
the writings of jurists. The words of the code alone are
binding, but decisions of judges of eminence and the
opinions of distinguished professors of the law may
gradually tend to establish a certain mode of approaching
and interpreting the sacred words which a tribunal will
not lightly reject. Similarly, in this country though the
chief authority in our private law is the reports of decided
cases, several branches of it have been codified by statute,
while in others, such as the law of property and the conflict
of laws, considerable weight is attached to the practice of
conveyancers and the opinions of jurists. Further, our
public law is largely statutory.

We have said something in our earlier chapters of the
growth of case law in this country.[1] The foundations of
the common law were laid by the decisions of the royal
judges in the century after the death of Henry II, and
naturally from the first former decisions played a part
in shaping the decisions in subsequent cases. There
were as yet no published reports of decisions, but the
pleadings and judgments in all cases were recorded on
the plea rolls to which the judges and more eminent
pleaders had access. The Year Books of the later Middle
Ages were not reports in the modern sense, since they
were not so much concerned with the decisions reached
as with the course of the oral pleading in court by which
the issue to be decided was formulated, but we can see

---

[1] On this subject see generally Allen, *Law in the Making*, and Rupert
Cross, *Precedent in English Law*.

from the Year Books that the citation of decided cases was already very common. This citation was based partly on cases already reported in earlier Year Books, and partly on memory and professional tradition. As yet, however, there was no suggestion that a previous decision was binding on the courts, and even with the advent in the sixteenth and seventeenth centuries of published reports of a more or less modern type the doctrine of binding precedent was very slow to develop. Thus John Vaughan (Chief Justice of the Common Pleas, 1668–1674), after pointing out how necessary it is to distinguish between that part of the reasoning of the court which is essential to the judgment given and that part which is mere *obiter dictum*, goes on to say that even the essential reasoning of the court may be rejected if it is in conflict with fundamental principles, and in the eighteenth century Lord Mansfield held that while precedents served to illustrate principles, yet the principles on which the law depended were not to be sought in individual cases.

But in the nineteenth century it came gradually to be established that a principle to be extracted from a previous decision of a superior court was binding on an inferior court, and further, that the highest tribunal was bound by its own decisions. This development was aided by the reorganisation of the judicial system by the Judicature Acts and by the contemporaneous changes in the character of the Law Reports. In the eighteenth century there were a number of separate courts which had little hesitation in differing from one another, and a supreme tribunal which was so constituted that its decisions did not command any great respect in the profession. After 1875 there was a well-regulated hierarchy of courts— High Court, Court of Appeal and House of Lords—and it was natural to conclude that decisions of the Court of Appeal should be binding on the High Court, the decisions of the House of Lords on the Court of Appeal, and that the House of Lords was bound by its own decisions.

Down to 1866 the publishing of reports was a matter of private enterprise, and there were great differences in their quality. A far greater respect would be accorded to a decision reported by Burrows or Campbell than to one reported by Comberbach or Espinasse, and judges were sometimes able to ignore decisions which they disliked by suggesting that they were incorrectly reported. In 1866 private reporting in the old sense of the word came to an end and the Incorporated Council of Law Reporting was established. This is indeed a private body, but has a quasi-official character, since its members are representatives of the Inns of Court and the Law Society. The Council employs an editor and a staff of reporters and produces a uniform series of reports of cases in all the superior courts. Of course only a small minority of cases heard are reported. It rests with the discretion of the reporter in court to decide whether any case seems prima facie to deserve a report, and with the editor to select from the cases noted by the reporters those which shall in fact be reported. If it is decided to report a case the judge has an opportunity of revising the wording of his judgment. In addition to the reports published by the Council of Law Reporting, which are known as " the Law Reports " *par excellence*, there are a number of proprietary series issued by journals and legal publishers.[1] The great majority of cases reported in these series of reports are also published in the Law Reports. All the reporters are barristers, which gives counsel the right to cite the reports in court, and there is little if any difference in the character of the reporting in the various series. But a great difference, which strikes any one who compares a report of a century ago with any modern report, is that

---

[1] The most important of the general series are or were the Law Times Reports (referred to as L. T.), the Law Journal Reports (L. J.), The Times Law Reports (T. L. R.) and the All England Reports (All E. R.). There are also several series devoted to special subjects—*e.g.* Patents and Trade Marks (R.P.C.), Tax Cases (T.C.), etc.

nowadays far less space is accorded to the pleadings and arguments, while the judgments have increased enormously in length. In the old days the judges tended simply to give the final words capping a long discussion in court, whereas to-day they rehearse the facts at length in their judgments, and since these judgments are generally reported verbatim in shorthand notes which are easy to obtain, whereas the arguments of counsel are not, there is a natural but regrettable tendency for the one to be reported and the other ignored.

But though the reorganisation of the courts and the semi-official character of modern reports may have aided the development of the doctrine of binding precedent, it is clear that a stronger motive must have been at work in establishing it. It may be suggested that this motive was the desire of English judges to point to some certain foundation for English law comparable to the various codes which were coming to form the basis of the law of most European states in the nineteenth century. After the publication of the " Code Napoléon " and its imitation throughout the length and breadth of Europe, it was natural for men to draw a contrast between the system of a code and the system of case law. Bentham had been a great advocate of codes and a great opponent of judge-made law, and English judges of the nineteenth century were sufficiently in sympathy with his views to repudiate the notion that they made law by their decisions and always to insist that they were merely applying law which already existed. A doctrine of binding precedent aided them in their contention that the law of England was something certain which did not merely reside in the breasts of the judges.

Meanwhile, in the nineteenth century, statute was gradually coming to rival decided cases as a source of English law. We have seen that the reorganisation of the judicial system and procedure in the nineteenth century was the work of statute, but statutes affected the substance of the law as well. In the sphere of private law there were three classes of statute which we may specially mention. First the type of statute such as the Partnership Act, 1890, or the Sale of Goods Act, 1893, which took a branch of the law which had been developed by a long series of decisions of the courts and cast the outcome of a mass of cases into the form of a few principles set out in the sections of an Act of Parliament. Secondly, those statutes such as the Conveyancing Act, 1881, or the Settled Land Act, 1882, which aimed at codifying the labours of conveyancers by importing into all documents of a certain class the provisions which were common form in all well-drawn instruments of that class. The conveyancers of the eighteenth and early nineteenth centuries had evolved the typical mortgage and the typical settlement, documents of immense length giving a great variety of essential powers to the mortgagee and the tenant for life or the trustees. The Acts of Parliament in question greatly shortened and simplified these documents by providing that such powers need not be expressly given but should be read into all mortgages and settlements. Thirdly, we have the statute which deals with an isolated point of private law where, for instance, a rule which has become established by decisions of the courts is recognised to work injustice but cannot be altered by the courts in view of the doctrine of binding precedent. Thus to take an early example the Contingent Remainders Act, 1877, was passed in view of the hardship revealed by the decision in *Cunliffe* v. *Brancker*. Some forty years ago a standing Committee of judges and lawyers called the Law Reform Committee was set up which issues reports from time to time on the desirability of legislation in any field of private law which is submitted to it for consideration. Some valuable legislation—*e.g.* the Limitation Act, 1939—has resulted from its labours. But the members are all people with other duties to attend to and the Committee has neither the time nor the staff itself to initiate projects of Law Reform. Eventually by the Law Commission Act, 1965, a body of whole-time salaried Commissioners was established " to keep the law under review with a view to its systematic development and reform including in particular its codification, the elimination of anomalies, the repeal of obsolete and unnecessary enactments, the reduction of the number of separate enactments and generally its simplification and modernisation." The Commission has already done much valuable work. We may instance in particular that it ventured into the contentious field of Divorce Reform and that its Report led to the Divorce Reform Act, 1969, which came into force on 1st January, 1971.

Thus over the last hundred years Statute has played a considerable part in the development of our private law and is plainly destined to play an increasing part in this field in the future. In the field of public law the part played by statute is even more evident. The whole structure of our local government was reformed by statute in the nineteenth century and the greater part of our law of public administration is statute law. There is, of course, nothing surprising in this. Our modern social services could only be provided by creating new public authorities with powers far more extensive than the prerogative powers allowed to the government by the common law. Recourse to Parliament was, therefore, essential.

Acts of Parliament are often very complicated documents, and it is natural to ask how they come into being. Parliament sometimes rejects bills and often amends those which it passes, but obviously it does not itself draft the bills which it considers. It possesses no machinery for such a purpose, even supposing that its members were qualified for the task of operating it. In the past the drafting of statutes amending private law was sometimes the individual work of distinguished lawyers, invited to undertake the task. Thus the Settled Land Act, 1882, was drawn by Mr. Wolstenholme and the Partnership Act, 1890, by Sir Frederick Pollock.

Nowadays most statutes are drafted by the government draftsmen—known as the Parliamentary Counsel to the Treasury—acting in collaboration with civil servants in the Ministries concerned or the body which has recommended a reform in the law. During the greater part of the nineteenth century the government possessed no single body of expert draftsmen, but in 1868 Lord Thring, who had drafted several government measures in the 50's and 60's, was appointed standing draftsman to the government, and round him the office of Parliamentary Counsel grew up. To-day it consists of some twenty counsel who are recruited from among members of the bar.[1]

There are now, it is calculated, over 300,000 reported cases and each year adds substantially to their number. Similarly the volume of " live " statute law and of " live " delegated legislation—*i.e.* orders and regulations made under statutory powers—is now enormous and is growing steadily. That the quantity of law in England to-day should be vast is inevitable. Huge sums are raised each year from the property and earnings of part of the population to finance services designed to benefit the community or the poorer sections of it. So one gets complicated Revenue laws and complicated regulations for the administration of the services in question—Health, Education, Social Security and so on. Then those who are, or are thought to be economically stronger must be prevented from exploiting their superior bargaining position. So one gets Rent Acts, Hire Purchase Acts and so on. Yet again legislation has to be passed to prevent or seek to prevent the manifold abuses which spring from increased knowledge and its application to life—the legislation with regard to motor cars and drugs to take two obvious examples. But though its bulk must needs be vast it is said with some force that it

[1] See the article on Lord Thring by Sir Courtenay Ilbert in the *Dictionary of National Biography*. He was one of several great civil servants whose names are little known but who left a deep mark on English administration.

need not be so hard to find or so obscurely expressed as it often is at present.[1] The need to refer to numbers of cases could perhaps be reduced somewhat by codification, and codification is one of the tasks to which the Law Commission is addressing itself. Further, our statute law would certainly become less unintelligible if it was anyone's business to see that it was drafted so as to be as readily intelligible as possible. As it is, Parliament does not concern itself with the form of legislation. It is prepared and drafted by experts—the civil servants in the Ministry concerned and the Parliamentary Counsel —who are not concerned to see that the Act should be intelligible to anyone who is not himself an expert in the particular field but simply that it is so expressed as to cover every contingency which they can foresee. One would certainly like to see Acts of Parliament which were less encumbered with detail and more concerned to enunciate principles which Members of Parliament could understand and judges seek to apply to concrete cases; but that would involve a great change in the attitude to legislation of all the chief parties concerned—the civil servants, the Parliamentary draftsmen and the judiciary.

This leads one to consider the part played by the judges in law making. Men to-day expect of the law two qualities which are hard to combine. They expect it to be certain, but at the same time they expect it to correspond to current notions of what is just. In the past when men's ideas of what was just in social relations did not change as quickly as they have come to do of late a high value was placed on certainty. Men valued a fixed rule which would be applied impartially in all cases as opposed to arbitrary decisions depending on the whim of authority. To-day when men's ideas of what is just are in a state of flux a decision according to law may easily appear unjust, an adherence to a fixed rule mere obscurantism, and the maxim " Hard cases make

[1] See Sir Leslie Scarman—the Chairman of the Law Commission in *What's Wrong with the Law* (B.B.C. 1970), pp. 8–15.

bad law " heartless nonsense.   Yet, for all that, in some
situations men still like the law to be certain.   No one,
for instance, on consulting his solicitor is pleased to hear
him say, " Until last year the cases were all one way and
in your favour.   But then came the case of X v. Y, and
now I am really at a loss to advise you.   It really depends
on which judge we get and, if we go to the Court of
Appeal, which division of the Court hears the appeal."

It was the glory of Lord Mansfield that he, more
than any English judge before or since, infused the
administration of justice with the spirit of his age and
strove to make his decisions reflect the current needs and
expectations of men.   But conservative judges like Lord
Kenyon and radical reformers like Bentham were at one
in condemning his methods, and the writer of the "Letters
of Junius " spoke for a substantial body of opinion when
he accused the great Chief Justice of unsettling the law
by the introduction of vague notions of equity and
natural justice.[1]   In the past when it took a long time
for reforms in the law to be effected by statute the disadvantages of a system of binding precedent which
hampers judicial legislation may well have outweighed its
advantages.   But with the advent of the Law Commission the position has been radically changed.   It is true
that Parliament has not yet decided—as it ought to
decide—to allot a certain amount of Parliamentary time
each year to non-political law reform, but even so reforms
advocated by the Commission can be carried into effect
with reasonable speed.   It would appear, therefore, to
be well arguable that nowadays the advantages of strict
adherence to precedent outweigh its disadvantages and that
the recent decision of the House of Lords no longer to be
bound by its own decisions was unfortunate.

[1] See Letter 41.

XXI

THE LEGAL PROFESSION

WE have now completed our account of the courts in which English law has been administered from Anglo-Saxon times down to the present day. In this chapter we will trace quite shortly the history of the legal professions, members of which preside or practise in our tribunals. This history falls naturally into two periods, the mediæval period and the period beginning about the sixteenth century, when the main lines of the modern organisation of the legal profession begin to be discernible.

In the communal and feudal courts of the Middle Ages there were no professional judges. There was indeed a presiding officer, but judgment was given by the whole body of the suitors of the court in accordance with the customary law of the district. Nor was it possible for the litigants in those courts to appear by representatives. They had to appear in person and personally make " the proof " which the court decreed in their case. It is to be imagined that some suitors of the court would on account of their age or abilities be regarded as authorities to whose opinion on local custom great weight would attach, and that litigants would seek and perhaps pay for the advice of such men in the conduct of their suits, but the time of an organised legal profession had not yet come.

In the Royal Court in its original feudal form of a meeting of the king's tenants-in-chief, there were similarly no professional judges. The peers of England gave judgment in cases which concerned one of their number just as they did until 1948 in the trial of a peer for felony. But as the Royal Court extended its jurisdiction to include the suits of ordinary litigants, and as at the same time the law administered by it grew more complex,

381

the necessity for professional judges to deal with this volume of difficult work became apparent. In the early years of Henry II his commissioners " in eyre " were often drawn from the ranks of the baronage, but by the end of his reign we find that a class of legal experts—the justices of the Royal Court—had come into being. Later we can trace just the same change taking place in the communal and feudal courts. The suitors lose their position as judges and sink to the position of jurors, finding the facts while the law is applied and judgment given by the sheriff's bailiff or the lord's steward.

The class of royal judges which grew up in the latter part of the twelfth century was recruited from among the clerks in the royal household and chancery, that is to say from the ablest and best educated men in the kingdom. They were all, or almost all, of them ecclesiastics with generally at least a smattering of either the civil or the canon law, but they were not like modern English judges, men who had practised as advocates in the courts, and came to the bench with a knowledge of English law. In their day, there hardly was a class of professional advocates from which they could have been drawn and there was no provision made anywhere for the teaching of the English law. It was, indeed, these very judges of the twelfth and thirteenth centuries who were themselves laying the foundations of the common law, and we may almost say that they made and learnt it at the same time. The most famous name among the clerical judges of the thirteenth century is, of course, Bracton, but we may perhaps recall the names of two of his predecessors, Martin Pateshull and William Raleigh.

When considering the origins of our modern professions of barristers and solicitors it is essential to bear in mind the distinction between the man who appears as the representative—the attorney—of a litigant and the advocate who speaks for him and puts his case before the court. If one remembers that in the Middle Ages all the chief steps in an action had to be taken in court and that no step could be taken in the absence of either of the parties, it is easy to see that when litigation became at all common it was essential to allow the parties to appear constructively by " attorneys," on whom they had conferred the power of binding them by their acts. The default of the attorney is then regarded as equivalent to the default of his principal and what the attorney pleads on his principal's behalf binds the principal. Meanwhile, however, as the law became more complicated litigants found that it was not always enough to employ an attorney however conscientious. The services of an expert in the law were required to tell the litigant's story to the court or to make his defence in the appropriate forms, and not all attorneys had the necessary skill. In the "narrators" or "counters" employed for this purpose we find the origin of the profession of barristers.

About 1300 the counters and attorneys practising in the royal courts began to get a professional organisation. The attorney came to be regarded as an officer of the court in which he practised. The Courts of Common Pleas and of the King's Bench each had a number of attorneys attached to them whose services were at the disposal of litigants using the court and whose admission to practice in the court was controlled by the judges. Some care was taken to ensure that unqualified persons should not practise. Thus a statute in 1402, after lamenting that many attorneys were " ignorant and not learned in the law," required all candidates for inclusion on the roll to be examined by the judges. Meanwhile within the body of counters or narrators two clearly marked grades had come into being. The older and abler of them formed a small class apart, the order of " Serjeants-at-Law," while the rest formed the societies which we know as the Inns of Court (Lincoln's Inn, Inner Temple, Middle Temple, Gray's Inn).

We find the order of serjeants-at-law in being at the beginning of the fourteenth century. It was a small close guild to which the most eminent advocates were appointed by patents from the king, and the day of his appointment became, in later times, the occasion of a magnificent entertainment given by the new-made serjeant. The serjeants lived a corporate life together in Serjeants' Inn, and wore a special dress of which the most prominent feature was the white silk " coif " or cap fastened under the chin. Members of the order had the exclusive right of audience in the Court of Common Pleas, the busiest of the three courts in the Middle Ages, and, by reason of this monopoly, the mediæval serjeant was generally a very rich man. In 1379 they were taxed at the same rate as the baronage. The greatest proof of the importance and influence of the order of serjeants is that the king came gradually to choose the judges of his courts exclusively from among its members. Already, in Edward I's reign almost half the bench was recruited from this source, and in Edward II's reign ecclesiastics in the royal civil service were very rarely made judges. Hervey de Stanton, who was a justice of the Common Pleas from 1306 to 1327, and founded Michaelhouse, one of the two foundations out of which Henry VIII formed Trinity College at Cambridge, was the last famous clerical judge. From the middle of the fourteenth century until the passing of the Judicature Acts it was an unbroken rule that to be a judge of one of the common law courts a man must first have been made a serjeant-at-law. Here we have the origin of the peculiarly English system by which the judges are recruited from among leading barristers and not from a class of legal civil servants. As a result the relations between Bench and Bar in England are far closer than in continental countries. The serjeants, though not judges, were regularly put on the various commissions of assize and thus often acted as judges on circuit, while the mediæval serjeant when raised to the Bench continued to live as before in Serjeants' Inn. The other serjeants remained his " brothers," and the day of his appointment as a judge made not nearly so marked a change in his life and position in the world as the day that he left his Inn of Court to become serjeant-at-law.

Barristers other than serjeants were known in the Middle Ages as "apprentices." Originally no doubt, as the word indicates, they were learners sitting at the feet of the serjeants, but as the work of the courts increased and the Courts of King's Bench and Exchequer, in which the serjeants had no monopoly, extended their jurisdiction, many apprentices became men of substantial position. In the Statute of 1379 to which we referred the "great apprentice of law" is taxed on the same scale as the serjeants and other apprentices at half the rates. No doubt it was the ambition of every successful apprentice to be made a serjeant, but if he was one of the governors or "Benchers" of his Inn of Court he was already a figure of importance in the world. The four Inns of Court and a number of satellite bodies known as the Inns of Chancery came into being in the fourteenth and fifteenth centuries as centres in which the barristers (other than the serjeants) lived a collegiate life. Each Inn consisted of a governing body of Benchers, the ordinary or "outer" barristers, and the students who were not yet entitled to practise. The Inns were centres of education. "Readers" drawn from among the Benchers gave the students instruction in the law, and other subjects as diverse as music, dancing and history were studied in them. Indeed, many young men of good family who did not intend to practise the law were entered by their parents as students in one of the Inns of Court, much as their modern counterparts were until recently sent to Oxford or Cambridge in search of a liberal education. When the student who desired to practise in the courts was considered by his Benchers to be qualified for his profession he was "called" to the Bar by his Inn, and then became entitled to practise in court. We see, then, that while the admission of attorneys to practice was controlled by the judges themselves, the admission of barristers was delegated by them to the

Benchers of the several Inns, though since 1837 the rejected student has had a right of appeal to the Lord Chancellor and the judges against his Inn's decision in his case.
But despite this distinction in the mode of their qualification for practice, the professions of attorney and
barrister were not entirely separated in the Middle
Ages. Attorneys were often members of one or other
of the Inns of Court, and, if not, were generally members
of one of the smaller Inns of Chancery.

In the later sixteenth and seventeenth centuries we
can see the beginnings of a number of changes in the
mediæval system which we have outlined above. To
begin with the attorneys, we find that the profession
became quite separate from that of the barristers, and
that as a result they were excluded from membership of
the Inns of Court.[1] Instead of working hand in hand
with the barrister in the conduct of a case, the attorney
now became an intermediary between the barrister and
the client. The rule grew up that a barrister must not
do work for a client without the intervention of an
attorney and, as a further mark of his superior status,
that in theory he worked for nothing and could not sue
for his fees. Meanwhile the attorneys gradually amalgamated with another body of persons whose work was
analogous to theirs—the solicitors.

Attorneys, as we have seen, dated back to the Middle
Ages and were attached to one or other of the courts of
common law, though by the eighteenth century many
attorneys procured their admission on the roll of attorneys
of all three courts. In the sixteenth century, however, a
number of rival courts were becoming popular—the Star
Chamber, the Admiralty and, above all, the Chancery—
and litigants in these courts required services such as
were rendered by attorneys in the courts of common law.
It is true that in the Court of Chancery, at least, there was
a large staff of clerks, one of whose functions was supposed

---

[1] On the history of attorneys and solicitors, see Michael Birks, *Gentlemen of the Law*.

to be that of acting as advisers to the parties to the suits ;
but the reputation of the clerks in the Chancery for
honesty and diligence did not stand high, and it is not
surprising to find that many litigants employed a law
agent of their own as well.   Thus there came into being
a class of men known as " solicitors," whose title sufficiently indicates the somewhat undignified nature of the
services which they originally rendered.   Briefly stated,
it was their business to further their clients' suits by oiling
the wheels of the Court of Chancery.   In the course of
time, however, the profession of solicitor acquired a distinctly higher status, and by the middle of the seventeenth
century the solicitor admitted on the Roll of the Court
of Chancery was recognised as professionally the equal
of the attorney at law.   A third class of men with a professional affinity to the attorneys and solicitors were the
" proctors " at Doctors' Commons.   In the ecclesiastical
and admiralty courts the doctors took the place of the
serjeants-at-law and were termed according to the tradition of the civil and canon law " advocates," while the
counterparts of the attorneys were known by the civil
law style of " proctors "—a title which still survives in
the office of the "Queen's Proctor," now amalgamated
with that of Treasury Solicitor.   We may observe that
many proctors were also " notaries public."   The
notary was an official of the ecclesiastical courts who
both drafted and authenticated documents to be used in
the international world of the Western Church.   Abroad
the practice of having documents notarially certified
spread from the ecclesiastical to the commercial world,
and is still much in vogue.   In this country the practice
never obtained to the same degree, but there are still a
certain number of " notaries " mainly in seaport towns
and, as of old, they are still appointed by the Master of the
Faculties of the Archbishop of Canterbury.
     In the eighteenth century a great step towards the
amalgamation of the three branches of what is now the
single profession of solicitors was taken by the foundation

in 1739 of the Society of Gentlemen Practisers in the Courts of Law and Equity, a voluntary association to which attorneys, solicitors and proctors might all belong. At about the same time a statute of 1729 made universal in all courts a system, which had already been imposed by the Common Pleas as early as 1633, of five years' apprenticeship under written articles as a necessary preliminary to admission to the rolls of attorneys and solicitors. Further provision was made for allowing persons admitted as attorneys to be admitted also as solicitors, and vice versa. In the nineteenth century the profession began to take its modern form. The name of proctor disappeared with Doctors' Commons after the Acts of 1857, and that of attorney gradually gave way to that of solicitor,[1] which thus became the sole designation of members of the profession. In 1831 the Society of Gentlemen Practisers and some other smaller associations of a similar character were amalgamated to form the Law Society which, though only a voluntary association to which solicitors may or may not belong as they choose, has been gradually entrusted by Parliament with control over all solicitors whether its own members or not. Thus the Law Society has the custody of the Roll of Solicitors of the Supreme Court and provides for and controls the education of articled clerks and holds the examinations which qualify for admission to the Roll. Further, the Discipline Committee of the Society [2] investigates

---

[1] It is curious that the historically less dignified name of " solicitor " should have prevailed over the more dignified style of " attorney." The explanation may perhaps be that for the ordinary practitioner in a country town it was sufficient to be an attorney attached to the courts of common law, whereas the leaders of the profession in London were invariably also solicitors of the Court of Chancery. The humbler practitioner may have wished to be known by the style peculiar to the more eminent.

[2] The gradual steps by which the solicitors' branch of the legal profession emancipated itself from the immediate control of the judges is well illustrated in the body popularly known as the " Discipline Committee of the Law Society," for though in fact that body is invariably composed of members of the Council of the Society and is housed at their hall, it is technically not a committee of the Society at all, but consists of a

charges of professional misconduct brought against solicitors and has the power, subject to an appeal to the High Court, to strike a solicitor off the Roll or suspend him from practice. The solicitor is an officer of the Supreme Court. He has, however, no right of audience there in open court or at the assizes, or even at quarter sessions if there is a local bar. On the other hand, he has a right of audience in chambers in the High Court and in the county courts and petty sessions. As well as conducting litigation personally for his client, the solicitor, of course, employs and instructs counsel where necessary, and advises his clients in a great variety of non-litigious legal business. The scale of charges which he can exact for his services is laid down by statute, and the client who is dissatisfied with his bill can have it taxed by one of the taxing masters of the court.

We must now return to take up the story of the barristers in the Inns of Court after the exclusion of the attorneys, and first we may notice that from quite early times the members of the Bar have tended to specialise. Thus the circuit system naturally gave rise to " circuit bars " composed of those barristers who habitually went a particular circuit. Circuit bars were quite unofficial bodies—strictly speaking no more than dining clubs— but since their rules prohibited any member from holding a brief on circuit with or against a member of the Bar who was not a member, unless the outsider had received a special fee, members of the circuit bar did in fact enjoy a monopoly of ordinary work on circuit. So again the growth of the Court of Chancery gave rise to a " Chancery Bar." There has never been a Chancery Bar " mess " corresponding to the circuit messes, and members of the Chancery Bar have always had to rely solely on their superior knowledge of the system of equity to maintain such monopoly as they enjoy in the Chancery Courts.

number of leading members of the profession nominated for the purpose by the Lord Chancellor.

¹ This " restrictive trade practice " has now been abolished.

The fact that while the Common Law Courts sat at Westminster, the Master of the Rolls sat in his official residence in Chancery Lane and the Chancellor often sat in Lincoln's Inn Hall, led to Lincoln's Inn being the Inn of Court to which barristers practising in Chancery have always tended to belong.   After 1857 there came to be a group of barristers specialising in work in the Probate, Divorce, and Admiralty Courts.   They were, of course, the descendants of the Doctors of Civil Law who practised in the Ecclesiastical and Admiralty Courts at Doctors' Commons, and were not necessarily barristers or members of an Inn of Court at all.

Then the growing complexity of the system of pleading in actions at law gave rise to a class of practitioners known as " special pleaders " who specialised in the drawing of declarations and pleas.   Some great pleaders, such as the famous Saunders, also practised in court, but others of them, though members of an inn of court did not trouble to be called to the Bar, and were known as special pleaders " below the Bar."   The simplification of pleading in the nineteenth century abolished the necessity for this separate body of practitioners devoted to the science, but the conveyancers, another class of specialists who grew up side by side with the special pleaders, are still with us.   The possibility of making elaborate dispositions of the legal estate operating under the Statute of Uses and the re-emergence of the system of trusts after the Restoration added very greatly to the complexities of conveyancing and called for expert handling. Sir Orlando Bridgman (Chancellor from 1667 to 1670) is generally reckoned the father of modern conveyancing, and he was followed in the eighteenth and nineteenth centuries by a long line of eminent lawyers who gradually elaborated and published an infinite variety of precedents capable of being adapted to all ordinary dispositions of land and stocks.   The conveyancers, unlike the special pleaders, were always members of the Bar, but until recently many of them were not prepared to conduct cases in court and confined themselves to their practice in chambers. This, however, is no longer the case to-day.[1] Since Roman Catholics were disabled from practice, conveyancing offered them an opening for their talents, and two of the most famous conveyancers of the eighteenth century, Fearne and Butler, were Papists. Under the Supreme Court of Judicature (Consolidation) Act, 1925, s. 217, as amended by s. 14 of the Administration of Justice Act, 1956, between three and six eminent conveyancers are appointed " Conveyancing Counsel to the Court" to whom the judges can refer the drafting of documents which require to be settled by the court in the exercise of its administrative jurisdiction.

In the course of the seventeenth and eighteenth centuries the Inns of Court changed very much in character. In the Middle Ages they had been colleges in which the barristers and students lived a communal life, but in this period their members gradually ceased to live within their boundaries. At the same time the educational system formerly provided fell into decay. The office of Reader, which had originally been an object of ambition and a stepping-stone to the Bench, became at first an irksome burden and finally, as lectures ceased to be delivered, a sinecure. Moots were no longer held, and the student was left to educate himself for his profession as best he could. The universities at this time provided no facilities for learning English as opposed to Roman Law, and consequently the education of the law student of the eighteenth century was largely empirical, consisting of the experience which he gained as a pupil in the chambers of a busy barrister. This state of affairs was only very gradually remedied. Lectures on English law were given in Oxford as early as 1755 by Sir William Blackstone, the first Vinerian Professor, who subsequently

---

[1] It seems to have been about 1800 that some of the conveyancers began practising at the Chancery Bar. The famous Edward Sugden, afterwards Lord St. Leonards, was one of the first to do so. See Atlay : *The Victorian Chancellors*, vol. 2, p. 4.

incorporated the substance of them in his famous *Commentaries on the Law of England*, but it was not until the latter part of the nineteenth century that the universities began to give degrees after an examination in English Law. Meanwhile legal education came to be once more provided by the Inns of Court, and in 1852 the Council of Legal Education was established, consisting of representatives of the four Inns of Court under whose control the Bar Examinations are now held. The Benchers of the Inns of Court have retained throughout their history the exclusive right of " calling " students to the Bar, and of " disbarring " those of their members whom they find guilty of professional misconduct. In 1894, however, the General Council of the Bar was formed (consisting of representatives elected by the profession as a whole) as a single body entrusted with the safeguarding of the interest of the profession and the maintenance of the rules of professional etiquette.[1]

Next we must pass from the barristers in the Inns of Court to the serjeants and judges in Serjeants' Inn. The seventeenth and eighteenth centuries saw a gradual decline in the importance of the order of serjeants-at-law and the rise of a new class of king's counsel headed by the Law Officers of the Crown. In the Middle Ages the king was often engaged in litigation, and he required his attorneys and solicitors like other litigants. In place of many royal attorneys and royal solicitors, we find by the end of the fifteenth century a single Attorney-General and a single Solicitor-General. As yet, however, these offices, though lucrative, do not compare in dignity with that of a serjeant. The Attorney- and Solicitor-General were not barristers but attorneys and solicitors, and to plead his case in court the king would employ one of the senior serjeants, designated

[1] Recently a body known as the Senate—consisting of representatives of the four Inns and the Bar Council—has been set up in order to promote uniformity of policy between the Inns themselves and between the Inns and the practising bar.

the King's Serjeant. But with the " Tudor despotism " in the sixteenth century a change came. The
home of the serjeants was the Court of Common Pleas,
their special province was the land law, and their political
prejudices were in favour of the common law and
opposed to the royal prerogative and the conciliar courts.
The Tudor sovereigns wanted legal advisers of a different
stamp from this—they wanted men who were in sympathy
with the royal policy and could further it in Parliament,
in the Council, and in the Star Chamber—and to meet
their need they began to appoint as their Attorneys- and
Solicitors-General eminent barristers outside the order
of serjeants.

Gradually it became clear that the avenue to the highest
judicial posts lay through the offices of Attorney- or
Solicitor-General. These " law-officers of the Crown "
advised the Council on legal questions, conducted State
prosecutions and explained and defended the royal
interests in Parliament. The Attorney-General in the
sixteenth and the first half of the seventeenth century was
in regular attendance in the House of Lords, not, of
course, as a Peer with a vote but as an assistant at the
deliberations of the House, while the Solicitor-General
had a seat in the Commons. After the Restoration the
Attorney-General came also to sit in the Commons, as he
does to-day. As a reward for their services the law
officers of the Crown came to be regularly promoted to
one or other of the chief justiceships or the Chancellorship, so that the ordinary serjeant could hardly hope for
anything better than a puisne judgeship. It is true
that by custom no man could be a common law judge
who had not previously been a serjeant, but this technical
difficulty was overcome by making the new judge, who
had never joined the order of the coif, a serjeant immediately before his elevation to the Bench. It must not,
of course, be supposed that the order of serjeants fell
into complete decay. It retained its monopoly in the
Common Pleas, and some of the most learned common

lawyers of the seventeenth and eighteenth centuries were serjeants. But it no longer played the part in the legal system which it had played in the Middle Ages. Eventually the order was dissolved on the passing of the Judicature Acts, the site of Serjeants' Inn sold and the proceeds divided among the surviving members.

Towards the end of the sixteenth century it was found that the two law officers sometimes needed assistance in the conduct of legal business in which the government was interested, and the practice grew up of appointing distinguished barristers of suitable political sympathies to the new rank of " King's Counsel," with the obligation of placing their services at the disposal of the government if required to do so. These king's counsel did not form a class apart from other barristers, as the serjeants did. They remained members of their Inn of Court and had no precedence there on account of their title, but in court they took precedence over ordinary barristers. Gradually, in the course of the eighteenth century the king's counsel ceased to be habitually consulted on government business, and the title was given to leading barristers merely as a mark of distinction giving them precedence over what came to be called the " junior " bar. The modern Q.C. wears a silk gown, not a stuff one, sits within the Bar of the court, and never appears without a junior to assist him. In practice the junior counsel does the preliminary work in an action, advising whether the action should be brought, drawing the pleadings, advising on evidence, etc., while the actual case in court is largely conducted by the Q.C. Barristers are appointed queen's counsel by Letters Patent under the Great Seal issued on the advice of the Chancellor, and juniors who think that their position at the Bar warrants their pretension, apply to the Chancellor to be allowed "to take silk." It is, however, only in a minority of cases that the application is granted.

It only remains for us to say something of the later history of Her Majesty's judges. We have already seen

that since the fourteenth century the king has always
appointed them from among leading barristers and that
until 1875 it was necessary for the new judge to have
been a serjeant-at-law, though the law officers and other
king's counsel were often made serjeants for a day or
two expressly to qualify them for the office. A judge of
one of the royal courts was, of course, a servant of His
Majesty and under his patent of appointment he held
office " during the King's pleasure "—" durante beneplacito nostro."   In the reigns of James I and Charles I,
when constitutional cases of great importance involving
the extent of the royal prerogative came frequently before
the courts, the fact that the Crown could dismiss the
judges at pleasure may have played some part in securing
judgments favourable to the claims of the Crown.   Such at
all events was the opinion of the Parliamentary opposition, and after the defeat of the king the form of the
judges' patents was changed so as to make their tenure
of office depend only on their good conduct, " quamdiu
se bene gesserint."   This form continued in use for some
years after the Restoration, but in 1668 Charles II once
more began to appoint his judges " durante beneplacito,"
and he and his brother James II made a free use of the
power of summary dismissal for the purpose of packing
the Bench with supporters of the extreme " prerogative "
claims, without regard to their ability or character.   This
practice was carried to such a height that at the trial of
the Seven Bishops in 1688 the Court of King's Bench
was composed of four judges none of whom was a lawyer
of eminence and one of whom was a man of infamous
character, while among the great lawyers who appeared
as counsel for the bishops were men who had formerly
been judges and had been dismissed from office.   As
Lord Halifax said, " Westminster Hall was standing on
its head."

   The Revolution of 1688 effected a great improvement
in the quality of the common law judges and by the Act
of Settlement (1701) it was laid down that the tenure of

their office should be " quamdiu se bene gesserint," but that they should be removable by the king if an address was presented to him with this object by both Houses of Parliament.   This is the tenure by which all the judges of the High Court and Court of Appeal hold their office to-day, though county court judges—as we have seen— are removable by the Chancellor for incompetence or mis-behaviour, and any justice of the peace can be removed from the commission at the royal pleasure.   County court judges retire at seventy-two ; judges of the High Court and Court of Appeal and the Lords of Appeal at seventy-five.   In appointing High Court judges the Crown acts on the advice of the Chancellor, who in the case of the judges of the Queen's Bench Division generally consults the Lord Chief Justice, but the Lord Chief Justice, the Master of the Rolls, the President of the Probate Division, the Lords of Appeal and the Lord Justices of the Court of Appeal are appointed on the advice of the Prime Minister, as of course is the Chancellor himself.

In the Middle Ages the royal judges were paid very small salaries and made up their income out of the fees paid by litigants in their courts.   As we have seen, a desire to add to their income in this way played a con-siderable part in the fierce competition between the three courts for business.   Gradually the fixed salary became a more important item in the judicial income, and finally, in the nineteenth century, the taking of a share of the fees was abolished altogether and the judges' salaries were fixed at figures which were calculated to equal the total emoluments which they then received.   In fixing the salaries of the Chancellor and the Chief Justices regard was also had to the value of the official patronage which was being taken from them at the same time.   The salaries of the puisne judges were fixed at £5,000 a year, which was then a large income.   They remained at that figure until 1954 when they were increased to £8,000. Now they are £14,000.   The salaries of the judges of the Supreme Court are charged on the Consolidated Fund.

This was no doubt intended to be a protection against arbitrary reduction by the Crown, but it was also an obstacle to increase to keep pace with the declining value of the pound. In 1939 the Heads of Government Departments were paid £3,000 against the £5,000 paid to judges. But as the salaries of civil servants can be easily increased by Treasury Warrant without recourse to Parliament the Heads of Departments got ahead of the judges in the inflationary rat race and the latter are having difficulty in catching up with them.

XXII

THE LEGAL SYSTEM AND THE STATE

THE legal system of a country is only one of the organs of its government and cannot usefully be studied in complete isolation from the rest of them. In tracing the history of the English legal system in the earlier chapters of this book we have tried to bear this fact in mind and to bring what we had to say of the growth of the law courts, and of the law administered by them, into relation with the general development of the English State. In this chapter we will discuss quite shortly the relations which subsist to-day between our legal system and the two other chief branches of the constitution—that is to say Parliament on the one hand and what is generally called the Executive[1] on the other.

In some countries the structure of the main organs of government including the principal law courts is defined in a document known as "The Constitution," which is not capable of alteration by ordinary legislative processes. Thus, in the United States the existence and some of the functions of the Supreme Court are provided for in the Constitution of 1787, and these provisions can only be altered by a special process which in effect involves the concurrence of a very substantial majority of the electors. If Congress and the Senate passed an ordinary bill purporting to abolish the Supreme Court it would be a nullity and would be declared to be so by the Supreme Court itself. In England, by contrast, the

[1] The term Executive is not very apt to cover the manifold activities of Whitehall, which are by no means confined to executing decisions taken elsewhere. The Administration would be a better term were it not that in England it is often used as an equivalent of the Ministry.

sovereignty of Parliament has been for at least the last
two centuries and a half unlimited, and even our highest
courts of law are subject to it.   Parliament could abolish
our Supreme Court of Judicature just as easily as it
could raise the salary of the metropolitan police magistrates.

Of course, the law courts have not always been subject
to Parliament.   Before the thirteenth century neither
Parliament nor law courts existed as independent bodies.
Both were phases of one and the same body—the Curia
Regis of our Norman kings—and as they grew into an
independent existence in the later Middle Ages it would
not be true to say that the law courts felt themselves to
be subject to the sovereignty of Parliament.[1]   Even as
late as the seventeenth century, with the activities of the
Reformation Parliament to look back upon, Sir Edward
Coke seems to have regarded the common law and the
common law courts as a sort of " tertium quid," independent alike of Crown and Parliament, and well fitted
to hold the balance between them.   But the supremacy
of Parliament over the royal prerogative was finally
established in 1688, and by a side wind, as it were, the
supremacy of Parliament over the courts and the judges
was achieved at the same time.   Perhaps eighteenth-
century Parliaments were hardly conscious of this
supremacy.   Certainly they seldom tried to exercise it,
and accorded the courts almost complete autonomy.
In the nineteenth century, however, there came a change,
in form, at least, if not in substance.   The reforms in the
organisation and procedure of the courts of which we
have spoken in Chapters 17 and 18 were carried out
either by the express terms of statutes or by legislative
powers delegated by statute to judges and other lawyers.
Thus the Supreme Court and the county courts and the

[1] It is, of course, true that the law courts recognised Parliament as
a higher court which could reverse their judgments by writ of error, see
p. 217, above, but Parliament was not thought of as an omnicompetent
legislative body.

procedure to be followed in them are all alike the creatures of statute.

But all this, one may say, is of little practical importance. In fact, our judges do not feel themselves galled by this parliamentary supremacy. Parliament only passes statutes affecting the organisation of the courts on the advice or suggestion of the legal profession, and the Rule Committee feels itself as free when acting, as it does to-day, under the provisions of section 99 of the Judicature Act as Chief Justice North and his puisnes can have felt in adding an " ac etiam " clause to the " capias " of the Common Pleas, without any statutory authority at all, but simply in virtue of their prerogative to control the procedure of their court. The reduction of the judges' salaries in 1931 by a measure which classed them with ordinary civil servants may perhaps show that Her Majesty's Courts of Justice and Her Majesty's judges have not quite the lustre that they once possessed, and that the active exercise of its supremacy over the legal system for the last century has taught Parliament to use a different language towards them than it would have used to Lord Eldon and Lord Ellenborough. But broadly speaking one may say that the mere fact that Parliament can do as it will with the legal system is not a fact of any great constitutional significance. It is otherwise with the relations between the legal system and the other main organ of our constitution—the Executive. The relations which subsist between them in England are exceedingly unlike those which obtain in other European countries, and from the difference flows consequences of considerable constitutional importance. To bring these consequences to light it is necessary to give quite shortly an account of the organisation of the legal system of some other European country, and we will choose that of France since it was in fact on the French model that the legal systems of most European countries were reorganised in the nineteenth century.

In France the provision of justice is a government service like the provision of education or main roads.[1] For its provision there are some 4,000 civil servants employed throughout the length and breadth of the country, and at the head of the service in Paris is the Minister of Justice (the Garde des Sceaux), who is a politician changing with the rest of the Ministry. The permanent civil servants who administer the service are known generically as " magistrats " and are employed for the most part in one of three ways. First, some 2,500 of them are judges sitting in one or other of the tribunals of first instance or appeal in various parts of France or in the supreme tribunal (the Court of Cassation) in Paris. To an Englishman used to some 100 county court judges and some 90 judges of the Supreme Court and House of Lords 2,500 may seem a very large figure. It must be remembered, however, that France has no single tribunal of first instance whose judges spend part of their time on circuit. Each French department has several courts of first instance, and for every three or four departments there is a court of appeal. Further, the lay J.P. who in England relieves the English judges of a great deal of criminal work, has no real counterpart in France, and French judges do not sit alone but in groups of at least three. These considerations largely suffice to explain the size of the French judiciary as compared with ours.

But besides judges there are a great many other " magistrats " engaged in the provision of justice. Each tribunal of first instance or appeal has attached to it several " magistrats," forming what is called the " Parquet," whose duty it is to represent the State both in the prosecution of crimes and in any civil proceedings in which its interest may seem to be affected. Indeed, no case is heard without the presence of a member of the

[1] For this sketch of the French legal system, see Barthélemy : *Le Gouvernement de la France*, Chapter X, and Ensor : *Courts and Judges* (Oxford), 1933.

" Parquet," though often, of course, he takes no active part in the proceedings.   Further, the Ministry of Justice in Paris, which exercises a general control over the whole system, has itself a small staff of " magistrats " immediately under the Minister.   It must not be supposed that these three categories—judges, parquet and staff of the Ministry of Justice—are in any way separate services.   They form one service—the " magistrature "— and members of the service may change about from one to another of the branches at different periods in their career, as they gradually rise from the lowest rung of the ladder towards the top.   Thus, entering the service at five-and-twenty a man might start his career in the " parquet " of some small tribunal, pass on to be a judge in a higher court, on again to be head of the " parquet " at some court of appeal, and so on until, if he was very able or lucky, he reached the Court of Cassation.   Contrasting this system for a moment with our own, it will be observed first that whereas in England a man who is appointed a judge, whether of a county court or of the High Court, has little chance of further promotion, promotion is the life blood of the French magistracy ; next that all appointments and promotions come from the same hand, that of the Minister of Justice, who has no counterpart in this country ; and finally, that in France the professions of barrister (*avocat*) and solicitor (*avoué*) have little connection with the magistracy.   A young man of five-and-twenty with a legal training will choose whether he will enter the " magistrature " or whether he will go into private practice.   If he does the latter he is not likely to obtain any ordinary judicial post, though, of course, if he goes into politics—and successful barristers go into politics more often in France than in England— he may perhaps become Minister of Justice and for a few brief months control the whole legal machine and exercise the enormous patronage attached to the office.

The picture which we have painted, though sufficiently unlike the English system, does not, however, give the full measure of the difference between it and the French, for in France there is not only one system of courts but two. So far we have only spoken of the ordinary courts in which civil business between private individuals and the prosecution of crimes are conducted. These courts, however, cannot, generally speaking, deal with any of the varied questions which may arise between a private individual and the State or its officials—cases, for instance, where a private individual says that he has suffered damage by the improper action of officials or seeks to restrain some governmental authority from taking some step which is in his view beyond its power. Side by side with the ordinary court of justice there is therefore a system of administrative courts which deal with these questions. There are local administrative courts (" conseils de préfecture ") and a central administrative court (the " Conseil d'État "), which sits in the Palais Royal in Paris, hears appeals from the local administrative courts and itself hears the heavier administrative cases at first instance. The Conseil d'État is a body of the highest importance in the French constitution. It is composed in part of magistrats, who might have entered the ordinary magistrature but who succeeded as young men in the very stiff competitive entrance examination and in part of eminent officials appointed to it from outside on the recommendation of the Minister of Justice. Its work is by no means confined to the hearing of administrative cases. Indeed the greater part of it consists in advising the various Ministries on the form and content of the schemes and regulations, the framing of which is such an important part of governmental activity to-day.[1]

When we compare the relations between our legal system and the rest of the government machine with those which obtain in France there are three differences which especially strike the eye.

[1] For an account of the " Conseil d'État " see C. J. Hamson's Hamlyn Lecture, 1954, *Executive Discretion and Judicial Control*.

The first is that our judiciary stands quite apart from the ordinary civil service and is intimately linked with the private profession of barristers-at-law. A young man with a legal training in England has no choice between private practice and the judiciary. It is through private practice, if he is successful enough, that he may in middle or old age attain to the judiciary, and when he goes on to the Bench he will not feel himself to have become a civil servant and to have passed into a different world from that in which he lived at the Bar. Justice in England is not really a service administered by State servants in the manner of an ordinary government department, but is rather a service based on a private profession, the leading members of which are clothed by the State with authority to preside in its tribunals.

The second great difference, and it is perhaps a consequence of the first, is that the legal system in England is not an organised service as it is in France. We have, for instance, no single figure at the head of our system comparable to a Minister of Justice. With us such control as there is, is dispersed among a number of persons. Some of the highest judicial posts are filled on the recommendation of the Prime Minister. The exercise of the prerogative of mercy and the control of the prisons rests with the Home Secretary. Then the Lord Chief Justice of England has considerable patronages in the Queen's Bench Division and an important voice in the organisation of its work. Undoubtedly our nearest approach to a Minister of Justice is the Lord Chancellor, who recommends the appointment of High Court judges, controls the county court system, and since the Judicature Acts has been gaining an increasing control over the organisation of the Supreme Court; but there are still some departments over which the Chancellor has no control. Again, we have no " parquet " in England. The Attorney- and Solicitor-General conduct important prosecutions and appear as leading counsel for the government in important civil proceedings, but they have no staff of lawyers under them who devote themselves exclusively to government work. In most criminal matters the police instruct barristers in private practice to appear for them, and the same is true of civil proceedings by government departments and local authorities.[1]

The third great difference between the two systems is, of course, that here we have no system of administrative courts [2] nor any body comparable to the Conseil d'État. If a private individual wishes to recover damages from his local council or to restrain the Minister of Health from confirming a clearance order, he will issue an ordinary writ, or apply for the grant of a prerogative order, (as the case may be) in the same courts as those in which he would sue his neighbour for breach of contract. Further, none of our courts act in an advisory capacity for the Government. They will decide concrete cases in which the Government is involved as and when they arise, but they have neither the right nor the duty to advise as to the form or content of governmental orders or regulations.

Now that we have pointed out some of the more important differences in the organisation of justice in England and France, we will in conclusion suggest very tentatively what perhaps may be the chief merits and demerits of the two systems. It is, of course, only when two countries are akin in civilisation and methods of government that any comparison of a single branch of their institutions can be of much value. Thus to compare the legal systems of England and China would probably be a rather useless task, since the objects to which the two systems are directed are so very different. But when

---

[1] The Director of Public Prosecutions undertakes a certain number of important criminal cases, and gives advice on the prosecution of many more, but he often instructs counsel in private practice to appear for the Crown.

[2] There are, however, nowadays many "administrative tribunals," which have jurisdiction over certain classes of dispute between the individual and the state; see pp. 409–410, below.

one finds that a country as akin to us as France has a legal system which is in many ways very unlike our own, it is by no means useless to compare the two, for it is probable that each will have something to teach the other.

Under a system such as ours the judiciary is likely to have more influence and to be more independent than under a system such as obtains in France. Our judges are comparatively few in number. Before they are appointed they have spent a substantial part of their working life in a highly competitive profession in which they have achieved some measure of success. On appointment they come at once into receipt of an adequate salary. Finally they have, generally speaking, little chance of promotion—nor will promotion, if they get it, necessarily benefit them financially or in any other way.[1] It follows that an English judge is likely to be a man with an adequate, some would no doubt say an exaggerated, sense of his own importance and that he is not likely to be in the least impressed by the fact that one of the parties or counsel in a case before him is possessed of influence of one sort or another or that a given decision would be acceptable to the powers that be. The position of a judge in France is very different. When he comes on to the bench he is a young man with no experience of the world and no claim to its respect. His salary is very small and his only hope of increasing it is by gaining promotion. A man so situated must have exceptional integrity and strength of character if he is not to care a rap for the good opinion of the local deputy or the local business magnate or for the contents of his personal file at the Ministry of Justice. No doubt there are such men in plenty in the magistracy of France, but it cannot be said that the system is as well adapted to produce them as that which obtains here!

---

[1] County Court judges are seldom promoted to the High Court. About one in every four High Court judges goes to the Court of Appeal, but there he has to work harder for the same salary.

That a judge should be no respecter of persons and himself enjoy some measure of respect must be desirable under any form of government. Whether he ought to be detached from politics and independent of the executive depends on the form of government in question. In a state in which there are no political parties, where it is expected that all good citizens will think alike on important issues and government control extends deep into the lives of the people, all those in authority, be they schoolmasters, judges, bureaucrats or ministers, may be said to be engaged in the same task. They are all trying in their several spheres to give practical effect to the dominant political philosophy—be it communism or fascism or what you will. To talk of judges in such a state being detached from politics or independent of the executive would make no sense at all. In a parliamentary democracy, on the other hand, the position is obviously quite different. In England those who are for the time being in control of the executive are simply the temporary representatives of a part, possibly a minority, of the electorate; there is no political creed which claims the allegiance of all good citizens; and the law is conceived not so much as an expression of the will of the government as as a safeguard of the liberty of the subject. In such a state it makes very good sense to say that judges should be detached from politics and independent of the executive.

But the problem of the proper relations between the executive and the judiciary in this country is far more difficult to-day than it was a hundred years ago. In those days the chief functions of government were defence and the maintenance of order. The area of possible collision between the organs of the state and the individual was therefore comparatively small and when collisions occurred the ordinary courts could deal with them. To-day, on the other hand, the " Welfare State " provides many elaborate services—health, housing, education, national assistance, and so on—for those who need them. To secure the provision of these services it has been necessary to confer on Ministers, that is to say in practice on the civil servants in the Ministry in question, very wide powers the exercise of which may affect large numbers of people in a great variety of ways. How is a balance between fair play for the individual and efficiency of administration to be achieved ? What is to happen if the person affected thinks that the Minister had no power to make the order which he made? Or that though he had the necessary power he exercised it improperly in the sense that he was influenced by matters which he ought not to have taken into account? Or again that though he had the necessary powers and was not actuated by improper considerations he reached a decision which an impartial body would consider to be plainly wrong ?

In France none of these matters can be considered by the ordinary Courts ; but, as we have seen, provision is made for their consideration within the executive itself. The Conseil d'État is a body of civil servants most of whom have had a legal training and many of whom have had considerable practical experience of administration. It has nothing to do with the initiation of policy or with its detailed execution. Its function is two-fold. First to give advice and help to the Government with regard to the way in which any given policy can best be implemented and secondly to ensure that the powers conferred on Ministers and their subordinates are properly exercised in accordance with principles of due administration which the Conseil has itself developed over the years. In exercising this latter function the Conseil d'État sits in judgment on the executive in the sorts of case to which we have referred above. An English lawyer is naturally tempted to think, as Dicey thought, that a body so constituted and functioning as it were at the very heart of the administration must inevitably be prejudiced in favour of the executive and against the complaining citizen. There seems, however, to be no doubt that this is not the case and that the Conseil d'État has succeeded in a remarkable way in having the best of both worlds. It has the inestimable advantage of expert knowledge of administration and at the same time it has sufficient self-confidence and prestige to express freely and to make the Ministries respect its views as to how administrative decisions should be made.

With us the position in this field is somewhat unsatisfactory. Our courts are not, of course, precluded, as are the ordinary courts in France, from deciding disputes between the citizen and the executive or its officers. Freedom of the person, for instance, over which the battle between the individual and the executive raged in the past, is adequately safeguarded in the Courts by " Habeas Corpus " and actions for damages for wrongful arrest or false imprisonment. But the new powers conferred on the executive by statute to enable it to administer the services provided by the " Welfare State " largely escaped judicial control. It is easy to be wise after the event and looking back one may say that the Courts had themselves to blame. If when the activities of the state began to increase at the end of the last and the beginning of this century the judges had extended the scope of the prerogative writs and adopted a less literal approach to the construction of statutes and statutory instruments they might well have been able to establish an effective control over administrative decisions and to build up a body of administrative law. In fact, however, they did not realise what was happening until it was too late. When they awoke to it they were at first full of indignation, which found expression in Lord Hewart's book, *The New Despotism*, but with the passage of time they have become resigned to their own impotence. Indeed sometimes, especially in the war years, they have shown an almost servile deference to the claims of the executive. " Certiorari " continues to apply only to decisions which can be said to be in some sense " judicial " not simply administrative and even in that narrow field its scope is very limited. Meanwhile our law of public administration, if it can be so called, has developed without regard to any principles. Sometimes the relevant statute provides for decisions on objections being made by an administrative tribunal, which the Minister tends to regard as an appendage of his department. Sometimes it provides for such decisions being made by the Minister in accordance with some defined procedure. Often, however, no procedure whatever is provided for objecting or deciding on objections. The Tribunals of Inquiry Act, 1958, passed as a result of the report of the " Franks " Committee,[1] did something to improve matters as regards the first two categories. But it remained true to say that over a very wide field the executive was a law unto itself. Until recently the only check on maladministration was the fear that some aggrieved individual might be able to complain loudly enough to force the government to appoint an " ad hoc " commission of inquiry with power to examine the departmental files and bring to light such errors in administration—to use a charitable term—as were revealed in the " Crichel Down " case.

In 1967, however, the Parliamentary Commissioner Act created an official called the Parliamentary Commissioner for Administration. On receipt through a Member of Parliament of a complaint by a member of the public that he has suffered injustice through maladministration the Commissioner is empowered to investigate any action taken by on behalf of a number of departments of state and other authorities in the exercise of their administrative functions, and for that purpose to require the department or authority in question to produce to him any necessary information. It is not his function to criticise the merits of any decision taken ; but only the way in which the department or authority has gone about its duties. Unfortunately, many authorities —including, in particular, local authorities—are still outside his jurisdiction.[2]

[1] Report of the Committee on Administrative Tribunals and Inquiries, 1957, Cmnd. 218.
[2] Out of 790 cases which he considered in 1969 he held that some

The upshot of the matter then is that so far as concerns the points upon which we instituted a comparison there are merits and defects in each system.   Our system under which the judges are not ordinary Civil Servants but are appointed in middle life from a class of professional men tends to give us a more influential and independent judiciary which in its turn is likely " pro tanto " to improve the administration of justice in the ordinary courts.   On the other hand the French appear to have solved far better than we have the very important problem of bringing the executive in a modern state under effective judicial control.

500 were outside his jurisdiction—on the ground either that the department or authority concerned was not mentioned in the Act or that administrative functions were not involved or that there was a right of appeal to a Tribunal.   Of some 300 cases which he investigated he found that in 48 (*i.e.* some 16 per cent.) there had been elements of maladministration which had led to some measure of injustice.

XXIII

LOOKING AHEAD

1. THE STRUCTURE OF THE COURTS AND CIVIL PROCEDURE

THE structure of the courts as it will be when the Courts Act, 1971 which gives effect to the proposals of the Beeching Commission is in operation is shown on the diagram on page 430. There is one obvious inelegance in it which could be cured by a change of name. If the Queen's Bench Divisional Court is to continue to hear appeals by way of " case stated " by magistrates' courts and by the Crown Court (as successor of quarter sessions in appeals from magistrates' courts) the existing anomaly of appeals from the Divisional Court in criminal matters going straight to the House of Lords, although there is now a criminal division of the Court of Appeal, will be perpetuated and a fresh anomaly of cases stated by one branch of the Supreme Court being heard by a co-ordinate branch of that court will be created.

Both these anomalies would disappear if criminal appeals by way of cases stated went to the Criminal Division of the Court of Appeal and no real change would be involved since they would continue to be heard by the same people, namely the Lord Chief Justice and two judges of the Queen's Bench Division or occasionally the Lord Chief Justice, a Lord Justice and one Queen's Bench Judge.

While on the subject of Divisional Courts one may, perhaps, ask oneself whether there is any sufficient reason for their continuing to hear any appeals from inferior tribunals. At present a Divisional Court of the Chancery Division hears appeals from the County Courts in bankruptcy matters, the Queen's Bench Divisional Court hears appeals from a number of tribunals set up under various Statutes, and a Divisional Court of the Probate, Divorce and Admiralty Division (soon to become the Family Division) hears appeals from magistrates in domestic proceedings. In all these cases there is a possibility of a further appeal to the Civil Division of the Court of Appeal. The possibility of two appeals short of the House of Lords was taken away in the case of the ordinary jurisdiction of the County Court as long ago as 1934 and one wonders whether an appeal to a Divisional Court between the tribunal of first instance and the Court of Appeal is really necessary in the cases above mentioned.

But these are comparatively minor matters. The important question is whether as a counterpart to the single Crown Court which is to take the place of the criminal assizes and quarter sessions a single civil court should not be set up to take the place of the High Court and the County Court so that the difference between High Court judges and circuit or County Court judges would not be in civil any more than in criminal cases, that they were members of different courts but that the High Court judge would try the more difficult and important cases. Such a change would have a bearing on the vexed question of civil procedure and also on the need to retain separate divisions of the High Court.

The Beeching Commission considered the question of a merger of the civil courts; but though they were attracted by the idea they concluded that it would involve a partial or even total assimilation of High Court and County Court procedure, a matter which lay beyond their competence and terms of reference (see para. 205). The proposals which they do make (paras. 206–220) are however directed to ensuring that the question whether any civil case is tried by a High Court or a County Court judge will depend on its difficulty or importance and not whether it was started in the High Court or in the County Court. They propose, in particular, (a) that a High Court judge, whether sitting in London or on circuit, shall have power to release for trial by a circuit judge any case in his list which he considers suitable to be so tried and (b) that uncomplicated defended divorce cases may be tried by County Court judges and, conversely, that difficult ancillary questions, e.g. as to custody of children, arising in undefended divorce cases may be dealt with by High Court judges.

But the question what judge is to hear a case, important though it is, is not so important as the question of the procedure to be followed in trying it. There is good reason to think that many just complaints of people who are not poor enough to get legal aid are never brought to court at all because of the expense involved. Mr. Justice Megarry has suggested that all cases should be conducted under County Court procedure unless good cause is shown for applying High Court procedure to them.[1] Lord Devlin, as we have said, thinks that even County Court procedure is too elaborate for many cases.[2] What is certain is that if any real saving of time and expense is to be achieved, every civil case should come at an early stage before someone with authority to decide— subject to appeal—how it should be tried so as to cut expense and delay to a minimum consistent with justice to the parties.

Finally comes the question whether there is any longer any point in retaining separate divisions of the High Court. The general principle advocated by the Beeching Commission is that difficult and important cases, whether criminal or civil, should be dealt with by High Court judges and all others by circuit or County Court judges. In the civil, unlike the criminal, sphere there are some types of case which are not only more suitable to be tried by a High Court than by a circuit or County Court judge but can be more satisfactorily tried at first instance by a judge who has specialised in the field in question when at the Bar than by one who is not a special-

[1] *Lawyer and Litigant in England* (Hamlyn Lecture, 1962), p. 194.
[2] See p. 328, above.

ist. Commercial cases, patent cases and pure Chancery cases are obvious examples. But the great mass of High Court cases do not need to be tried by specialist judges. Few High Court judges have practised to any appreciable extent in the Criminal Courts and some who have made the best criminal judges were never in a criminal court before they presided in one as judges. Again, many High Court judges have had little experience of personal injury cases before going on the Bench. Yet again although there are some "family" matters which are more suitable to be dealt with by a High Court than by a County Court judge, for example " kidnapping " cases where the court has to decide whether to send the child back to the foreign country, it cannot be said that a specialist High Court judge is needed to decide such cases.

All this leads one to think that the High Court should be a single and much smaller body than it is to-day, some of whose members are specialists in certain fields and can deal with High Court cases which need to be tried by a specialist judge at first instance, but all of whom (including the specialists) take a part in trying the ordinary run of High Court cases, civil and criminal, both in London and on circuit. In point of fact, as we have said, it looks as though the distinction between Queen's Bench judges and Family Division judges will soon disappear; so the problem really relates only to the Chancery Division. If a barrister who is a " commercial " expert and has never appeared in a criminal case can be trained in criminal work by sitting with the Lord Chief Justice and another experienced Queen's Bench judge in the Criminal Division of the Court of Appeal and can take his share in ordinary criminal and civil work on circuit while concentrating on specialist commercial work in London, there is no reason in the world why a Chancery barrister should not be appointed to the Bench on the same terms. Of course, the existing Chancery judges who were not appointed on those terms and who in the opinion of some of their brother judges are the spoiled children of the judicial family would have to be spared the drudgery of circuit; but there is no reason whatever for the anomaly to be perpetuated and it will be in the long run disastrous for the Chancery Bar if it is perpetuated.[1]

2. Criminal Procedure

This subject falls into three parts (*A*) the period before a suspect is brought before the court which is to try him, (*B*) the trial of those who plead not guilty and (*C*) the sentencing of those who plead or are found guilty.

(*A*) *The period before trial*

The points which excite most interest at present are (i) whether the so-called privilege against self-incrimination should be restricted to any extent and (ii) whether the prosecution should be precluded from using statements made or alleged to have been made by suspects to police officers unless such statements have been made before magistrates or "tape recorded". No one suggests that the privilege against self-incrimination should be abolished altogether. No one, that is to say, suggests that any direct pressure (for example, by detention in prison) should be put on suspects in order to induce them to make statements admitting that they have committed an offence or implicating others in it. The question which is debated is how far, if at all, a suspect who refuses to make a statement should be protected against inferences unfavourable to him being drawn from his refusal to do so. The present state of the law on this point is, on any view, quite illogical. When he is about to be charged the suspect is "cautioned", told, that is to say, that he need say nothing but that anything which he does say may be given in evidence at his trial. He is not warned that if he chooses to say nothing adverse inferences may be drawn from his failure to make a statement and so, quite logi-

[1] It is a hopeful sign of the times that a Chancery "silk" has recently been appointed a judge of the Family Division.

cally, neither prosecuting counsel nor the judge is entitled to comment to the jury on the fact that he said nothing when charged. Again consistently with this principle, if the accused chooses to give no evidence at his trial, counsel for the Crown is not entitled to comment on the fact. On the other hand, quite inconsistently, the judge is entitled to comment on it and generally takes advantage of his right to do so. Yet if the privilege against self-incrimination were to be pressed to its logical conclusion, it should be the duty of the judge not simply to refrain from adverse comment on the failure of the accused to give evidence, but to exhort the jury not to be influenced by the thought that an innocent man would not keep silence but would be anxious to proclaim his innocence as soon and as often as possible. " It is ", he should say, " one of the most cherished rights of an Englishman not to be under any obligation to answer questions which the police or the Crown lawyers would like him to answer. Who knows but that the man in the dock could readily dispel any suspicions which the prosecution evidence may have raised in your minds but prefers to rely on his right not to give his own account of what happened and to force the prosecution to prove the charge which they have chosen, perhaps quite mistakenly, to bring against him without any help or hindrance from him."

Bentham, in a well-known passage, pointed out what a God-send to criminals the privilege against self-incrimination is and when one realises the fantastic results to which it would lead if consistently applied, it is at first sight surprising to find that it has any whole-hearted supporters outside the criminal classes. There is, after all, a vast difference between punishing a man for refusing to assist the police in their task of detecting crime and saying to him : " You need not make a statement, but it is only fair to warn you that if you are prosecuted your failure to make a statement when charged will certainly be commented on and may lead to unfavourable inferences being drawn against you." Undoubtedly what makes many people unwilling to see the privilege restricted in any way is their belief, possibly well-founded, that police enquiries are often not fairly conducted. But it is no remedy for this to maintain a set of rules which police officers rightly consider to be unreasonable and to which they will never pay more than lip service. After all, a police officer who was an honest supporter of the privilege against self-incrimination would say to every suspect whom he stops in the street: " I hope that as a good citizen you will answer some questions which I would like to put to you; but I am bound in honesty to point out to you that it may well be in your interest to refuse to tell me anything." The only remedy for unfair questioning by the police is to ensure that the version of what passed which is laid before judge and jury is undisputed and accurate. One way of achieving this result (which is adopted in some countries) is to provide that only statements made by the accused in the presence of a magistrate can be given in evidence at his trial. But with crime running even at its present rate the introduction of such a system would cast a very heavy, perhaps an intolerable, burden on the magistracy. It would seem preferable to provide that statements should, as far as possible, be tape-recorded when made. Of course, objections can be raised to this solution both from the point of view of the suspect and of the police. On the one side it is said that it would not be much more difficult for the police, if so minded, to insert fictitious confessions in the record than it is for them, if so minded, to insert fictitious confessions in their note-books. On the other side, it is said that suspects, though not in fact suffering any ill-treatment, would be able when inconvenient questions were being asked them to make, for the record, fictitious complaints of illusage. But it is surely not beyond the wit of man to produce a " knave proof " system of recording and it seems likely that this is the solution of the problem of police interrogation which will eventually be adopted.

(B) *The Trial*

Two points excite discussion here : (1) to what extent and in what circumstances the character of the accused should be disclosed to the court and (2) whether trial by jury should be retained. As to (1) the present position is, broadly speaking, that the prosecution cannot give evidence of previous convictions of the accused for similar offences unless he has given evidence of his own character or attacked the character of the witnesses for the prosecution. This is not, of course, because evidence of his previous convictions is irrelevant. If " A " says that he saw " B " take a note-case out of " C's " pocket and slip it to " D " who ran away and " B " denies that he did so, anyone called upon to decide whether " B " may be telling the truth would certainly consider it relevant to his decision to know that " B " was a Sunday-school teacher of unblemished reputation or that he had six previous convictions for picking pockets. The reason advanced for the exclusion of such evidence is that juries would attach undue weight to it and never acquit any accused person who had previously been convicted of a similar offence. If and so far as that is true, it is an argument against the retention of trial by jury. But one may fairly doubt whether it is true. No doubt the knowledge that his previous convictions would be disclosed would lead many defendants who have committed the offences with which they are charged but who now plead not guilty to plead guilty. Further, anyone who pleaded " not guilty ", whether in fact guilty or not, would be forced to give evidence, since the recital of his previous convictions coupled with a failure on his part to go into the witness-box would ensure his conviction. But the fact that a man who had previously been convicted of similar crimes gave evidence in proof of his innocence on the occasion in question would, one would think, dispose any body of men who were not utterly unreasonable to give him an attentive hearing. Moreover, the judge would be at pains to impress on them that they must not treat the

previous convictions as evidence that the accused had
committed the offence with which he was charged; that
if they had any reasonable doubt of his guilt they must
acquit him; and that the previous convictions were simply
relevant in considering the weight to be attributed to his
evidence. Again, if and so far as the disclosure of
previous convictions does inevitably tell against an accused
is that fact really any injustice to him? Why should he be
spared the disadvantage consequent on his previous misconduct?

Moreover, as things are, it is by no means true to say
that if the accused has previous convictions that fact remains unknown to those who are to determine whether he
is guilty. Defendants who have no previous convictions
invariably parade the fact. The first question which
their counsel puts to the police officer is: " Has this man
been in trouble before?" Consequently anyone who
knows the ropes infers at once from the fact that such a
question is not asked that the accused has " a record " and
he may well assume that it is worse than it is. The vast
majority of criminal cases are tried by magistrates who
know the ropes and who therefore are well aware that the
defendant who has not put his character in issue has a bad
character.[1] Again it is by no means safe to infer that all
jurors are completely innocent in this matter. If they
have served before or even listened to some cases in the
particular sessions they may well have come to realise how
easy it is to know whether the accused has previous convictions. To exclude evidence of them, unless he puts
his own character in issue or attacks the characters of the
Crown witnesses, is to exclude relevant material which in
the majority of cases certainly will, and in the rest may well,
be known in a general way to the tribunal but which the
tribunal may well infer, in the absence of evidence to the

---

[1] Milton points out (at p. 71) that if the defendant is unrepresented and
does not give evidence of good character magistrates are left guessing.
They cannot know for certain—as they can if he is represented—that he
has a bad character.

contrary, to be more unfavourable to the accused than it is in fact.

We turn now to (2), the question whether trial by jury should be retained. Only a tiny fraction of civil cases is now tried by jury and a steadily increasing proportion of criminal cases is now tried summarily by magistrates; but the more serious criminal cases are still tried by jury. Granted that it is necessary that in such cases there should always be a trained lawyer as presiding judge, is there any good reason why the facts should not be found by the judge and a number of lay magistrates sitting with him, as in quarter sessions when it is hearing appeals from Petty Sessions? It would be difficult to maintain that the average jury was as competent or more representative than such a tribunal. But even if trial by jury works reasonably well in the ordinary run of cases which do not last for more than a day or at most two or three days, it is at all events incontestable that it is quite unsuitable for really long cases and in particular for cases of fraud which often not only last for many weeks but involve the consideration of many documents and much expert evidence.[1]

(C) The sentence

Here again there are two questions : (i) who is to impose the sentence and, (ii), what is it to be ? With regard to (i) the position as it stands is anomalous. At County Quarter Sessions whether as a court of first instance or as a court of appeal from Petty Sessions, the sentence is fixed by the magistrates acting by a majority. At Borough Quarter Sessions, on the other hand, the sentence is fixed by the Recorder alone and at the Assizes by the Judge alone. The Beeching Commission had to consider what the position is to be in the Crown Court which is to take the place of the Assizes and Quarter Sessions. With some hesitation they recommended that lay justices should

[1] See for the cases for and against trial by jury GLANVILLE WILLIAMS, *The Proof of Guilt*, p. 271–303.

assist the professional judge in sentencing but only as
assessors. It would certainly be unfortunate if lay
justices ceased to play any part in the trial of serious
criminal cases. The professional judge must, of course,
decide all questions of law and when it comes to sentencing his knowledge of the sort of penalty which offences of
the kind in question normally attract should ensure that
the sentence passed is not unjust in the sense that it is out
of scale, either in severity or in leniency, with sentences
passed in similar cases by other courts. But though the
" tariff " is a very important consideration in sentencing,[1]
every case is unique and there may be special features in any
given case which justify a departure from the " tariff " and
it is here that the lay justices have a contribution to make
for if several minds study the problem there is less likelihood of some special feature being disregarded. Again
to work with the judge in the Crown Court is likely to
help the lay justices in their work in Petty Sessions

But granted that a professional judge and a few lay
justices aided by social enquiry reports and medical reports form as good a tribunal for fixing a sentence as we
are likely to find, there remain a number of fundamental
questions which need to be faced. What is the justification for imposing any sentence on anybody ? What
is the sentence intended to achieve ? Is the range of
possible sentences adequate ? Our outlook on these
questions has changed very much in recent years. In the
19th century the general view was, broadly speaking, as
follows : " Apart from ' madmen ', who form a clearly
definable class, and young children, everybody is responsible for his acts. Those who commit crimes are doing
what is morally wrong—sinning—and deserve to be
punished. Some, no doubt, are more likely to be

---

[1] Again and again in applications for leave to appeal against sentence the
applicant says, in effect : " Of course I deserved a severe sentence and if
everyone who behaved as I did got four years I would not mind ; but it
is monstrous that Bill whose crime was every bit as bad as mine and has an
even worse record only got two."

prompted to commit crimes than others. The poor are more likely to steal than those who are not in need and the ill-educated are more likely to indulge in violence than the better educated. So as poverty diminishes and education spreads crime will decrease. Meanwhile, both because criminals are wrongdoers and because it is necessary to deter those who are under a strong temptation to commit crimes from doing so, crimes must be punished and the punishment must be unpleasant. Retribution and deterrence are the objects which the judge must have in mind in imposing a sentence."

Turning to the present day, we find first that the hope that less poverty and more education would mean less crime has been sadly disappointed. There is much less poverty in England to-day than there was even 50 years ago and we are a better educated people in the sense in which the word is commonly used ; but there has been a vast increase in crime, both in crimes of dishonesty and in crimes of violence. At the same time, the beliefs that everyone is responsible for his acts, that to commit a crime is morally wrong and that retribution is a proper consideration for a judge to have in mind in imposing a sentence, are much less generally and less firmly held than they used to be. Gradually we are coming to think that a man, being the sort of man that he is, and being in the circumstances in which he is placed at any given moment, must inevitably act as he does. No doubt he would have acted differently if he had chosen to act differently, but his choice was determined by his character and the circumstances in which he did what he did. So no one can be blamed for anything that he does if and so far as the notion of blame involves the idea that he could have acted otherwise.

In face of such trends of thought, conceptions of moral responsibility and retribution fade away. Of course, even the most forward thinking of us fight shy of the logical conclusions to be drawn from these lines of thought in cases which shock us deeply or where we are personally

involved.   It is easy enough to understand, and to pat
ourself on the back for understanding, how young Johnny
with his sad home background and his urgent desire to
dazzle his girl friend came to break into the café and steal
money from the till.   But anyone who could regard the
Moors murderers or Hitler and his gas chambers with
complete detachment and understanding would be either
more or less than human.   Again, if a psychiatrist were to
tell us (as one may well do in the not very distant future) that
the best way to cure some man convicted of a particularly
revolting sexual crime would be to give him, at the public
expense, 10 days' holiday in Copenhagen with plenty of
money to spend, it would not be only the victims' friends
and relations who would object to such " treatment "
being imposed on him by way of sentence.   Nevertheless,
although we fight shy of the logical conclusions to be
drawn from the modes of thought which we favour many
of us are opposed to severity in sentences—and passion-
ately opposed to the death penalty—because we connect
severity with ideas of " sin " and " retribution " which we
regard as outworn.   This is, of course, utterly illogical.
There is no inconsistency between accepting that no one
is to blame for being a social nuisance and taking such
steps as may seem appropriate to eliminate social nuisan-
ces.   The truth is that we are living in a twilight between
the old-fashioned severity based on religious conceptions
and the severity which is to come when breeding will be
selective and the old and unfit will not be allowed to encumber the ground.   Living, as we do, in this twilight,
it is not surprising that we find ourselves faced with
problems with which we are unable to cope.   Our young
people receive little or no moral education in the sense of
being trained to admire some forms of behaviour and to dislike other forms of behaviour, because most parents have no
very strong feelings on such subjects themselves and the
state takes no interest in them.   What used to be regarded with horror as " crime " is now called " anti-
social behaviour " and the more we come to realise that

those who indulge in it are not to blame, the more we shrink from treating them with severity. As Milton says, if shoplifters were hanged outside the shops which they had plundered there would soon be an end of shoplifting.[1]   But to put to death a shoplifter whom you do not regard as morally to blame for her actions would require a degree of " toughness " of which we are not yet capable. Consequently, even though most criminals are never caught, our prisons are full to overflowing and we are faced with the immediate question of what to do about it. It is sometimes said that imprisonment " does no good ". That, of course, is nonsense.   Prisons perform at least two very useful functions.   First, they keep out of circulation for long periods a number of people who would be not simply a nuisance but a menace to their neighbours if at large.   Secondly, since many, if not most, people who go to prison once do not get into trouble with the criminal law again, imprisonment plays an important part in keeping down the volume of crime.   But between these two classes there is the large class of those who are not deterred from crime by one spell of imprisonment but serve another and yet another term as and when they are caught but yet cannot be regarded as real menaces to society.   No one can honestly maintain that imprisonment does anything to make these people " better citizens ", and one has to ask oneself whether some other method of dealing with them could not be devised ; whether for, example, it would not be better instead of spending money on new prisons, to spend it on an extension of the probation service so that such people could live in home surroundings but yet under far more intensive supervision than " probation ", as at present understood, provides.

3. The Legal Profession

Whether the two branches of the profession should be fused into one is a well worn topic of discussion.   The

[1] *The English Magistracy*, p. 81

client naturally tends to regard the question from the
angle of costs.   He assumes that it must be more expensive to pay two people than one and views the rule that
he must employ a barrister as well as a solicitor in a High
Court case as a device to put money into the pockets of the
lawyers.   Professional opinion, among solicitors as well
as among barristers, is on the whole opposed to fusion—
not wholly for selfish reasons.   It is in fact doubtful
whether fusion would result in any appreciable saving of
costs and it might well affect adversely the quality of the
service available to the client.   But the main argument
against it is that it might affect the quality of the justice
meted out by the court.   Although the layman is often
ignorant of the fact and surprised, sometimes even in-
dignant, when he learns it, an advocate owes a dual allegiance.   He has his duty to his client but he has also
his duty to the court—that is to say to the community.
The boundary between the two duties cannot be laid down
with precision and it is sometimes difficult for an advocate
to know what he ought to do.[1]   But it is far easier for him
to view the problem objectively and to give due weight
to his duty to the court if he occupies a somewhat detached position and has as a buffer between him and his
client another lawyer who has prepared the case and inter-
viewed the witnesses.   Again the task of the judge is
made far easier if those who address him are drawn from a
small body most of the members of which are known to
him personally or by repute.   This enables him to know
which advocates he can trust never to mislead him and
which he must view with some degree of caution.   These
two safeguards would disappear with fusion.

But though only comparatively few solicitors really
want fusion and though the strength of the arguments
against it are perhaps more widely appreciated than they
used to be, the increased demand for advocates and judges
consequent on the increase in crime and to a lesser extent

[1] The ethical problem is discussed with refreshing candour by the late
Cyril Harvey, Q.C., in *The Advocate's Devil* (Stevens, 1958).

on the increase of civil litigation brought about by legal
aid may well lead to a state of affairs in which the maintenance of two separate branches of the legal profession
will become difficult.   At present, solicitors have a right
of audience in county courts and magistrates' courts and
in a few quarter sessions where it is thought that the
supply of barristers normally available at those sessions is
inadequate to meet the needs of the public.   Further,
solicitors are eligible for appointment as chairman or
deputy chairman of county quarter sessions and as stipendiaries, but not as Recorders or county court or High
Court judges.   The Beeching Commission estimated (see
para. 236) that if the new Crown court is to be adequately
manned it will be necessary for some 40 new whole time
circuit judges to be appointed.   Further, it is proposed
that there shall be some 120 part-time criminal judges
(styled Recorders, though no longer having a connection
with any particular town) who will sit continuously for at
least a month each year.   No doubt most of these part-
time posts will be filled by existing Recorders ; but, even
so, there will evidently be a crop of fresh judicial appointments.

The number of practising barristers has been increasing
somewhat of late, but the increase is not commensurate
with the increase over the same period in the number of
judicial appointments reserved exclusively for barristers or
with the increase in the work of the courts in which barristers have exclusive right of audience.   So it is only
natural that many people who are not advocates of
" fusion " should ask : " Why should not solicitors have a
right of audience in the Crown Court as they have in the
county court ?   Why should not solicitors be eligible for
appointment as circuit judges and county court judges ? "
The compromise embodied in the Courts Act, 1971 is (a)
that solicitors shall have a right of audience in the Crown
Court when it is hearing appeals from magistrates' courts
or cases which have been committed by magistrates to the
Crown Court for sentence, but not when it is trying in-

dictments and, (b), that solicitors of 10 years' standing will be eligible as well as barristers of 10 years' standing to be appointed Recorders and that after five years' experience Recorders will be eligible for appointment to the circuit bench.

Whether this compromise will prove satisfactory and lasting remains to be seen. Of course, many solicitors (including probably the ablest members of the profession, such as the partners in big London firms) have not the slightest wish to practise as advocates or to becone judges. On the other hand, there is no doubt that many solicitors who practise in magistrates' courts and county courts would be in every way fit for appointment as county court judges or circuit judges and are perfectly competent to conduct criminal cases in the crown court. But if solicitors were given an unrestricted right of audience in all courts and made eligible for all judicial appointments, the Bar would soon cease to exist, for why, in such circumstances, should any young man take the risk of limiting himself to a barrister's work in preference to joining the branch of the profession in which every avenue was open ? For anyone who believes that the quality of the justice administered in English courts would be likely to suffer by the disappearance of the Bar there is here a real problem.

There is another problem facing barristers and solicitors alike which though not immediately pressing is likely to prove in the long run more serious than that of the relations between the two branches of the profession. In the 19th century the lawyer served the needs of the upper and middle classes, including in the latter tradesmen and farmers. Members of the lower classes—farm labourers and town workers—had troubles in plenty to cope with but, except when they were charged with criminal offences their troubles were not often of a kind in which a lawyer, even had one been available, could have helped them and when they were defendants in criminal proceedings they were generally unrepresented. To-day, on the other hand, the working classes have become, through legal aid, potential clients of the legal profession. As we have said it is unusual for any defendant in the higher criminal courts to be unrepresented and even in the magistrates' courts the granting of legal aid is becoming more common. Again in a high proportion of the matrimonial and family disputes which have increased so greatly in number in recent years, the parties are in comparatively humble circumstances and are legally aided. Further, the working classes have been brought—so to say—within the ambit of the law as beneficiaries under a mass of legislation designed to afford them protection in one shape or another. It is, however, one thing to confer rights and another to ensure that those entitled to them know of them and invoke them, Undoubtedly there is a need to " bring the law to the people " and schemes are on foot for setting up, particularly in areas where solicitors in private practice are in short supply, centres staffed by salaried lawyers to give legal advice and assistance including the conduct of proceedings.[1] Meanwhile, during the last half century or so the importance of the lawyer to his old clients, the upper and middle classes, has been tending to diminish. For example, much work which used to be done by lawyers is now done by accountants and banks and it may well be that with the spread of Registration of Title, conveyancing will cease to be the lucrative monopoly of solicitors which it is to-day. So the legal profession is likely gradually to be faced with the sort of problems with which the medical profession was suddenly faced on the introduction of the National Health Service ; how to adjust itself to the fact that it is becoming more and more a social service and in particular how to maintain the professional standards built up in an era when all lawyers were self-employed in an era when most lawyers will be in reality largely employed by the state.

[1] *The Report of the Advisory Committee on the Better Provision of Legal Aid and Assistance*, 1970, Cmnd. 4249.

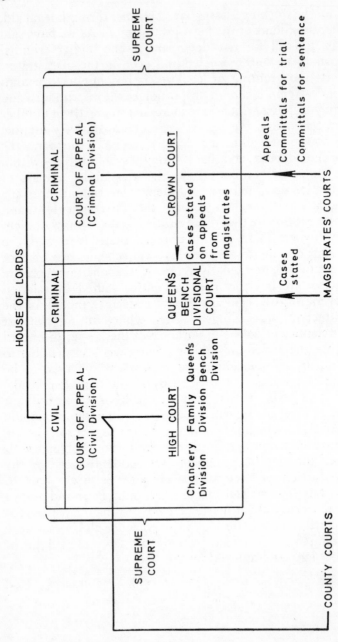

SUPREME COURT

HOUSE OF LORDS

| CIVIL | CRIMINAL | CRIMINAL |
| COURT OF APPEAL (Civil Division) | | COURT OF APPEAL (Criminal Division) |

HIGH COURT

Chancery Division, Family Division, Queen's Bench Division

QUEEN'S BENCH DIVISIONAL COURT

CROWN COURT

Cases stated on appeals from magistrates

Cases stated

Appeals
Committals for trial
Committals for sentence

MAGISTRATES' COURTS

SUPREME COURT

COUNTY COURTS

INDEX

A.

D.

Q.

R.

T.

W.